NOT IN MY BACKYARD

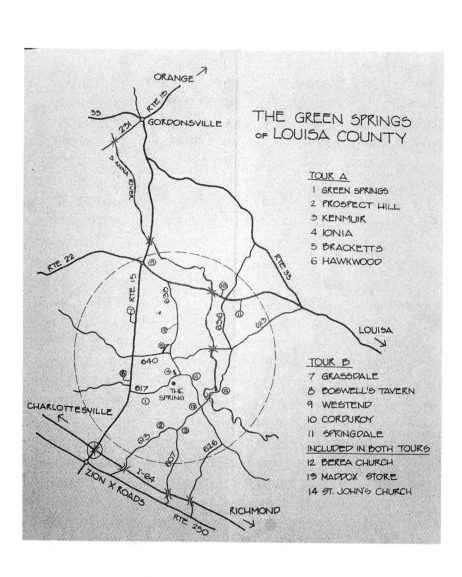

BRIAN BALOGH

Not in My Backyard

HOW CITIZEN ACTIVISTS
NATIONALIZED LOCAL POLITICS
IN THE FIGHT TO SAVE GREEN SPRINGS

Yale
UNIVERSITY PRESS
NEW HAVEN AND LONDON

Published with assistance from the foundation established in memory of Philip Hamilton McMillan of the Class of 1894, Yale College.

Copyright © 2024 by Brian Balogh.
All rights reserved.
This book may not be reproduced, in whole or in part, including illustrations, in any form (beyond that copying permitted by Sections 107 and 108 of the U.S. Copyright Law and except by reviewers for the public press), without written permission from the publishers.

Yale University Press books may be purchased in quantity for educational, business, or promotional use. For information, please e-mail sales.press@yale.edu (U.S. office) or sales@yaleup.co.uk (U.K. office).

Set in Scala type by IDS Infotech, Ltd.
Printed in the United States of America.

Frontispiece: Map from Green Springs house tours pamphlet, 1971. (The Green Springs Association)

Library of Congress Control Number: 2023936630
ISBN 978-0-300-25378-8 (hardcover : alk. paper)

A catalogue record for this book is available from the British Library.

This paper meets the requirements of ANSI/NISO Z39.48-1992 (Permanence of Paper).

10 9 8 7 6 5 4 3 2 1

For KC

CONTENTS

List of Abbreviations ix

Introduction 1

PART ONE: ESCAPING THE PAST

1 A Reform-Minded Republican 13

2 Escaping Cul-de-sacs 21

3 Competing Histories 32

4 "He Was Not Always Right—But He Was Never Wrong" 42

PART TWO: MAKING HISTORY

5 Peppery Women 53

6 Federalism's Fissures 68

7 Virginia's Preservation Network 76

8 Federal Court 83

9 The Women's Ground War 95

10 Courting Bureaucrats 100

11   Public-Private Partnership   111

12   Vermiculite   122

13   The Conflict Expands   133

14   Echoes of Vietnam   144

15   Genteel Civility   156

PART THREE: PRESERVING HISTORY

16   Guys and Dames   171

17   Repurposing Civil Rights Strategies   183

18   The Problem of Asbestos   198

19   A Formidable New Foe   206

20   Local Affairs and the Law of the Land   214

PART FOUR: HISTORY RHYMES

21   Preservationists as Lobbyists   227

22   Wife or Environmentalist?   240

23   A Silk Jungle   254

24   "A Female in Your Face"   267

Epilogue   285

Notes   301

Acknowledgments   345

Index   349

ABBREVIATIONS

BOS	Louisa County Board of Supervisors
DWI	Virginia Department of Welfare and Institutions
EPA	U.S. Environmental Protection Agency
FmHA	Farmers Home Administration
HGSI	Historic Green Springs, Inc.
JRWA	James River Water Authority
LEAA	Law Enforcement Assistance Administration
NEPA	National Environmental Policy Act
NIMBY	"not in my backyard"
NHPA	National Historic Preservation Act
NPS	National Park Service
SLAPP	"Strategic Lawsuit Against Public Participation"
UVa	University of Virginia
VHLC	Virginia Historic Landmarks Commission
VRA	Voting Rights Act
VVL	Virginia Vermiculite, Ltd.

NOT IN MY BACKYARD

Introduction

"THE VERY FIRST THING I THOUGHT TO DO, and I told our board of directors instantly, we must all buy shares of stock. And they looked at me like I was crazy," Rae Ely recalled. She bought a few shares thinking "those ten shares are going to carry me far, and they did."[1]

Rae had never seen *The Solid Gold Cadillac,* Hollywood's 1956 version of one woman taking on a giant corporation by purchasing a handful of shares, but twenty years after the Oscar-winning movie she turned a real-life W. R. Grace & Co. shareholders' meeting to similar advantage, although it would take decades for the strategy to pay dividends. That Grace "was a corporation headed up by a man with a *name*—and it was an old family name, unlike 'Mr. General Motors' or 'Mr. General Electric' " made it a "*target*."[2]

By the May 1976 shareholders' meeting in Boston Rae was on CEO Peter Grace's radar. His staff warned that "Apparently, Mrs. Hiram (Rae) Ely . . . has gotten to the Secretary [of the Interior]," who had written a typical "eco-freak letter . . . asking us to give up our vermiculite reserves in Virginia." There was every reason to expect fireworks at the meeting, and a cluster of Grace lawyers and security staff was dispatched to meet the anticipated band of angry women.[3]

Instead, they got what Rae described as a solitary slim and pretty southern gentlewoman "dressed like a fairy princess. I mean really eye-catching clothes, not conservative . . . because I knew I'd be on TV." "Good morning gentlemen," Rae drawled in her best Virginia lady accent. "So sorry about your lawyer." "What?" one of the men asked. As she headed for her seat Rae casually mentioned, "Well, you know he was arrested yesterday; I'm sure you'll hear about it."[4]

The lawyer, Bill Perkins, had diligently labored to clear Grace's legal path to strip mine in the recently created Green Springs National Historic Landmark District. Perkins had been rounded up with ten other notables at a cockfight on Inglecress Farm near Charlottesville, home to the University of Virginia. The incident had been entertaining enough to elicit the *New York Times'* headline "Uproar Over Cockfight Ruffles Virginia Gentry." The top brass at Grace were embarrassed by the arrest; learning about it from Rae Ely only made matters worse.[5]

Rae had arrived at the shareholders' meeting early to get a "really choice spot ... in Peter Grace's line of sight." As soon as the public comment period began Rae jumped to her feet. "Well, Mrs. Ely," Peter boomed, "so nice to see you here again this year." "So nice to see you," Rae replied with her big cheery smile, turning sideways so that the photographers and hundreds of shareholders could see her.[6]

"Mr. Grace," Rae began, "I'm just here this morning to tell all these shareholders how grateful the people of Green Springs are to you, sir, for the efforts that this fine company is making to preserve the beautiful historic Green Springs valley in Virginia from efforts that this company *had* been considering making to extract vermiculite." Rae knew that W. R. Grace still planned to mine in what she described as the most beautiful eighteenth-century grouping of historic buildings "nestled in the shadow of Monticello." But she also knew that relationships mattered. That morning's mission was to establish a good one with a powerful opponent.[7]

The tactic worked when the entire auditorium burst into applause; people stood and cheered. Peter Grace beamed. As shareholders boarded buses that whisked them to a bicentennial luncheon in Lexington, some men raced up to Rae and announced: "Mr. Grace would like to know if you would be kind enough to ride with him today." "Certainly," Rae replied, "what a nice invitation." She soon glided off in his limousine.[8]

"He's just a jolly, hard-drinking, Catholic elf—raised by nuns," Rae concluded. "This, of course, is the theme of the rest of our relationship.... You're never going to persuade anybody by angry ranting." Rae Ely's vivid demonstration of the good will that the company could garner with shareholders by paying lip service to preserving history and the environment was just one

INTRODUCTION

gambit of many in her long-range strategy to drive the company out of the historic district that she had created.[9]

Years later, after moving to a farm in Green Springs, I began to hear what seemed like fantastical stories about Rae Ely. She had defeated Governor Linwood Holton's effort to site a prison there in the early 1970s; she had prevailed over W. R. Grace's attempt to mine; she had created America's first national historic landmark in a rural district that encompassed thousands of acres; she had graduated from the University of Virginia School of Law without an undergraduate college degree; she had burned down her house in an attempt to murder her husband. Intrigued, I looked into these rumors, and much to my surprise, discovered that all but the last one proved to be true. I even noticed the bullet-pocked brown signs that announced the borders of that landmark district and realized for the first time that I lived inside it. Few people seemed to know much about Rae Ely's life before she arrived in Green Springs in 1967. What I learned about her early years made her political success all the more remarkable.

Rae Hatfield was born in the Coconut Grove section of Miami on May 13, 1941. When Rae was five years old her mother was killed in a traffic accident. From that point on Rae was raised by a series of her father's girlfriends and wives—three of them soon to be ex-wives. Her father, Ray Hatfield, captained yachts for unsavory characters, including, it was rumored, Al Capone. Hatfield only had an eighth-grade education, "but there was no smarter man that ever lived," Rae recalled. "If he hadn't been a drunk, he [would have] done something with himself." He could be a mean drunk—so much so that the state of Florida removed Rae from her home in the spring of 1954. She was placed in foster care and a few years later shipped to a high school for girls in distress in Thomasville, Georgia. When Rae turned eighteen she graduated (or aged out of) the Vashti Industrial School for Girls, took a job at a local business, and soon married her boss, Hugh Duncan. She did not stay in Thomasville or married to Duncan for long. In 1962, when she learned that Colonel Hiram Ely, the husband of a recently deceased prominent Dachshund breeder, was seeking an appropriate mate for his wife's dogs, she showed up at his house in Flemington, New Jersey, with two candidates.[10]

Hiram's 1692 gray stone manor house seemed magical. Likewise its dozens of acres, its horses, not to mention the fine Dachshunds and Colonel Ely himself. He was good-looking and accomplished; Rae was sold, despite the near-half-century age difference between them. They were married that same year, happily at first. Yet, as New York City's exurban sprawl crept closer, the Elys sought safe harbor. In 1967 they moved to Louisa County, Virginia, a rural backwater whose seat a county supervisor described as "a one-horse town . . . and the horse died in 1936."[11]

Although Rae knew nothing about politics—when they moved to Virginia she didn't know if she and Hiram were Democrats or Republicans—her powerful will, capacity for learning, and knack for long-term strategy enabled her to shift from dependent to political action figure. She soon battled a series of powerful men who, in her opinion, threatened to destroy the unique rural character of her neighborhood and her rights as a fully empowered citizen. Her first antagonist was, at the time, Virginia's first Republican governor in the past century, Linwood Holton. In May 1970 he announced plans to close Richmond's decrepit state penitentiary by building a new "diagnostic center" to sort and rehabilitate convicted felons. It would be located directly across from the Elys' front yard in Green Springs. An island of wealth in otherwise impoverished Louisa County, Green Springs, with its many surviving plantations, had begun to attract northerners like Rae and Hiram fleeing exurban sprawl.

The fight against the prison was so prolonged that the *Washington Post* labeled it "Holton's Vietnam." Rae next took on multinational mining conglomerate W. R. Grace & Co., which wanted to mine Green Springs' vermiculite, a rare absorbent mineral used in construction, manufacturing, potting soil, and sometimes as cat litter. The neighborhood activists eventually defeated Grace in a battle that lasted even longer than the prison fight.[12]

Along the way, Rae Ely and her allies established the first national historic landmark to be honored explicitly for preserving the heritage of thousands of acres of rural history, joining a small group of American landmarked icons including the Alamo and Mount Vernon. The Green Springs National Historic Landmark District was created when property owners placed scenic conservation easements on thousands of acres of private land, sacrificing their right to subdivide their property or interfere with the rural environment that surrounded the houses and other structures. Creating a landmark to preserve rural history was all the more remarkable because nobody in Louisa's political establishment believed that Green Springs had any notable history. As the district's own supervisor told *Time* magazine, "Virginia is full of old houses like that."¹³

The citizens' group led by Rae challenged the local branch of an old political machine, Virginia's Byrd organization. Circuit court judges ran the organization in rural counties, and in Louisa that judge was Harold Purcell. The local courthouse crowd had been coerced by Federal courts to integrate the Louisa County High School in 1970, but the all-white male group of public officials remained in firm control of other local prerogatives like land use. The majority of the county's voters vigorously supported the courthouse crowd's agenda: protecting male and racial privilege as well as property rights, prioritizing economic development, and most vocally, keeping the Federal government out of the county's business—at least business that was not profitable for political insiders or that might bring jobs.¹⁴

Green Springs' middle-class white women may have leaned heavily on history to preserve the rural quality of their property, but they bridled at the Byrd organization's historically insulated style of politics. Instead, they engaged the full range of political venues directly (rather than merely at the ballot box or through their elected representatives), from mass meetings, to petitioning, to lobbying distant Federal agencies and litigating in Federal courts. By 1980, local land-use policy in Green Springs—a government prerogative kept as close to home as Jim Crow segregation had been—was shared with the "Feds" and a nonprofit organization led by Rae Ely and powered by female citizen activists.

How did Rae Ely beat the odds and defeat the local machine, a powerful governor, and a Fortune 500 company? Some of the answers were obvious: her talent, skill, and persistence. It helped that she was white and upper middle-class. As I dug deeper into the extensive documentary evidence and began to interview locals, many of whom were afraid to talk about the courthouse crowd fifty years later, I realized that the full answer required an appreciation for the historical context in which this story unfolded. Rae was successful because the political, social, and economic landscape was shifting rapidly when she jumped into politics in 1970. Her personal story wound through some of the key changes experienced by Americans in the last third of the twentieth century. Indeed, it illuminated them. Rae conquered that shifting landscape and leveraged the new resources for citizen activists it unearthed. She was the right woman in the right place at the right time.

Her story provides a unique perspective on American politics in the last third of the twentieth century. The most important change she turned to her advantage was the rising demand—especially among progressives—for an improved quality of life, manifested most visibly in the surging environmental movement. So too her recognition that the national government had penetrated a centuries-old local monopoly on racial matters by 1970. Why not engage the Federal government to protect the quality of life that she and her neighbors enjoyed in Green Springs?

That such a quest was endorsed far more heartily by national elites both in the environmental protection sphere and among historical preservationists only increased the incentive to circumvent local control. The Green Springs activists harnessed legislation like the National Environmental Policy Act (NEPA) of 1970, Federal agencies like the Department of the Interior, and the Federal judiciary to override local majorities who resented both the Feds' intervention in their business and any restrictions on their property. Although the white female activists in Green Springs had never been denied the right to vote, their voices had been silenced by the same ruling oligarchy that until recently had presided over Jim Crow segregation.

Gaining access to national venues had never been easier given a decade-long commitment to opening national administrative agencies, regulatory review, and most importantly, Federal courts to citizen comments, concerns, and legal standing. Rae plunged into politics at a moment in American history when autonomous rights-bearing individuals increasingly *dis*placed place-based communities, as did groups who identified by race and gender, regardless of where their members happened to live. In an age of jet travel, interstate highways, national broadcast networks, and most significantly, the demise of legally enforced Jim Crow segregation in the South, the connection between place and political jurisdiction meant far less than it had even a decade earlier. By 1975, the most visible pillars of the Jim Crow regime had been dismantled, clearing a path for citizens with far different backgrounds and agendas than civil rights activists. These newly minted activists demanded that *their* national constitutional rights be protected as well, even when local oligarchies like the one that governed Louisa County insisted otherwise.[15]

Although place as political jurisdiction meant less than it had a few years earlier, many middle-class white women were introduced to politics when something both dear and near to home was threatened. Rae was only one of hundreds of thousands, perhaps millions, of citizens who engaged directly in political action for the first time in the 1970s. Although they adapted strategies and tactics forged by the national civil rights, anti–Vietnam War, environmental, and second-wave feminist movements, these activists advanced far different agendas over the next three decades than the social movements of the sixties. Much of this activity occurred at the local, often neighborhood level. Newly engaged citizens reconciled the demise of place-based governance with the rise of neighborhood-based agendas by identifying more closely with likeminded Americans thousands of miles away than with certain neighbors just down the road.

Governor Holton announced his plans for the diagnostic center shortly before the *New York Times* quoted highway and public utility officials criticizing "backyard obstructionists." The phrase slowly morphed into "not in my backyard" (NIMBY). Those advocating for new construction or changes in land use usually applied the term to somebody else's backyard—protesters who opposed a range of initiatives, from mobile home courts to the transportation of nuclear waste; from shelters for the homeless to drug treatment centers. It was just this kind of intrusion that prompted Rae Ely's initial foray into politics. What critics of NIMBYs have missed because their causes are so often neighborhood-based are the common concerns that many NIMBYs share across geographic boundaries. Those shared concerns about quality of life issues reshaped national political agendas.[16]

Perhaps the most surprising resource seized by Green Springs' citizen activists was triggered by changing conceptions of what constituted history. It was only after a Ph.D. student at the University of Virginia introduced a newly minted framework for understanding Green Springs' past that residents embraced it as the best way to authenticate the area's distinctive characteristics. Prison opponents argued that history consisted of more than famous political leaders and military battles. An approach that captured the relationship between old structures—even if nobody famous ever slept there—and the surrounding landscape encouraged Green Springs residents to dig deeper into their own past. It ultimately shaped the district's future.

By the 1970s these tectonic shifts in the relationship between citizen and state were taking place against a backdrop of long-term economic decline in the United States. Yet policymakers continued to promise more, especially when it came to issues like the environment. Doing more with less money is precisely what the Green Springs activists promised to achieve through the public-private partnership they crafted. Private easements would now protect 14,000 acres from intrusions like prisons and strip mining. To be sure, the Federal government played an important role. But the Feds were joined by those private landowners who voluntarily restricted the use of their land, and by Historic Green Springs, Inc., which connected landowners to the National Park Service (NPS).

The urge to do more with less explains, in part, the fluid state of partisan politics during the 1970s. By 1975, fiscally constrained Federal administrators no longer contemplated massive projects like the national parks built during the New Deal. Both liberals and conservatives, Democrats and Republicans, emerged from this era with a renewed commitment to public-private partnerships. This was hardly the triumph of the free market so often associated with the "Reagan Era," but it *did* accommodate growing voter frustration about rising taxes, budget deficits, and centralized control.

Nor did political parties demand the kind of strict partisan allegiance that paralyzed politics by the twenty-first century. Rae Ely was backed by Republican secretaries of the Interior under Presidents Richard Nixon and Gerald Ford, even though that support pitted them against Virginia's Republican governor. It could not have been comfortable for Interior Secretary Rogers Morton, a former Republican National Committee chair, to back Linwood Holton's Green Springs opponents. Nor was it easy for President Ford's secretary of the Interior to publicly pressure a major Republican donor like Peter Grace to forgo mining.

Republicans and Democrats had already begun to diverge in 1970 over local control, especially when it came to integrating public schools. President Nixon's signature domestic program, the "New Federalism," promised to reverse the flow of power to Washington. In an extraordinary jujitsu move, Ely used the Federal legislation that funded Holton's proposed prison, support that was explicitly designed to *cut* Federal strings, to circumvent local courts. The result was a landmark decision in the United States Court of Appeals for the Fourth Circuit that imposed a virtual spider's web of restrictions on how Virginia could use those Federal funds, ruling that other national legislation passed to protect the environment and preserve the nation's history trumped Nixon's pledge to return decisions to "local officials responding to local conditions and local constituencies."[17]

Nixon appealed to the growing number of Americans who insisted that improving the quality of life for middle-class citizens directly threatened their own economic progress. Louisa County's citizens battled over two contrasting visions of progress. Pushing back against the Green Springs crowd, most Louisans, whatever their attitude about prison reform, recognized an opportunity for job creation when they saw one. Every public official in Louisa County agreed and supported both the prison and mining.

What began as Nixon's tentative effort to reverse the powerful trend toward nationalizing politics fanned broad rural support for a set of ideals that had long defined the courthouse crowd's agenda. When I started my research in 2010, I viewed many of the arguments mounted by Louisa's ruling oligarchy about race, the sanctity of private property, and the evils of centralized government as the last gasp of a part of America that was vanishing. Rather, these beliefs soon became (many would argue had already become) the foundation for one of the two major political parties in the United States, along with the rural base of voters that supported these appeals.

One relentless, talented person can make a big political difference when history, strategy, and determination are on her side. Rae Ely faced long odds when Louisa's governing establishment supported Governor Holton and W. R. Grace. Their collective appeal to the residents of this impoverished county was jobs. Ely prevailed because she tapped a new style of participatory politics first crafted by the civil rights movement. She tethered direct citizen engagement to the expertise and regulatory authority of the National Park Service and Department of the Interior. She circumvented local courts, going directly to the Federal judiciary. In redirecting the national government's resources toward preserving history and the environment, she challenged long-standing commitments to government-stimulated economic growth at any cost.

What began as a personal quest evolved to break a political machine's stranglehold; carve out a space for legitimate debate about ill-conceived plans; and ensure the proper balance between economic growth and concern for the environment as well as cultural resources. Ely's lessons and strategies now resonate across the country and political spectrum in ways she trailblazed but might not have intended. That is because she created the template today deployed by thousands of neighborhood groups who resist any form of development—thwarting, for instance, initiatives to make housing more affordable.

By the twenty-first century it was easy to poke fun at NIMBYs, as suggested by the growing list of more caustic acronyms such as BANANA (build absolutely nothing anywhere near anything) and NOPE (not on planet earth). Virginia's current governor, a dark horse for the Republican presidential nomination, has been tagged YIMBY (yes in my backyard) in Chief. However, the half-century-long Green Springs battle is a reminder that self-interested motives do not preclude public benefits. Women who had never engaged politically mobilized effectively to fight the courthouse crowd, Governor Holton, and W. R. Grace. Increased political engagement, whatever its motivation, surely counts as a civic gift. So too the tangible alternatives to government or corporate insistence that is "my way or the highway."[18]

Protecting their own property was hardly the only motivation for the citizens who worked with Rae Ely in Green Springs. They also wanted to preserve what they believed was a national treasure. For some, this was merely the beginning of their political engagement. *Because* they got involved, residents discovered a history that they had not previously been aware of. Creating and preserving that history enhanced the *nation's* backyard by protecting a slice of rural history that grows more valuable with the construction of each new Starbucks, especially the one just a few miles down the road from historic Green Springs.

PART ONE

ESCAPING THE PAST

1
A Reform-Minded Republican

LYNDON JOHNSON'S LANDSLIDE 1964 victory over his Republican challenger for the presidency, Barry Goldwater, promised to cement a Democratic majority in Congress well into the future. Yet the five states that Goldwater carried outside of his home state of Arizona, in the so-called Solid South, demonstrated the fragility of the Democratic Party's century-long hold on that region. Goldwater's national humiliation juxtaposed against his southern triumph ignited a fierce battle within the Republican Party. Some rising stars, like Ronald Reagan, picked up where Goldwater's state's rights rhetoric left off, while others, like New York governor Nelson Rockefeller and Michigan governor George Romney, aimed for moderate Republicans and independents. In 1968, Richard Nixon sought to blend both—pursuing a moderately progressive domestic policy agenda while dog-whistling to white southern voters on issues like local opposition to busing and the surging national concerns about crime. His strategy underscored just how ideologically malleable the GOP had become for the moment.

In 1969 Linwood Holton capitalized on Nixon's appeal to moderates when he ran to the left of his Democratic opponent in the race for governor of Virginia. The link between party and ideology, tenuous at best between 1945 and 1968, continued to unravel with Holton's victory. There was every reason for the new governor to believe that reforming the Commonwealth's antiquated prison system might appeal to the coalition that had just elected him. "Border state" Virginia had not gone for Goldwater, but Nixon's success in appropriating the crime issue from southern Democrat George Wallace in

1968 left little doubt about its salience a year later. Doing something about crime was at the top of the incoming governor's agenda. Holton's approach to crime, however, embraced a long-standing progressive framework for reducing it: rehabilitation. His crime policies resembled the New Deal and Great Society approach far more than the "tough on crime" and "lock them up" approach that both national political parties would soon embrace to build what scholars call the carceral state.

Holton had not devoted much attention to the other domestic policy that had captured the nation's attention by 1969: protecting the environment. A note from his good friend and political ally, Republican Delegate Ray L. Garland, focused the governor's mind. Garland wrote to "Lin" suggesting two seemingly disparate issues that were political sure bets. "If your Administration would take a strong and effective stand against our increasing crime rate and the deterioration of our environment the people of Virginia would overflow with gratitude." Holton did just that, but in Louisa County a few residents who cared about the environment overflowed with rage, not gratitude. They entangled his crime policy with their quest to preserve the natural and cultural environment and plunged Holton into a controversy that outlasted his four years as governor.[1]

Abner Linwood Holton, Jr., was born in 1923 in the Appalachian village of Big Stone Gap, Virginia, whose 3,000 residents lived tucked into a gorge between mountains in the heart of coal country. Linwood's father's management position for the Interstate Railroad company placed the family squarely in the middle class, but the future governor must have observed plenty of rural poverty despite his own comfortable childhood.[2]

Holton claimed that he couldn't remember a time in his life when becoming governor of Virginia "wasn't simmering in the back of my mind." Republican loyalty made sense for a boy from western Virginia, where that party had deep roots, but it was one of the few places in the Commonwealth where it did. When he was courting Jinks Rogers, "the love of his life," she was embarrassed to be seen with a Republican and refused to ride on Dwight D. Eisenhower's campaign train as it rolled through Virginia in 1952. Resilient, persistent, or simply stubborn—all three adjectives applied to Linwood Holton—he convinced Jinks to marry him in 1953.[3]

Ike's victory in Virginia buoyed Holton's hopes for a Republican Virginia. When he ran for the House of Delegates in 1955 and 1957, losing both times, his party's platform embraced gradual school desegregation. Though barely moderate, it stood in stark contrast to the Democrats' "massive resistance" to integrating public schools. Holton continued party-building and in 1965 accepted the dubious reward of the Republican nomination for governor in the wake of President Lyndon Johnson's landslide victory. Linwood well understood that he had little chance of defeating his Democratic opponent, Lieutenant Governor Mills Godwin. Once again that combination of resilience, persistence, and stubbornness drove him toward a seemingly impossible dream.[4]

A shrewd strategy helped Holton realize it. He hoped to augment a Republican minority with the burgeoning African American vote, topping it off with a growing number of white Democrats disaffected by their party's staunchly segregationist stance. Holton was rewarded with enough of the vote—38 percent—to run again in 1969. This time the divisions within Virginia's Democratic Party and Holton's endorsement from President Richard Nixon put the Republican over the top with 53 percent of the vote.[5]

The first Republican elected governor since 1874, Holton would soon claim another first for his family. Doubling down on his inaugural claim that "the era of defiance is behind us," Holton became the first governor of a southern state to send his children to an integrated public school, a moment so extraordinary that the *New York Times* memorialized it in a front-page photo (Fig. 1). Slim and erect, thin-lipped smile firmly in place, Governor Holton strode beside thirteen-year-old Tayloe as she entered the previously all–African American Kennedy High School. "It's always hard for a child to change schools," the governor said. "They don't want to leave old friends. But my children go where they are assigned."[6]

Holton's victory may have been anomalous, but it epitomized a remarkably fluid period in American partisan politics. Just a year earlier, segregationist Democratic Alabama governor George Wallace ran as an independent, carrying five states in the deep South and lengthening the odds for Democratic presidential nominee Hubert Humphrey. The solid Democratic South no longer looked quite so formidable. Holton joined a host of moderate Republicans in the GOP, headlined by the "New Nixon." The former Cold

Figure 1. Governor Linwood Holton walks his daughter Tayloe to a recently integrated public school, September 1971. (Librado Romero/*The New York Times*/Redux)

Warrior was eager to demonstrate that he could work with an increasingly progressive-leaning Democratic Congress. Especially compared to the intense partisanship that characterizes twenty-first-century national politics, party loyalty was tepid at best in 1969, with the ideological tilt of each party often difficult to discern.

Governor-elect Holton quickly acted on both of Garland's suggestions, first previewing a prison reform plan, and soon after, capitalizing on the growing popularity of the environmental movement by creating the Governor's Council on the Environment. Indeed, Holton was naturally drawn to the conservation issue by virtue of a happy childhood spent swimming in the rivers and fishing in the mountain streams of Big Stone Gap. Although chief of staff John Ritchie had to twist his arm to get him to attend the first Earth Day in 1970, an event that was to engage more Americans than the biggest civil rights or antiwar demonstrations of the 1960s, Holton later conceded that attending Virginia's celebration had "turned out to [be] a very good move."[7]

Addressing crime and the environment appealed to Holton because they both had limitless "upside," with little risk for controversy. After all, avoiding controversy had been one of his campaign's hallmarks. "I just said, 'Look, you need to have [the] competitive force of two parties. It's a two-drugstore town.' " Unfortunately for Holton, his signature crime initiative would soon undermine his reputation as a friend of the environment.[8]

Americans listed crime in 1968 as their top domestic concern for the first time since Gallup began asking that question in the 1930s. In the South, and in some urban areas racked by several years of urban rebellions, attitudes had hardened and calls for "law and order," egged on by George Wallace, Ronald Reagan, and Vice President Spiro Agnew, were on the rise. Progressives, however, among them recently retired Supreme Court Chief Justice Earl Warren (a former Republican governor of California), still controlled the incarceration agenda. They believed that prisons should reform rather than punish. Holton opted to address crime in a manner that had the hallmarks of liberal penal reform.[9]

Governor Holton's approach had something for every segment of his diverse constituency. Felons got jail time. Yet Holton blamed poverty and psychological factors for crime—conditions that could be remedied. In the long run, remediation would make Virginians safer, provide an economic stimulus to host communities, and ultimately shrink the size of government by properly diagnosing felons—returning them to society as productive taxpaying citizens.

Whatever Holton's approach, no governor could ignore the festering situation at the state penitentiary. Opened in 1800 on the outskirts of Richmond, by 1970 the "Pen" stood near the center of town, a block or two from the Governor's Mansion, where the Holtons had ample opportunities to see, smell, and hear what went on there. The gigantic complex with its stacked rows of windowless cells fronted by barred doors, combined with its dungeonlike basement for the "worst of the worst," was "hardly a place to send a man and expect him to return to society having learned he must behave or be confined," as one reformer put it.[10]

Holton's first step, and the centerpiece in dismantling the penal dinosaur, was a proposed state-of-the-art "reception and diagnostic center." Initially estimated to cost roughly $3.7 million, the diagnostic center would be the "first stage in the development of an entirely new approach to dealing with the convicted offender in Virginia." It was backed by expert research on crime that recommended smaller specialized units and proper classification as the way to reduce recidivism. Local news media embraced the approach: "The sooner

Virginia can restore the criminally convicted to society equipped for something better than continuation of a life of crime, the better off Virginia will be."[11]

Holton's point man on prison reform was Otis L. Brown, just a round-faced thirty-two, and looking even younger, when Holton's predecessor, Mills Godwin, appointed him director of the Department of Welfare and Institutions (DWI). Brown was part of the "can-do" generation infused with President John F. Kennedy's "Camelot" spirit whose grail was to improve the lives of citizens through government action. He seemed the perfect pick for the job of ensuring that prisoners were properly classified and assigned the correct treatment plan. All adult male felons in the state would "undergo sophisticated classification processing in a system that utilizes every pertinent discipline, functioning among pleasant surroundings calculated not to dehumanize the offender." Holton and Brown planned to apply space-age tools to an age-old problem and tackle the nation's number one domestic concern in a fashion likely to appeal to a broad cross-section of voters.[12]

Brown had served in state and local government long enough to understand that nobody wanted a prison close to their home and that siting the diagnostic center might get tricky. When he chose a Louisa County location fifty miles west of Richmond, he must have been aware of the fuss a few Louisans had raised when the Virginia Electric and Power Company (VEPCO) announced in April 1968 that it planned to build a nuclear reactor near there. That this momentary kerfuffle ultimately failed to stop VEPCO's plans must have reassured Brown: compared to the intense, prolonged citizen opposition to reactor siting in California and New York State—protests that thwarted both projects—the nuclear issue was less contentious in Louisa County. The county needed the tax revenue, the construction jobs, and the roughly one hundred permanent jobs that the utility promised. The reactor cooling pond, soon christened "Lake Anna," created valuable waterfront property overnight and, as the *Central Virginian* gushed, "perhaps one day, even a destination resort."[13]

Reassuringly, Brown and Holton could count on Louisa's political leadership. Little had changed over the last half-century in the way citizens expressed their political preferences. The hierarchy established by Senator Harry F. Byrd, Sr.'s political organization was designed to dampen voting and quash citizen engagement. It left local decisions in the hands of circuit court judges like Louisa County's Harold Purcell. Although this was a Democratic machine, even a reform-minded Republican governor could count on Louisa's courthouse crowd to take care of business if that meant jobs for the county. There is no record of discussions with the man who sat atop the local power structure, but Brown and Holton had good reason to assume that the judge would like the 200-acre site selected for the diagnostic center. The Commonwealth planned to purchase it from Harold's brother Richard, at twice the price that "Dickie" paid just a few months earlier.[14]

Advocates for the diagnostic center touted Green Springs as the ideal location for several more publicly palatable reasons. A few miles north of the new interstate exit, the pasture surrounded by miles of similar rolling fields, edged with cedars and dotted with black Angus cows, promised fresh air for inmates. Governor Holton's son Woody later recalled his parents saying that the men would "not have to smell all the tobacco smell that we smelled all the time from the factories in those days." With the completion of Interstate 64 through Charlottesville, Green Springs was half an hour east of a first-rate hospital and the professionals working at the University of Virginia. Heading in the opposite direction from the Louisa site on I-64 put prison administrators in the Commonwealth's capital in less than an hour.[15]

The diagnostic center was promoted as a crucial economic stimulus for Louisa County. Like the nuclear power plant, it promised to bring a multi-million-dollar annual payroll. Louisa County surely needed those jobs. The county's population stood at 14,004 in 1970: 61 percent was white and 39 percent was officially classified as "nonwhite." Roughly one quarter of families in Louisa County lived below the poverty line—compared to 9.3 percent statewide. The per capita income in Louisa County in 1969 was $1,089: $764 below the statewide average. Forty percent of Louisa's residents who did have jobs traveled outside the county to reach them. Compared to wealthier counties, a disproportionate number of Louisans who worked there were employed in agriculture and forestry, which still accounted for 7 percent of Louisa's work force. Dean Agee, the county's first administrator, summed up Louisa's economic condition by describing his aunt's reaction when he told her that he was moving there in 1970: "My god, have they gotten electricity there yet?"[16]

Originally, Holton's plans called for a facility that would house roughly 200 inmates and employ a staff of approximately the same size, generating an annual payroll of $2 million for Louisa County and the surrounding area. Its scope soon grew. Rumors swirled that the DWI administrative offices might be moved to the site as well. Nine months later the number of prisoners planned for the facility had doubled to 400.[17]

Although there was no architect's rendering yet, Otis Brown was "positive it will fit in"; residents "won't even know it is there." A pamphlet published by DWI explained why it would *not* be "an environmental eye-sore to mar the natural beauty of Virginia" and how the facility would "blend in with its surroundings." The sketch that eventually was released redefined the term "blend in": 600 feet in diameter, the facility was to be surrounded by a six-foot-high steel fence. Clearly visible over it, thirty-foot maximum-security concrete windowless cell blocks radiated out from a sixty-foot control tower, itself dwarfed by the 120-foot-high water tank (Fig. 2).[18]

Otis Brown wanted the governor to see the site, so the week before the public announcement they jumped in the state helicopter for the short flight to Green Springs. Holton barked, "I like what I see: let's go with it." Still, Brown could be forgiven for scanning the horizon, as he had done earlier when he asked some Louisa politicians if there would be any opposition. One assured him there would be none: except "the lady up on the hill—we'll hear from her." That lady was Rae Ely.[19]

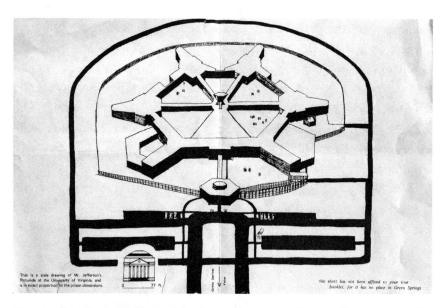

Figure 2. A preliminary sketch of the diagnostic center and "Mr. Jefferson's Rotunda" "in exact proportion to the prison dimensions." (Historic Green Springs, Inc.)

2
Escaping Cul-de-sacs

RAE AND HIRAM ELY HAD MOVED TO Green Springs in central Virginia from New Jersey in 1967 to escape New Jersey's threatening exurban creep. They wanted to move to a place that would protect the rural quality of life they had once enjoyed, and also to flee from deteriorating relationships with Hiram's children who were not pleased with their new stepmother, a generation younger than they. In fact, Hiram had to remind his two adult children about the new chain of command: "Rae is the First Lady in this family," he instructed.[1]

Rae's readily visible qualities, her mass of auburn hair, her girlish figure, unaffected by the births of her three children, her beguiling manner, and most of all, the forty-five-year age difference between her and Colonel Ely undoubtedly were subjects of amused gossip in Louisa County. They paled in significance, however, compared to several other factors that explained how and why she became the powerhouse that ultimately derailed Governor Holton's diagnostic center. Her mother's death under mysterious circumstances and her father's drinking and abuse meant that Rae learned self-sufficiency at an early age. Removed from her father's care after he assaulted her, Rae was sent to a jail-like foster care facility by the time she was thirteen. It was there, after Bible study, that she decided God had put her on this earth to achieve something and that God would watch out for her. From then on, she decided that she was never going to be afraid of anything; she was never going to be intimidated. Rae did have several sanctuaries during her childhood, including the home of her elementary-school best friend, George

Engel—an Italianate house complete with three-story tower overlooking Biscayne Bay.[2]

Rae's adolescence, largely spent away from her father, replicated the chaotic conditions of her childhood. Her uneasy place in the class structure gyrated from near the bottom ("poor white trash") to near the top, and comprised of some of the wealthy people she met through her father's questionable line of work and Engel's classy tower. So too did her notions of family and home as she bounced from institutional foster care to short paroles with wealthy Christian foster parents; from an industrial school for girls to her short-lived first marriage; and finally, to a new husband and hostile stepchildren. Over the first five years of her marriage to Hiram, Rae developed the appetites and demeanor that, when combined with her white skin, would assure her place in society's upper echelons, whatever her actual income and net worth.

Things were not perfect between her and Hiram after they moved to Virginia. She was hosting spectacular parties and running the house like it was an embassy. "As long as he was the lord of the manor and had his darling little children running around his knee and his pretty wife making him look really, really good," Rae chuckled, "he was a happy man." Then Holton announced his plans for the prison. Rae found a new sanctuary in an old tower and forged pathbreaking political ground to ensure that never again would she live in the shadow of a penal institution.[3]

Ethel Abercrombie Hatfield, Rae's mother, grew up in Muncie, Indiana, the daughter of a vice president of the Pennsylvania Railroad. She apparently had a lively history of her own, including a rumored affair with Babe Ruth and "at least" one failed marriage before meeting and marrying "Captain Ray" in Fort Lauderdale, Florida. Rae's father, Ray Vinton Hatfield, earned a living by piloting sport fishermen, test driving Porsches, and captaining yachts for owners who were rumored to have made their money illegally.[4]

When Rae was five years old Ethel "disappeared and didn't come back." Rae recalled that "for some reason they decided not to tell me she was dead." Ethel had been struck by a car on McArthur Causeway in Miami Beach while walking late one November night. It was an unlikely place for a stroll at any time of day, and the time and place of her death, combined with the type of people that the Hatfields associated with, fueled speculation about foul play.

When Rae was told of her mother's death nine or ten months afterwards, she recalled that "they asked me not to cry." She didn't.[5]

After Ethel's death, Ray took up with, married, then divorced a series of women who became Rae's more or less willing caretakers during her father's frequent absences piloting yachts and driving fast cars long distances. Between the marriages Rae soaked up Miami-style glamor as her dad's "sidekick," accompanying him to his favorite high-end watering holes. Sometimes he would take her on long cruises, piloting "incredible big yachts over one hundred feet in length all made of mahogany with brass fittings." She sailed to Cuba and the Bahamas, dining on giant shrimp and huge lobsters. Rae grew up assuming that "everybody lived that way."[6]

This was the fun part. Not so pleasant were her father's frequent drinking bouts and violent temper. Nor the winters spent in a hospital oxygen tent because of her asthma, exacerbated by Ray's chain smoking. Emaciated, and debarred by her health from gym class, Rae's nickname at school was Bone Rack Hatfield.[7]

There were two sanctuaries in Rae's Coconut Grove childhood. The first was a secret hiding place hollowed out of the coral rock wall behind her house where she stashed the bottles of maraschino cherries bought with dimes intended for the church collection plate. Rae self-medicated when needed, delighting in this syrupy treat whenever she decided that she deserved one. As she put it years later: "Others might have liked cocaine," but "my particular drug of choice were jars of maraschino cherries."[8]

The other refuge was George Engel's house. Rae met George in her second-grade class at Coconut Grove Elementary School. His fashionable house with a three-story tower by the bay served as a much-needed escape from the daily trials of Rae's own home and the never-ending parade of stepmoms. George's mom, a queenly Grace Kelly look-alike, always greeted Rae as though she was a visiting dignitary. "Joined at the hip," the children talked and giggled late into the night in George's magnificent bedroom in the tower.[9]

By the time Rae was twelve or thirteen, school officials at Ponce De Leon Jr. High School could no longer turn a blind eye to her domestic situation. The authorities removed Rae from her father's home and placed her in the Dade County Children's Home in Kendall. Combination orphanage/reform school/juvenile detention center, the one thing that many who passed through its gates agreed upon was that it was no place for a child.[10]

Rae's recollections from the three months she spent at Kendall were fragmentary—"huge two- to three-story barracks surrounded by high fences and outside of that was miles of alligator swamp"—a physically and mentally abusive director, who immediately told Rae that she knew her from before, when Rae was "two years old and found abandoned in a Miami hotel room." Everything was locked at all times. Matrons carried masses of keys.[11]

While at Kendall Rae joined Youth for Christ, a Billy Graham–led evangelical program dedicated to inspiring young people to preach to others their age. Ray Stanford was the director of the Miami branch of Youth for Christ. He and his wife, Sue, maintained their home as a Christian Youth Ranch where, according to the *Miami Herald*, "kids come and go whenever they please, and sometimes they come with their problems long after midnight." The Stanfords rescued Rae from Kendall and took her in at the Christian Youth Ranch.[12]

Rae recalled her stay with them fondly. They "were wonderful to me and treated me like their own child." In spite of their kindness, which led Rae to believe that she really had been adopted, this was no permanent refuge. "I think that in my little-girl mind I thought I'd found a permanent home and I don't think I understood that that was really just a temporary home for me and I was very sad when the time came that I had to leave there." After leaving the Christian Youth Ranch, Rae was handed off from one foster family after another, most of them upper middle-class and connected to Miami Beach Presbyterian Church, where the Stanfords worshipped. The series of moves ended abruptly when Rae, at fifteen, was sent to Vashti Industrial School for Girls, a charitable institution in Thomasville, Georgia. Vashti was not an accredited high school at the time, but Rae described it as a place that "took good care of the girls" and "was a good home for girls like myself who really didn't have a reliable family . . . where they could live." One of Rae's friends at Vashti recalled that she was "the prettiest girl on campus." Her auburn hair was striking, and she always dressed beautifully. Beyond those traits, there was something about the way she presented herself that made her stand out.[13]

Like many men at the time, Hugh Duncan took an immediate fancy to Rae. She described her first husband as nondescript—average height, brown hair, no distinguishing features: "not embarrassing." By the time Rae met Duncan, doing what she had to do to survive had become a deeply ingrained feature of her life. There were indications that she did not expect the marriage to last—and she was right about that: Hugh Duncan turned out to be an echo of her father in some respects. Not long after the birth of their daughter Sherri, Rae got rid of him.[14]

Rae may have been stuck in Thomasville, Georgia, having just jettisoned a good-for-nothing husband, but she did not stay there long. Always a dog lover, when Rae learned that Zellie de Lussan Porter Ely had suffered a fatal heart attack while viewing the Westminster Dog Show at Madison Square Garden and that her husband was now seeking an appropriate mate for their purebreds, Rae pounced. She paid a visit to Colonel Hiram Ely at Hihope, his estate in Flemington, New Jersey. For one seeking new sanctuaries, the Elys' manor house, rumored (probably correctly) to have housed George Washington, seemed magical.[15]

She stayed for three days and may have left with her second marriage proposal in as many years. If not, it did not take long to receive one. Hiram showered Rae with gifts after her visit and begged her to return to New Jersey as quickly as possible. As he put it, there was no need to bring anything—all would be provided. She married Hiram in October 1962 and, with her Thomasville landlady minding six-month-old Sherri, Rae and Hiram sailed off to Europe for their five-month honeymoon.[16]

Born in March 1896, Hiram was descended from Nathaniel Ely, who came over on the *Mayflower*. Hiram's father, Addison, fought in the Spanish-American War and practiced law in Bergen County, New Jersey. After graduating from West Point in 1917, Hiram went into ordnance. A photograph from 1922 displays a handsome young uniformed Ely holding a phone connected to a washing machine–sized black device covered with dials—the "Ford Target Computer" (Fig. 3). It was a cutting-edge precursor to the computer used by the Navy to correct artillery fire for a ship's movement.[17]

Hiram went on to study acoustical engineering at MIT, then worked at Bell Labs, in New Jersey, where he patented two inventions: a sound-locating device (1930) and fire control apparatus (1933). He rubbed shoulders with Helen Keller there and with Thomas Edison in West Orange. At home, Hiram loved tinkering: he could make anything and fix everything. He was a renaissance man who spoke multiple languages, appreciated fine silver and

Figure 3. Captain Hiram Ely operating the "Ford Target Computer" in Washington, D.C., October 1922. (Licensed from Juniper Gallery/Shorpy/Vintagraph. A National Photo Company Collection glass negative.)

art, loved gardening, and had a certificate from Le Cordon Bleu, the famed Parisian cooking school.[18]

The Colonel stood six feet two inches tall and did not have an ounce of fat when Rae met him. As she put it, he carried himself elegantly, though never foppishly. She was proud to be seen with this accomplished man who clearly delighted in showing off his young bride. Rae thought of him as a walking *Encyclopedia Britannica* and was eager to turn his pages. He opened doors for her that she did not even know were there. Walking through those doors and locking them behind her assured Rae's presence in the upper middle class.[19]

One door accessed the upper echelons of the military. Rae was soon introduced to illustrious men and their wives at the Army and Navy Club in Washington, D.C; she even sat next to Mamie Eisenhower. To prepare for such events Rae pored over *Assembly Magazine,* the West Point publication that contained pictures and background on Hiram's schoolmates. She memorized each name and face and quickly emerged as the belle of the ball. Hiram flaunted the obvious age difference between himself and his wife; he enjoyed fooling his buddies, who assumed that Rae was his granddaughter.[20]

The Colonel's own children were less welcoming. His daughter Hope had filled the social vacuum that Zellie's death created, but a stepmom twenty-two years her junior upended Hope's relationship to her father as both daughter and companion/hostess. Before the wedding Hope wrote a letter to her father expressing her concerns. It all seemed "too soon and too fast." Hope wanted to see "the qualifications," like family and capabilities: "Not just that she has pretty red hair and sparkling eyes. Remember, we all have to live with her too." Hope's husband weighed in even more candidly, dwelling on his wife's hurt feelings, which weren't going to be "pooh-poohed away," and questioning Rae's motives. No "young thing, particularly if she is anywhere's [sic] near attractive, is going to marry a 65 year old man for love, or for pity, or for companionship, or sex, and if not these—then for what?"[21]

Hiram never answered that question, but he did sign a prenuptial agreement soon after receiving their letters. It stipulated that the Colonel had fully informed Rae Hatfield of his present real property holdings and ensured that Rae would inherit the house and at least fifteen acres of surrounding property if she remained married to him and outlived him. The agreement required that Rae forgo any rights to Hiram's remaining property.[22]

This apparently did not temper the sniping. A year later Hiram announced that there was a new chain of command and that Hope had better fall in. He wanted both his adult children to know that "any crack, or action, or discourtesy of any sort against Rae is a direct slap at me and will not be tolerated. You may think your father is a poor, decrepit old man and that he has married a foolish young woman," but they should know that he was "in full possession" of all of his faculties, that Rae had "a much more mature philosophy of life" than most women, whatever their age, and that "we are going to live together for a long time."[23]

Hi Jr. (as in the first syllable in Hihope farm) had his own issues with his father. A vehement and public dispute evolved when Junior added a modern wing to his cottage next to Hiram's property. A stockade fence between the properties and a "ham-shaped swimming pool" that crossed the property line soon led to a "No Trespassing" sign, threats of dynamiting from the former ordnance officer, and finally, bulldozers and a lawsuit that settled the matter. While fences could be dismantled and pools rebuilt, the relationship between father and son was damaged beyond repair.[24]

Hiram Jr. was not the only one building modern "monstrosities" in Flemington during the mid-sixties. The town was rapidly turning into an exurb of New York City, exploding with subdivisions, some of which were built on land that Hiram Sr. sold off to pay the higher taxes supporting this residential development. Every year Hihope looked out on more homes and fewer hills. "We had these subdivisions popping up all around us," Rae recalled, "which destroyed the lovely setting where the farm was."[25]

Flemington was not unique. Although its distance from New York City initially spared it from the sprawl that inched out from urban centers following World War II, a combination of highway construction and rising land prices gripped many such villages in the homebuilding frenzy that catapulted the percentage of Americans who owned their own homes from 44 to 63 percent between 1940 and 1970. The June 18, 1966 cover of Hiram's copy of the *Saturday Evening Post* summed up the national trend and featured a photograph of a giant bulldozer that appeared to be pushing the headline—"The Rape of the Land"—into the reader's lap. The quieter, smaller subheadline warned, "As our cities spread out cancerously in all directions, we are destroying—for profit—too many of the green and open places we need to make them livable."[26]

Soon, there were more Elys at Hihope. Addison's and Todd's births exacerbated the open warfare between the couple and Hiram's older children. With development inching closer each day, Hiram and Rae began to look for tranquility in locations beyond the reach of both adult children and suburban cul-de-sacs.[27]

The prospect of a special Arabian took her to Virginia, where she found Rikki, the horse of her dreams, at Lewis Field Farm. James Fielding Lewis, who owned the farm and the horse (his father had once owned the Champion Spark Plug Corporation), insisted that Rae buy a farm in Virginia. It would go nicely with the horse. His pal, realtor Eugenia Adams, had a must-see farm that Rae could check out on her way back to New Jersey.

Figuring that it would take more time to argue than to drive by the farm, Rae consented. With Rikki in the trailer, she followed Eugenia out Route 15 to Louisa County.[28]

The house—stucco, tower, and red-tile roof—leaped straight from her childhood into her future. "We had the horse and now I had George Engel's estate!" she remembered. Only this time, *Rae* would be Grace Kelly. Returning to New Jersey, Rae informed Hiram that she had found the perfect place. The couple drove down to Washington for the annual Army and Navy Club West Point Dinner, and then on to Charlottesville. After checking into the Jefferson Inn, they drove out to Louisa County the next day for a closer look. The asking price of $150,000 included the manor house, 400 acres of some of the best farmland in Louisa County, and four tractors. Hiram's $110,000 offer elicited a quick response: "Congratulations: Hawkwood is yours," including the rugs, draperies, and chandeliers (Fig. 4).[29]

The couple decided that Rae and the kids would move to Virginia while Hiram remained in New Jersey to sell Hihope. In July 1967, Rae piled Sherri and Addison into her grey Mercedes, found a sturdy box for baby Todd, and all four headed south. Rae and the older children slept on mattresses on the floor, while Todd got an upgrade from his box to a large drawer. The Ely family moved itself, making at least four trips in a used truck emblazoned with a huge pig resting on a crescent moon.

Rae and Hiram enrolled Sherri at Robert E. Lee Elementary School in Charlottesville. One of the enticements that Eugenia Adams had touted was the Tuition Reimbursement Plan—an outgrowth of Virginia's massive resistance to desegregation that reimbursed white citizens who enrolled their children in one of the many private "segregation academies" that sprang up across the state.[30]

As millions of Americans added their voices and sometimes their bodies to the civil rights movement of the mid-sixties, the Elys were untouched by this ferment. Rather, they joined the hundreds of thousands of white southerners who enrolled their children in state-subsidized private segregation academies, fueling the largest increase in private school attendance in that region's history. Hiram was pleased to hear that the Commonwealth of Virginia would pay for his children to attend a private school.[31]

Having retired in 1954, Hiram occupied himself primarily by gardening and managing his investments. He was also in charge of the shopping,

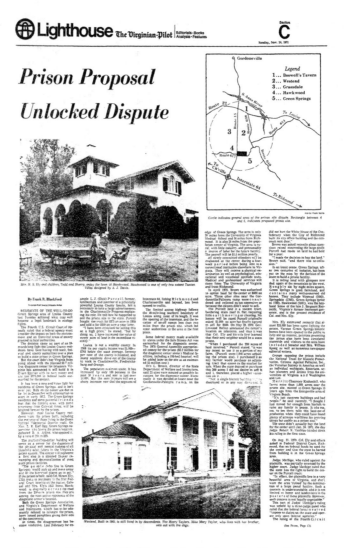

Figure 4. The top half of the article displays Rae Ely with her children in front of Hawkwood, November 1971. The bottom half displays Westend Plantation. (Licensed by Tribune Publishing. Photo: Frank Blackford.)

which he executed with military precision. Every other month the Colonel would drive the International Harvester truck down to Fort Lee, near Petersburg, Virginia. He returned with provisions, always spending exactly $600. Rae was determined to best her stepdaughter at cooking and within a few years, she recalled, she had refashioned herself into an excellent chef.[32]

Although the Elys had escaped subdivisions and Hiram's adult children, things were far from perfect at Hawkwood. Rae and Hiram had contrasting parenting styles. Hers was casual and, in the opinion of some, bordered on neglectful. Hiram, on the other hand, was a nineteenth-century disciplinarian who sometimes forgot that he was no longer in the military. For the most part, Rae compensated for inattentive mothering by catering to Hiram's other needs, including the most important one as lord of the manor.[33]

3
Competing Histories

A WEEK OR SO AFTER HOLTON'S 1970 helicopter reconnaissance, Rae and Hiram Ely settled down for the evening at Hawkwood, ready to enjoy the early spring evening and to catch the news on their big Magnavox television set. This is how they learned of the "facility"—and where the governor planned to put it. Stunned, Rae envisioned prison walls in full view of her own home—her haven. She looked to Hiram: "What are you going to do about *this*?" A good military man, Hiram took preemptive action and within hours had assumed a leading role in organizing the resistance. It would take far longer for the residents to discover the history of the community they lived in, its geology, and in some cases, the genealogy of their own homes. The property values of their individual estates, however, would not have withstood Governor Holton's prison reform agenda or the courthouse crowd's quest for jobs had Angus Murdock, a graduate student in history at the University of Virginia, not penned a two-page essay titled "A Private Opinion of the Future of the Green Springs" that explained why Green Springs was distinctive. It was the area's *history* that distinguished it from other parts of Louisa County, and indeed, much of Virginia.[1]

To make his case, Murdock deployed a different conception of what constituted history than the one commonly held by most Americans. This new approach focused on the everyday interactions of a *community*—the people who built it and the relationship between the structures they built and the landscape they cultivated. Although Murdock wrote about Green Springs in the nineteenth century, the historical lens he trained on that community was crafted in the 1960s.

He insisted that Green Springs was unique because this rural community had survived as a "contiguous whole." History was about more than the famous white men who had lived there or passed through on their way to war. Because so many of the original structures and their surrounding environment remained intact in Green Springs, that community was uniquely positioned to offer a history lesson about how people worked and lived before the Civil War in the rural South. Once glimpsed through this lens, preserving the community's past became a powerful argument for putting the prison elsewhere.[2]

Named for a spring that offered medicinal cures (according to Thomas Jefferson), Green Springs was an oval-shaped 14,000-acre region that hugged the western border of Louisa County. Politically, it was a magisterial district within Louisa County, but Green Springs also had a geological and agricultural coherence that explained why much of Louisa's best farmland was located in this six-by-eight-square-mile section of the county. Landowners throughout the Commonwealth had long enjoyed a prosperity that rested upon the work of enslaved people. Green Springs landowners also benefited from a volcanic intrusion that had carved out a bowl-shaped area, creating soil that was more fertile than the surrounding Virginia Piedmont. In the words of a 1973 study, that soil gave "continuous economic vitality to the area," which, after European farmers had displaced native populations and a scattering of trappers, yielded hefty profits for plantation owners who cultivated tobacco, wheat, and cattle in succession. Early tax records documented that more than half of the land in Green Springs was "extraordinary." Progressive farming techniques, the McCormick reaper, a new railroad line, and the emergence of Richmond as a global wheat and slave-trading center leveraged Green Springs' natural advantages.[3]

Those advantages led to centuries of enmity between Green Springs and the rest of Louisa County. The "bitterness," Clare White, a reporter for the *Roanoke Times,* chronicled, stretched back to the early 1800s, "when the planters of Green Springs grew rich on their fertile land while the rest of the county struggled with poor land." The bird's-eye view of Green Springs she sketched in 1970 underscored just how little physical change had occurred. Cattle grazed on the rolling pastures, "corn tasseled in the fields, and the old houses, some thirty-six of them generously spaced from one another, were still there as mute testimony to the building practices of 250 years." By 1970, however, most of the former plantations had been divided into farms that ranged from forty-five to 1,000 acres.[4]

The population of Green Springs was largely white and Protestant, but that is where the similarities between neighbors ended, as incomes and wealth spanned the economic spectrum. Property owners in 1970 "were no longer a class apart as were the planters in the heyday of enslaved labor. They were a mixture, some of humble origin, some aristocratic, and some in between." According to White, there was no longer "a web of relationship . . . to create a kind of closed society."[5]

The growing resistance to Governor Holton's announcement rekindled that web overnight. Passing drivers who had merely raised an index finger off their steering wheel, in the universal rural greeting, suddenly got to know each other a lot better. Complete strangers showed up at the Elys' doorstep for gatherings and meetings. Shared phone lines—"party lines"—hummed. For the most part, the men reached out to elected officials, who, they quickly learned, stood firmly behind the governor. The men also planned a community gathering to express their outrage at the plan, the choice of site, and the secrecy that had surrounded the whole process.

It was the women's job to make calls, spread the word, take notes and host fundraising events. Rae was no different in this regard than the other wives. She deferred to her husband when it came to politics. In fact, her deference went well beyond politics. "If somebody asked me, what did I think?" she recalled, "I would look at him and ask, what do we think? I had no independent identity separate from him. I literally stood in his shadow and basked in his glory."[6]

On June 2, 1970, roughly 175 citizens packed Green Springs Elementary School to express their unanimous opposition to the governor's plan. Many had already signed a petition containing 280 names requesting that the Louisa County Board of Supervisors "do everything in their power to prevent this Center from being located in Louisa County." The meeting also elected Hiram as the chair of the "Green Springs Penal Protesters."[7]

Hiram insisted that he and his neighbors were being punished because they had been good stewards of the land "in an era of thoughtless use of the bulldozer for the sake of a few dollars' profit." He charged that they were being penalized "for having kept our beautiful valley uncluttered with developments." Charlottesville's newspaper, the *Daily Progress,* asked skeptically: "Can a small number of Louisa citizens muster enough support to thwart the seemingly already concrete plan of the state?"[8]

Colonel Ely again spoke on behalf of concerned Louisans at a public meeting with Otis Brown, this time excoriating bureaucrats' failure to consult the people who would be affected most directly by the prison. "We have seen them flying overhead in their helicopter and they have come in their limousines and there is not any one of them that has had the decency or the courage to walk across the street and talk to me and say, 'We're going to put a penal institution here across from your house. What do you think of it?' "[9]

A June 11 public meeting with Brown attracted a couple who wielded both wealth and national stature. Richard S. (Major) Reynolds, the chair of the board of Reynolds Metals (as in aluminum foil), had once owned the land now sited for the prison, along with Hawkwood across the road. Major Reynolds testified that the site could not support a large complex like the prison. His wife, Virginia Sargeant Reynolds, a native of Louisa County, was "flabbergasted" that "the land which the state was offering $800 per acre [for] was sold less than two years ago for $200 an acre." Indeed, a January internal memo from Otis Brown estimated the cost for site acquisition at $75,000—roughly the same amount Dickie Purcell (Harold's brother) had paid in December—less than half the $160,000 that the Commonwealth now offered.[10]

The opposition soon raised a host of other issues. Large Green Springs landowner and staunch opponent of the diagnostic center Donald Lee Atkins (known as D.L.) emphasized threats to real estate values. Several other opponents worried about the children: not only would they now have to live near a criminal element in the prison itself, they would be exposed to the *families* of criminals moving to the district to be near their relatives. Mrs. John B. Askew of Grassdale, one of the largest estates in Green Springs, a teacher and native of Louisa, pleaded, "Please do not let these youngsters be forced to grow up with the stigma of being from the prison neighborhood."[11]

Conservationists and environmentalists also weighed in. Bracketts Plantation owner Elisabeth Aiken Nolting's conservation roots were nurtured by her uncle, Carl Nolting, the driving force behind the Thomas Jefferson Soil

Conservation District. Conservation, his niece believed, did not mean hermetically sealing the land—Louisans had fished and hunted at Bracketts for generations. Rather, it demanded the highest and best use. Nolting reminded Governor Holton of that other sure bet he had made, along with reducing crime, writing, "up to this time we have been so heartened by your stand for 'Conservation.'" The Sullivans, both biologists, deployed the language of contemporary environmentalists, warning that Holton's plans would "utterly destroy one of the few remaining ecologically sound rural areas of the Virginia."[12]

The Krahenbills, farmers whose land abutted the proposed diagnostic center, urged the Commonwealth to consider "some other sites, where hard working, god fearing people like us will not be hurt and have to give up their homes." After all, the town of Mineral, also in Louisa County, wanted the facility. A town in neighboring Orange County had also expressed interest. One of the few prison opponents who acknowledged the larger dilemma of siting public works was John W. Askew. Although he asked Governor Holton to revise his plans, Askew hoped "we are not saying 'do this to somebody else but don't do it to us.'"[13]

Otis Brown had heard these kinds of complaints before. Murdock's essay introduced a new wrinkle. Although Angus had only recently moved to Green Springs, he embodied a new understanding of history that incorporated some of the central social, cultural, and intellectual currents coursing through the 1960s. He applied this perspective to Green Springs' history at the very moment that some academics and preservation professionals were beginning to embrace it as well. Following Murdock's path from Kenyon College frat boy in 1957 to his 1970 Green Springs essay illustrates the seismic shift in who and what should be included in history and the catalyst for this transformation.

A 1957 photograph of the young "Bob" in the *Kenyon Collegian* shows him, crop-haired and berry smeared, winning the Freshman Pie Eating Contest. Suspended in his senior year following a particularly destructive party involving a Steinway piano dropped from a fourth-floor window, Angus "did the honorable thing" and enlisted in the U.S. army. After he married Deborah Harrah, who left Vassar to join him, Angus used the Army's generous benefits to complete his undergraduate education, taking night courses in history at San Francisco State College. Deborah and Angus lived in San Francisco, close to the City Lights bookstore founded by Beat poet Lawrence Ferlinghetti when it, and he, were the epicenter of the countercultural movement. Although Angus and Deborah were not "hippies," it was impossible to avoid the zeitgeist.[14]

Had he gone directly from Kenyon to the Ph.D. program at the University of Virginia in 1961, Angus would likely have remained just as oblivious to the history of Green Springs as many of its residents were. Most history professors at that time focused on famous white men, wars, and the political machinations that animated them. A mere six years later, as he began graduate work at San Francisco State, Angus quickly learned that even professional historians were easily influenced by the winds of social change blowing across the nation. Historical scholarship was evolving, albeit slowly, and Angus was swept up in some of those changes.

The burgeoning civil rights movement, mounting protests against the Vietnam War, and second-wave feminism reminded scholars that politics was not confined to diplomatic correspondence or legislative debate. Politics took place in the streets and was waged by people who often had been left out of history—poor people, the working class, African Americans, and women of all classes and races. One of Murdock's professors, Joseph Illick, described his own reasons for shifting the lens: "My students had no family ties to the politicians, military heroes, and business leaders who appeared in textbooks; their predecessors were immigrants and farmers, slaves and wage workers and housewives, anonymous but real Americans."[15]

The same trends that affected Angus's professors at San Francisco State influenced architectural history in 1968, when he enrolled in a Ph.D. program at the University of Virginia in Charlottesville. Here, it was the environmental movement that proved influential, as some scholars began to pay greater attention to the relationship between the built environment and its surrounding "natural" environment. Although Murdock's advisor in the Corcoran Department of History pursued a traditional approach to political history—he was a leading expert on Teddy Roosevelt—a field in architectural history again exposed Angus to an intellectual current that challenged orthodox thinking about history. Though Jefferson's legacy ensured that classical architectural forms would not be neglected, growing attention was directed to structures that served everyday life in the state. When the School of Architecture initiated a review of the Commonwealth's notable architecture, the final survey encompassed industrial structures like Richmond's Tredegar Iron Works; it even included a 1926 gas station.[16]

Angus, who claimed that he just liked looking at old houses, was drawn to field work. The peripatetic Professor Freddy Nichols led many of these excursions. Dubbed "the Fred Astaire of architecture" by Deborah Murdock for his flamboyant ways and two-toned shoes, Nichols chaired the Architectural History and Preservation Program at the School of Architecture. Angus took two or three courses with Nichols; they consisted almost exclusively of road trips to the major plantation houses and churches of Virginia.[17]

Murdock's research expanded beyond houses themselves. He examined the relationship of the buildings to the surrounding natural environment, focusing on both their aesthetic meaning and utilitarian connections. Although history from the bottom up featuring Americans who previously had been ignored gained a foothold in the academy, much of the history that Murdock and the prison opponents discovered featured homes of wealthy white people. They were the ones who left records and lived in the structures most likely to survive, let alone be restored.[18]

Poring over the rental ads in 1969, Angus spotted a place in Louisa County. He and Deborah drove out to Eastern View, a two-story frame house built shortly before the Civil War, where they were met by the owners, D. L. Atkins and his wife, Frances Anne. For forty dollars a month, along with the eight rooms at Eastern View, the Murdocks got access to 300 acres, fresh-killed turkeys on Thanksgiving and Christmas (although Angus had to help the farm manager with the executions), and all the quail they could shoot. Like many of the plantations in Green Springs, the house had been neglected. It was, for all practical purposes, unheated; Angus simply hung the holiday turkeys from the dining room lighting fixture.[19]

The Murdocks learned that people got to know each other at church. That is where they met the Elys, and soon their five kids were playing together. As the only young mothers among their acquaintances, Rae and Deborah appreciated the support when it came to child tending, and the two energetic, intelligent young women easily became friends.[20]

Even those Green Springs landowners who knew something about the history of their own plantation, like D. L. Atkins, had not given much thought to the relationship between these old houses and their surrounding environment: they certainly did not think of them as comprising a broader historical community. When Governor Holton announced his plans for the diagnostic center, Angus connected the historic dots, and, more important, arranged them in compelling fashion, pointing to the collective architectural history of the area and rattling off all the names of historically significant houses within a carriage ride of each other: Westend, Grassdale, Bracketts, Hawkwood, Green Springs Plantation. "It was as though he handed me a key," Rae recalled. "Oh, I get it now."[21]

As "a historian, an architectural historian and a resident of the Green Springs district," Murdock believed that the development proposed by the Commonwealth was "an affront to the past and an insult to the future." Most significant, he specified the historical, architectural, environmental, and aesthetic qualities that distinguished Green Springs from other communities that might also object to a prison. His essay distilled Green Springs' history, from the spike in the price of wheat in the 1850s triggered by the Crimean War to the introduction of fertilizers like guano that dramatically improved the yield of Green Springs' already productive soil. Conspicuously missing in Murdock's account, from today's vantage point, was any mention of enslaved people other than as an expense to be avoided. With the advent of labor-saving devices, planters could now use their surplus capital to "build more elaborate mansion houses." This created an unblemished region "where the architectural historian can trace the evolution of the Virginia house from 1740 through 1860." History preserved in wood, brick, and stone was augmented by rich manuscript collections that documented the ideas and activities of the people who lived there.[22]

Gliding through the essay was an account of Mary Jane Boggs Holladay. On a summer day in 1851, the eighteen-year-old drove through Green Springs on her way to visit Prospect Hill plantation. Her diary described the "very pretty" land of Bracketts (1799) and Westend (1849) and reported on the excellent quality of the crops. For "a hundred years before Miss Holladay's drive through the Green Springs district and a hundred years later," Murdock wrote, "those who by accident or design have passed through this verdant region cannot escape the haunting charm of its rolling pastures, dusty roads and old dwellings."[23]

If surplus capital created those historic homes, the "genteel poverty of the post–Civil War years preserved many of these plantations from total decay or thoughtless remodeling." The essay also foreshadowed the kind of private initiative that would soon attract public partners in the quest to preserve Green Springs. Capital scarcity may have preserved the outer shells of Green Springs' plantations, but as Murdock put it, "Careful restoration by recent owners has brought most of them back to their original condition."[24]

The most distinctive feature of Murdock's case for Green Springs was an emerging scholarly interpretative lens through which historians identified what *constituted* history. Murdock insisted that the "*unique* aspect of the Green Springs is the survival, in their original form, of so many of these 18th and 19th century plantations many of which have all of their old outbuildings, and the fact that they all adjoin in a contiguous whole to form an *unblighted* unblemished example of a plantation community."[25]

Noting the Herculean effort poured into reconstructing and restoring Colonial Williamsburg, Murdock contrasted that icon with the organic evolution of Green Springs. "All the money in the world could not reproduce what nature and man and the passage of time have created in this neighborhood." Ultimately, Green Springs' claim to distinctiveness rested on its residents' ability to give its land, its houses, and its way of life a history. Applying a new and capacious framework for appreciating its history might safeguard Green Springs' future in an era of rapid development and well-intentioned prison reform.[26]

Published in local newspapers as a letter to the editor, Angus Murdock's essay soon dominated the public narrative about the diagnostic center. In a piece quoting Murdock extensively, the *Daily Progress* suggested just what was at stake: "the preservation of the area which is considered crucial for the state and the country." Once the new way of thinking about history was introduced, prison opponents unearthed deeper histories of the district's old houses, the relationships between these houses, and their ties to the land. They found a lot more dots to connect, and each one filled in the portrait of their new historical canvass.[27]

Plenty of homeowners in Green Springs did not even know the full history of their own homes—including the Elys. When they bought Hawkwood, Rae assumed that it was a 1920s knockoff of an Italian villa, similar not only to her childhood chum George Engel's home but to dozens of other "Italianate" houses. Murdock soon exploded that assumption. Working in the UVa archives he stumbled across correspondence with the renowned Civil War–era architect Alexander Jackson Davis that contained drawings dating back to the 1850s documenting the construction of Hawkwood.[28]

Rae recalled Murdock's excitement when he called. In a high-pitched voice, barely able to contain himself, Angus asked: "Do you know what you've got?" Given Murdock's excitement, she assumed one of her kids was contagious: "Chicken pox?" she asked. What Angus reported was good news—perhaps more exciting to the architectural historian than to Rae Ely at the time. He informed her that she was living in a house that had great historic significance, a house designed by the renowned nineteenth-century architect Alexander Jackson Davis. Before Holton's prison announcement and Murdock's guide to Green Springs' history, discovering Hawkwood's pedigree was a source of great pride, but hardly the basis for any action, and certainly not a catalyst for reimagining Hawkwood's relationship to the surrounding rural community.[29]

Murdock's perspective on history gave prison opponents a tool that provided an overarching rationale—one that accommodated a set of disparate motivations, from the desire to protect property values to deep convictions about sustaining the environment and preserving the neighborhood's quality of life. For a handful of citizen activists, it was more than another argument that protected their property; it was a cause that they passionately embraced. Prison opponents suddenly noticed previously obscured connections, making real the historic community that they now sought to preserve. Historic preservation was also a valuable resource because it resonated beyond the boundaries of Louisa County. Indeed, it was valued far more in Washington, D.C., than in Louisa County.

The Green Springs fight also connected the stodgy world of historic preservation to the environmental movement, highlighting beauty and permanence—two of the three components (along with health) that defined environmentalism in the last half of the twentieth century. The effort to embrace the rapidly expanding history of the Green Springs community soon attracted the attention of allies far beyond Green Springs. It also enflamed enemies closer to home.[30]

4
"He Was Not Always Right—But He Was Never Wrong"

CLAIMING THAT THE RELATIONSHIP BETWEEN Green Springs' old buildings and their surrounding environment offered unique insight into a historical rural community struck many of Louisa County's residents as absurd. They and every elected official believed that this newfangled understanding of history was bunk. Local favorite son Patrick Henry was history—not the relationship between the house he once lived in and a bunch of trees. In their opinion, history paid homage to some of the famous white men who had once lived in Louisa County, the houses those notables lived in, the occasional famous man, like Lafayette, who passed through, and the battles fought nearby.

Nor did most Louisans see any conflict between protecting history and modernizing the landscape that surrounded it. W. W. Whitlock, who served as an attorney for the county, pointed to Bear Castle, home to Thomas Jefferson's brother-in-law, Dabney Carr. It was now located in the shadow of the North Anna nuclear power plant. Yet, W. W. believed that it was "more attractive than ever, and is receiving more historical notice from the public, because of the increased traffic that comes to the area." As the nation approached its bicentennial, County Administrator Dean Agee scored the Green Springs crowd for their tepid participation in that celebration: that was history, not abstract concepts like a "contiguous whole."[1]

The more proximate history that most Louisans recalled, however, was their county's history of economic deprivation and the ways in which local government had always been run by the Byrd organization and their deputies in Louisa's courthouse crowd who took their marching orders from Circuit Court Judge Harold Purcell. Despite their strident defense of states' rights and opposition to anything that smacked of social welfare, both Senator Byrd and men like Harold Purcell were politically and economically positioned to steer jobs to Louisans because they sat at the intersection of the market and the public sector. Louisa may not have had a stoplight in 1970, but it did have Harold Purcell informally directing economic traffic. Although Louisa remained one of the Commonwealth's poorest counties, the ruling elite's access to potential jobs and revenue-creating private initiatives and public largesse combined with the long-standing conflation of public and private interest in the service of economic development seemed to many to be the best path forward. That way of doing business (and politics) reached back to the New Deal, if not earlier. Indeed, Harold was the son of Bank of Louisa president John S. Purcell, who understood that "the banks were much involved in politics." Harold "followed his lead."[2]

Angus Murdock's understanding of Green Springs' history "just came out of the woodwork," Otis Brown recalled. Developer Robert Whitlock, W. W.'s brother, did not believe that Green Springs was any more historical than the rest of the county, although after elected to office he learned to see it as a beautiful area. Recent arrivals like the Elys could afford to ignore material considerations because they "were not concerned about [Louisa's] economy. They had ... other means of income." These "newcomers" relocated "because it was a beautiful area," and "they did not want to see it change."[3]

For the most part, those who had lived in Louisa County the longest were also the most skeptical of Murdock's so-called history, starting with the man who represented Green Springs on the county's board of supervisors, Earl Ogg. He was a bachelor who lived in a hundred-year-old farmhouse with his sister and brother. They were the fourth generation of Oggs who lived there; for good reason Ogg claimed to know a thing or two about Green Springs' history.[4]

Earl Ogg doubled down on his remark to *Time* disparaging claims that Green Springs was historic, telling another reporter, "I never heard about all this history those people ... are talking about. The Battle of Trevilians is the only history here." Earl's sister, who was shelling walnuts with a neighbor in the kitchen, jumped in: "I've never heard of this history either. The Battle of

Trevilians: there's where the history is, if it's up here." The siblings were referring to the largest battle of the Civil War fought exclusively by cavalry, in June 1864. Brother Earl had the last word: "If it's history they claim, I've not been able to see it."[5]

Whatever their views about history, the courthouse crowd insisted that it should not impede economic opportunities for Louisans. County Administrator Dean Agee was blunt about the reasons for his constituents' overwhelming support for the prison: jobs. With the completion of I-64 through Louisa County and two nuclear reactors under construction, many residents backed the diagnostic center because it would keep the economic momentum going.[6]

Most Louisans believed that they had the courthouse crowd to thank for the jobs that came with this kind of modernization. Purcell led a tight-knit group of growth-oriented public officials who could attract and guide that economic development. Even the Federal government's intervention in local affairs was welcomed when it came to job creation or improvements in infrastructure like highways, bridges, and nuclear reactors. Governor Holton's reform ambitions aside, the diagnostic center fit squarely into this government job-creating pattern.[7]

The New Deal conjures images of a series of alphabet soup–labeled Federal programs designed to jump-start the economy and put money in the pockets of workers. These interests were pitted against staunch opposition from the private sector, the story goes. Overlooked by this portrayal of politics, however, was the fact that New Deal programs and their Cold War heirs stimulated the growth of the private sector. Some programs, like the Tennessee Valley Authority's efforts to stimulate demand for electricity, and spinoffs, like the Electric Home and Farm Authority, which provided credit for the purchase of electric appliances, were emulated by private utility companies across the South.[8]

The broader economic objective of Governor Holton's proposal was indebted to another way in which the New Deal stimulated economic growth—alliances between the Federal government, regional and local politicians, and private-sector elites. Each of these partners trumpeted the crucial tie between public investment and the kind of economic benefit that the diagnostic center promised. Roosevelt did not mince words when it came to the role of state and local governments. "You are the great decentralizers," he told his National Emergency Council tasked with coordinating Federal programs with state and local governments. Nor did he confine his message to insiders. He told the millions who tuned into his second Fireside Chat that his initiatives were not seeking "Government control." Rather, they jump-started a "partnership between Government and farming and industry and transportation."[9]

Even the most successful examples of these partnerships—high-tech defense industries in southern California, Silicon Valley in northern California, and the Research Triangle in North Carolina—elided the Federal government's role in these endeavors and certainly did not garner much public attention. Hundreds of similar Federal interventions into local and regional economies, like the one on the nuclear reactor–heated shores of Louisa's Lake Anna, flew entirely beneath the radar.[10]

Even though Harry F. Byrd battled Franklin Roosevelt for the Democratic presidential nomination in 1932 (and again in 1944) and eventually made a name for himself by criticizing the New Deal for its profligate spending, when Byrd was originally appointed to a vacant Senate seat in 1933, he supported virtually all of FDR's legislative initiatives in the first hundred days of the New Deal. A staunch critic of any program that might be considered a handout even during this desperate time of need, the senator rarely met a patronage position or infrastructure assistance from the Federal government that he was not happy to accept. The conservative *Richmond Times-Dispatch* summed things up best in describing Virginia's Byrd-dominated public officials: "They are great advocates of state rights when such advocacy meets their convenience, but when it doesn't they believe in letting Uncle Sam hold the bag."[11]

The Byrd organization began to unravel with Harry F. Byrd, Sr.'s death in 1966, even though his son, "Little Harry," was appointed to his father's seat in the U.S. Senate. The organization fell victim to the tidal wave of Black voter registration stimulated by the Voting Rights Act of 1965. Nevertheless, fragments of the machine remained firmly in place well into the 1970s, including in Louisa County. The local political infrastructure had not changed much since the 1930s. Louisa County's elected officials heartily embraced Byrd's "massive resistance" to school desegregation and his local control rhetoric. The courthouse crowd served as a reliable cog in the Byrd organization.[12]

The Byrd organization was designed to maximize the authority of the public officials, not the voices of voters, and it achieved that by suppressing turnout, especially Black voters. A shared perspective on politics, governance, and the market was the glue that held the Byrd organization together. As

Virginia governor Lindsay Almond, Jr. put it in 1958, "It's like a club . . . except that it has no bylaws, constitution or dues. It's a loosely knit association, you might say, between men who share the philosophy of Senator Byrd." More succinctly, a *Washington Post* reporter wrote, "the road to political success begins not on the hustings but at the circuit judge's Christmas party."[13]

Maintaining white supremacy in the racial hierarchy was the foundation of the Byrd organization men, along with a fierce commitment to local control. Even at the local and state level, taxes were to be kept low and services limited, except when they promoted local business, especially the enterprises run by organization leaders. Throughout his long career, Senator Byrd was best known for his commitment to road building, transportation infrastructure that was essential to the success of his apple orchards and many of the farmers in his rural constituency. As Byrd's biographer Ronald L. Heinemann explained, "Byrd entered politics not primarily out of sense of service to the larger community . . . but to preserve or advance that which was beneficial to himself and his interests."[14]

Circuit court judges were the organization's field marshals who ensured that this shared vision was carried out as they vetted new recruits to the "club." One for each of Virginia's forty counties, the judges were appointed by men like themselves in the Virginia General Assembly. The circuit court judges, in turn, controlled a host of appointments at the county level, including real estate assessors, the welfare board, and, most significant politically, the board of electors. Influence also radiated out from the county's circuit judge to the state senator, General Assembly delegate, and eventually county supervisors in the organization. Green Springs' supervisor, Earl Ogg, was a case in point. As one former Louisa County supervisor put it, Earl was one of those people "who appears to be power . . . but in fact he wasn't. He was controlled by the Purcell family."[15]

No field general had matters buttoned up more securely than Louisa Circuit Court Judge Harold Purcell. Linwood Holton may have been the first Republican to occupy the Governor's Mansion since Reconstruction, and he may have garnered 49.4 percent of the vote in Louisa County, but that did not mean that the Democratic stranglehold on local politics had lost its grip. At least not while Harold Purcell was in charge.

Purcell was born in 1920. Except for prep school, college, law school, and military service during World War II, he would spend his life enjoying and expanding his birthright prominence as far as possible in the Louisa County pond. The judge was known for driving the latest-model Cadillac. "He was very aristocratic . . . he had a very high opinion of the Purcells." They ran Louisa County. A lifelong Democrat, Purcell served for two decades as a Virginia state legislator. Harold Purcell's service to the 26th District, and perhaps his personal friendship with Mills Godwin and Harry F. Byrd, Sr. paid off in 1966 when he was appointed to the 16th Judicial Circuit. Purcell presided over Louisa County from that post until he retired in 1979.[16]

In Judge Purcell's view, business and politics were closely related. Indeed, few things of political consequence in Louisa County happened without the judge's knowledge and approval. Like Byrd, Purcell was a staunch conservative: he disapproved strongly of "people and generations that live on government money." Government money, however—advanced knowledge of which often reached circuit court judges in the Byrd organization—was not a bad thing when it constructed roads like I-64 that promised to put Louisa County on the economic map. It was especially welcome if it brought jobs *and* a healthy profit for the judge's brother, as was the case with the diagnostic center.[17]

Judge Purcell saw little need to separate his land business from his politics. It was rumored that at one point, he and his son owned tens of thousands of acres in Louisa County—covering an area more than twice the size of Green Springs. How they had come by this land was the subject of much speculation. Many people who had business dealings with Judge Purcell praised his honesty. One associate stated that Harold was "a very sharp man" who had a reputation for "being a hard man." However, the associate continued, "for all my business dealings with him, I couldn't have dealt with nobody no better."[18]

One persistent rumor was that the former state legislator used his political position to get a jump on land that would soon appreciate in value due to state-subsidized or state-regulated development. The nuclear power plant going up in Mineral was one example. It was rumored that Purcell and his friends started buying land three years before anybody knew about the project, and certainly before the public knew that the South Anna River would be damned, creating valuable lakefront property that hosted dockside gracious living. By one account, Judge Purcell paid $50 an acre for the land and sold it for $200,000 a lot. "He went after all this land three years before anybody knew that the power company was coming here. Of course, he was a judge: he *knew* it was coming."[19]

Dean Agee, between his experience as county administrator and then clerk of the court, probably knew Judge Purcell as well as anybody. According to Agee, the judge was "as good as gold" to him. Yet there was no doubt that Purcell ruled with an iron fist. Agee described him as a very strong man who loved to exert pressure. "Like Lyndon Johnson, he didn't give up."[20]

One elected official described Purcell as a good neighbor but a tough judge who could be domineering: "He was not always right—but he was never wrong." Judge Harold Purcell was not pleased with those activists in Green Springs whose conception of political participation was radically at odds with his.[21]

"He got revved up one morning before court," Dean Agee recalled. Judge Purcell was so mad that Agee assumed his boss had been working on his taxes. The real source of his anger soon became apparent. Purcell kept a full courtroom waiting while he orchestrated his campaign and ordered his clerk to carry it out. "The whole focus was zeroing in on Rae Ely." The judge only relented the next day when one of the supervisors sat down with him and told him, "Harold, I don't believe in getting into a pissing contest with a skunk because you can't outstink 'em." That logic resonated with the judge—at least that morning. Decades later, Agee did not mince words in describing the relationship between Rae Ely and the Purcells: "I'm telling you what, it is a *war* between she and the Purcells; *that* will never heal."[22]

Although the public was never polled on the issue, pro-prison candidates fared well in subsequent elections, confirming that a substantial majority of Louisa's voters supported the diagnostic center. It was not just Judge Harold Purcell's father who believed in the seamless integration of business and politics. When it came to public investment that would stimulate the local economy, the New Deal formula had long been embraced; indeed, it was one of the few areas of consensus that crossed racial lines. The claims that such policies would diminish the quality of life for a few people in Green Springs, or that economic development could possibly run counter to the national interest—in this case, preserving the environment and nation's past—did not impress most Louisans.

Dean Agee summed up the perspective of most Louisans: "Some people saw a means of making money. And if we can make money we're going to solve a lot of ills." Agee then repeated an assessment of the Green Springs battle that I heard again and again from those who supported the prison and mining: "It was a fight of the haves and the have-nots. The people who were opposed to it, they had made theirs, they had bought here and they wanted to be exclusive. Those that wanted it [the diagnostic center] were still working and they saw it as a means of getting a little more out of life. Now, what does that do to the environment? I ain't going there."[23]

Like their white neighbors, Black Louisans supported this quest for jobs but not the courthouse crowd that pursued those jobs. These were the same men that had presided over Jim Crow segregation and sought to maintain Louisa County's racial hierarchy well into the 1970s. Blacks were disadvantaged by a governing regime that maintained both racial and political hierarchies. Long-standing New Deal formulas for economic development in the South were buttressed by even older attitudes about race, gender, and their powerful remnants.

A distinguished Black teacher who worked in Louisa County at the time of the controversy offered a good summary of Black public opinion. Lewis Stephens did not support Historic Green Springs, Inc's political agenda. Most of the local jobs for Black men were on farms or in sawmills, lumbering, and the pulpwood business. Like lower-middle-class whites, many African Americans traveled as far as Washington, D.C, a two-hour drive away, for employment. In Stephens's opinion, most Blacks in Louisa believed that the prison and vermiculite mining would bring far better-paying jobs closer to home. White politicians did not benefit from this potential support, however, because Black opinion did not matter to the political establishment. "Nobody's listening; there is no outlet; [Blacks] were pretty much ignored." Stephens and many other Blacks just sat back and watched.[24]

Those who opposed Governor Holton's prison plans faced more than outdated conceptions of history and a reform-minded rising Republican star. They took on an entrenched governing team that held virtually all the political, legal, economic, racial, and gendered cards in 1970. When the conflict was framed as historic preservation versus jobs, as the courthouse crowd insisted, Louisans of every demographic stripe supported their local officials. Beating the machine was not going to be easy.

PART TWO

MAKING HISTORY

5
Peppery Women

THE THREAT TO RAE ELY'S FRONT yard and the growing recognition that more than Hawkwood's 400 acres was at risk propelled her into a leadership position in the Green Springs Association. Millions of women had plunged into politics through left-leaning direct action, or at least support for the civil rights movement, the antiwar movement, second-wave feminism, or the environmental movement. "There was something about that period," public interest law pioneer Ralph Nader recalled, "Vietnam, Civil rights. Coming off the struggles of the 60s—it did something to people that age." At the other end of the ideological spectrum, thousands of politically disengaged women were drawn into politics even earlier through conservative networks that operated on the local level.[1]

Though Rae's journey no doubt reflected her unique path and skill set, she arrived at the same place as many previously apolitical white middle-class women who entered politics during the 1970s to protect their immediate environment from perceived threats to the land or air, or from noise, or traffic congestion. A good number were labeled "peppery" or "feisty" for pursuing political agendas—from preserving history to protecting the environment—that simultaneously protected their property values. These were women like seventy-five-year-old Putnam Valley, New York, resident Mrs. Arthur Kinoy, described by the *New York Times* as "peppery," who had worked for forty years to save enough money to build a house that was now threatened by highway construction. Or Michelle Madoff, another "peppery" housewife living in the primarily white, middle-class Pittsburgh neighborhood of Squirrel Hill, who led a movement to improve air quality in 1969. At first reluctant to take on the role (she later remembered, "I didn't want to go and testify and be branded as another idiot housewife—hysterical Squirrel Hill housewife in tennis shoes"), Madoff eventually formed a local branch of GASP—the Group Against Smog and Pollution. Or Claire Ellis, who in 1972 wrote to the *Concord Journal* in Massachusetts rallying her neighbors to block plans to widen a highway that would run through her town. She urged them to use a bit of Concord's Yankee ingenuity and draw upon their Thoreauvian roots to protect what made Concord unique and special.[2]

Unlike minority and economically disadvantaged communities, middle-class white women like Rae Ely brought financial and racial advantages to political arenas. Would those resources offset their inexperience and the hostility they encountered in the uniformly male (albeit white) political venues they breached? That men were rarely labeled "peppery" or "feisty" for pursuing political agendas that served the public yet simultaneously advanced self-interest signaled the challenge that lay ahead. Rae Ely overcame daunting obstacles faced by any woman entering the political sphere: there were plenty of sexist obstacles in a nation where leading newspapers still identified her as Mrs. Hiram B. Ely. She used gender, defined by her in a distinctly pre–second-wave feminism fashion (and fashion was a crucial tool in her toolbox), as a potent resource. She led a female army in a war in which "fighting like a gentleman" had failed to stop the prison.

When Colonel Ely became the first president of the Green Springs Association, Rae's name was not even listed among the organization's officers or members of the executive council. While Hiram buttonholed public officials, wrote letters to the editor, and presided over meetings, Rae assumed that he would take care of the politics—he always had. Rae and the other women who opposed the prison had been consigned to jobs that might fall into the social or secretarial category—chatty phone calls to remind neighbors to attend public meetings, taking notes, hosting, cooking, and cleaning up for gatherings. One of Rae's chores was helping nine-year-old Sherri write to Governor Holton. Noting that she would have to move if the prison was built, Sherri described the natural beauty, wildlife, and pets that would be lost, along with her 128-year-old house. Rae's influence was particularly evident in the last sentence of the letter: "If you help me now, when I grow up I will vote for you."[3]

Rae's opportunity to demonstrate her leadership skills came soon enough. The men had talked about getting a lawyer, so she thought it would be permissible for her to follow up on that straightforward chore. Rae targeted Bill Perkins at a prestigious law firm. She was sure he would be on their side. Instead, he stunned her by laughing and shaking his head before he told her, "I don't think that there is any way in the world you all are going to get anywhere with that case," adding, "Don't you know you can't fight city hall?" Rae was left with the impression that he thought "this was the . . . silliest thing he had ever heard of."[4]

That's when Rae recognized that there was "a real problem . . . that it wouldn't just all be easy to take care of. It never occurred to me that we wouldn't just get a lawyer and stop it." Rae had overcome greater personal challenges than fighting city hall and she kept pressing, telling Perkins, "well, there must be *somebody*." He could see that Mrs. Ely wasn't going to leave until he offered a name. Finally, he relented: "If there's anybody in the state of Virginia who could do it, it would be Emanuel Emroch in Richmond."[5]

Emroch was a Richmond institution. Born in 1908, he practiced law there after graduating from the University of Richmond in 1931, specializing in personal injury litigation. Within this often-derided field Emroch was known for publishing in professional journals such as *Personal Injury Annual* and lecturing on product liability law. He relished tackling difficult cases; Green Springs certainly fit that bill.[6]

Emroch looked and sounded the part. "Impeccably put together," according to Rae, from his custom-tailored Savile Row suits to his manicured fingernails, he looked like "twelve judges rolled into one lawyer." Soft-spoken and kind, Emroch listened thoughtfully to this political novice and agreed to help her. By the end of their first meeting Rae was hooked. It was the same as if "his ideas were tinged with silver and covered with fairy dust," Rae recalled. "That changed my history totally . . . because I spent the next ten years of my life in his office." Rae may have felt like another door had swung open as the portals of wealth, style, and culture had been opened by Hiram during the early years of their marriage. She described her situation in the summer of 1970 as that of "a newly hatched chick," an "observer," who was picking up clues quickly.[7]

"We have a lawyer," Rae reported to the Green Springs Association. What she did not reveal was the time she spent quietly fending off bargains. When the fight against the prison garnered pro bono offers, Rae made her first executive decision: "Get rid of these other guys," she told herself, "before somebody in the group decides that a free lawyer is better than a lawyer you have to pay." She sensed that the "thing that was going to make the difference here was the highest level of skill possible." Emroch did not offer his services for free—over the next five years, the Green Springs Association incurred legal expenses in excess of $100,000. Nevertheless, his work was a labor of love that compensated him at a rate far below his standard fees.[8]

If Rae had expected support from everybody who lived in Green Springs, she was quickly disabused of that notion. Going door to door among her neighbors along the dirt road immediately west of Hawkwood, Rae headed into the woods and encountered a very different world. These neighbors did not own historic houses. Indeed, many did not own houses at all—they lived in small cabins and trailers. Convinced that the prison meant jobs, they raged against the association members' stately mansions, privately schooled children, and well-filled pantries, not imagined threats to Green Springs' fanciful history.

Even God-fearing and hard-working farmers like Chauncey and Doris Krahenbill suffered the hostility directed at hobby farmers. The Krahenbills bought 150 acres in Green Springs in 1955 as the booming Virginia Beach real estate market was turning coastal farms like theirs into subdivisions. Eventually, they purchased and cleared additional land, creating a 400-acre farm. Initially, the Krahenbills could not even afford to buy a tractor. They rented one, worked hard, and raised their six children to do the same. Chauncey was a workaholic whose kids called him the "Red Rooster" because he worked from sunup to sundown seven days a week. Daughter Helen was trained to use a tractor as soon as her feet could reach the pedals. The kids worked before going to school and returned to the fields as soon as they arrived home, with Doris joining the rest of the family.[9]

The Krahenbills had just returned from the day's work when the phone rang. It was D. L. Atkins. "Doris," he said, "the state is planning to put a Federal prison right in your front door, it's gonna be right across [from] your driveway." The Krahenbills quickly joined the fight to stop the prison, adding their own perspective in a letter to the editor of the *Daily Progress* in July 1970: "We only asked to farm our land, to rear our children, to live in peace with our many friends and neighbors, to enjoy the beauty of this God-given valley." Instead, the Krahenbills warned, they might soon look out on "high steel fences" restraining a mass of convicts.[10]

Rae enlisted Doris in the petition drive; she quickly ran into resistance. Among the roughly fifty people Doris approached, few, if any, signed the petition. Some were polite, some rude—and one or two were aggressive, like the man who set his dog on her. What hurt the most were those friends who not only refused to sign, but belittled Doris for wasting her time. One evening while entertaining long-time friends from Virginia Beach, her frustrations boiled over when the friend laughed at "what fools" the Krahenbills had been to "spend all that time and money and effort to try to stop the state and he said you cannot stop the government." Doris dumped spaghetti on his head.[11]

Rae soon moved beyond canvassing friends and neighbors. Her budding relationship with the press, combined with her natural talent for this medium, her determination, and her boundless energy, soon converted publicity into political capital far beyond Louisa County. That public role began inauspiciously with a letter to the editor in July 1970. Synthesizing Green Springs' history and the importance of conservation if "we are to provide an adequate quality of life for those yet unborn," the letter was part of a broader publicity campaign that included paid advertisements placed in local papers.[12]

Bumper stickers and signs began to pop up early in the campaign. Colored green, the stickers proclaimed, "Save Green Springs," while the signs flashed, "SAVE Beautiful Historic GREEN SPRINGS from Distruction [sic] by the Penitentiary." In addition to the voluntarily affixed stickers, Rae later confessed, the organization had procured some killer glue. She acknowledged that while yet another public hearing about the prison droned on, "We had teenagers out plastering these cars with bumper stickers." Prison supporters soon countered with "EAT AN ENVIRONMENTALIST FOR BREAKFAST" stickers.[13]

The cornerstone of public fundraising, publicity, and private pressure rested on tours of Green Springs' historic homes. Rae directed that initiative, serving as the head of the publicity committee, which soon catapulted her to chief spokesperson for the Green Springs Association. That she was a young, vivacious hostess who welcomed the press into her home and shuttled them around Green Springs did not hurt. Deborah Murdock recalled that Rae's "verbal persuasiveness was awesome. She was energized; almost with a mission." Murdock meant this both figuratively and literally.[14]

Rae had confided to her friend that she had once belonged to a church that sent missions "out into the neighborhood" and "didn't leave until they were on their knees." Rae was no doubt referring to the work she did on street corners in Miami's skid row during her Christian Youth Ranch days. The kids delivered their message of redemption at the Miami Rescue Mission. The teens brought musical instruments and sang gospels while Rae showed off her impressive voice. She was often asked to "give the word" about Jesus. A good preacher even as a child, Rae adapted those skills to more secular ends. "Bingo," Deborah thought. "That explains a whole lot."[15]

Reeling in Manny Emroch was just the first catch in Rae's career as talent scout. "My job suddenly became pulling people's skills and urging them to go forward. . . . Every human being I met—I found out what could they do." For instance, she sensed who the aristocrats were and how best to deploy them. Henry Taylor of Green Springs' Westend plantation was a good example. He was known as "Henry the Eighth"—ostensibly the eighth Henry in his line. "They know everybody—they didn't need the internet." Not fully recognizing the extent of her other skills, Rae believed at this time that the best she could do was "get other people to do something. I was a facilitator. Write a letter . . . bake a cookie."[16]

She recognized that Elisabeth Nolting was a remarkable asset, one of those "aristocrats" who, deployed properly, could help the cause. Born in 1906, Elisabeth had been by her own account "quite a tomboy," climbing the trees and riding her horses bareback at sprawling Cobham Park Estate just east of Charlottesville. Her father had died when she was two and half years old and her Uncle Carl, a conservationist who owned Bracketts Plantation in the heart of Green Springs, became her guardian and father figure. When Carl died in 1958, Elisabeth moved into Bracketts and ran it as a working farm.[17]

Nolting was the quintessential Virginia Lady, spelled with a capital L. She wore linen dresses and spoke in a blue-blooded "Nolting accent." Deborah Murdock described the way her "perfect" teas were served in high-ceilinged rooms filled with light from many-paned twelve-foot windows.[18] More than style made Elisabeth Nolting a lady. "Every week people who were out of work and out of luck would quietly come to her back door and she'd give them money." Rae Ely recalled that Nolting "knew who in the community was having a hard time." Elisabeth Nolting was a quiet, selfless woman, Rae continued. "She put the Christ in the word Christianity." Rae summed up their joint contribution to Green Springs: "I was the energy; she was the soul."[19]

Rae deployed neighbors like Nolting to balance her own more youthful appeal as she began to craft the public image of Green Springs. "We had all these lovely elderly ladies in Green Springs," Rae observed. This appealed to those who were fascinated by the "little old ladies in tennis shoes" engaging in political action. As for the media's reaction, Ely noted, "I think that they liked me. I was really young and I think I was photogenic at the time." She and Deborah Murdock were fetching in their identical Empire dresses, custom-made for the association's "house tours" by Charlottesville's "Mr. Hank." Combining youth, tradition, and blue-blooded lineage, the tours provided Rae the opportunity to configure Green Springs' human assets along with its physical ones to the association's advantage.[20]

This strategy paid dividends with the press. Richmond's most conservative newspaper, the *News Leader,* remained editorially cool to the upstarts in Green Springs but could not resist the blandishments of wealthy scions who opened their houses to the public. The *News Leader* featured an article headlined "Leisurely Style of Life Flows from Green Springs" in the section reserved for stories about women and food. Although it eventually mentioned the prison fight, the article was awash in "Southern charm." It quoted plantation notes from Westend listing all the mouths that had to be fed there: "700 hens and chickens, 150 ducks, 269 turkies [sic], 212 pheasants, 100 sheep, 19 cows, 18 calves, 62 cattle, 18 mules, 13 horses, 10 cats and dogs, 28 darkies, 14 folks." That "darkies" came somewhere between dogs and "folks" was probably not lost on some of the *News Leader*'s readership.[21]

Food was an essential ingredient at the house tours. Rae engaged the skills of association member Eunice Fisher, who cooked for the local elementary school; she served lunch to hundreds of visitors. Using the kitchen at Berea Baptist Church and assisted by many of the other women in the Green Springs Association, Fisher offered up Brunswick stew and biscuits for hungry visitors.[22]

The association reported that over 1,200 people toured the homes. Virtually every local newspaper in Virginia covered the tours, which grossed over $5,000. Colonel Ely's personal contributions, and the levies of $2,500 on ten of the biggest landholders in the association, were still its mainstay financially. But small contributions mattered. "You could raise money from the public while educating the public," Rae observed, "and then the public would go forth and spread the word."[23]

Local law enforcement did not sit by idly as outsiders poured into Louisa County. The day before the tour association members put up directional signs to guide visitors. Henry Kennon, Louisa's veteran sheriff, ruled that the signs violated Virginia Department of Transportation regulations and ordered them removed. Patrol cars hid in the bushes, on the lookout for communists, according to Rae.[24]

She continued to develop her skills as a talent scout, reaching out to a network of historians—especially architectural historians—beginning with Angus Murdock's UVa mentors. Whenever possible Rae arranged visits to Green Springs for these experts, and a good number attended Green Springs Association meetings.[25]

Rae was also developing into an individual who was not confined by her position as Hiram Ely's wife or the mother of Sherri, Addison, and Todd. When Deborah Murdock first met Rae at the pool she wore an old-fashioned swimsuit with a skirt. But she soon changed her style, letting her hair down and wearing pants. Deborah Murdock later recalled that "she came out . . . as a young, effective, not feminist by any means, but a woman who was attracting." And "it was very effective," emanating "energy and a little bit of sex" (Fig. 5).[26]

Fashion may have helped; "she used it," Deborah observed. Rae took care to select the right outfit for every encounter, and her alluring qualities were highlighted in the gatherings she hosted at Hawkwood. One professor of architecture recalled such an event, especially Rae's grand entrance. "She was a very attractive woman, beautifully dressed."[27]

Years later, Rae readily acknowledged standing in front of her closet, choosing between dozens of possible outfits and deciding what she would wear that day. As Rae peered into her closet, she asked herself, "Who am I going to be today?" Rae compared herself to a "Zelig," adjusting appearance and behavior to win the approval of whoever she needed to please that day. She later linked that need to please directly to her early childhood experiences of neglect, abuse, and foster care. Rae transformed the child's need for affection into a more utilitarian goal—part of a deliberate strategy in the Green Springs war that was beginning to consume her life.[28]

Figure 5. Rae Ely, circa 1975. (Photographer unknown. Photo provided by Roberta Patton.)

Many of the men that Rae lobbied or recruited for the cause commented on the same compound of energy, fashion, and "attracting" identified by Deborah Murdock. Once Rae emerged as the leader of the fight against the prison, her allies and even a few of her enemies added intelligence, preparation, and persistence when describing the mix that Ely wielded so effectively. No single word described her, although had Rae been a male political operative the adjective that would likely have been used is "charismatic." Rae also leveraged a long history of women's traditional role as guardians of home and hearth, along with the heavily gendered tradition of female leadership in garden clubs and historic preservation. She mastered long-range strategic thinking and opportunistic tactics; press relations; an impressive grasp of lobbying; and the willingness to defy gender norms by consistently operating in all-male political, bureaucratic, and media venues.[29]

For all those reasons, Rae began to supersede Hiram as the spokesperson for the prison opponents. Her relationship with Emroch had already positioned her as the chief legal strategist for the association, and as she spearheaded the tours her role in both fundraising and publicity grew as well. Litigation, bureaucratic politics, and media savvy had not been terribly important components of effective rule in Louisa County in the past, but they would prove increasingly influential in the last third of the century.

For the first six months of the fight against the prison it had been the men of Green Springs who met with public officials. Those public officials were also men, whether they represented the magisterial district, county, or state levels of government. Federal public officials in decision-making positions were virtually all men as well. Women had been the foot soldiers and, in some instances, behind-the-scenes generals of the campaign against the diagnostic center from the start. Led by Rae Ely, women now emerged as the official leaders and spokespersons for the movement.

That shift corresponded with male leadership's failure to stop the diagnostic center through traditional representative politics at the local level. If "gentlemen" like Colonel Hiram Ely were not able to get their way through the kind of politics that had usually protected their interests in the past, perhaps it was time for a change. If Holton, Purcell, and Ogg refused to fight like gentlemen, maybe this was not a gentleman's fight.

Rae's speech to the governor's Environmental Council in January 1971 signaled this change. That Rae used the governor's chosen vehicle for improving the Commonwealth's environment as a platform to spell out just how a diagnostic center would destroy Green Springs put two of Governor Holton's signature initiatives on a collision course. Ely waxed rhapsodic about the area's "peace and tranquility ... harmony of God and man and nature," and the "inner calm" they offered. The "ecology and good environment of the Green Springs was being carefully guarded," she told the council, "long before most folks even knew what those words meant."[30]

Rae then warned that even this environmentally and historically resilient oasis was not immune to progress and its attendant degradation. She suggested that perhaps word had gotten out that there was one place in central

Virginia that had *not* been spoiled. "So we now find that we have been chosen by the State of Virginia to receive one of the most effective polluters of them all." Having weathered droughts, floods, and the Civil War, "it now seems that the death sentence has been pronounced for the beautiful and historic Green Springs." Although some labeled the situation hopeless, "if it is, and 200 years of man's efforts to preserve and protect that which is good and that which is refreshing to the soul has been in vain, then God help us all!" Mrs. Frances Martin also challenged the council to take a stand on the prison and preempted a charge commonly levied at women activists. She called out state agencies for dismissing those who expressed environmental concerns as being "too emotional." The "really emotional persons are those in and out of government who clutch the security blanket of habit and outworn ideas."[31]

It was not just opponents who cloaked women in emotional garb. When the Virginia Commission for the Arts met to review the proposed prison site in April 1971, opponents turned out in force. Ignoring the opposition, the commission approved the governor's plans. *Daily Progress* reporter Jerry Simpson, a strong behind-the-scenes Green Springs Association ally, reported that "[t]wo women wept" after the ruling. One was Mrs. James Gallagher, a schoolteacher in Louisa County, who told the commission, "I am crushed by what happened here this afternoon." Simpson continued, "Mrs. Ely, sitting in a corner, was also crying."[32]

"Mrs. Ely" certainly knew how to dramatize her message when it helped the cause. Asked years later about this moment, however, she simply laughed. "I know I didn't cry; I think I *was* fuming mad." Rae suspected that "it would appeal more to the reader to have me crying." Simpson's decision to highlight the emotional nature of the women at the meeting stood in sharp contrast to his coverage of the men. It epitomized the gendered lens through which some foes, and even a few friends, viewed the battle. Although Colonel Ely remained the titular head of the Green Springs Association, the extended battle was probably more than the seventy-five-year-old Colonel originally bargained for. A generation or two older than many of the reporters covering the story, Colonel Ely did not connect with the press as well as Rae. Both behind the scenes and out front, Rae was taking over while looking for the person she could hand the reins to—keeping everything afloat until she could find the right person to take charge. She had no doubt that person would be a man.³³

While gender roles had changed very little among those who held office in Louisa County, Richmond, or for that matter Washington, D.C., the electorate's policy preferences and the way that they were conveyed shifted quickly by 1970. More citizens embraced measures that enhanced their "quality of life." That term covered a broad range of concerns, from toxic threats to health to the environmental movement's commitment to preserving nature, open space, and reducing the mountains of waste that Americans produced each year. Though "quality of life" sounded innocuous enough, one person's genuine commitment to "open space" might be another person's chosen instrument for racial exclusion or barrier to mixed-income housing. That had been the effect of so-called exclusionary zoning laws for decades, requiring lot sizes designed to price millions of Americans out of building in that town, for instance. Zoning had always been, and still is, locally controlled. As the Federal government ramped up its ability to protect both the environment and history, the tension between improving the quality of life for some and access for all to a middle-class quality of life and income increased.

Quality of life concerns were a crucial, if overshadowed, component of Lyndon Johnson's Great Society. The president's 1964 address at the University of Michigan, in which he enumerated the elements that would make society great, is correctly remembered as a catalyst for his war on poverty. Yet, LBJ directed a good portion of his speech to improving the quality of life for those who were *already* in the middle class.³⁴

Johnson's Great Society speech challenged graduating students to "enrich and elevate our national life, and . . . advance the quality of our American civilization." With imagination and initiative, they could strive "not only toward the rich society and the powerful society, but upward to the Great Society." That kind of society would also fulfill the need for beauty, "community," and "contact with nature": in short, it would promote beauty, health, and permanence. Congress soon passed legislation that made good on elements of Johnson's vision. It pushed through measures that protected the quality of air that Americans breathed and preserved wilderness areas. Congress also expanded aid to college students and created the National Endowments for the Arts and for the Humanities.³⁵

The U.S. Conference of Mayors Special Committee on Historic Preservation kept up the momentum to improve American civilization, publishing *With Heritage So Rich* in 1966. "If the preservation movement is to be successful," the report insisted, "it must go beyond saving occasional historic houses" and "concern itself with the historic and architecturally valued areas and districts which contain a special meaning for the community." *With Heritage So Rich* quickly led to passage of the National Historic Preservation Act of 1966, which applied the term "cultural" for the first time to preservation legislation. The act wielded an "action-forcing" mechanism, Section 106, that required every Federal agency to consider the impact of its actions on properties and districts in the National Register of Historic Places. It also created an Advisory Council on Historic Preservation to oversee this process.[36]

Grassroots neighborhood protests were often the first line of defense for a variety of threats. Citizen activists, particularly in white, middle-class neighborhoods, intervened in land-use decisions, usually squaring off against real estate developers or government officials. The frequency and scope of such grassroots mobilization increased dramatically by 1970. So, too, did the victories scored by citizens fighting city hall.

Post–World War II highway construction that fueled suburban sprawl was perhaps the most powerful catalyst for grassroots neighborhood activism. Neal Potter was an early example, even though his efforts failed initially. An economist with the Ford Foundation–funded Resources for the Future think tank, Potter led a wave of citizen environmentalism in Montgomery County, Maryland. His family's farm on the Potomac River had been annexed as part of the massive roadbuilding project that created the Capital Beltway outside Washington, D.C., in the early 1960s. "Engineers were everything back then, engineers and building roads. The hell with the landscape, the hell with the people."[37]

Potter founded the Citizens Committee for Fair Taxation in 1960 and by the end of the decade was enmeshed in environmental causes as a member of the Montgomery Citizens Planning Association and the co-chair of the Metropolitan Coalition for Clean Air. In 1970, Potter was elected to the Montgomery County Council, where he became a staunch advocate for slower, planned development. That same year, a *New York Times* front-page story headlined "Many Big Projects Near City Stymied by Protests" chronicled a litany of complaints by neighborhood groups, some that partnered with national environmental groups like the Sierra Club.[38]

Women led many of the protests reported by the *Times* and other media outlets. Responding to the kinds of protests mounted by the "peppery" Mrs. Arthur Kinoy, frustrated officials working for highway departments and utilities pointed to pressing regional needs—ensuring against blackouts in the case of a power line, for instance—that these "backyard activists" were gumming up. "You know what I've begun to realize?" the head of the East Hudson Parkway Authority told the *Times*. "If the [interstate] highway system were just starting now, it couldn't be built."[39]

By 1973, Michelle Madoff's GASP air pollution–fighting membership had grown to 40,000. Another organization labeled GASP, Group Against Smokers and Pollution, was founded by Clara Gouin, whose daughter was severely allergic to cigarette smoke at a time when everyone, smokers or not, felt obliged to provide ashtrays in their homes and offices. "What doormats we nonsmokers were!" Gouin recalled. By the spring of 1972, the charter branch had mailed over 500 "New Chapter Kits" to activists around the country.[40]

The largely middle-class agendas of these groups were fueled by several decades of economic growth that lulled many of its beneficiaries into assuming that it would continue uninterrupted. Demands for clean air and water, scenic vistas, protecting the environment, and improved health were voiced by millions of Americans who now enjoyed higher disposable income, expected to live longer lives, and had more leisure time on their hands. These were the very kind of constituents who applauded Governor Holton's commitment to conservation. Citizens like Rae Ely, many of whom had only recently entered the political fray, injected a new set of issues into the public arena, ultimately skewing conceptions of progress from an emphasis on economic mobility and income redistribution to a broader array of demands that often featured enhanced quality of life. For the large number of Americans who had not yet climbed into the middle class, these demands often seemed to be self-serving, especially when they ignored the disproportionate environmental insults visited upon impoverished regions of the country and communities of color.[41]

The fight against the prison was hardly the only example of backyard activism in central Virginia. Shortly before the Green Springs Association hosted its fall house tours, the General Electric Company announced that it planned to build a new research and manufacturing facility in another predominantly white, well-heeled area in central Virginia—the "Ivy Valley." The valley lay at the base of the steeper hills and dramatic landscape west of Charlottesville. A *Daily Progress* headline soon asked: "GE Plant: Menace or Manna?" One opponent insisted, "For God's sake, don't start industry [in] that beautiful valley," while an advocate claimed, "All I see in that valley is . . . brush. . . . We need jobs. . . . This is dollars from heaven coming to us."[42]

It did not take long for local pundits to connect the Green Springs fight to this new assault on the environment. *Daily Progress* columnist Bryce Loving, one of the journalists Rae Ely had cultivated, yoked Green Springs to the Ivy Valley a few weeks later. "Both these cases present a somewhat similar problem," Loving wrote, asking, "is there to be no privacy, peace of mind, or gracious living?"[43]

Both Governor Holton and Otis Brown believed that sleepy Louisa County, under the tight control of the courthouse crowd, was an ideal location for the diagnostic center. Yet, in the seven months following Holton's initial announcement neither side had budged; indeed, each shored up its position. That a good number of newly politically engaged middle-class citizens in Green Springs were female, and the group was now led by a "peppery" woman, may have reinforced Linwood Holton's determination to site the diagnostic center in Green Springs.

6
Federalism's Fissures

FOR MUCH OF THE TWENTIETH CENTURY, local government had denied basic rights to large swaths of citizens, especially in the South. The civil rights movement had powered a decades-long crusade to loosen the stranglehold imposed by segregation. Lyndon Johnson was instrumental in harnessing the power of that movement to pass the landmark Civil Rights Act (1964) and Voting Rights Act (1965), undermining Jim Crow, though hardly ending racial discrimination in multiple other forms.

With the formal trappings of Jim Crow waning by 1970 and the Federal courts finally beginning to enforce the landmark *Brown v. Board of Education* decisions desegregating public schools, the meaning of local control no longer automatically conjured associations with Alabama sheriffs, vicious German shepherds, and fire hoses. President Nixon jumped on this opportunity to reshape the meaning of local control in the post–Jim Crow era and turn it to his political advantage. As trust in the Federal government plummeted, Nixon loudly rebranded the term "local control," turning it from a euphemism for racial oppression to a Republican version of "power to the people," dog-whistling to white Southerners that "the people" meant *them*.

Although prison opponents in Green Springs had *not* been disenfranchised as had most Blacks, these white activists believed that their rights merited national protections as well, even if support for historical preservation and the environment was not shared by the majority of Louisa County's voters. In their quest to mobilize political resources against the courthouse crowd and Virginia's governor, the preservationists explored multiple points of access provided by federalism's distribution of political accountability between national, state, and local jurisdictions. Whenever possible, they steered clear of Judge Harold Purcell's courtroom in Louisa County, seeking out Federal judges instead. Ironically, they acquired standing in Federal court because the diagnostic center was funded by the very kind of "no-strings-attached" Federal grants that Nixon created explicitly to return decision-making to state and local officials like Linwood Holton and Harold Purcell.

In August 1969 newly elected President Nixon delivered a nationally televised address that placed local control at the center of his domestic agenda, declaring: "After a third of a century of power flowing from the people and the States to Washington it is time for a New Federalism in which power, funds, and responsibility will flow from Washington to the States and to the people." The last thirty-five years had "produced a bureaucratic monstrosity" that presided over "entrenched programs that have outlived their time."[1]

Nixon turned the phrase "New Federalism" into action by bundling dozens of "categorical grants"—so called because there was one for every *category* of government program Congress and entrenched interest groups could think of: jellyfish control, water treatment, social programs, police equipment, you name it. Each category came with Federal strings attached. Nixon promised to convert these categorical grants into "block grants" that would pump Federal tax dollars into the states without all those Federal requirements. Nixon also proposed "revenue sharing," which returned Federal tax dollars to the states to use as they pleased.[2]

President Nixon's New Federalism was a good example of just how fluid partisan politics was by the late 1960s. Walter Heller, Chair of the Council of Economic Advisors under Presidents John F. Kennedy and Lyndon Johnson, had been a proponent of revenue sharing long before Nixon. Elected officials from both sides of the aisle with diverse ideological perspectives had supported the idea, from Republican senator Barry Goldwater of Arizona to Democratic senator Edmund Muskie of Maine. Nonetheless, Nixon was the first president to make the issue one of his top domestic priorities.[3]

His 1971 State of the Union address charged that placing trust in a bureaucratic Washington elite that believes it "knows best what is best for people everywhere" meant "that you cannot trust people to govern themselves." The president submitted a plan to Congress to remedy the "delay and duplication

"... waste and rigidity" of Federal grant-in-aid programs. "There is simply no good reason why a Federal official should have to approve in advance a local community's decision about the shape a new building will have or where a new street will run or on what corner it will put a new gas station." Decisions should meet local needs. "No group of remote Federal officials—however talented and sincere—can effectively tailor each local program to the wide variety of local conditions." It was time to bring "more tailors into the act, tailors who are elected to make sure that the suit fits the customer."[4]

Nixon acknowledged that "a number of State and local officials will prove to be unresponsive or irresponsible," only to brush aside the legacy of a racist Jim Crow system in the South because "moving toward greater freedom" always entailed risk. No doubt a wink and a nod to some racist white voters in the South, the President's targeted message resonated with a far broader group of Americans because memories of German shepherds or fire hoses in the streets had begun to fade.[5]

Letting people govern through their "local public officials," as the New Federalism promised, would make possible "a peaceful revolution in which power was turned back to the people—in which government at all levels was refreshed and renewed and made truly responsive." Nixon soon went to Philadelphia to sign the State and Local Fiscal Assistance Act of 1972, the formal name for revenue sharing. The president stressed that when "we say no strings, we mean no strings." Local officials could now "concentrate on pleasing the people—so the money can do more good." Governor Linwood Holton was just the kind of local official the president had in mind. Much of the Federal revenue that Nixon had liberated from the grasp of overweening Democratic congressional subcommittee chairpersons and intrusive string-pulling federal bureaucrats would flow through state and county elected officials like Holton who were far more likely to be Republican than the congressional subcommittee chairs in a Congress that had been controlled by the Democrats for decades.[6]

In the case of the proposed diagnostic center, the Federal government would pay roughly one quarter of the construction costs, slashing the usual red tape because the funds came from the Safe Streets Act. In another example of bipartisan consensus, the legislation was passed in the waning days of the Johnson administration but heartily embraced and vigorously implemented by the Nixon administration. This expansion of the war on crime showcased the kind of no-strings-attached block grant funding that Nixon had been talking about since his 1968 campaign. It returned crucial decisions to elected officials like Governor Holton and places like Louisa County—decisions such as where to site a prison. It was an offer that no reform-minded Republican governor could, or would, refuse.[7]

The secretive, introspective Nixon, who ordered the Federal government to spy on protesters, is hardly remembered for embracing direct citizen participation. Yet even Nixon had to acknowledge, or at least pay lip service to, the wave of citizen activism that had swept across the nation, from its wellspring in the civil rights movement to its tributaries that stretched from college campuses to feminist protest, to a growing number of backyards. New Federalism was Nixon's far more moderate nod to citizen participation. It would revitalize "grass roots government"; it would multiply "the centers of effective power in our country . . . multiplying the opportunities for involvement and influence by individual citizens." It was even plausible to argue that local control would return power to the people. Which people, however, remained a highly contested matter.[8]

Rae Ely and the Green Springs Association were part of the larger pulse of citizen participation that disrupted the best-laid plans of state and local officials. If the U.S. Supreme Court, aided and abetted by the U.S. Department of Justice and pressed by organizations like the National Association for the Advancement of Colored People (NAACP), could systematically dismantle an oppressive system of racial segregation, why shouldn't Green Springs activists use the same tools to chip away at the remnants of local fiefdoms? The Green Springs activists did not view local government the way Richard Nixon hoped they would. Indeed, they forged alliances with national agencies and Federal courts, *subverting* the decisions of local elected representatives.

The Green Springs Association used the very tools described by a leading scholar of racial politics who noted that when it came to preventing racial discrimination the courts and the Equal Employment Opportunity Commission (EEOC) "were not simply the upper reaches of a hierarchy whose dicta, pronounced from on high, were law. Rather, they were opportunities to be exploited, points of access to the structure of state power, openings that could be entered to try to pry policy loose and to advance an approach to antidiscrimination enforcement." Senator James Abourezk (D-South Dakota) was more succinct: the success of civil rights legislation depended upon "enlisting citizens as law enforcement officials."[9]

By 1970 there were national analogues to the NAACP Legal Defense Fund that pursued a broad range of public interest law, and more specifically environmental litigation, like the Environmental Defense Fund and Natural Resources Defense Council that Ely and company were pleased to enlist as "law enforcement" officials. She took a page out of the civil rights playbook and soon reached out to national environmental and preservation law groups engineering legal victories in "distant" Federal courts that would never have been possible at the state and local levels. The Green Springs Association embraced those distant bureaucrats and forged national alliances arrayed against the very local officials that Nixon claimed were "closest to the people." The association looked to the Federal courts and administrative agencies to challenge the same men who had presided over Jim Crow segregation in Louisa County just a few years earlier.[10]

Nor was the Federal government's utility limited to the courts. Just as the NAACP Legal Defense Fund worked hand in glove with the Office of Civil Rights in the Department of Justice and other outposts of the "entrenched Federal bureaucracy," Ely and her fellow activists tapped deep sources of expertise and influence buried within the Department of the Interior and the newly created Environmental Protection Agency. Nixon sought to staunch the flow of power from local to Federal government, to create a "people's government." Yet, some of the president's own programs provided an entrée for the Green Springs Association to Federal resources that proved crucial to overturning the clear will of their elected local and state representatives, not to mention the majority of Louisa County's voters. The game-changer proved to be a citizens' lawsuit brought in Federal district court and appealed to the Fourth Circuit, twice. That the citizens of Green Springs were granted standing in the Federal courts in what arguably was a quintessentially local dispute, and that the Federal judiciary ultimately required a host of federal agencies to weigh in on the matter, proved decisive.

The path to Federal jurisdiction led from Hawkwood along I-64 to the law offices of Emanuel Emroch in Richmond. In those heady days of conducting interviews with the national press, reading five newspapers a day, lobbying state legislators, and the never-ending quest to raise sufficient funds to pay the legal bills, Rae met with Manny Emroch several times a week. While her husband funded many of the association's expenses, tended the garden, and took care of their kids, Rae pointed her Mercedes Benz SEL toward Richmond. Down a long hallway on the eighth floor of the city's only skyscraper, Rae sat in the mahogany-lined suite for hours discussing the world, politics—and the law.[11]

Ely and Emroch often lunched at Miller and Rhodes Department Store's Tea Room. After he warned Rae to check her sandwich for toothpicks—Emroch had once represented a client who failed to take this precaution—they would watch the daily fashion show and talk shop. Emroch always ordered a cup of soup and a BLT sandwich. Rae did not eat much—because "girls" were not supposed to do that. She did drink up the experience. Her immersion in the law was like a new universe, as she put it. The lessons did not stop in Emroch's office or over lunch at the tearoom. Rae usually left with an armful of documents and digested them at home, soon returning for the next lesson.[12]

Rae dressed to match her elegant partner's expensive suits and monogramed shirts. She often donned a Jackie Kennedy–style suit and matching pillbox hat. Like many of the professional men that Rae encountered on her path into politics, Manny Emroch was captivated by more than the outfit. There was a wholesome, wide-eyed quality to Rae's infatuation with politics and the law, enhanced by the fact that she was a quick study. It did not hurt that she made men feel like they were the only person in the room, or that Rae was slender, attractive, and dressed for "attracting," as Deborah Murdock put it. The infatuation was often mutual: Rae, with law and politics, the men who provided access to them, with Rae.

During one of these sessions, Manny asked Rae if she recalled reading about that new law that passed. He was referring to NEPA, signed into law by Richard Nixon on January 1, 1970. Emroch and Green Springs would use the Federal government's failure to consider the environmental impact of the diagnostic center along with similar neglect of requirements imposed by the National Historic Preservation Act of 1966 (NHPA) to gain access to federal district court.[13]

Federal funding for the Safe Streets Act punched their ticket to Federal jurisdiction that offered a venue far more hospitable than Judge Purcell's courtroom. The Safe Streets Act of 1968 created the Law Enforcement Assistance Administration (LEAA) to direct the president's war on crime. From the Kennedy administration through Johnson, punitive measures were balanced with social programs designed to eradicate what liberals considered to be the roots of crime. In the wake of urban rebellions in the second half of the 1960s, and especially with the reelection of Richard Nixon in 1972, that balance veered starkly toward punitive measures, from tough-on-crime policing to massive investments in prisons. There was strong bipartisan support for the entire trajectory of this war on crime. By the time the LEAA was disbanded in 1981, it had disbursed roughly $10 billion to support 80,000 crime control programs across the country.[14]

On August 18, 1970 the Green Springs Association announced that it would file a lawsuit in Federal court, which only hardened the state's position: it immediately dropped consideration of other sites. The Ely in *Ely v. Velde* was Hiram, not Rae; the defendant was Richard Velde, associate director of the LEAA. Velde was a former staffer for Republican senator Roman Hruska of Nebraska, best known for defending the doomed nomination of Harold Carswell for Supreme Court justice by declaring that even if the nominee was mediocre, "there are a lot of mediocre judges and people and lawyers. They are entitled to a little representation, aren't they, and a little chance?" Velde helped guide the Safe Streets Act through the Senate Judiciary Committee.[15]

Ely v. Velde sought to enjoin the state from building on the proposed site and block the $775,000 grant that had been authorized by the LEAA. The plaintiffs also claimed that their constitutional right to protection from unnecessary and unreasonable environmental degradation under the Ninth and Fourteenth Amendments had been violated. The defendants pointed to the "block grant source of Federal funding" as evidence that the "location of the Center is immaterial to the L.E.A.A.," since it was "entirely a local concern."[16]

For the next two months Emroch prepared for his day in court. Rae identified and procured expert witnesses and prepared some of them to testify at the trial. "Mr. Emroch taught me how to take a farmer and turn [him] into an expert," she recalled. Rae also tracked down leading architectural historians, especially authorities on preserving historic landscapes. She was like a vacuum cleaner, sucking in every possible ally, making cold calls to anybody. Most of the experts donated their services, but when one land-use planner requested compensation Rae was shocked. "My utter conviction [was that] our cause was so noble . . . it stunned me that anybody would think in terms of money."[17]

Murdock's two-page history of Green Springs and the growing recognition that context mattered informed Emroch's brief. So too the National Historic Preservation Act's shift in emphasis, from protecting a "few precious national shrines" to respecting the cultural significance of a wider swath of American history. The act's explicit mention of historically significant "districts" signaled congressional interest in preserving collections of buildings. It stressed the integral connection between place and community by protecting districts that possessed "integrity of location, design, setting . . . feeling and association."[18]

On November 2, 1970, the first day of the hearing in Federal court, Assistant U.S. Attorney David Lowe introduced a motion to dismiss the case. Because there were no strings attached to the Federal block grant, Lowe argued, the court had no jurisdiction. He appeared to be on solid ground when he characterized the unique nature of the statute that authorized LEAA funding. Would Nixon's reliance on block grants and plans for revenue sharing truly loosen Federal control? Or would other Federal obligations bind the money, regardless of the statute's intent?[19]

The defense's argument supported some of the rumors that swirled through the Green Springs Association about the White House carefully following *Ely v. Velde*. Should the courts decide to subject the diagnostic center to requirements like an environmental impact statement or review by the Advisory Council on Historic Preservation, Federal strings might be cinched tighter than ever. The high stakes also explained why the U.S. attorney threw so many resources into the case. Rae Ely recalled a parade of filing cabinets rolling through the courtroom on carts. She had "the mental image . . . that they were bringing in their whole office on roller skates." Whatever the decision, the Green Springs Association had cleverly used the Federal funding contained in Richard Nixon's chosen vehicle for empowering localities to shift the battle from a local to a Federal venue.[20]

7
Virginia's Preservation Network

STATES OFTEN ADMINISTERED THE PROGRAMS CREATED by Federal legislation, and the 1966 National Historic Preservation Act was a typical example. It spawned the Virginia Historic Landmarks Commission (VHLC) charged with preserving the Commonwealth's historic treasures. Shared professional perspectives between Federal and state administrators that forged thick networks of mutual public policy interests easily trumped loyalty to public opinion as interpreted by the elected officials representing geographically bounded locations.[1]

One political scientist labeled this phenomenon "picket fence federalism" because overlapping agendas, shared interests, and mutual professional disciplines bound "highway guys" more reliably, for instance, than allegiance to the state or Federal elected officials their agencies reported to. These professionally infused communities could easily steer public policy toward functionally defined agendas—highways, water, housing, historic preservation—in ways that undermined any governor's or, for that matter, president's preferences. From a distance, the Federal government's or individual state's fences might look solid; yet, there were large gaps between the boards in those fences. Each picket protected only its own narrow set of interests, not necessarily the collective interest as expressed by those elected to represent the people who resided behind the fence.

The Virginia Historic Landmarks Commission was part of just such a preservation picket. Although it officially reported to Governor Linwood Holton, it was more tightly bound to the national preservation community, including the Department of the Interior, especially its National Park Service, which oversaw many of the nation's historic preservation programs. The influential nonprofit National Trust for Historic Preservation was also an integral nongovernmental actor in that network.

The Green Springs activists reached out to the architectural historians at the VHLC who shared their commitment to historic preservation. The VHLC proved to be an important source of expertise and path of least resistance to more powerful allies in the Federal government, who in turn worked at cross-purposes to their Federal counterparts within the criminal justice picket at the Law Enforcement Assistance Administration.

The prison guys had political leadership on their side. The Green Springs diagnostic center was a signature initiative for Holton, and its funding source—block grants—was crucial to Nixon's agenda as well. For good reason, the executive director of the VHLC quashed publicity about the growing number of Green Springs plantations that his agency had nominated for the National Register of Historic Places, warning that it was best to avoid "much newspaper speculation and embarrassing queries" and "make as few waves as possible." Far better to advance the cause quietly and hope that nobody in the Governor's Mansion noticed.[2]

Angus Murdock was not the only Green Springs resident who had professional ties to the historic preservation community. A week after Holton's prison announcement, Henry Taylor, scion of Westend plantation, wrote a letter to Governor Holton. Taylor was the former president of Taylor and Parrish Construction Company, responsible for restoring some of the Commonwealth's most venerable historic properties. They included, as Henry gently reminded the governor, "the Capitol you now occupy." After a brief history lesson about Green Springs, Taylor warned that the diagnostic center "would be gross pollution of this area." He also wrote to the executive director of the Landmarks Commission, James Moody, urging him to pressure Holton to delay any decision about the prison site until the commission could meet. The commission responded swiftly: the top brass headed out to Westend for a tour of Green Springs.[3]

Jane Davies, the leading expert on architect Alexander Jackson Davis, also alerted the VHLC. She reminded them that Davis had introduced the "picturesque, romantic style for country houses" in the United States, and that Hawkwood was "one of the most important Italian-style houses in the country." Just as important as the house itself was Hawkwood's "romantic setting . . . overlooking an idylic [sic] scene of fertile, rolling, cultivated fields and small groves." Destroying that setting "would surely cause the eventual loss of the house itself." She did not need to remind anybody that the scene she described was the proposed prison site.[4]

Angus Murdock also alerted other key members of the state-level preservation community, writing to his soon-to-be boss, the president of the Association for the Preservation of Virginia Antiquities. Angus never expected to "be embroiled in struggle to save my own front yard." He wondered how Holton, who claimed to care about conservation, could propose a diagnostic center for this site. Murdock underscored the political bind facing Virginia's preservation community: the VHLC could not afford to antagonize "the powers that be," yet if the Commonwealth was "insensitive" to the state's architecture and scenic resources, "we can't expect private parties to respect these natural and historical assets."[5]

It was not long before Rae Ely contacted the National Trust for Historic Preservation directly. Her phone call produced immediate results. None other than James Biddle, the trust's president, weighed in directly. In a letter to Otis Brown, Biddle, "representing more than 22,000 individuals and organizations interested in the preservation of our American heritage," registered his concern over the proposed prison. The chair of the VHLC, Edward Alexander, also put Brown on notice, writing that the prison would "constitute a serious intrusion"; Brown should find a more appropriate site.[6]

The signals from the preservation world were unmistakable: the VHLC needed to fight for state-of-the-art conceptions of historic preservation. As the battle garnered more publicity, Alexander and Moody balanced their commitment to historic preservation against the likelihood that articulating their professional conclusions would upset their boss. They knew that Governor Holton would bridle at a relatively obscure state commission scuttling the diagnostic center, especially on grounds that tarnished his reputation as a conservationist.

Even without political obstacles, making the case for Green Springs' history was not going to be easy. Calder Loth, an architectural historian who joined the VHLC in 1966, reported that when the protests began, only *one* property in the vicinity had been registered with the commission—Boswell's Tavern. Originally constructed circa 1735, somebody famous really had slept there: the Marquis de Lafayette. That well-documented structure, however, was four miles from the proposed prison site.[7]

Loth first encountered Green Springs when he heard that "some woman was upset because the prison was going to be near her." All he knew about Rae Ely was that she had escaped rapidly exurbanizing New Jersey only to discover that a prison was planned for her front yard. Loth readily acknowledged that protecting the symbiotic relationship between rural settings and historic structures was a new way of thinking about preservation in 1970. "We didn't have any idea about cultural landscapes, we did not cover this at all in grad school." Documenting the history of Green Springs set the precedent for this kind of thinking—even among highly skilled professionals in the field. The VHLC soon began making history at a rapid pace, although it was careful to keep its efforts under wraps.[8]

On July 28, 1970, Executive Director Moody forwarded a short report on Green Springs to Governor Holton. Dating back to the 1720s, the report began, a "region of prime agricultural quality" saw the development of prosperous plantations. Crucially for its historic value among cutting-edge arbiters of what *should* constitute history, "a homogenous body of small and large landowners" emerged. "As a result," the report continued, "this section, virtually unchanged and relatively compact, represents the evolution of rural life in Virginia from pre-Revolutionary days to the present."[9]

The report acknowledged that the number of Green Springs buildings recorded in either the Virginia Landmarks Register or the National Register of Historic Places was small: one, to be exact. But it quickly noted that both Westend and Hawkwood were being considered for nomination. More important than any individual structure, however, was the group "in a related context, representing a century and a half of architectural development." Because Green Springs had been spared development, the report noted, the architecture could be observed in its original settings.

The authors then penned a phrase that would resonate in virtually every document that supported the case for Green Springs' preservation for the duration of the battle over the prison and long after. Green Springs was a "gently civilized countryside where the land had been enhanced rather than despoiled by the presence of man." Injecting an "incompatible object" into this "carefully balanced" area would have a "negative effect on both the appearance and life of the area." Although it stopped short of offering a specific policy recommendation, like Murdock's "Private Opinion," the report was gentle in tone but firm in its commitment to preserving the history of Green Springs. Unlike Murdock, who emphasized his private-citizen status in the very title of his essay, the VHLC's report provided the stamp of official authority. It did not take Manny Emroch long to incorporate the experts' perspective into his brief. It quoted extensively from the VHLC report, underscoring its conclusion that Green Springs "is of great historical importance and national interest to all of the people and citizens of the United States."[10]

Otis Brown did not sit idly by as a rival state agency criticized his decision. He urged the VHLC to consider all the facts—not just the objections of "certain people living in the vicinity." Change was inevitable, Brown continued, and Green Springs was slated for a great deal of it because it was located between two urban areas and near a recently completed interchange for an interstate highway. Brown also shared a lesson gleaned from his experience with such matters: "This facility is like all other facilities, in that although people desire to have them, they want them close to someone else."[11]

Otis Brown's response only emboldened the VHLC. At its August 4 meeting the commission recommended that Brown discuss the matter with the Governor's Council on the Environment—a step sure to slow the approval process and force the governor to choose between criminal justice reform and protecting the environment. Meanwhile, VHLC Assistant Director Junius Fishburne refreshed his ties with the preservation network beyond Virginia, trading a copy of the VHLC report for correspondence between the National Trust for Historic Preservation and the Holton administration.[12]

Moody simultaneously reached out to the key Federal department aligned with his mission—Interior. In the guise of seeking advice, Moody wrote to Interior's Advisory Council on Historic Preservation about a looming violation of Federal law. The Landmarks Commission, Moody explained, twice had urged Otis Brown to build his reception and diagnostic center elsewhere—to no avail. Prison opponents were now threatening to seek an injunction, Moody warned. Because Brown's criminal justice Federal partner, the LEAA, funded the project, the plaintiffs planned to invoke the National Historic Preservation Act. This would set the stage for a battle between Governor Holton and Federal legislative protections for historic sites.[13]

Although the VHLC went through the motions of keeping the governor and his key staff members informed, the professional historic preservation network had been alerted and was now actively shoring up its picket, which was grounded locally but rose vertically through state to Federal agencies and their most effective voluntary-sector advocates like the National Trust. As each element in that vertical picket closed ranks, the gap between it and a contiguous picket in both state and federal fences—criminal justice professionals, in this case—widened. Elected gatekeepers, from Nixon to Holton, had a lot of fence-mending to do.

Like enemy troops scrambling for the last acre of territory before a cease-fire, prison opponents picked up the pace. Their efforts were rewarded when Hawkwood and Westend were added to Virginia's Landmarks Register on September 1, 1970. The recommendation was immediately forwarded to the Department of the Interior. Seventeen days later both properties were placed on the National Register of Historic Places. History, it turned out, could move quickly when threatened.[14]

Although the news quickly spread through the preservation grapevine, VHLC's role in documenting Green Springs' history was confined to those in the know. Moody's letters to the Taylors and Elys informing them of the good news concluded with a telling apology for failing to issue a press release: "I am sure you understand." Taylor, a charter member of the preservation network, and the newly engaged but politically savvy Rae Ely undoubtedly did.[15]

One VHLC board member, Frederick Hartt, did not feel constrained by that organization's careful efforts to walk a fine line with the governor. The eminent architectural historian pressured Holton to abandon his plans for the diagnostic center in Green Springs, prompting a detailed response from the governor. Holton had personally reviewed the matter, was satisfied it was correct, and believed that "plans and work have progressed so far that it is no longer realistic to talk about change of this decision." Opponents, Holton insisted, did not appreciate the care the Commonwealth was taking to preserve the historical setting, nor did they acknowledge the inevitable growth and development the region would soon experience due to the completion of I-64. Indeed, given the green space that would be preserved around the prison there was a unique opportunity to leverage this "anchor" to manage growth in a more orderly fashion. Holton quipped that the controversy had even yielded unanticipated benefits, needling, "[W]e have almost literally discovered a new historically valuable area of our Commonwealth."[16]

Hartt challenged "every major point" raised by the governor. Attempts to landscape the facility and its sixty-foot guard tower "would be about as effective as trying to camouflage the Pentagon." The prison was no anchor; "a depth charge would be a more accurate simile." Nor would Hartt let the swipe at the recent discovery of Green Springs' history stand unrebutted, firing back that the "historic value of the area has long been known to students of Virginia architecture." Hartt warned Holton that he was endangering the legacy of his "excellent administration." If "such an intrusion" was permitted to disfigure Green Springs, "that monstrosity above all will stand in the minds of Virginians as a permanently visible monument to your term in office."[17]

Addressing Holton's contention about the inevitability of growth and development, Hartt disclosed an idea that the VHLC had long supported but only discussed internally, fearing that it might anger the governor. "The legal device of scenic easement," Hartt told Holton, could staunch development and preserve historic Green Springs. Hartt was no depth charge, but as a scholar and tenured professor, he was a loose cannon when it came to fealty to Virginia's chief executive. Moody and the other employees of the VHLC did not have that freedom.[18]

With the lawsuit filed and two more properties certified as state landmarks, the National Trust again tested the waters with Brown and Holton. In a brief note to the governor, the trust's president noted the recent formation of the Governor's Council on the Environment; it was the proper venue for weighing the possibility that "a less disruptive and more compatible location for the penal complex could be found." Far from reconsidering, Linwood Holton was more anxious than ever to get moving—especially now that the opposition had sued the state. On August 26, Ed Temple, the governor's commissioner of administration, warned Brown that Holton was growing impatient. The governor wanted to know "why this project had not moved faster." Ominously, Temple noted Holton's handwritten note: "I don't see how any of this [historic landscape] could possibly be adversely affected by the reception and medical facility. Let's go!" Cautiously, Otis Brown tried to persuade the governor to consider another site. Brown identified one and gently suggested that it "might be to our advantage to move down the road." There is no record of Holton's response, but the governor's subsequent actions spoke loudly: full speed ahead with the Green Springs site.[19]

8

Federal Court

GAINING ACCESS TO THE FEDERAL COURT system was one thing. Winning there was another matter. When the Federal district court ruled against the plaintiffs in January 1971, it looked like venue shopping had failed to deliver any tangible benefits for the Green Springs Association. Prison opponents soon learned, however, that legal setbacks could serve as effective tools for political mobilization, especially when pursued in conjunction with national preservation and environmental networks. Green Springs' national allies feared that the district court decision, paired with President Nixon's determination to return control over Federal funds to local and state officials, might undermine the National Historic Preservation Act, or the more recent National Environmental Policy Act. Both Rae Ely and the Virginia Historic Landmarks Commission effectively leveraged that concern.

The VHLC had to proceed cautiously, as James Moody acknowledged to a key nongovernmental ally. "Our position has been uncomfortable, as I am sure you understand, for intramural disagreements between state agencies is not encouraged. So we have sat by and held our tongues, hoping that our role would be carried out by others." Grassroots citizen groups like the Green Springs Association and Moody's confidant, the executive director of the most influential nongovernmental preservation organization, were free to speak out and eager to do so.[1]

Federal District Court Judge Robert R. Merhige presided over *Ely v. Velde*. Born in Brooklyn in 1919, Merhige grew up in the comfortable subdivision of Merrick Gables on Long Island, but quickly adapted to his new home in the South. After completing his undergraduate work at High Point College in North Carolina, where he received an athletic scholarship, he moved to Richmond and attended the University of Richmond Law School while moonlighting as an assistant basketball coach. After flying on B-17 bomber raids into Nazi Germany, Merhige returned to Richmond, where he eventually founded his own law firm.[2]

In 1967, Lyndon Johnson appointed Merhige to the bench as a U.S. district court judge, where he served for the next thirty-one years. Recounting his meeting with LBJ, Merhige recalled the president's amiable chitchat and his foul mouth. On his appointment of liberal judges, Johnson complained, "Everybody thinks I am so keen on Federal judges. Truth of the matter is that most of the Federal judges I met have been shit asses." At Merhige's confirmation hearing a Mississippi senator had only one question: "What's a fellow from New York doing as a judge in Virginia?" The nominee answered cleverly, but respectfully "My mother was there when I was born; but I am a Virginian by choice."[3]

Merhige's pragmatic approach to the law was quickly tested by an avalanche of civil rights cases. The judge was no civil rights crusader; he later wrote that he was embarrassed that he had been too distracted in private practice to focus on the "problems of racial discrimination." Nonetheless, in the wake of the Supreme Court's 1968 landmark *Green v. County School Board of New Kent County* decision that voided a nearby "freedom-of-choice" plan because it violated *Brown v. Board of Education,* Merhige issued a series of rulings that immediately drew fire from Virginia's avowed white supremacists and Richmond's more artfully biased "Main Street" establishment.[4]

Although Merhige believed his "cautious and accommodating approach" would give communities time to adjust to the rulings, he soon required around-the-clock protection of U.S. marshals due to threats from the Ku Klux Klan, which held weekly parades outside his house and staged faux funeral ceremonies. Writing in 1992, Judge Merhige noted that he was hardly the only Virginia public official to face the wrath of segregationists, crediting Governor Linwood Holton with extraordinary bravery for publicly escorting his children to a desegregated public school. "Indeed, his actions helped to alleviate my concern that I had unfairly subjected my own family to danger."[5]

Solidly built, with deep-set eyes, Merhige augmented his flashy personality with equally flamboyant dress. Rae Ely described him as a "feisty little guy . . . always dressed like a peacock." Merhige "needled" lawyers from the bench and could be sassy at times—a "smart Alec." He delivered his instructions in a light voice with a hard "New Yawk" accent. His biographer labeled Merhige the "King of Richmond" who treated his courtroom and chambers as "hallowed ground." To protect that sanctuary Merhige once ordered a Federal marshal to remove a man who had fallen asleep in the courtroom. It was Merhige's father.[6]

On the first day of the *Ely v. Velde* trial roughly thirty Green Springs supporters, the lawyers, witnesses, and reporters filled the carved mahogany benches of the U.S. District Courthouse for the Eastern District of Virginia in Richmond. The stately Italianate courthouse had once housed Jefferson Davis's office during the Civil War. Rae had cultivated many of the witnesses for the plaintiffs; the staff of the National Trust for Historic Preservation and the Nature Conservancy needed no coaching. The defense must have been encouraged when Judge Merhige concluded two days of hearings by stating, "We should look for ways for the state to handle its own affairs."[7]

Years later, Merhige elaborated on his views about federalism. Glancing out his office window, he contemplated the "intriguing physical arrangement of government buildings in Richmond." The Virginia General Assembly, State Supreme Court, and Governor's Mansion sat on the crest of a hill; at the bottom of that hill sat the Federal courthouse. Merhige wondered "if that physical arrangement was designed to encourage modesty on the part of the federal judiciary." The judge's courageous stance in the desegregation cases, however, belied any automatic "states' rights" predisposition. Those cases offered a different perspective on the wisdom of leaving matters up to state and local officials. "Many a time when I am forced into a confrontation with state government, I can glance up the hill at the State Capitol and think, so near, and yet so far. . . . Integration is not only the law, it's the right thing to do."[8]

It looked as though the decision in *Ely v. Velde* would turn on just how modest the Federal government was in Robert Merhige's view and how far short of doing the right thing state government fell. To get the balance right he would have to consider the degree to which protecting Green Springs' history was comparable to the right of Blacks to attend the school of their choice. If he looked for the state to handle its own affairs, it would be an uphill battle for the Green Springs Association.

As it turned out, Judge Merhige's opinion exonerating the defendants sidestepped the Sisyphean task of balancing the prerogatives of local and national government. Rather, it focused on chronology and parsing congressional intent. The decision weighed three Federal statutes to determine which ones should dictate the actions of the LEAA and how best to balance competing objectives contained in those statutes. How might the LEAA reconcile its obligations under the Historic Preservation Act of 1966, the Safe Streets Act of 1968, and the National Environmental Policy Act of 1970?

Merhige declared the Safe Streets Act the winner. That meant that the LEAA won too, along with the Commonwealth of Virginia and President Nixon's New Federalism. By Merhige's logic, the Safe Streets Act prevailed because it was enacted *after* the Historic Preservation Act. Presumably, the judge reasoned, Congress was familiar with the existing laws it overrode when the subsequent legislation was passed. Chalk up a victory for birth order—sometimes. The amount of leeway a statute offered agencies, Merhige pivoted, could trump birth order. Even though the Safe Streets Act was enacted *before* the National Environmental Policy Act, the judge ruled that the Safe Streets Act also overrode NEPA because it used "non-discretionary" language. The Safe Streets Act *mandated* action—leaving the agency no discretion: "The administration *"shall* make grants."9

But administrators only had to pursue NEPA's objectives "to the fullest extent possible." "Shall" edged out NEPA's "to the fullest extent possible" no matter the legislation's date of birth. "When two statutes of equal efficacy conflict, one non-discretionary and one discretionary," Judge Merhige explained, "the non-discretionary one must prevail." The 1968 Safe Streets Act trumped both its challengers.10

Although Merhige avoided any explicit discussion of federalism, the implications were clear. In sharp contrast to the dozens of desegregation cases that the judge presided over, his decision in *Ely v. Velde* chose local over national control—just as the Nixon administration had advocated. At least when it came to protecting history and its surrounding environment, the "intriguing physical arrangement of government buildings in Richmond" got it just right. The Federal courthouse was still at the bottom of the hill.

The district court's decision affirmed Nixon's promise: there were no strings attached to block grant Federal funding, which meant that Virginia could locate the diagnostic center where it wanted to, regardless of its impact on the site's historic environment. Otis Brown quickly launched a charm offensive, as any new neighbor might. He promised that the "facility will be in harmony with the community." If the Green Springs activists were disappointed, they did not display it publicly. They did, however, announce that they planned to appeal.[11]

Judge Merhige's ruling mobilized the preservation network because it threatened to undermine the Historic Preservation Act. It also alerted environmental interest groups concerned about the impact on the National Environmental Policy Act. The possibility that this decision threatened to roll back hard-won victories soon triggered national press coverage. No doubt, Rae Ely would have preferred that Merhige simply block the prison site. Nonetheless, his decision solidified her budding relationship to the state and national preservation network, forged new alliances with the national environmental movement, and opened the door to national media outlets.

The counterattack began in Linwood Holton's own backyard when the VHLC spread the word of the looming danger. Executive Director Moody forwarded Merhige's decision to Robert Garvey, executive secretary of the Advisory Council on Historic Preservation, and asked Garvey how he planned to respond. Garvey well understood that any effort to resist the judge's interpretation of the NHPA cut against a policy initiative dear to his boss, Richard Nixon. Nonetheless, he defended the preservation picket—albeit cautiously.[12]

The VHLC also kept the lines of communication open to voluntary-sector advocates for historic preservation, prompting National Trust president James Biddle's letter to the chair of the Arts Commission of Virginia. Biddle recommended that he reject the prison site at the commission's April 1971 meeting. Several months later the trust took more formal action, filing a brief with the Fourth Circuit as a "friend of the court." The trust was joined by a prominent national environmental group, the Natural Resources Defense Council.[13]

Like these voluntary organizations, the Green Springs citizen activists who opposed the prison were a valuable asset to the preservation network precisely because they did not report to governors or presidents. Days after Merhige's decision the *Daily Progress* reported that citizens from Green Springs were planning to meet with the influential U.S. senator from the state of Washington, Henry (Scoop) Jackson. A key architect of NEPA, presumably Jackson opposed Judge Merhige's ruling preempting the application of that legislation. While it is not known if Jackson got involved, fellow Democratic senator and NEPA supporter William B. Spong of Virginia did. He expressed his displeasure with the district court decision in a meeting with Rae Ely, Deborah Murdock, and Elisabeth Nolting. Louisa's U.S. congressman, William L. Scott, reacted differently. "He was sitting there looking all pasty faced, and with what looked like black shoe polish in his hair," Rae recalled. The women should take up the matter with their local supervisor, Scott told them. If their supervisor did not reflect the views of the majority of the district, "then you should elect somebody else."[14]

The ubiquitous Frederick Hartt reached out to First Lady Pat Nixon, inviting her to visit the beautiful historic homes in Green Springs. Politely declining, she expressed her hope that "this picturesque and historic region will continue to be preserved for future generations to enjoy." Whether Mrs. Nixon was aware that her perfunctory response directly undercut her husband's domestic initiative is not clear. She did not report to him, but she did have to live with him.[15]

On April 25, 1971 the conflict drew national attention via a feature story by *Washington Post* staff writer Helen Dewar. She succinctly summed up the contentious issues: "whether the prison is more important than preservation, whether its presence would necessarily despoil the countryside and whether the bucolic purity of Green Springs isn't marked for extinction anyway—if not by a prison, then by a factory, a subdivision, a trailer park." Dewar believed that some prison opponents made a compelling case for the unique quality of Green Springs' historic rural culture and that those concerns were accentuated because many had moved to Green Springs in the first place to escape just the kind of development the Commonwealth now planned to jump-start. Dewar gave equal space to the prison's advocates, quoting Earl Ogg, who spoke passionately about placing human need—in the form of local jobs for his constituents—above buildings.[16]

In August, a national television network came to Louisa to film a two-part series on the controversy. Representatives of the Green Springs Association fanned the publicity by reading the acknowledgment that Pat Nixon had sent to Frederick Hartt. "The 'Save the Green Springs' fight possibly could go to the White House," *Daily Progress* correspondent Dorothy Mench reported breathlessly.[17]

The Fourth Circuit Court of Appeals heard arguments in *Ely v. Velde* on August 23, 1971. A three-judge panel, consisting of Harrison Winters, Simon E. Sobeloff, and soon-to-be Supreme Court nominee Clement Haynsworth, presided. Rae Ely recalled, "We came away feeling like it's a whole new ball game." She had good reason to be optimistic. On November 8, a decision authored by Judge Sobeloff reversed the district court decision: administrators did indeed need to consider the environmental impact of the facility and its effect on the historic properties near the site before Federal funds could be allocated.[18]

Sobeloff opined that "[i]n the presence of unmistakable language to the contrary, we should hesitate to read the congressional solution to one problem—protection of local police autonomy—so broadly as unnecessarily to undercut solutions adopted by Congress to preserve and protect other social values such as the natural and cultural environment." The decision was unequivocal on the key issue at stake: because the LEAA was a Federal agency it must comply with National Historic Preservation Act and NEPA requirements before authorizing the expenditure of Federal funds. This cinched some of the strings that Merhige's ruling had loosened.[19]

The opinion questioned Judge Merhige's insistence on choosing between competing Federal statutes, ruling that such a choice should be the last resort. The three-judge panel opted instead for a closer examination of the underlying intent of each statute, followed by a more rigorous effort to reconcile conflicting elements. Applying that logic, the opinion concluded, "It is not to be assumed lightly that Congress intended to cancel out two highly important statutes without a word to that effect." Rejecting Merhige's interpretation of NEPA, the appeals court decision cited the recent *Calvert Cliffs* decision that imposed the procedural *requirement* to balance environmental considerations against other interests on all Federal agencies. Although the appeals court ruled in *Ely* that this same balancing requirement applied to the LEAA, it never dictated what the substantive conclusion of that process should be. That outcome remained the prerogative of Federal administrators at LEAA. Their obligation was merely to carry out, in good faith, the agency's procedural duties to conduct the proper balancing act before arriving at their final decision.[20]

Though a resounding victory for the Green Springs Association, the decision stopped short of enjoining the Commonwealth of Virginia from proceeding with construction as requested by the plaintiffs. The appeals court agreed with the district court decision that the Federal statutes exempted state and local officials from compliance if the project did *not* accept Federal funds, leaving open the possibility of proceeding without them.[21]

Both sides claimed victory. Rae Ely told a *Washington Post* reporter that the decision "makes the point we were most anxious to establish." George Minter, director of information for the state Department of Welfare and Institutions, proclaimed that "we are pleased that the legal attempt to block the construction of the Virginia Correctional Center was rejected by the appellate court."[22]

The decision resonated far beyond Louisa County and the Commonwealth of Virginia. A case comment in the *Notre Dame Lawyer* published in April 1972 noted that the appeals court decision in *Ely* would extend the reach of NEPA. This robust defense of the National Historic Preservation Act and NEPA—despite the "no strings attached" rhetoric of the Safe Streets Act—established an important precedent with broad applicability. The Fourth Circuit's decision "makes it clear that in 'the absence of *unmistakable* language to the contrary' (emphasis added) all federal agencies will be forced to comply with NHPA and NEPA." The comment concluded that "[i]n its broadest sense, the decision provides a new impetus to citizens' suits intended to halt environmentally degrading projects." The appeals court decision went "farther than any case to date" toward using these statutes to protect the environment.[23]

That same comment, however, pointed to what many environmental advocates would come to view as the major flaw in the appeals court decision—its failure to levy an injunction against the Commonwealth of Virginia blocking construction should the state choose to *forgo* Federal funds. This was bound to encourage "wait and see" tactics by states: they could simply apply for Federal funds and hope that projects would not be challenged by environmentalists or preservation advocates. If challenged, "they can then use state funds for that project and replace those funds by redistributing the money from federal grants."[24]

The Fourth Circuit's decision laid down an important marker: block grants, and presumably revenue sharing more generally, did not override other Federal obligations, no matter how eager President Nixon was to cut red tape. Federal funds came with an obligation to abide by *all* Federal statutes. Yet, the appeals court would not cross a bright line that haunted the compound republic. States that did not take Federal funds need not comply with a host of nationally imposed obligations. What's more, savvy state operatives—and when it came to federalism, there were plenty—could simply apply for Federal funding, hoping that the Federally funded project would not be challenged. If it was, states could continue the project as planned by simply returning the Federal funds or cleverly redirecting them to another, less controversial project.

Governor Holton was just such a savvy state official. He had already suggested that he was prepared to bear the financial burden by forfeiting Federal funds. One day after the appeals court decision was handed down, Assistant Attorney General of Virginia Vann H. Lefcoe announced that the state would proceed with construction, using its own money while it conferred with the Department of Justice on how the decision would affect future federal funding.[25]

The *Richmond Times-Dispatch*'s lead editorial argued that the Commonwealth could "use the decision as a sound reason for taking a fresh look at the damage it might do to that charming area." Should this review confirm what "an impressive array" of architects, historians, and real estate brokers had already recommended, "the state could gracefully shift its important program to another, less aesthetically significant site in Louisa." The newspaper urged the governor to take a page out of his own Council on the Environment's recent report calling for the creation of "historic districts" protected by open-space easements, underscoring that "not the tiniest peep has been heard from the Council about Green Springs."[26]

Somebody in the governor's administration was listening. DWI Director Otis Brown insisted that no final decision had been made. He added that the state was again exploring alternative sites. Richard N. Harris, director of the state agency through which all LEAA funds passed, soon announced that future requests for Federally funded projects in this field would have to submit statements about the facility's potential impact on the environment. Harris added that "nobody in his right mind is going to start building a jail now until he gets cleared on the question of environmental impact statement on the Green Springs facility."[27]

The court's refusal to pull the plug on a diagnostic center built entirely with state funds left the VHLC in a political bind. While some commission members and staff were eager to protect Green Springs through a state-designated historic district that relied upon a "large-scale easement program," the minutes summed up the commission's determination to maintain a low profile, even as it worked with national allies to oppose the governor's plans. "Further discussion of this concept will take place as occasions demand." Moody held his tongue. But his hope that others would speak out against the prison was fulfilled. As Moody wrote Biddle: "it has been [carried out] splendidly ... by groups such as the National Trust."[28]

As Holton's point man on the diagnostic center equivocated, the governor remained resolute. His determination may have been bolstered by the knowledge that the state agency that had selected the Green Springs site in the first place—DWI—would be the first to release an environmental impact statement. Initially, the DWI analysis produced positive headlines for the governor's team. Taking a victory lap, Otis Brown insisted that "a full study of this report will demonstrate to any impartial person that the proposed reception and medical center will not harm either the historical character, rural character, or the ecology of the Green Springs community." That favorable press quickly soured when a *Richmond Times-Dispatch* editorial pointed out that the report's authors were DWI employees. Even more questionable were the report's "consultants," who included Louisa County prison supporters Dean Agee and Earl Ogg. "How's that for objectivity?" the newspaper asked.[29]

Rae recognized that the *Times-Dispatch* was a crucial opinion leader, especially when it came to balancing the left-leaning slant of the *Washington Post* and *New York Times*. As one of the leading political columnists in Virginia characterized it, the *Times-Dispatch* "was a leading conservative fixture in Virginia during the period, reliably pro-business." It was "a self-appointed guardian of tight-fisted government and a glorious state history that could overlook transgressions against poor and minority populations." Rae made it her business to get to know Ed Grimsley, who recently had taken charge of the editorial page.[30]

When she walked into his office unannounced, his secretary tried and failed to put her off. Sheepishly, Grimsley confessed that he did not even invite her to sit down. Like many others lobbied by Rae, he noted how effectively she presented her case: she was "a very dynamic person" who could back up her statements. Rae lured Grimsley to Green Springs for "the tour," confirming the editor's impression that she was an effective, tenacious advocate for her cause. She was charming, not angry; never strident, in his opinion.[31]

Rae deployed a battery of experts to counter the DWI report, like Irwin Taylor Sanders II, a professor of history at Washington and Lee University. She urged him to "write a few comments for inclusion into the Association's rebuttal of the Otis Brown manifesto." Sanders's letter addressed the ways in which the "awakened interest in ecology, conservation and the environment has trickled over to the problem of historic preservation." He went so far as to suggest that Congress must have had an area just like Green Springs in mind when it crafted the National Historic Preservation Act because it "reflected the movement toward the preservation of entire historic districts . . . that offer such acute reminders of the nation's heritage."[32]

James Biddle soon added his voice to the growing chorus criticizing the DWI report. He lobbied the chair of the Virginia House of Delegates Appropriations Committee to pressure DWI to find another site. Rae testified at committee hearings, pleading that Green Springs not be sacrificed on the altar of economic expediency. It was no fun litigating, she conceded, but that is what citizens had to do when local officials abdicated their responsibilities. The "most obscene" waste could not be estimated in dollars and cents, another *Times-Dispatch* editorial warned. No price could offset the "degradation the state would bring to a beautiful rural area that has been preserved much as it has existed in pre-Revolutionary times."[33]

While some representatives in both the House of Delegates and the Senate took the opportunity rhetorically to criticize the prison, legislative backing for the governor's plan survived. Local control was no longer synonymous with "massive resistance," but in Virginia it still meant deferring to local officials whenever possible. Legislative support for the diagnostic center even endured (poorly) rhyming verse published in the *Daily Progress*: "Louisa's oligarchs have ruled so long, / (in conscience weak in economics strong), / That swarms of local lackeys leap, when told, / To lick their masters' boots."[34]

As the second anniversary of Governor Holton's prison announcement neared, Rae could legitimately claim that the Green Springs Association had accomplished "more constructive good, particularly in the field of environmental law, than many of us could ever have imagined." Noting that some claimed that "average citizens can't fight City Hall—much less State and Federal governments—," Ely insisted that "it can be done and will be done and we will do it!"[35]

9

The Women's Ground War

WHILE THE GREEN SPRINGS ASSOCIATION wedged its way into Federal court and eventually won a path-breaking victory in the Fourth Circuit, the women who had been giving tours and gathering signatures to stop the prison pursued a relentless ground war that ultimately took them, uninvited, to Governor Holton's balcony. Rae's all-consuming dedication to the cause, however, led to a good number of arguments with Hiram at home. That Rae's leadership took her away from her duties as wife and mother was undoubtedly part of the problem. That she had finally found her "voice" was a more significant reason for the increased domestic strife.

In January 1972 Green Springs women took the fight directly to Linwood Holton. They had been collecting signatures for a petition asking that Holton change the site of the prison. Gathering signatures was no easy task in the pre-internet days, and the sparse population—even Charlottesville's population was under 40,000—added to the challenge. Fanning out to shopping centers and grocery stores in Richmond and Charlottesville, women went door to door as well, accumulating 8,500 signatures. In January 1972, when the women requested a meeting with the governor to present their petition, he refused to meet with them. Two days later a delegation of over sixty women visited the Capitol, trailed by the press.[1]

"[A] deluge of mildly irate women descended upon the governor," Jerry Simpson reported. They ringed the balcony of the old Capitol. The governor relented when he saw them outside his second-floor office. "Not even Caesar's legions could have come and seen and conquered with such grace. . . . Like an Army master sergeant selecting soldiers for patrol duty, Mrs. Hiram B. Ely selected those who would sit down at the table with Governor Holton." Rae picked up the story from there: the governor "came sheepishly out of his little office." Two of the chosen thirteen women handed him the stacks of paper.[2]

The petition requested that Governor Holton take immediate action to prevent the construction of the prison in Green Springs, and "to provide every State protective measure available to preserve this area for the enjoyment of future generations of Virginians." There is no one here who does not agree that an institution like the diagnostic center was badly needed, Rae told the governor. Because Green Springs was irreplaceable, however, she asked Holton to intervene to preserve that national treasure by siting the prison elsewhere.[3]

Governor Holton, who walked around the table to shake the hand of each member of the "chosen few," accepted the petition, listened to Rae's appeal, and then pushed back. "There have been other delegations here supporting our plan to put this facility there." Pointing out that "no one wants a prison near him," the governor stressed that there were many historic areas in Virginia. He reiterated that all of the county's elected officials supported the facility. Insisting that he remained open to the possibility of changing the site, the governor said he welcomed the Federal government's assessment of the court-mandated environmental impact report that DWI had recently sent to the LEAA and the National Environmental Quality Council. He stated that the U.S. Department of Justice's evaluation "will be helpful as an out-of-state recommendation."[4]

Holton also addressed rising costs, blaming them on delays. By now, the original $3.7 million price tag had more than doubled. Perhaps alluding to the loss of Federal funds and litigation-induced delays, Holton reported that the costs would be substantial, whether the site was moved or not. Though hardly the blanket rejection of the current site that the women lobbied for, the governor left the door open. He followed up, writing Deborah Murdock to say that he enjoyed meeting her and the other "ladies."[5]

Symbolism was more important than the substance of the exchange, especially because this was the first time that the governor had met in person with opponents. Holton tried his best to be gracious, telling the women, "I appreciate your massive efforts and concern." Yet, his patience wore thin at times. Those moments exposed the ways in which the norms of genteel gendered

Virginia politics continued to shape this conflict. When Mrs. Gallagher challenged Holton, he responded with southern chivalry: "Now I don't want to get into an argument with you ladies, and I have no intention of getting into an argument with you. I don't want to argue with ANY ladies." Rae shot back: "We at Green Springs have defended the area for twenty months. We shall continue to defend it. It will be most regrettable if the state's action requires additional legal or legislative action and effort on our part."[6]

During her ascent from the Vashti Industrial School for Girls to the sophisticated worlds of the Army-Navy Club and upper-middle-class Virginian respectability, Rae had mastered the art and appeal of the Southern Lady, and could embrace it instantaneously, when advantageous. After a few more pleasantries she informed the governor that "there are many, many more of us out in the gallery who couldn't come in here. Would you like maybe to just step out and. . . ." She then "wiggled her fingers at the governor, and looked hopeful." Governor Holton could not refuse. He "smiled and rose from his high-backed chair," stepping into the balcony gallery to greet the remaining "ladies." They too followed the script, applauding the governor's entrance.[7]

After the women conducted two television interviews, Simpson reported that some of them "went shopping and some went to lunch." As they left, one of the governor's aides said, " 'Thank you so much for coming. Come back any time.' Mrs. Ely's eyes popped." No Southern Lady would have taken that colloquial farewell literally—but Rae was only a Southern Lady when it served her purpose. She returned to the Capitol often, invited or not.[8]

Things were less polite when it came to the courthouse crowd's reaction to Rae, who contested the very rules of the game. Hiram Ely had opposed the prison as well and was more of a "Yankee" than Rae. Yet, even those who disagreed with him claimed that they liked the Colonel, called him a gentleman, gave him the benefit of the doubt. He played by the rules; fought like a gentleman; had worn the uniform. The attitude toward Rae Ely was different. Locals gossiped about her even before the diagnostic center was announced. When people who talked about the age difference between Rae and Hiram, it was always Rae, not her husband, who bore the brunt of the "blame" for this departure from norms.[9]

For her part, Rae was allergic to hierarchy. She was as stubborn and assertive as the men she opposed. In every instance she was their intellectual equal, often their superior. Like many of her opponents, Rae was willing to do whatever it took to win. Doris Krahenbill summed up the courthouse crowd's attitude toward Rae. "I do think that they resented her from day one, they really did. And the more they resented her, the more she liked it." Krahenbill explained the dynamic: Rae "was feisty and she stood up to them and she was smart. You know, she had an answer for everything they threw at her.... I don't think they'd ever had anybody to stand up to them, man *or* woman, like that." Nonetheless, Krahenbill was "pretty sure" that the fact that Rae was a woman "had a lot to do with it."[10]

Rae's rise as leader of the prison opposition created conflict at home. There had always been differences between Rae and Hiram when it came to parenting styles, but the tension was offset by Hiram's willingness to perform many tasks that men of his age and background might have shunned in the 1970s. This was his second go-around as a parent and he enjoyed many of the tasks typically assigned to mothers at the time, like cooking and shopping. There was also paid help to take care of the house, the farm, and the kids. Ruby Verdier wore a uniform and was paid eight dollars a day in the early 1970s. If somebody came to the door to see Rae, Ruby would tell the visitor, "I will see if my madam is in."[11]

By 1972, Rae's devotion to the Green Springs cause, and possibly the fact that she had begun to overshadow Hiram, tipped what already was a delicate balance in their relationship. Rae believed that "he was certainly challenged ... once I found my voice." When Green Springs came along, Rae continued, "and Governor Holton became his competitor, he was not so happy. That was the beginning of the end." Lobbying in both Washington, D.C., and Richmond often required long stays away from home. Hiram was angry all the time—raging, according to Rae. He also began to leave for two-month visits to his daughter in Tampa. Hiram added a separate wing of the house at Hawkwood; he lived in one end of the house, Rae in the other.[12]

The Colonel took precipitous, unilateral actions that reflected his growing dissatisfaction with the relationship. For instance, he presented Rae with a brochure for a castle built out of stone on top of a mountain in Tryon, North Carolina. They were moving there, he informed his wife. "Well, enjoy yourself," Rae told him, "but I'm not going." Hiram grew agitated and retreated to his separate quarters. That was the first serious indication, in Rae's opinion, that "there was big-time trouble afoot."[13]

One day she came home to find a prominent Charlottesville realtor and Hiram in their living room. The realtor was a big guy—a former football player. The two men presented her with a contract to sell Hawkwood. "I am confronted by this guy and Hiram, and I am told to sign this paperwork." They told Rae that if she knew what was good for her, she would sign the papers. "Unfortunately for them, by now I had *found* my voice. They were a couple of years too late. And I did understand that the property was in my name."[14]

Rae found her voice and used it in a wide range of venues. As a girl, that public voice had often been confined to singing and spreading the gospel. When Governor Holton announced that he planned to build a prison across the road from her newfound sanctuary, Rae asked Hiram what he planned to do about it. Now thirty, gaining confidence in herself and her rights as a woman and as a citizen, Rae was doing more telling than asking.

10
Courting Bureaucrats

PROFESSIONAL COMMUNITIES THAT SHARED POLICY AGENDAS had long worked across local, state, and Federal borders, forging the relationships necessary to build highways, deliver social services, or, as Rae Ely soon discovered, preserve history. Prison opponents tapped into a network of Federal preservation and environmental protection administrators who authenticated Green Springs' history and certified the natural landscape surrounding historic buildings as an essential part of its environment.

These forays into Federal courtrooms and conference rooms turned Speaker of the House Tip O'Neal's aphorism that "all politics is local" on its head, leaving the courthouse crowd and Linwood Holton wondering whether all politics was at least partially national as well. To be sure, opposition to the diagnostic center began in the front yards of Rae Ely, D. L. Atkins, the Reynoldses, the Krahenbills, and other Green Springs residents. Nothing could have been more parochial. Yet six months into the battle, it was clear that the Green Springs Association was holding its own in the fight against "city hall" because it had tapped into a powerful new framework for understanding what counted as history worth preserving, and that interpretation of history resonated with a host of powerful Federal public officials and their allies in national voluntary organizations like the National Trust for Historic Preservation.

Rae expanded her network to reach many of the Federal agencies now required to comment on the environmental and cultural impact of the proposed facility. Her mission was clear: she had to "make sure that every Federal agency came up with a thorough and penetrating and damning review; and that every state agency did the same thing." Rae believed that she "couldn't afford to lose a single agency, not even one." Whenever a report delivered bad news for Governor Holton and the courthouse crowd, Ely alerted the growing number of reporters she had cultivated.[1]

She also drew upon her class connections, in this case forged through Hawkwood itself, to reach the upper echelons of the Federal government. For instance, Richard S. (Major) Reynolds, the man the *Washington Post* dubbed the "grandson of Reynolds Wrap," put her in touch with his good friend William Ruckelshaus, head of the Environmental Protection Agency (EPA). Reynolds's Princeton buddy promised to look into the situation.[2]

Introductions to men like Ruckelshaus, in turn, provided an entrée to key nodes of influence populated by what one political scientist labeled "mezzo-level" administrators who advanced the cause deep inside of the bowels of the Federal government. Rebecca Hanmer at the EPA and Bruce Blanchard at the Department of the Interior were hardly household names, but they knew their way around environmental impact statements.[3]

Besides the Ruckelshaus connection, Rae was able to reel in Hanmer because she grew up in a small, rural Virginia county. That background gave Hanmer "a feeling about the way things were done which I later would call oligarchy." Hanmer believed that she could recognize oligarchy the moment she saw it and had no doubt about the way Louisa County was governed. "There was no hope that they could possibly prevail with the Louisa County Board of Supervisors."[4]

Ely got to Blanchard through Hanmer. When Hanmer first asked him to look into the Green Springs case to see if there were any environmental grounds for federal intervention, Blanchard yelled, "Becky, I have HUNDREDS of these things; I do not trek out and see fields for a two bit proposal in the middle of nowhere." Eventually Hanmer convinced him to drive out with her for a picnic. Blanchard and Hanmer were exactly the kind of Federal bureaucrats Rae had to persuade if she was going to "win" every one of those agency reviews.[5]

While Rae worked behind the scenes at the EPA, Interior, and National Park Service, public attention shifted to Federal criminal justice bureaucrats when the LEAA issued its Draft Environmental Impact Statement. The Federal agency had simply copied large portions of the report issued by its state-level counterpart at Virginia's DWI. This did not sit well with the *Richmond Times-Dispatch*. Its editorial began with two identical quotations, one from the state DWI, the other from the Federal LEAA. "Like Lewis Carroll's Alice," the paper quipped, "Green Springs finds that its adventure in wonderland—a wonderland administered by state and federal bureaucracies—just keeps getting 'curiouser and curiouser.' " Excoriating the Federal agency for parroting the DWI's "whitewash," the *Times-Dispatch* noted that it had taken the LEAA six months to issue a report that copied "entire pages" of the state's in-house report.[6]

Public references to a suppressed independent study commissioned by the LEAA soon filtered out. Returning to its go-to adjective for the whole mess, the *Times-Dispatch* warned that "the 'curiousest' part of this waltz of the state and federal people may not be out in the open yet." While the LEAA "so assiduously copied the information furnished it by the Department of Welfare and Institutions, there is not one mention of the existence of an Illinois study in the draft report LEAA has offered for public consumption." The newspaper wondered why a publicly funded study was being withheld from the citizens who paid for it. On August 14, 1972, Judge Merhige quashed Manny Emroch's request for a restraining order. The judge did, however, require that the LEAA explain why the University of Illinois study had been withheld.[7]

The Virginia Historic Landmarks Commission, which had been choosing its words carefully to advance its mission without inflaming its political masters, capitalized on the public flap. Junius Fishburne, who had replaced James Moody as the commission's executive director, chastised the LEAA. "The situation is grave when agencies of government in Richmond and Washington issue environmental-impact statements which all but ignore ... an issue which has been the heart of the controversy from the beginning." Governments could not be " 'do as we say, rather than as we do' environmentalists."[8]

The details of the consultant's report were devastating. At the LEAA's request, and on the public's dime, the National Clearinghouse for Criminal Justice Planning and Architecture at the University of Illinois really *had* conducted an objective and comprehensive analysis of the site. The diagnostic center flunked both the penological and the environmental tests. Green Springs was the wrong site; a diagnostic center there would cause "irretrievable" damage to the historical and architectural environment, which "would commence to deteriorate and might well be lost to future generations."[9]

More damaging, coming from a cutting-edge authority on criminal justice reform, was the judgment rendered by the University of Illinois experts on Virginia's *approach* to diagnosing and treating felons. The think tank's research suggested that facilities should be located in populated areas because that is where the professional staff and services were. The critique of DWI's underlying approach to diagnosis and treatment could be read as conclusive evidence that grassroots opposition had caused delays, making once-innovative approaches obsolete; *or* as a fortunate wakeup call that saved the Commonwealth of millions of dollars by delaying a facility that was outdated before construction even began.[10]

The report also questioned the underlying economic premise that motivated so many supporters in Louisa County. The Illinois professors doubted whether the economic impact would be as great as DWI estimated, although it likely would be greater than opponents conceded. Whatever its impact on employment, the report dismissed the notion that building such a facility would encourage young people to remain in Louisa County. Coming from the LEAA's own hand-picked consultants, this was an embarrassing blow.[11]

Now "that an objective environmental analysis is before the public for the first time," the *Times-Dispatch* concluded, "let us hope that officials will not be too proud to admit that a mistake was made and that it needs to be corrected promptly." No wonder Rae's September 25, 1972 letter to the Green Springs Association was upbeat. The LEAA consultant's study "bore out everything we have been saying about the destruction to the area." Ely underscored that only the association's legal action had secured its release.[12]

Rae spent the summer of 1972 focusing on Federal agencies charged with commenting on the environmental and historical preservation assessments. She first targeted EPA Administrator Ruckelshaus, who passed Rae onto Rebecca Hanmer at EPA vouching for the citizen activist as somebody who had done her homework. A harried, midlevel bureaucrat like Hanmer could easily have overlooked a tiny local matter like the diagnostic center. Already introduced through her Hanmer's boss, a combination of Rae's lobbying skills and Hanmer's determination to join the fight against Louisa's ruling establishment ultimately hooked the administrator.

As a middle-class white woman who was roughly the same age as Rae Ely, Hanmer faced similar obstacles. She relied more heavily than Rae, however, on her education—a college degree from William and Mary—a Federal initiative to hire women, and the expertise she developed in the field of water quality. B.A. in hand, Hanmer procured a position in 1963 as a clerk at *Druggist Magazine*. She planned to apply for a writing assignment until her boss told her there was no chance that they would ever hire a woman for a professional position. Hanmer moved from New York City to Washington, D.C., because her boyfriend lived in Georgetown and making choices based on the male partner's needs was typical at that time. Hanmer found a rare parking spot on her way to an interview at a trade association and noticed a sign that read, "Health Education Welfare." Two hours early for her scheduled interview, she decided to inquire about jobs there.[13]

Years later, Hanmer recalled her "naive belief in 1964 that the government would hire me even though I was a girl." Her instincts were correct: the Department of Health, Education, and Welfare (HEW) was under pressure to diversify. Still, she was surprised when she got an immediate interview in HEW Secretary Anthony J. Celebrezze's office. She was even more surprised that the interviewer was an African American woman. Hanmer was offered a position in a new analysis unit the same afternoon.[14]

Hanmer was drawn to the water pollution control folks in the Public Health Service because the issues they tackled seemed attractively concrete compared to the murky nature of education policy. When offered a job in the water pollution control program, she dove in. Hanmer moved to the Environmental Protection Agency when it was created in 1970, where she oversaw environmental impact statements and pollution control at Federal facilities. She also implemented foundational environmental legislation, such as the U.S. Clean Water Act.[15]

Rebecca Hanmer wasn't the only talented woman who found her first professional opportunity in the public sector after being denied opportunities elsewhere. Despite graduating third in her class in 1952 from Stanford Law School, for example, the only position that Sandra Day O'Connor was offered at a law firm was secretary—and even that offer depended upon her typing speed. O'Connor's husband, who graduated from Stanford with a far lower class ranking a year later, was immediately offered a job in a top law firm. The future Supreme Court justice eventually got a job in the San Mateo County district attorney's office in California.[16]

Hanmer rubbed shoulders with an impressive role model, Alice Rivlin, who served as assistant secretary for planning and evaluation at HEW in 1968. Rivlin went on to run the Congressional Budget Office and the Office of Management and Budget. While Rivlin joined a handful of women who were able to elevate the glass ceiling a bit, Mildred Lille, whom President Nixon seriously considered appointing to the Supreme Court in 1972, was not so fortunate. Nixon was torn. He believed that it might be time for a woman's view to be represented on the court, but he also questioned whether any woman had the right temperament for a government job, let alone Supreme Court justice.[17]

Nixon stated privately, "I don't think a woman should be in any god damn job in government, frankly . . . mainly because they are erratic, and emotional." The president also wondered if Chief Justice Warren Burger would be able to deal with this affront to the court's male monopoly. Nixon told Secretary of the Treasury John Connolly in September 1971, "Poor old Burger couldn't work around a woman. Now, there'll come a time, maybe . . . maybe one or two appointments later we'll find one that's ready. But there isn't one now that's ready."[18]

Rae Ely found Rebecca Hanmer by navigating two interconnected hierarchies —one class-inflected, the other administrative. Reynolds checked the first box: his parents had once owned Hawkwood. Rae was soon face to face with the nation's first EPA chief. That she was referred by a college friend who had attended Ruckelshaus's wedding surely made an impression on Hanmer. More impressive was his high regard for Rae, her grasp of the issues, and skills as a lobbyist. Ruckelshaus stressed these assets when he asked Hanmer to explore the situation in Green Springs. He told her that the folks in Green Springs had done their homework, "they weren't just whining. . . . This was an unusually competent bunch of folks for an environmental issue." That homework took the form of a huge, bound compendium of testimonials from experts like Taylor Sanders.[19]

Both Ruckelshaus and Hanmer praised the way this tiny group used Federal statutes to shift the conversation from a neighborhood brawl to a national debate. As Hanmer put it years later, "They had seized upon this idea and this law as a way of getting access to the Federal government. . . . They had gone far beyond 'let's just have a meeting.' . . . Whether they called it their anti-EIS (Environmental Impact Statement), or their counter-EIS, [they] . . . had made the best case they could for why [it would be] a major Federal action." Neither Ruckelshaus nor Hanmer believed that the EPA had jurisdiction over this local situation. But Hanmer recalled that Ruckelshaus "had obviously promised Rae he would look into it; he wanted it looked into, so it was simply handed to me to look into."[20]

Class connections and entrée to the environmental impact statement bureaucracy aside, it was Rae's good fortune that Hanmer realized that she had a personal stake in the issue as well. As she vetted the documents provided by Rae, Hanmer recalled her father's struggles as mayor of Keysville, a railroad town in Charlotte County, Virginia. With a population of roughly 750, the Chamber of Commerce anointed the town "a small wonder." Hanmer recalled vividly her father's battles against the tight-knit group that controlled Keysville. When the town landed a new water supply system, pursuing the kind of New Deal investment in localities that also created jobs, Rebecca noticed that their state senator just happened to be the first in line for a new reservoir on his property, compliments of the Feds. The courthouse crowd in Louisa County brought back memories of the oligarchy her father had fought decades earlier in Keysville.[21]

On her drives between the town she grew up in and D.C., Hanmer sometimes took the slower route—along Route 15. She knew "that at a certain point . . . you passed into an unusually scenic part of U.S. 15 that was unusually free of highway schlock that we all associate with Virginia highways." The connection clicked as Hanmer perused the Green Springs file. Green Springs was that unusually beautiful part of the drive—"What a shame it would be to have it messed up."[22]

Recognizing that this was a land-use issue, not one that involved water use, she called up her friend in Interior, Bruce Blanchard. "If there was any agency that could do anything," Hanmer recalled, "maybe it was some area of National Park Service responsibility." Even if Hanmer had known somebody in the NPS, she would not have called them first because any Park Service administrator would have viewed the situation through a tangle of rules and regulations. Blanchard would glimpse the problem with a "bird's-eye view." Also, Hanmer added, "he's an aggressive kind of guy, we had that in common." As the official coordinating the National Environmental Policy Act's implementation for the entire Department of the Interior,

Blanchard was one of the most powerful middle-level administrators in America.[23]

Bruce Blanchard was born in the Philippines in 1932. Raised as an Army brat, he moved with his family from the Philippines to Fort Knox, Kentucky. His growing interest in engineering led him to MIT, where he received both his Bachelor of Science degree in civil engineering and his masters in that field. He worked for the Bureau of Reclamation in Denver during the early 1960s and moved to Washington, D.C., in 1966, where he was assigned to the U.S. Water Resources Council, chaired by the secretary of the Interior. Days after the National Environmental Policy Act was signed into law, Blanchard was transferred to Secretary of the Interior Walter Hickel's office. He was reassigned later that year after Nixon fired Hickel for publicly criticizing the president's position on the Vietnam War. When Rae met Blanchard in the summer of 1972, he was directing Interior's Office of Environmental Project Review, a unit Blanchard designed himself for the new secretary of the Interior, Rogers Morton.[24]

Blanchard read the *Ely v. Velde* decision but didn't pay much attention to it. As he put it, the case "wasn't on my plate." When the LEAA's draft EIS was eventually served up it looked more like a side dish than a main course. Blanchard ran an office that reviewed and revised hundreds of these. The Green Springs EIS sat at the bottom of his in-box because, in his opinion, there were no environmental issues: "Nothing." At that point, Blanchard recalled, historic preservation issues "were just not recognized as environmental issues."[25]

Then the phone rang. It was Hanmer. She asked Blanchard if he had seen the Green Springs EIS. You mean the one for that center? he asked. "It's not a center: it's a god damn PRISON," Hanmer yelled. "What do you mean?" Blanchard asked. "They're going to put a prison with X number of people in it with staff and all, right in the MIDDLE of an HISTORIC DISTRICT!" So, he muttered, "our historic preservation people will look at it." "I want YOU to look at it," Hanmer persisted.[26]

Hanmer acknowledged this was not really an EPA issue, but it might be an Interior issue, which is why he should go out there. "The hell I am!" Eventually, however, he relented and the two bureaucrats soon cruised down Route 15 in Hanmer's 1965 Ford Mustang convertible.[27]

Becky Hanmer described her first impression of Hawkwood as "breathtaking." Rae escorted them both around Green Springs, moving from one well-preserved historic home to the next. She hosted, while they gazed out at the bucolic vistas. "Bruce and I are ordinary middle-class bureaucrats; we are not treated like that for the most part," Hanmer recalled. As Rae recounted the more sordid details of the price paid for the prison site, Hanmer thought: "this is Charlotte County stuff." She quickly added: "But it's one thing to have a feeling about that; it's another thing to have jurisdiction. . . . It was clearly the despoliation of a unique historic area: period; the end." But as much as she wanted to help, Hanmer could not think of any legal basis for action. She left it in the hands of Bruce Blanchard. She chose well.[28]

Bruce's first impressions of Green Springs were less enthusiastic. Blanchard was not particularly taken by Hawkwood; as for the other houses: "all nice . . . scattered around." Rae herself was a different matter: "She was just so enthused with the area and eloquent about the properties and the landscapes, as well as its history." Nonetheless, he was "still not terribly wrapped into this thing at this point." He was getting a "good tale," but was unsure about just how deeply Interior should get into it. Blanchard struggled to "figure out if the proposal had any national significance." Rae kept the matter alive after the visit: she "had gotten into the Park Service People—the historic preservation people"—she had them all stirred up. Between Rae's direct lobbying at the NPS and her preservation-world allies, the Park Service's comments were "strong," so there was something to work with. Still, the matter only rose to the top of Blanchard's in-box because he soon received the full Rae Ely treatment. "She would come to Washington regularly and bring me up to speed on the proposal." Rae's efforts bore fruit in the fall. By the time the Department of the Interior formally responded to the LEAA's environmental assessment, Blanchard did not accept the proposal to place a prison in a historic district.[29]

That spirit infused Interior's eight-page single-spaced letter dated September 21, 1972. It criticized the LEAA report for a general tone that "tends to be one of economic justification and expedience," which "severely impaired" the report's ability to convey an accurate assessment of the environmental effects. The LEAA had failed "to consider the integrity and significance of the visual and cultural values" of the prison site. Underscoring that Green Springs was a "significant example of historic rural America" and noting that the "community setting has been maintained by the private sector," Interior declared that the prison facility was "incompatible" with that setting. Bottom line, the *Washington Post*'s Helen Dewar concluded: spending Federal funds would be "inconsistent with the national policy of preserving the nation's historical and cultural heritage."[30]

Rae Ely piled on, declaring that Interior's response "confirms exactly what the Green Springs Association has been saying to the administration in Virginia for 2½ years." This was "only the first of a number of major federal agencies which will strongly oppose the funding of such a project in Green Springs." It was no accident that Interior's criticism mirrored that of the Green Springs Association or that it was the first federal agency to critique the LEAA's draft environmental impact statement. Rae had been busy. The *Richmond Times-Dispatch* continued to pummel Governor Holton. More pointedly, the paper asked editorially, how much longer "will it be necessary for the residents of Green Springs to turn to federal agencies for relief?" For a newspaper that had long supported states' rights, inviting a Federal agency to help with a local matter was perhaps the ultimate insult.[31]

The Louisa County Board of Supervisors agreed, but in this case, it defined "local" quite differently than the *Times-Dispatch*. The supervisors did not believe that local control meant deferring to a handful of rabble-rousers. The BOS published a letter in the home-team *Central Virginian* offering Ed Grimsley a tutorial on local control. Accusing him of acting like an authority on matters best left to the people of Louisa County, the supervisors criticized the *Times-Dispatch* for intervening in local affairs without consulting those public officials who knew best. Not one local, state, or Federal elected official who represented Louisa County opposed the diagnostic center. Indeed, those who had stood for election since coming out in support of the site had been re-elected.[32]

Invoking language worthy of Vice President Spiro Agnew, the BOS expressed amazement that the country had gotten to a point "where a handful of people could stir up what has aptly been referred to as the pseudo-intellectuals in this country, to the extent that this project is being caused to be mired into the Federal muck." The BOS compared the *Times-Dispatch* editorial board to the pseudo-intellectuals who criticized the Vietnam War and "give aid and comfort to the enemy." The BOS did not specify just who the enemy was in this analogy—although there is a good chance her initials were R.E.[33]

On October 6, 1972, the DWI announced that the state was withdrawing its application for Federal funds. Although the DWI did not blame the decision on the body blows delivered by the University of Illinois and Department of the Interior critiques, the *Daily Progress* suspected that both were key factors in the decision. The draft LEAA environmental impact statement "reportedly generated strong opposition to the site, not only from federal agencies and private environmental groups, but also from several state agencies." A few days later, Governor Holton confirmed that the EIS was at the heart of the decision to forgo Federal funds because the process had turned into "an endurance contest."[34]

Rae declared that the facility would never be built in Green Springs: she was sure that "this is a turning point in the battle." It was—at least momentarily. By now, both sides in the thirty-month battle surely understood that no twist or turn was likely to be the final one. More gyrations soon followed.[35]

11
Public-Private Partnership

IN OCTOBER 1972 GOVERNOR HOLTON AGREED to move the site of the proposed diagnostic center *if* he received "positive assurance within a reasonable time that the historically critical area of Green Springs will be preserved." One of the few details contained in the vaguely worded challenge was the governor's preference for "open-space easements." Easements were legally enforceable voluntary restrictions on privately owned land authorized by the 1966 Virginia Open Space Act.[1]

Typically, they restricted subdivisions on property and prohibited new construction that interfered with scenic views. Landowners voluntarily agreed to restrict development, presumably depreciating their property's market value. In return, they were assured that the existing landscape and its viewshed would be preserved in perpetuity. As Governor Holton explained, easements guaranteed that privately owned lands "will be used only in keeping with their historic or scenic character."[2]

The governor did not specify what constituted the historically critical area of Green Springs or what percentage of that land had to be placed under easement to satisfy his challenge. Rather, he tasked the VHLC with these crucial decisions. He did announce that March 1973 was the deadline for procuring those easements. VHLC architectural historian Calder Loth was unequivocal in his assessment of Holton's offer: "we all took it as blackmail."[3]

Not Rae Ely. She had discovered easements in July 1970, when she thumbed through *Life* magazine. "Sometimes the fight to save our natural beauties seems doomed by its very magnitude," the article began. Yet, there was cause for hope because all across the land "dedication and determination are beginning to pay off." Paging through the glossy photographs of hawks soaring, marsh grass rippling, even a rare historic southern magnolia tree thriving in Brooklyn, protected by a phalanx of African American youth, one ubiquitous organization repeatedly saved the day: the Nature Conservancy. Rae could hardly contain herself. "It was kind of like a column of light came down from the heavens onto me and I thought, *this* will save Green Springs. This is it!"[4]

"Right then and there, I took my magazine, I walked ten steps to the telephone . . . got the number for the Nature Conservancy in Washington, put a call through—I was almost shaking—and got the secretary." Rae asked to speak to Mr. Richards, the top man in the Nature Conservancy. "In a few seconds, this deep voice came on, and said, 'This is Tom Richards, may I help you?' " From that moment, Richards served as Green Springs' guide to preserving the land through easements. If Governor Holton was blackmailing the Green Springs Association by insisting that a record-setting amount of acreage be placed under easement in an impossibly short period of time, at least he and the preservationists agreed upon the currency that would pay the ransom: easements.[5]

The Green Springs Association also endorsed Holton's decision to let the VHLC decide whether sufficient easements had been procured. The governor no doubt counted on the fact that the VHLC reported to *him* and that its leadership was acutely aware of his determination to build the diagnostic center in Green Springs. As the VHLC's decision ultimately confirmed, his bet paid off in the short run. The VHLC deemed the thousands of acres of easements procured in five months insufficient to positively assure that Green Springs would be preserved.

The VHLC's professional ties, however, soon turned the governor's victory into a pyrrhic one. Even as the VHLC delivered the answer that Governor Holton yearned to hear, the commission also sped down back roads—well-traveled paths that ran directly from Hawkwood to Washington, D.C. The VHLC nominated the entire Green Springs district for the National Register of Historic Places, which successfully positioned Green Springs to become the nation's first rural national historic landmark district.

Easements were a way to merge private and public purpose, potentially saving the government the cost of buying huge swaths of land while benefiting from the capital, free labor, and good will of citizens. An October 1970 letter to the editor of the *Daily Progress* from Christopher and Pamela Gale praised this kind of private stewardship in action. They had observed it firsthand on one of the Green Springs tours, and it changed the way the Gales thought about historic preservation. "Up to now we have assumed that it was the government's role to preserve important historic areas." Green Springs demonstrated "that individuals—with their personal dedication—can not only accomplish a major preservation, but more important, give warmth and a genuine feeling of the living past which is so often missing from museums and monuments." The Gales realized that public history might be best preserved by unleashing private initiative.[6]

Their observation came at the very time that a good number of public officials were openly exploring ways to deliver services in a less costly fashion. Influenced by economists like Milton Friedman, some conservatives, California governor Ronald Reagan among them, advocated scaling back what government could do, making a case, at least rhetorically, for market solutions. Far more frequently, both conservatives and progressives sought to sustain public programs and services by forging public-private partnerships—the very kind of arrangement that voluntary easements on private land, held by a nonprofit organization like the Green Springs Association and overseen by the VHLC or a Federal partner like the National Park Service, embodied.

Caught by surprise, Rae Ely still was not at a loss for words after Governor Holton issued his October challenge. "It's been a long hard struggle . . . but we hope the end results will be adequate land use planning throughout the state that will prevent this sort of thing from every [sic] happening again." It was a "beautiful and happy thing for Green Springs," and she "look[ed] forward to a good working relationship with the governor." Indeed, Ely immediately claimed credit for introducing easements as the mechanism that would preserve Green Springs. "[W]hat has been lost sight of is that the people of Green Springs originally offered scenic easements 2 ½ years ago." The offer was still good, Ely insisted, "not as a response to a challenge by the governor, but because it is the right thing to do." Earl Ogg was skeptical about procuring all those easements. "How in the world are they going to do that?" He gave would-be easement holders some free advice: "I think it would be hard for anybody to sell a place if it is tied in with something like that. I wouldn't buy a place under any such conditions. I know that."[7]

Ogg's advice suddenly carried more weight because of the other October bombshell: the international mining conglomerate W. R. Grace & Co. was exploring the possibility of mining vermiculite, a rare mineral used in potting soil and construction materials, in Louisa. The Louisa County Board of Supervisors was so excited about this windfall that, in apparent violation of the state's freedom of information law, it met in a closed session to discuss the prospect. "Is there any limit to what the supervisors will allow in this county?" Rae asked. "First a nuclear power station . . . then a prison, now strip mining. It's an outrage. . . . We're not about to sit back now and see the whole land torn up."[8]

Because Governor Holton had set a tight deadline for procuring sufficient easements, while W. R. Grace claimed that mining was years away, the race for easements eclipsed concerns about vermiculite for the moment. Nevertheless, the potential for millions of dollars in profit from the vermiculite that lay beneath their land certainly encouraged some Green Springs landowners to think twice about placing their land under easement or restricting its use in any way.

With her *Life* magazine in one hand and the phone receiver with Tom Richards on the line in the other, Rae took a breath and thought to herself, "you better be better than you've ever been in your life in this cold call. And I tried, as smoothly as I could, to explain my situation." Rae invited him to Green Springs, "never thinking in this world" that there was any chance of this happening. He visited Green Springs a couple of weeks later.[9]

"From that day forward," Rae recalled, "I was obsessed because I *knew* . . . that this was the way—I mean screw the prison—I knew . . . that this was the way to permanently preserve the area. Suddenly it all made sense to me; suddenly, it all fell into place. Suddenly in my mind Linwood Holton became just an irritant. . . . We suddenly had a grand vision." Until then it was just "we don't want you to do this." When somebody mentioned the possibility of paying landowners to place scenic easements on their property, Rae immediately quashed the idea as far too costly. Those easements would have to be donated, "for love [of] the land; love of the future; love of future generations." Rae then volunteered to be the first one to put her land under easement, although convincing Hiram to go along was not easy.[10]

In April 1971 the *Washington Post* reported that Green Springs residents were prepared to place easements on thousands of acres of land, and by September easements on 5,000 acres had been pledged. Simultaneously, the VHLC staff quietly laid the groundwork for creating a rural district preserved through voluntary easements on private land. The first public hint appeared innocuously in the caption for a December 1970 *Richmond Times-Dispatch* photograph of the commission's visit to Green Springs. The caption reported that "area residents want the Commission to declare the vicinity a 'preservation zone' in an effort to halt the prison plan."[11]

Executive Director James Moody and Commission Chair Edward Alexander breathed a sigh of relief when other state officials failed to notice this unanticipated—and unwelcome—publicity. Even though this was the very idea that Holton used to challenge prison opponents in October 1972, had it originated in a commission charged with preserving history that reported to the governor in 1970, it would have been interpreted as a naked attempt to undermine plans for the diagnostic center.[12]

When Alexander wrote to his successor, Stanley Abbott, in January 1972, Alexander named a "Landmarks Plan" as the VHLC's most important goal. "We have been moving too slowly and passively in this area," the director warned. To address this problem Alexander proposed setting up pilot projects. Foremost among these were at least one "historic district" and one "historic neighborhood."[13]

Moody soon reached out to National Register of Historic Places Keeper William Murtagh. Moody asked Murtagh for his views about "the propriety/practicality of placing a large area on the National Register." Since the "situation in Green Springs . . . could be duplicated many times over in other parts of the country," Moody wanted to know: what were "the ramifications of such action? Caveats? Advice?" Although the letter laid the groundwork for this precedent-setting move, it did so cautiously.[14]

On April 18, 1972, Keeper Murtagh made it official: historic districts *did* qualify for consideration on the National Register. If scenic easements were the "column of light" that revealed the role of private citizens in preserving Green Springs, the Register of Historic Places was the Federal government's contribution, aided and abetted by its state counterpart—the Virginia Historic Landmarks Commission.[15]

* * *

When Virginia legislators passed the statutory basis for easements—the Open-Space Land Act (1966)—they bet that private ownership of historic properties protected by prohibiting subdivision rights would be a more effective and less costly preservation tool than public ownership or subsidies. Although these properties might be eligible for local property tax deductions "earned" by placing restrictions on their use, the property remained on the tax rolls, unlike museums and publicly owned landmarks. Adding "warmth" and a "genuine feeling of the living past" for visitors like the Gales was a bonus for this approach to preservation.[16]

Although the Gales did not realize it, sites placed on the National Register of Historic Places relied on cooperation between private citizens, the states, the voluntary sector, *and* the national government. As the booming post–World War II economy, burdened by the cost of Vietnam and social spending, slowed to a crawl during the 1970s, public officials at both the Federal and local levels faced greater austerity. However, they rarely abandoned their ambitions. Rather, they encouraged private and voluntary-sector initiatives—the kinds of partnerships that had long been a staple of the nation's collective endeavors, from the Red Cross, to health insurance, to higher education. By the 1970s, Federal policymakers also deferred tough choices by expanding credit to multiple sectors of the economy—financing policy choices rather than prioritizing and raising the revenue to pay for those priorities during a sagging economy.[17]

Privatization and public-private partnerships were even more common at the state and local levels. For instance, the number of "community associations" that delivered the kinds of services once provided by municipal governments—from snow removal to park maintenance—ballooned from 4,000 in 1970 to more than 60,000 by the late 1980s. New York City, facing a looming fiscal crisis, was ground zero for many of these "private" efforts. Some nongovernmental actors were veterans of the broad social movements spawned in the 1960s. For instance, "radical" horticulturalists and recreationalists drawn from Black and Puerto Rican nationalist organizations took matters into their own hands, planting community gardens in New York's vacant lots and building "adventure playgrounds" out of materials strewn about economically distressed neighborhoods. Partnerships filled a vacuum created by the city's fiscally hobbled Parks and Recreation Department. Within a decade, some of these community groups joined forces with the city that they only recently had attacked, creating enduring public-private partnerships.[18]

Predominantly white middle-class residents who were gentrifying brownstones in neighborhoods near Brooklyn's Prospect Park and in Fort Greene also stepped up. They fought to preserve the history that was rapidly disappearing in those parks, saving Victorian buildings and not coincidentally, enhancing the property values of their own homes. They too created durable alliances with public administrators, using taxpayer dollars and voluntary institutions like the Estee Lauder Foundation. By the mid-1970s, beleaguered Mayor Abe Beame launched a "citizens' campaign" that drew on many of these community groups to save the city's parks. The mayor bragged that "the project is a four-way partnership involving two levels of government and two private groups."[19]

In an age of tight budgets, Green Springs could not count on a massive Federal investment like the one that had led to the creation of Shenandoah National Park during the New Deal. Harnessing the Green Springs Association members' "personal dedication" and "warmth" to partners in state government, like the VHLC, voluntary organizations like the Nature Conservancy, and the National Park Service and Department of the Interior was a politically effective approach in the 1970s.

Once Governor Holton claimed the idea of creating a preservation district through private easements as his own, the commission was free actively and publicly to pursue the agenda it had long advocated behind the scenes. The VHLC seized that moment, promising to issue a report within thirty days that would define the historic area and specify actions required to assure that it was preserved. Whatever the misgivings about the precedent-setting scale of the challenge and tight deadline, the VHLC "welcomed" Governor Holton's "interest" and endorsed his easements-based approach.[20]

While the Green Springs Association and the VHLC could claim credit for promoting a preservation district created through private easements long before Holton's challenge, the governor wielded a tool more powerful than authorship—jurisdiction. His challenge shifted a battle that had veered dangerously out of his control back to Virginia soil. His landmarks commission —not the federal courts or Department of the Interior bureaucrats—would determine if the prison opponents in Green Springs had satisfied his demands for relocating the diagnostic center. For the next four months the preservationists in Green Springs scrambled to meet the governor's challenge by pledging easements on thousands of acres. They were aided by the VHLC, which designated even more Green Springs properties "historic." Whether this would be enough to deliver "positive assurance," however, was a question that only Governor Linwood Holton would ultimately answer.

The Green Springs Association geared up for the easements battle by reorganizing as a tax-exempt group under section 501 © (3) of the Internal Revenue Code. The association was reincarnated as Historic Green Springs, Inc. (HGSI). Private landowners placed their land under easement and then donated those easements to HGSI, subject to a long list of conditions. First on the list was a guarantee by the Commonwealth that no penal facility would be built within three miles of the historic area. Easily lost among the other conditions was a requirement that ultimately would shift the debate back to a Federal venue. Before HGSI could exercise its option on an easement, the Commonwealth of Virginia had to designate Green Springs a "Historic District" *and* "agree to nominate it to the U.S. Department of the Interior for inclusion on the National Register of Historic places."[21]

This was a bold move, since it would make Green Springs the nation's first rural historic district. Yet, the VHLC had repeatedly tested the waters for just such a nomination and Rae Ely never met a body of water that she was not prepared to jump into—headfirst—if it served the cause. Nominating the entire *district* for the National Register was HGSI's and the VHLC's response to Holton's "blackmail." The governor was free to dictate the terms of his challenge, and both the prison opponents and the VHLC worked tirelessly to satisfy his vague conditions. The preservation network responded with its own version of blackmail, however, bypassing Richmond and teeing up an arbiter of historical value located in Washington, D.C.

HGSI suggested guidelines for defining the area to be preserved under the terms of Governor Holton's challenge, taking care that it would also pass muster for the state and national registers of historic places. In October 1972 Elisabeth Nolting wrote to Junius Fishburne suggesting an oval area that would define the boundaries of the historic district. It encompassed all five properties already registered on the National Register of Historic Places and radiated out from a center very close to the proposed prison site. It also mirrored the map that the organization had used to guide visitors to its fundraising tours (see frontispiece). By getting there first, HGSI created the template for every subsequent effort to define the boundaries of the historic district.[22]

Nolting's letter embedded a deep-seated historical premise: the reason that Green Springs became distinctive in the first place had occurred millennia earlier, when volcanic activity—an "intrusion"—created the bowl-shaped land formation and the moisture-retaining soil that eventually made the area so attractive to plantation owners. The contour of that geologically defined bowl had been documented by Federal Soil Conservation Service studies and mapped neatly onto the oval-shaped district.[23]

Nolting informed Fishburne that owners of property already listed on the National Register would likely sign easements and other landholders would soon follow. She reiterated the conditions that HGSI demanded before it formally registered the easements, including designation as a historic district and nomination for the National Register. Over the next month, HGSI, the Virginia Historic Landmarks Commission, and the governor's office hammered out some of the details. Holton met with VHLC Chair Stanley Abbott, who agreed that the area would cover roughly 10,000 acres. HGSI also procured a grant from the National Endowment for the Arts to conduct a formal land-use study directed by prominent University of Virginia landscape architect Meade Palmer.[24]

HGSI's December 1972 newsletter reported that the organization had procured commitments for 6,300 acres of easements within three days of Holton's challenge and that more commitments were arriving daily. Rae kept up a steady drumbeat of public updates and commentary, while HGSI publicized the blue-ribbon preservation committee it created to vet easements and advise on best practices for administering them. Chaired by none other than "column of light" past president of the Nature Conservancy Thomas Richards, the committee contained other familiar faces like Angus Murdock, as well as luminaries like A. E. Dick Howard, a law professor at UVa and a leading authority on the Virginia Constitution.[25]

Rae also connected reporters to high-profile experts well positioned to confirm the unique nature of this undertaking. National Register of Historic Places Keeper William J. Murtagh could not "think of any other group of private citizens in the United States, who have agreed to put easements on such a large amount of acreage of their properties." The National Trust for Historic Preservation's Russell Keune agreed. "I am unaware of any other single offer of land in this great amount being offered for protection by easements at one given time. . . . It is also unique that the area (Green Springs) can be preserved both for historic and open space reasons."²⁶

Even recently trained historians were impressed by the concept. As Calder Loth put it, "We were just picking the individual parts without seeing the whole. . . . We didn't have any idea of cultural landscapes—and this *was* a cultural landscape." It was the rapid pace of exurban sprawl, the very kind that had driven the Elys from New Jersey, that made the case for Green Springs compelling. By 1970 "things were getting really nasty," Loth recalled. "It got to the point you better go look at something while it's there 'cause it's not going to be there the next day or it's going to be very different." The VHLC's Stanley Abbott and Junius Fishburne spent the winter of 1972–73 visiting Green Springs and examining old houses in their rural context. VHLC Chair Abbott, who had designed the Blue Ridge Parkway, was one of the leading landscape architects in the country. Fishburne recalled driving every available road with him, ensuring that the district was coming together visually.²⁷

VHLC staff worked furiously to turn its field work into the descriptive narrative, maps, and photographs to support their case. On February 14, 1973, Fishburne presented a draft nomination for the Virginia Landmarks Register and the National Register of Historic Places to the full commission. "Although this is the first time a historic district has been suggested for a rural area," Fishburne wrote, "the staff feels this is a valid proposal." Checking some boxes, though notably avoiding the governor's office, Fishburne cleared the draft with the state attorney general's office and discussed it with staff of the National Register. He warned the commission that they would soon have to decide "whether enough easements have been obtained" to justify the moving of the prison.²⁸

Although the executive director did not spell it out, his strategy for navigating between the historical rock and the political hard place *disaggregated* the VHLC's quest to certify Green Springs as a historic district from the governor's separate question about the threshold for acres under easement required to assure preservation. The VHLC propelled the nominations for state and national registers on the fast track. On February 20, 1973, with just one dissenting vote, the VHLC's Landmarks Register Committee recommended designating Green Springs a historic district. The full VHLC then approved the motion to designate Green Springs a landmark for the Virginia Landmarks

Registry and notified the governor's office. The VHLC also forwarded the nomination to the keeper of the National Register of Historic Places for his consideration.[29]

The commission underscored that its actions did not interfere with the private use of anybody's property. Prison opponents were thrilled by the VHLC's designation. Rae Ely predicted that the VHLC designation would "alert persons who might choose to bring in incompatible uses for the land." A *Richmond Times-Dispatch* editorial opined that the designation was significant, not because it had any legal impact on land use, but because it carried "moral weight." The editorial board found it "hard to believe that the Holton administration will pursue its ill-considered plan to build a prison within Green Springs." Quite a few Green Springs landowners, not to mention the county's public officials, disagreed.[30]

12

Vermiculite

"THE PLANS OF W. R. GRACE AND CO. of New York to mine vermiculite . . . hit the county in late December 1972 like a second wave of bombers," Peter Bacque reported. Overshadowing its story about Nixon's "Christmas bombings" of North Vietnam, the *Daily Progress* reported that Grace had purchased 500 acres near historic Boswell's Tavern, four miles from the proposed prison site. Coming just a couple of months after Governor Holton's first wave—the easement challenge—the mining assault changed the dynamics of the war.[1]

It opened a second front—intensifying the challenge that Historic Green Springs, Inc. already faced. It also introduced a powerful new combatant—a multinational conglomerate with over a century of experience in global resource extraction. That history and those financial assets came with plenty of political connections in high places—especially in the Republican Party. They started at the top with President Nixon, whose appointments headed the Environmental Protection Agency and the Department of the Interior.

Even though vermiculite mining promised dozens of jobs for the county—the publicly stated rationale for the courthouse crowd's support for both prison and mine—strip mining also offered a handful of fortunate landowners in Green Springs potential riches that dwarfed the potential profit from any other uses of their property. Some Green Springs residents who had large deposits of vermiculite on their land mobilized to capitalize on that "God-given" asset. The courthouse crowd's advance intelligence and political connections had always provided opportunities to benefit disproportionately from economic development. For the first time in recent memory there was now a pot of gold at the end of the development rainbow for Louisa citizens who were not necessarily political insiders.

The Byrd organization had wielded power by suppressing the vote and stifling citizen participation. As the battle over the prison, mining, and the creation of a historic district dragged on, however, Louisa's governing establishment adapted to a more participatory style of politics as it began to coordinate its actions with citizens eager to protect their right to mine. Millard Filmore Peers, for instance, badgered the VHLC, asking that his land be removed from the historic district and threatening legal action if it was not. M. F. owned a large farm in Green Springs and had opposed the prison before Grace's announcement. By February 1973 he was deep in negotiations with W. R. Grace and his position on the prison had changed significantly. He now attacked Rae Ely, writing to Governor Holton, "I can't understand how one woman who has been in the state about 5 years can stop the state, county and all operations in them." When a group of citizens filed a lawsuit in state circuit court to protect their right to mine, the county joined them in the litigation. If prison advocates had been looking to divide HGSI's supporters by peeling off those who stood to make a killing from mining vermiculite, landowners like Peers were the ticket.[2]

Tactics like citizen-driven litigation and allegations that due process had been denied by a tight-knit group of public officials looked a lot like the strategies used by HGSI. So too did a far more public media strategy. One of the litigants, Elizabeth Craig Nininger (Mrs. Elgin Nininger), was tired of the ridicule she believed defenders of property rights had been subjected to by the press. She fought back using the same means as the opposition. "We have kept silent all these years because we felt it was the wise and sensible thing to do." Friends and neighbors eventually convinced the Niningers that the public had already heard too much from the opposition: it was time for "our side" to speak up. The couple agreed, eventually granting a television interview. Things did not go well. According to Betty Nininger, they were "made to look like idiots" after their statements were edited.[3]

Self-interest was surely a catalyst for public action in the case of the Peerses and the Niningers—just as it was for the Elys. To assume that any of these citizens were motivated purely by self-interest, however, is to narrow severely the complex motivations for political engagement among citizens who previously had done little more than vote—if that. For most of the activists in HGSI, self-interest was balanced, and in some instances outweighed, by a genuine commitment to historical preservation and protecting the environment. For both prison and mining advocates, a mixture of self-interest and deeply held beliefs about the sanctity of private property and, in some cases, the dire need for jobs in an impoverished county, proved just as compelling.

Whatever the motivations for their political actions, so-called "amateurs"—citizens with little previous political experience—played an outsized role in politics by the 1970s. Regardless of their ideological slant or policy agenda, tactics began to converge. Nothing could have been more unlikely than direct citizen action in a prototypical remnant of the Byrd organization like Louisa County. Yet as the pro-Holton, pro-prison *Roanoke Times* observed sourly in March 1973, after the Green Springs district was placed on the National Register of Historic Places, the governor had been "outmaneuvered, out-weighed and done in, if not by editorial pages, then by the women's pages. A handful of dedicated, enthusiastic amateurs won the Green Springs battle hands down."[4]

The presumption that women were amateurs was par for the course for any mass media outlet, where female reporters and editors were rare. What Holton's hometown newspaper got right was the potential power of direct action by citizens. Its advice to the governor signaled the changing times. Even if Holton moved the prison site, citizens would object to the new site—"it will be historic, beautiful, or unjust, or something or other." There was an important lesson here. Next time around, the Department of Welfare and Institutions would be wise to "build up its case" and take it to the public right away. Roanoke was not Berkeley or Boston—it was a Republican-leaning railroad hub in the hills of western Virginia. Yet the *Times* understood that "amateurs" were here to stay and would be essential allies in any fight. Even public officials in Louisa County got that memo.[5]

Governor Linwood Holton did not. On March 30, 1973, he announced that HGSI had not positively assured him that Green Springs would be preserved if he moved the site for the prison. Holton leaned heavily on his own VHLC's determination that even though HGSI had obtained easements for more than half the acres in Green Springs, the "checkerboard pattern" of the easements did not adequately protect the district from development. Although HGSI's staunchest ally had provided the ammunition that Holton required to reject the 7,000 acres of proffered easements, those same easements provided a path to Washington, D.C., that kept HGSI's hopes alive.

Holton had effectively defended the fence that circumscribed the Commonwealth of Virginia. The preservation picket, however, protruded well beyond that geographically bounded fence line. The same evidence that failed to satisfy the VHLC in Linwood Holton's challenge had already gained traction with the keeper of the National Register of Historic Places and would soon be used to claim the most prized status of them all—national historic landmark. In spite of state and Federal assurances that this placed no restrictions on private property, the growing grassroots opposition was wise to question that pledge.

Green Springs was green because of the distinctive nature of its geology and soil. "About 600 million years ago," Meade Palmer's *Land Use Study* began, "much of the eastern portion of the United States, including Virginia, was covered by a shallow sea." Several hundred million years later, a volcanic intrusion was responsible for "the very existence and uniqueness of the Green Springs area" and shaped its "basin-like topographic feature." Although it had long been known that Green Springs's fields were more fertile than the rest of Louisa County, Palmer's study grounded the district's fertility in the ancient past. Volcanic and "basin-like" soon joined "gently civilized landscape" as foundations for Green Springs' claims to distinctiveness.[6]

The only consequential mineral deposit Palmer found in Green Springs was vermiculite. It had a number of commercial uses, including insulation, packing, and lightweight fillers. Because vermiculite was remarkably absorbent, it was also used in potting soil and cat litter. The high concentration of vermiculite in Green Springs, rare for the East Coast of the United States, piqued Grace's interest. The company already owned the largest reserves of vermiculite in the United States, located in Montana, South Carolina, and Texas.[7]

The identity of each side in the mining battle was readily discerned by its description of vermiculite's use: insulation and fireproofing, Grace explained; kitty litter, opponents sneered. Grace found the association between kitty litter and vermiculite particularly irksome; Thomas Lyall, vice president for manufacturing, even wrote a letter to the *Central Virginian* pointing out that less than 0.2 percent of Grace's vermiculite was used for this purpose. The association between Grace, vermiculite, and kitty litter, however, was catnip for opponents of strip mining.[8]

By 1972, W. R. Grace & Co. was one of a handful of companies, along with iconic names like DuPont, Kodak, and Shell, that had managed to retain strong corporate identities for a century or more. Founded in 1854 by an Irish immigrant to Peru, W. R. Grace built a fortune on bat and bird excrement, gracefully, or at least more tastefully, called guano. It was used as a fertilizer around the world (one of many factors that had contributed to the nineteenth-century productivity of the Green Springs wheat fields). Grace deployed its shipping network to transport sugar and tin, and in the twentieth century it parlayed that transportation expertise and its Latin American connections into partnership with Pan American Airways.[9]

Shortly before the second wave of bombers hit Louisa County, *Forbes* profiled Peter Grace, chairman of W. R. Grace. He took over the company from his father in 1945 and diversified still further into industries that ranged from chemicals to packaged foods. In 1972, Peter Grace still called the shots for the conglomerate, which was worth $1.6 billion and had 115 subsidiaries across the globe. The article praised Peter's ability to play defense, a skill he learned as Yale's hockey goalie in the mid-1930s. However, with declining profits, perhaps it was time to "stop playing the brilliant goalie and settle down to being captain of the team."[10]

Though few Americans had heard of vermiculite, natural resources—specifically oil—were on the minds of many in the spring of 1971, when the Organization of Petroleum Exporting Countries (OPEC) tightened its grip on the world supply of oil. Although the major spike in oil prices would not occur for a few more years, triggered by the "Yom Kippur" Arab-Israeli War, the price of oil was creeping up by 1973, along with concerns about conserving natural resources.[11]

Initially, Peter Grace left Louisa matters to his second and third lines in middle management, who sought to make a good impression on the locals. Thomas Lyall even reached out to Louisa County's ninth-grade science class. Vermiculite's special qualities made it "more important today—to reduce the consumption of other natural resources such as energy fuels." Besides promoting conservation through its use in insulation, the lightweight soil conditioner could be used to grow vegetation on top of buildings "to help keep the air cleaner." There were considerable economic benefits: the Green

Springs mine might eventually employ one hundred people and almost all those jobs would go to residents of Louisa County. As for negative impacts on the environment, Lyall assured the students that "it would be difficult to determine that the mining had taken place after the land was restored."[12]

The likelihood that Grace would mine vermiculite roiled existing tensions in Green Springs. Would landowners who claimed to care about preserving their historic rural community when a prison threatened their property values still support preservation if that meant forgoing millions of dollars in royalties from mining vermiculite on their property? If the Peerses were representative, the answer was no. Rae Ely responded to the financial incentives for those with vermiculite on their property by doubling down: "If anybody starts strip mining in Green Springs they first might try strip mining in Colonial Williamsburg because that might be easier."[13]

Grace's interest in mining vermiculite also raised the stakes for the VHLC. Soon after Governor Holton's October 1972 challenge, VHLC Executive Director Junius Fishburne dutifully wrote to Earl Ogg, who now chaired the Board of Supervisors. The letter politely asked for suggestions from the supervisors and enclosed a five-page "Preliminary Statement" that defined the historically critical area of Green Springs and enumerated the commission's publicly stated position that a major change in land use like the diagnostic center would "greatly affect" the historic quality of Green Springs.[14]

Ogg's response sizzled: the commission had not even shown the courtesy of discussing the matter. He believed the recent election gave him a popular mandate: he was a strong proponent of the diagnostic center, carrying every precinct in Green Springs' magisterial district and "thumping his opponent, who ran against it." From Ogg's perspective, representative democracy was working just fine until a bunch of nonelected so-called experts at the VHLC stuck their noses in local business.[15]

Louisa's political establishment echoed and amplified Earl Ogg's opinion. Incoming BOS Chair Carson Winston was "shocked" and "horrified" that the VHLC now controlled private landowners, who had "lost all rights." Democracy itself was threatened, especially since the state had taken this drastic action without even notifying the citizens directly affected by it. Supervisor John Butler cautioned that such actions "cannot long be tolerated if we are to remain as a free society."[16] When the BOS codified its sentiments in a unanimous resolution demanding that the VHLC rescind its action, Ogg underscored the point by insisting that W. R. Grace would not accept the commission's action. HGSI might have invited state and national agencies into this neighborhood squabble, but the supervisor who represented the Green Springs district upped the ante, invoking the clout of a global partner.[17]

While Louisa County's political establishment had long defended the rights of property owners, this was the first time that grassroots mining proponents began to coordinate their actions, even threatening litigation. J. Lewis and Martha H. Dobbins joined the Peerses and asked Junius Fishburne to remove their property from the historic district. Taking a page out of their opponents' handbook, the Dobbins' otherwise polite letter concluded with threatened legal action. When Fishburne suggested that the Dobbinses come to Richmond to meet and discuss the matter further, they responded, "Nothing is further from our minds." They let Fishburne know that if he wanted to talk, "you may come to Louisa, as you most likely will, as we understand that we are not alone in this matter and that dozens of other people included in your arbitrary boundary have already requested relief or expect to do so shortly." The VHLC was soon flooded with letters from property owners.[18]

Roughly two weeks after the VHLC placed the Green Springs district on the state register of historic places, Chief of Registration for the National Register of Historic Places Jerry Rogers approved Green Springs for the national list. Governor Holton must have been shocked to learn that the National Park Service rubber-stamped it so quickly. The only good news for prison and mining advocates was that the NPS added 4,000 acres to the district. That number mattered: it was the denominator for the percentage that Governor Holton would soon use to determine whether HGSI had placed sufficient acreage under easement. Rae Ely immediately declared victory: "there is virtually no chance that a prison or any major undertaking by the state or federal government will ever be constructed in the historic district. . . . I've never heard of a national historic district being strip mined and I wouldn't think that the W. R. Grace & Co. with the fine public image it has would want to be the first."[19]

Several days later, fifteen residents who owned 6,500 acres in the historic district asked the county circuit court to modify or void the Commonwealth of Virginia's designation of Green Springs as a historic district; the plaintiffs were joined by the Louisa County Board of Supervisors, which had already retained W. W. Whitlock—who happened to be the brother of the town of

Louisa's mayor—to handle the matter. The litigation charged that the VHLC's action "places a cloud against the property" of owners who wished to mine, affecting its marketability. It also claimed that the plaintiffs' property rights were infringed without due process and that the VHLC lacked the authority to nominate the district for the National Register.[20]

It was now the Louisa County Board of Supervisors that asserted judicial review was the only way it could force a public hearing on the matter. As the *Central Virginian* reported, the petitioners wanted to assure "an open forum, since neither the Virginia Historic Landmarks Commission or National Registry of Historic Places has ever notified or consulted the public and particularly many property owners involved." The Board of Supervisors and an increasingly organized grassroots opposition demanded greater transparency in government, turning to the state courts to ensure *their* rights.[21]

Some of the landowners even ventured into the unfamiliar territory of the Federal bureaucracy—just as Rae Ely had done earlier. M. F. and Norma Peers, for instance, hounded Associate Secretary of the Interior Ernest Allan Connally with questions about the process for placing Green Springs on the National Register and the speed with which this had occurred. The long letters concluded with a succinct bottom line: "We do not appreciate the listing of our property in the National Register [and] request same to be deleted therefrom." It fell to Keeper of the Register William J. Murtagh to offer what he no doubt hoped would be the final response. The Commonwealth's application for the National Register, he wrote, was subjected to a thorough review by historians before being approved by three levels of the Department of the Interior. Like the VHLC before him, Murtagh insisted that this did not, in any way, restrict the rights of property owners. His response only provoked more questions.[22]

Green Springs' addition to the National Register of Historic Places spooked citizens who hoped to cash in on the vermiculite, undermining their confidence that W. R. Grace *would* be allowed to mine now that the Feds were snooping around. J. M. Hill told Lyall that the company did not appreciate the bitter fight going on between neighbors over the historical classification. Hill balked at finalizing a lease allowing Grace to mine his land until he could be assured that this would be allowed in a historic district that was now on the National Register. An exasperated Lyall explained the catch-22: "it is necessary that we obtain some leases on vermiculite deposits in the area prior to going before governing agencies and requesting zoning changes and mining permits." Grace may have owned enterprises around the world, but standing in Louisa County required that the company own property (or lease the rights to vermiculite beneath the ground) there.[23]

On April 3, L. J. Hash, Lyall's assistant, reported to his boss that there were indeed "some very formidable obstacles ... to be faced in future years in obtaining a mining permit on land included in the National Register of Historic Places." Regrettably, even an ally like President Nixon was bending to environmental interests in this realm. Nixon's February 1973 radio address, for instance, backed a bevy of environmental bills in hopes of augmenting foundational legislation from his first term, such as the National Environmental Policy Act and the Clean Water and Clean Air Acts.[24]

The Nixon-backed legislation that would have affected Grace's operations in Green Springs most directly was the National Land Use Policy Act. The bill promised large-scale Federal investment in comprehensive planning, even if that meant overruling traditional local powers—such as zoning. "Historic districts" were one critical type of land-use planning specified in the bill. Secretary of the Interior Rogers Morton led Nixon's legislative push, ably supported by EPA Administrator William Ruckelshaus. Despite the full-court press, the bill stalled in the House of Representatives, succumbing to charges that it undermined states' and personal property rights and that it would "bring big government into everyone's backyard."[25]

Although Grace did not know the land-use legislation's fate in the spring of 1973, it did get a first-hand lesson in the ways that broad national policy intersected with local politics in out-of-the-way places like Louisa County. Grace counsel Mario Favorito's takeaway from the recent Federal developments persuaded him that the company should mine sooner than originally planned. Hash agreed, even if it meant curtailing production at existing facilities in South Carolina or Montana because the "profit potential" of the Green Springs vermiculite was so much greater. If the Louisa operation started small, made a good impression, and abided by existing laws and regulations, it would be well positioned to expand later.[26]

Citizen engagement had always been discouraged in the Byrd machine. Now, a county-funded lawsuit was driven by the passion of more than a dozen citizens. What's more, those citizens were taking the fight deep into the Federal bureaucracy. Nor was this citizen engagement manufactured— the kind of so-called grassroots facade latter-day pundits derided as "Astro-

Turfing." Given the rumors about the Federal government dictating land use, there was plenty of genuine concern, especially when vermiculite lay under that turf. Despite nonstop assurance from state and national officials that no property rights would be harmed, litigants, especially those who were in direct negotiations with W. R. Grace, had good reason to wonder if the National Register designation was purely symbolic. Grace certainly believed it threatened the company's bottom line.

Lyall and Hash attended the BOS meeting on April 18 even though there were no mining-related issues on the agenda. They did their best to ease into local politics. "W. R. Grace just felt that we owed it to the Board of Supervisors to stop by," Lyall said after the meeting, "let them take a look at us, see who we are." They again appeared before the BOS the last week in April to request that the Louisa County Planning Commission rezone 2,000 acres from agricultural to industrial use. This time they were joined by the Peerses and the Hills.[27]

Rae and Hiram Ely might not have been the kind of citizens that Richard Nixon was thinking about when he crafted his New Federalism domestic agenda, but surely the Peerses, Dobbinses, Hills, and Nininger were. And what better set of "closer to home" elected officials to decide such matters than the Louisa County Board of Supervisors? Yet the Fourth Circuit's decision, and now the VHLC's National Register nomination, exposed the ways in which even the most local decisions were integrally linked to Federal prerogatives, New Federalism or not. W. R. Grace & Co., for one, was not taking any chances.[28]

On March 30, 1973, Governor Holton announced that plans to build the diagnostic center at the proposed site would proceed. Holton noted that the residents of Green Springs itself were roughly equally divided on the prison question and reiterated that development was inevitable. However, the main reason for his decision was the prison opponents' failure to adequately guarantee preservation. The governor pinned that conclusion on a letter from none other than VHLC Executive Director Junius Fishburne, which stated, "In our opinion, the existing easements are inadequate to ensure the preservation of the Green Springs area." Although prison opponents had secured easements on 7,354 acres in the district, over 6,000 acres remained unprotected. The pattern of easements simply was not the right shape to guarantee that the area could stave off development, even if the prison was never built.

The "checkerboard pattern" of coverage was the culprit. John Ritchie, executive assistant to Governor Holton, pointed to the large tract of land in the "heart of the district" that had not been placed under easement. Though Ritchie did not name its owner, the acreage likely was the 1,000 acres Dickie Purcell still owned surrounding the prison site.[29]

Finally identified by her own name (as opposed to Mrs. Hiram B. Ely), Rae angrily labeled the decision a "sheer act of vandalism." She insisted that the easement campaign was unprecedented; just two months earlier, only 749 acres had formally been placed under easement in the entire state of Virginia. "In 1970 the decision to locate in Green Springs was an administrative catastrophe; now it's a madness."[30]

Louisa's public officials were thrilled by Holton's decision. Carson Winston immediately endorsed it, insisting that the diagnostic center would be "the nicest thing in the Green Springs district." Dean Agee emphasized the $1.5 million payroll. Beyond the much-needed employment, Agee claimed victory for the "democratic form of government" because the facility was "what the majority of people want."[31]

Several newspaper accounts highlighted the timing of Holton's statement. It was released at 6 p.m. on a Friday evening, a well-established ploy before the emergence of the 24–7 news cycle to bury inconvenient stories. It was also released just before the governor left the country for an extended trip to Europe. His press critics could not resist commenting, "Linwood Holton may be tangoing in Paris, but the natives are hopping in Green Springs"; and "[w]hen Gov. Holton returns from his Paris trip he will have to face the music."[32]

The *Roanoke Times* stuck by its native son, concluding that the "time has come to bury tomahawks dug up from Indian mounds in Louisa County and get on with this critical project." Yet, few believed that Holton's decision would settle matters. HGSI certainly did not; it issued a call to arms in its April newsletter. "The impossible has happened. The nightmare has returned. The situation is desperate." The newsletter asked: "*Is this your fight?* YOU BET IT IS!" If this could happen in Green Springs, "it can happen anywhere. No one is safe."[33]

13
The Conflict Expands

"ONCE THE STRIP MINING BEGINS," HGSI charter member Lennart Heimer's letter to the editor warned, "it is difficult, if not impossible, to restrain the miners. When the strip miners have made their fast profit, what will be left for the people of Louisa?" Though Lennart could not have seen the confidential memos circulating among Grace executives, he anticipated the strategy that Lyall and Hash pursued: get started before restrictions were imposed, prove that Grace was a good citizen, and expand incrementally. The *Daily Progress* bemoaned the looming environmental and cultural disaster: "It is almost as if this society, in its relentless march towards industrializing the universe, had glanced back over its shoulder and exclaimed, 'there's a postage stamp sized tract in Louisa County, VA, that we missed. Let's go back and get it.'" Yet, with the prison bogged down in litigation and Grace just starting the zoning approval process, the only thing moving quickly in Green Springs was history. HGSI sought to parlay that history into the most coveted preservation status recognized by the Federal government by seeking a national historic landmark designation.[1]

History proved to be HGSI's most effective weapon. From the original sketch offered by a Ph.D. student, Green Springs' history had become every bit as real as the vermiculite that now threatened to destroy it.

Those defending Governor Holton's prison initiative soon got a first-hand lesson in just how rapidly history could accrue. While cross-examining Rae Ely in July 1973, Assistant Commonwealth Attorney General Vann H. Lefcoe scoffed that only four individual properties in Green Springs were on the

National Register of Historic Places. Rae quickly rebutted this statement, pointing out that the number was *thirty*-four. Caught off-guard, Lefcoe sputtered—"When did this happen?" Earlier this year, Ely replied. Like vermiculite, Green Springs' history expanded when heated up.

Having successfully placed 14,000 rural acres on the National Register of Historic Places, HGSI now sought to enshrine Green Springs in the preservation hall of fame by procuring national historic landmark status. While national landmark status enhanced the stature of the historic district, it did not in and of itself offer legal protection from intrusions like prisons or mining. The best way to enhance that kind of protection was to ensure that the Department of the Interior had a greater stake in preserving Green Springs—that the Federal government literally owned property in the district. That property came in the form of easements that HGSI would gift to the department. Once Interior held those easements it would have a seat at the table in land-use disputes and direct access to Federal courts.[2]

To achieve that goal HGSI drilled deep beneath the surface of the Federal bureaucracy and once again hit pay dirt. HGSI's campaign had already successfully demonstrated that the assemblage of centuries-old houses and their surrounding landscape offered a unique window into a historic rural community. Permanently securing Green Springs' history required that the citizens' group embrace its friends in the Federal government more tightly than ever. Once again, the instrument that Holton had promoted—easements—proved to be a crucial ingredient in this initiative. This time around, however, it would be the United States of America, not the Commonwealth of Virginia, that decided if the donated easements could adequately preserve Green Springs' history.

HGSI already held easements on roughly half the land recently decreed historic. Unlike the highly visible battle with Holton and W. R. Grace, Rae Ely quietly nudged the Department of the Interior and its National Park Service to hold these easements. Accepting them would not be an easy decision because it came with the obligation to protect 14,000 acres from any activity that might diminish the district's historic value.[3]

Mining additional Federal support started soon after Green Springs was listed on the National Register of Historic Places in March 1973. Rae's allies in Interior like Bruce Blanchard, Pete Raynor in the Solicitor's Office, Assistant Secretary Nathaniel P. Reed, and Deputy Assistant Secretary for Fish and Wildlife and Parks Douglas P. Wheeler pushed their department to accept and administer Green Springs' easements. This approach to preservation would undergird a new program "under which the Secretary might foster historic preservation through the acceptance of easements on worthy properties."[4]

Rae Ely could not recall whom she first approached or how the idea of donating Green Springs easements to the Federal government was conceived. Already adept at leveraging Federal authority to win local battles, most likely Ely simply built upon her relationship with Bruce Blanchard. Owning the Green Springs easements would strengthen Interior's clout. Because easements were essentially property, accepting them would make the Department of the Interior a potentially litigious property *owner* in Louisa County.

Fortunately for HGSI, Douglas P. Wheeler, a young lawyer, who after a failed run at elected office and a brief stint as an assistant legislative counsel for Interior, moved up to deputy assistant secretary. Wheeler had been thinking about ways to advance the National Park Service's preservation efforts without busting the Federal budget. A report from the chairman of the National Advisory Board on National Parks, Historic Sites, Buildings and Monuments in September 1971 spelled out those constraints, which mirrored efforts by the Nixon administration to do more with less. "Our most important conclusion," the sober document reported, "is that for at least a decade, the National Park System has made progress on an infirm foundation [because] its growth and elaboration have far outpaced its funding."[5]

Wheeler was introduced to "conservation" or "scenic" easements, as they were often called, through Russell Brenneman's publications. An attorney who was actively engaged in preserving open land, Brenneman lobbied successfully for Connecticut's landmark Tidal Lands Preservation Act, passed in 1969. While some communities used zoning to preserve historic properties in their natural setting, this was often resisted "in communities that regard development as the solution to fiscal needs." As both Brenneman and Wheeler knew well, that was a lot of places.[6]

Easements, especially if they were donated to the National Park Service, might be the kind of public-private partnership that could protect the nation's historic treasures from commercial development while retaining opportunities for economic growth in the rest of the community. They might achieve this balance, Brenneman argued, because they could be narrowly targeted.

Which "community"—Federal, state, or local—should regulate the restrictions on land use, however, was a highly contested matter.

Wheeler's boss, Assistant Secretary Nathaniel Reed, was also intrigued by the idea. Tall and angular, Reed was called "Ichabod Crane" by some of his colleagues. The patrician Reed came to the Department of the Interior with a well-established record as an effective environmentalist. The *Washington Post* described him as "a courtly developer and investment banker born into wealth ... [whose] deep-seated appreciation for the environment had its roots in his mother's efforts to block the development of an early Florida theme park." Having spent most of his youth surrounded by nature, and deeply steeped in a sense of service instilled by Deerfield Academy in Massachusetts, where he prepped, Reed was inspired by Rachel Carson's *Silent Spring*.[7]

Reed emerged as a leading conservation advocate in Florida, credited with convincing Republican governor Claude Kirk to withdraw his support for a gigantic jetport in the Everglades. Appointed assistant secretary of the Interior for fish and wildlife and parks by President Nixon in 1970, Reed joined an ensemble of politically astute administrators (working across the aisle with leaders in Congress like Edmund Muskie) who wrote many of the environmental laws and regulations still in place today. Reed's personal contribution to this impressive protective infrastructure was the Endangered Species Act of 1973.[8]

The impetus certainly did not come from the president himself. "I don't give a damn about environmental issues. I've got too many things on my plate," Nixon once grumbled to Reed. But the president did want a better record on the environment than Jack Kennedy. Far closer to JFK's patrician roots than Nixon's working-class origins, Nat Reed was part of the team that ensured Nixon's environmental record dwarfed Kennedy's and Johnson's combined.[9]

As with so many other men in high places whom Rae ultimately recruited to the cause, "it started with a visit to my office," Doug Wheeler recounted. His initial reaction was similar to Bruce Blanchard's: the whole Green Springs issue was too small, "too retail," to gain traction. Rae soon converted him. Her timing could not have been better because Wheeler was already intrigued by the idea of using easements as an inexpensive way to get more bang for Interior's bucks. Green Springs might be a good test case. The prospect was discussed more formally at a meeting convened in August 1973. Accepting easements on the Green Springs properties would give the Feds a seat at the local table and a veto over any actions by other Federal entities that might damage Green Springs.[10]

The initial reaction from those midlevel bureaucrats who would have to administer such an easement program, not to mention all the easements in embattled Green Springs, was frosty. They balked precisely *because* Green Springs was controversial. Ernest Connally, the seasoned associate director of professional services in the Office of Archaeology and Historic Preservation, stated the problem bluntly: "the easements [in Green Springs] that have been collected do not protect the property from the threats facing it: the prison facility and vermiculite mining." Either Connally had not gotten "the memo" explaining that Morton and team hoped to *mitigate* these threats, or, well aware of the reason for their request, he was making an effort to stand his ground. In either case, this NPS veteran had every reason to believe that he could withstand a passing fancy of his patrician overseers in the Department of the Interior. At a minimum, raising some cautionary warnings would buy time to assess just how much the big shots cared. Connally understood that direct opposition was rarely the most effective way to kill what he clearly considered a misguided idea. Knowing that a full-fledged easement program would take years to develop, he focused on the immediate threat—accepting Green Springs' easements. "We believe that a carefully limited program could indeed prove worthwhile," he wrote to Reed on August 31, adding that there was legal precedent grounded in the Historic Sites Act of 1935.[11]

Connally then added the downside: only properties designated as national historic *landmarks,* a distinction limited to roughly 1,000 national treasures like the Alamo and Mount Vernon, were eligible. That was rarefied air for Louisa County. The property should also "have a high potential for inclusion in the National Park System if private ownership ever proved incapable of meeting the preservation restrictions of the easement." In other words, this was one gift horse that the NPS had better examine carefully.[12]

Connally believed that Green Springs failed both tests. Like thousands of other properties on the National Register, it was not a national landmark, and consequently not covered by the Historic Sites Act. Even worse than its bottom-feeder status compared to those sacred national landmarks, Green Springs invited trouble. "We do not believe the Secretary should take a widely publicized action in behalf of preservation that is unlikely to result in preservation." If the prison was built and Grace strip mined, Interior would be responsible for the district's inevitable destruction. Better, Connally suggested, that Green Springs gift its easements to the National Trust for Historic Preservation rather than the Federal government.[13]

Historic Green Springs, Inc. was not about to be deterred by a midlevel bureaucrat. Within days of Connally's dour prognosis, HGSI President Elisabeth Nolting wrote to Secretary Morton and proffered the roughly 7,000 acres in easement commitments that Green Springs had accrued, forcing the department's hand. Although Wheeler's conversations with Ely had continued since that first meeting, he had little way of knowing just how many Green Springs residents she represented, which is why he urged Rae to demonstrate broad support for preservation. The 7,000 acres of easements that HGSI offered Interior spoke louder than words, especially since donated easements were not deductible from Federal income tax until the tax code was revised in 1976.[14]

Wheeler and Reed immediately began to lay down the dual tracks that would guide the Department of the Interior's position on donated easements over the next four years. The first was broad-gauged: it delineated the legal authority of the secretary to accept easements for national historic landmark properties and weigh from a policy perspective whether it was wise to embark upon a program to encourage such donations. The second track was shorter and terminated in Green Springs. It authorized doing whatever it took, legally, administratively, and politically, to accept donated easements from HGSI.

In October 1973 Acting Solicitor for Conservation and Wildlife David A. Watts reiterated Connally's warnings: because Green Springs was a historic district, not a single property, the secretary should be prepared to "commit himself to preserving a nationally significant unit, not necessarily all of the properties, but a sufficient numbers of properties to preserve the national significance status of the area." Watts also warned, "As you are aware, the acquisition of an interest in land would in turn incur an obligation to insure the protection of this governmental interest"; that meant that the program "could result in a significant expenditure of funds."[15]

Few criticisms could have been more damaging, since one of the arguments for preservation through donated easements was that it would be a cost-effective way of protecting history and the environment. Several weeks later, Connally played the "congressional oversight" card. "[W]e do not believe [a program] can be initiated," he cautioned, "without formal discussions with our Subcommittee Chairman." Easements, Connally reminded Wheeler, were property, and "our legislative overseers" were very concerned with anything that entailed acquiring property and the obligation to protect it.[16]

In January 1974, NPS historian Robert M. Utley wrote his boss, Connally, to report that Rae Ely had visited the previous week. Ostensibly, she was merely dropping off the Meade Palmer *Land Use Study*. Utley, however, believed that the visit signaled trouble. Ely's visit "should be viewed in the light of the possibility if not probability that the Department will direct us to prepare a landmark study of the Green Springs for the spring meeting of the Advisory Board as a basis for considering whether to accept the easements on this property." Nor would Utley and Connally have a free hand in assessing whether Green Springs deserved this rare distinction: the secretary "wants to accept the easements," Utley cautioned.[17]

Utley's warning was followed by a letter to Rogers Morton from prominent architectural historian and diehard Green Springs supporter Frederick Hartt that offered congratulations "on your interest in accepting [the] historic easements," prompting Connally to scribble, "Has the Secretary accepted the easements?" Although the answer was no, Rae's visit, Utley's warning about the secretary's intent, and Hartt's letter demonstrated that this would be an uphill battle for Utley and Connally.[18]

When the higher-ups weighed in, Utley was ordered, first, to initiate a historical study of Green Springs' possible eligibility for national landmark status, and second, to formulate an easements program for Advisory Board endorsement and congressional clearance. Connally's boss in the NPS, A. R. Mortensen, recorded his many concerns in a March 22 memo. After noting that using easements has "much general merit," it only took him half a sentence to get to "however." If the program was popular it would require "countless man-hours of administrative and legal work," Mortensen warned. The department's limited experience with scenic easements suggested proceeding with caution.[19]

He then turned to some of the higher-order political considerations. The program could provoke widespread criticism of the NPS and Interior from the private sector. Ignoring the fact that the program was predicated on voluntary *donated* easements, Mortensen warned that many property owners might view an easement on their property as "the epitome of loss of individual rights and freedom, and a naked invasion of Federal authority." The easement program might be "the final straw to those owners of property who already see the specter of Government oversight looming in the future."[20]

Although easement advocates purported to align the program with the President Nixon's policy of "placing responsibility at the level of government nearest the affected citizen," it in fact would do just the opposite. "Any person with rudimentary knowledge with the President's New Federalism would immediately catch the inappropriateness of attempting to justify the proposed easement program as a part of that Presidential Policy. At the heart of it, the President's policy on New Federalism is based on control being exercised at the level closest to the citizen. The proposed easement program is based on control from a highly centralized Federal level." Administrative and legal technicalities aside, Mortensen criticized the very philosophy behind Federal administration of easements because it contradicted the president's objectives. Should Mortensen's fears be realized, it would be the second time that Rae Ely turned to the Federal government to foil President Nixon's local-control agenda.[21]

Because slow-walking the proposal was perhaps the only tool available to easement opponents in the NPS, Utley was pleased to report on April 3 that he had been able to forestall a request to the Advisory Board for formal program approval. There was also good news from Ben Levy, another NPS historian, who was tasked with preparing the study to determine whether the Green Springs Historic District qualified as nationally significant. The answer was yes, and "[t]hat's a relief," Utley wrote Connally, "for Doug [Wheeler] leaves no doubt that Morton would regard us as terribly narrow if we came in with a negative finding." It appeared that the Park Service could satisfy the secretary, at least for the time being, by designating Green Springs a national landmark while deferring the decision to accept Green Springs' easements and approve the broader easement program.[22]

While Ely, Nolting, and Hartt teamed with Interior higher-ups to provide air cover, infantry troops turned their attention to securing approval for their landmark recommendation from Morton's Advisory Board on National Parks, Historic Sites, Buildings and Monuments. From Levy's perspective, this was just another administrative hoop to jump through before the secretary could accept the Green Springs easements. To others, less familiar with the arcane requirements of the Historic Sites Act of 1935, however, landmark status signified an exalted place in the world of historic preservation. It could burnish the public case against the prison and add another layer of protection against mining vermiculite.[23]

When the Advisory Board met in April 1974, the Department of the Interior did not press for a vote on launching an easement program, opting instead to ask for the board's advice. NPS historians Ben Levy and Katherine Cole had teed up the special landmark study on Green Springs for the History Areas Committee, and as expected, the report recommended approving landmark status for Green Springs. They had a big gun and fierce advocate on their side: the agenda item was "Proposed by . . . Mrs. Hiram B. Ely and Secretary of the Interior, Rogers C. B. Morton."[24]

Although the Advisory Board rubber-stamped the recommendations of its staff, agreeing to "study" an easements program and recommending that Morton designate the Green Springs district a national historic landmark, the discussion was contentious. Bob Utley again warned that there "could be serious legal implications, especially in historic district situations." The opaque minutes reported "considerable discussion" of the legal, administrative, and tax implications of such a program. The History Committee chair, Lady Bird Johnson, asked if "all landowners were united in not wanting the prison." The answer, probably offered by NPS easement advocates Levy and Cole, was, by any measure, a stretch: "it was indicated that all but two or three were."[25]

New York Times readers, including members of the Advisory Board, learned about Rae Ely and the "Battle of Green Springs" in an article published the day before the board convened. While the timing might have been coincidental, Rae's relationship with the author, *Times* correspondent Ben A. Franklin, was not. She had cultivated friendships with a broad network of reporters, journalists, and editors over the past several years, and Franklin was one of her newest and most prized additions.[26]

Franklin started as a clerk at the *Times* in 1959, eventually rising to correspondent in the Washington bureau. The son of a *New York Herald Tribune* editor and graduate of the Columbia School of Journalism, Ben most likely was assigned to the Green Springs story because he covered mining issues in the mid-Atlantic states, among many other topics. It is also likely that

Franklin covered the story because he had taken a shine to HGSI's "underdog" battle against a long list of heavyweights, and because he was smitten with Rae Ely.[27]

"After 250 years of rustic prosperity there among the white-fenced plantations of Virginia's Green Springs Valley, an environmental time bomb is ticking," Franklin's article began, referring to W. R. Grace's plan to "surface mine" vermiculite. Using the company's estimates, Franklin projected that the value of that vermiculite to farmers might be as high as $10 million in royalties. However, "[n]ot since Patrick Henry ... openly challenged the rule of King George III in 1765 has this crossroads county seat struggled with such a bitter controversy." Franklin cited "city-bred 'newcomers,'" who made up roughly half the plantation owners, as the base of resistance. The battle over mining pitted "the new 'peace and quiet' landowners against the old vermiculite-owning landholders." The remainder of the article described the citizens' group led by Rae Ely and its successful effort to surround the land that Grace hoped to mine with scenic easements.[28]

Two days after the Advisory Board meeting, the *Daily Progress* headlined: "Green Springs in line for Historic Designation." Since there had been no public announcement of this action, and because Bruce Blanchard was quoted extensively, it is likely that Rae Ely orchestrated the coverage. The article reported that Mrs. Lyndon B. Johnson had nominated Green Springs for national landmark status. If ratified by Secretary of the Interior Rogers Morton, it "would catapult Green Springs into the select ranks of the 'most treasured' reminders of the nation's past," including "such famous places as Monticello, Mount Vernon, and Colonial Williamsburg in the Commonwealth," and nationally, the Alamo and Bunker Hill. Green Springs is "extremely important to us," Blanchard insisted, leaving no doubt that Morton would soon sign off on the board's recommendation.[29]

It was left to Park Service Information Officer Duncan Morrow to reassure disgruntled landowners that national landmark status would not threaten their property rights. He did his best, even insisting that the owner "can set dynamite to it and blow it away and there's nothing we can do about it." Whatever consolation Morrow offered was likely undercut by Bruce Blanchard, who signaled publicly for the first time that "the secretary [of the interior] is very interested in *acquiring* the easements." The *Daily Progress* article exposed the key elements of the subterranean initiative engineered by the Ely-Blanchard team, from designating the historic district a landmark, to the likely next step—accepting Green Springs' donated easements. No wonder the Park Service flack turned to explosives for damage control.[30]

On May 1, Grace President Felix Larkin wrote to Morton and asked him to reject the Advisory Board's recommendation to designate Green Springs a national historic landmark. Larkin excoriated the board's action, labeling it "arbitrary and capricious" and warning that it "would have an immediate adverse effect on the value of Grace lands and would constitute the basis for future Federal action to acquire the lands by eminent domain." Multinational Grace scolded the Federal government for interfering in a "purely local issue."[31]

Mr. and Mrs. M. F. Peers had a better claim to protecting local prerogatives: they had both lived in Louisa County all of their lives—101 years combined. Surely that should "be given some consideration," as should their family's centuries-long history of living on the land they currently owned. Their letter to Morton contrasted their deep local roots with those of the troublemakers in Green Springs. The "Federal government so often steps in and tells the local government what it can do. This seems to happen after a few newcomers with their most persuasive ways, can in some manner, get a following."[32]

"Wouldn't it appear to you as it does to us," they asked, "that the main reason that the Greensprings [sic] area historic designation is being pushed so furiously and hard is the fact that the opponents to the prison and mining are trying desperately to keep both operations out of the area[?]" The Peerses had been told that despite their land being listed on the National Register, they could use it as they "deem fit." They found this "very difficult to believe since other things have been railroaded through without our knowledge."[33]

14
Echoes of Vietnam

EVEN AS THE PARIS PEACE TALKS resumed in 1973, the last American troops were being withdrawn from Vietnam under President Nixon's "Vietnamization" program, and Congress moved to cut off funding for that war, the Vietnam metaphor spread to every aspect of American life.[1]

That was certainly true of editorial writers and cartoonists as they strived to make sense of the quagmire in Green Springs. A September 1973 *Washington Post* editorial headlined "Governor Holton and the Battle of Green Springs" spoke for numerous media outlets when it gave the governor advice on how to end "Holton's Vietnam." The "most honorable and just course" he could take "is immediate withdrawal from this scenic valley." For Charlottesville's *Daily Progress,* even Lyndon Johnson's and Richard Nixon's ill-fated decisions in Vietnam were not sufficient to capture Holton's stubborn determination to stay the course. Editorial page director George Bowles reached back to World War II. He mobilized a flotilla of military metaphors, zeroing in on the senseless waste that would ensue if Governor Holton did not pull back from the brink. Bowles targeted military occupation, landing parties, and beachheads. "We are somewhat reminded of the Colonel in the [1957 film] *Bridge on the River Kwai,*" the editorial concluded, who in his "single-minded determination to overcome the technical obstacles to its construction . . . completely lost sight of the fact that the bridge itself would do his cause irreparable damage." So too with the governor, who had "lost sight of the infinitely larger damage . . . that would result from this relatively minor personal triumph." The *Richmond Mercury* soon plastered Holton's likeness across its front page. Parodying

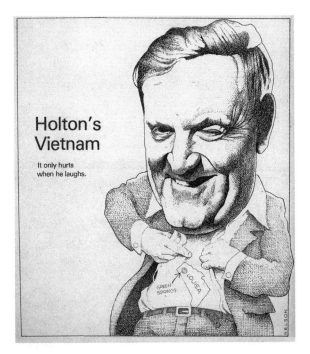

Figure 6. Parody of an iconic Lyndon Johnson Vietnam cartoon by the *Richmond Mercury*'s Bill Nelson, September 1973. (Permission from *Richmond Mercury* Publisher Edmund Rennolds. Cartoon: Bill Nelson.)

David Levine's iconic 1966 cartoon likening Lyndon Johnson's appendectomy scar to a map of Vietnam, Bill Nelson portrayed a winking Holton, shirt hoisted, pointing to a map of Louisa County that spotlighted Green Springs superimposed on the governor's stomach (Fig. 6). As the term-limited governor's tenure neared its end, Rae Ely resorted to guerilla warfare, surveilling Grace's vermiculite mine in South Carolina by land and air.[2]

Like the Vietnam War, the conflict in Green Springs roiled domestic relations—in this case, between Hiram and Rae Ely. She hoped not to get into a prolonged battle with Hiram, but warned that, if necessary, "I'm sure you know that I am not afraid to face it." Sometimes, Rae concluded, "we don't appreciate what we have until it is gone." In February 1974, Rae typed a long letter to Hiram, so that he might better understand her "feelings about our present situation." This was necessary since it "has become impossible to have constructive discussions anymore. . . . Do you have any interest in re-establishing the lovely relationship that we had for so many years, or not?" she asked.[3]

By the summer of 1973 W. R. Grace & Co. began to check off regulatory boxes in friendly local venues. First stop: the Virginia State Division of Industrial Development. Assistant Director William C. Simms made the company feel right at home, stating that Grace did not choose where to put the reserves in Green Springs. "It's just an act of God that vermiculite is only located there." Simms wished "the Good Lord hadn't put it on that spot, but He did." The Commonwealth's Labor and Industry's Mined Land Reclamation Division took a more secular tack, one that nonetheless was a blessing for Grace. Penalties for failure to properly reclaim mined land, it turned out, were less costly than restoring the land.[4]

On July 23, Thomas Lyall returned to Louisa County, appearing before the Planning Commission to formally present Grace's request to rezone 2,900 acres for industrial use. The Grace executive listed the uses of vermiculite (omitting kitty litter) and promised jobs for roughly seventy employees that would generate an $800,000 annual payroll. Potentially, Louisa could become the world's fourth largest source of vermiculite. Nor would this hurt the environment: "Fish, such as bass, swim in our clean water reservoirs," Lyall testified. Grace hoped to begin mining in a few years.[5]

Lyall was no doubt caught off-guard when Robert Whitlock asked if Grace would fly the Planning Commission and the Board of Supervisors to Montana. Parrying this publicly solicited "gratuity," as one mining critic put it, Lyall suggested that "some arrangement" be made instead to visit Grace's vermiculite operation in Enoree, South Carolina. The matter was resolved a few weeks later when twelve Louisa officials drove there, "Dutch treat."[6]

Rae Ely and Angus Murdock arranged their own trip to South Carolina. Rae was determined to "investigate every nuance . . . to find out everything there was about vermiculite mining." We "did some really outrageous things. I guess we were both young and filled with a sense of guerilla warfare." Reconnaissance was the first order of business. Surveying the scene by car, they scoped out the vermiculite processing plant that towered above the landscape. It looked like an immense grain hopper puffing out huge billows of smoke, surrounded by miles of fields that "looked like the surface of the moon." Those vermiculite tailings—a white, gritty sand-like substance—were punctuated by ponds full of stagnant water strewn with broken sections of black pipes. After surveilling the perimeter, the duo documented the battlefield from the air. Rae told a charter company agent they wanted to "fly low; and slow; and get great photographs."⁷

The Pilatus Porter PC-6 was perfect. Soon after takeoff they "were buzzing around and dive bombing this plant. And the guys were coming out of the plant and looking up." The plane banked sharply, Angus hanging out the side clicking away. Even though "all of a sudden all of the smoke stops coming out" of the plant, Angus and Rae had their photos. Taking advantage of the "severe clear," the pair decided to capture the entire vista from the sky. Dipping, diving, snapping photos, they crisscrossed the pockmarked landscape. "You could see pits forever." During one steep bank, Angus hung so far out of the plane that his wallet fell out of his shirt pocket. Rae could not stop laughing, imagining some poor child, living in one of the shacks below, watching the billfold and its contents "fluttering down from Jesus."⁸

Angus and Rae then drove as close to the plant as they dared, hid the car, hiked down one of the empty roads, and took evasive action. "We sort of saw the plant like a prison tower." In Rae's mind, "there were guards up there." Leopard-crawling on their bellies, they slithered along the ground to get a closer view of the processing plant. Rae had television coverage of a real war in mind as she approached the plant. "I felt like I was going to Vietnam."⁹

A *Daily Progress* editorial that appeared on the morning of the Planning Commission's second meeting referred readers to a "phototorial" displaying aerial photographs of Grace's South Carolina mining operation. "Only the pock-marked remains of this once beautiful piedmont land that once had been strikingly similar to that of Louisa" remained. The accompanying article touted the "first round of a heavyweight bout between Green Springs defenders and mining contender . . . the nation's 43rd largest corporation." More than 300 people, the vast majority opposed to Grace's rezoning request, filled Louisa High School auditorium, where verbal sparks flew and tempers flared.¹⁰

Of the thirty citizens allowed to speak, only one favored rezoning. "Let's not be hypocritical," J. Lewis Dobbins told the crowd. "You're not looking out for Louisa County, but yourselves." Of course, HGSI was hardly the exception when it came to protecting property views and valuations. Francis Chester, a farmer who had fled the exurban sprawl creeping toward Long Island in 1968, reported that several members of the Grace family had been his New York neighbors. Chester recounted their fight against the State of New York to protect their backyard from development. While Grace's "brief presentation" lasted for an hour, Rae Ely, limited to three minutes, was denied the opportunity to show slides of her aerial photographs. When HGSI's attorney rose to make a point of order, he was silenced by two sheriff's deputies.[11]

The hearing lasted well past midnight. "Let them talk," County Administrator Dean Agee remarked, "and forever hold their peace." When all the scheduled speakers were done, Rae was permitted to show her slides. She also revealed just how little Grace had paid in local taxes at its South Carolina operation—a grand total of $21,447 in 1972—an amount that one antimining supervisor later noted would not even cover the cost of a two-bedroom bungalow. Damage to the roads from trucks hauling vermiculite, on the other hand, amounted to $100,000 in the first six months of 1973. There was no response from the courthouse crowd to this unsettling financial balance sheet, although the Planning Commission did postpone action pending further study. The *Central Virginian* reported that despite "abuse, cursing, interruptions and screams of 'Sieg Heil' members of the Commission kept their dignity."[12]

On October 22, the Planning Commission voted 5–3 to rezone over 3,000 acres from agricultural to industrial. The matter now moved to the Louisa County Board of Supervisors for a final vote. Although the outcome of the Planning Commission meeting was no surprise, the split vote was. Melvin Turner, one of the three commissioners who voted against rezoning, stated that he wouldn't want such an operation near his property. He also acknowledged that the paltry tax revenue that Louisa County would receive from mining simply was not worth it.[13]

Rae Ely was in no mood for pyrrhic victories: she vowed to sue. The *Daily Progress*, also in a fighting mood, labeled the vote as "regrettable as it is ill-advised." The supervisors should not bargain away "this priceless birthright for a veritable mess of pottage." In this "year of unending government scandal" —Vice President Spiro Agnew's resignation under a cloud of corruption, the deepening Watergate crisis, Vietnam—the *Progress* urged the supervisors to put "pride above politics and vision above venality."[14]

Postponing a vote on Grace's rezoning request, the BOS instead discussed how best to regulate mining should it occur. The board amended the county zoning ordinance, doubling the Planning Commission's suggested maximum performance bond to $10,000 per acre. Adopting a magnanimous tone about the potential additional cost, William Perkins, who had informed Rae Ely that she could not fight city hall three years earlier and was now W. R. Grace's local counsel, claimed that he wanted "to work with the county and with landowners who are entitled to receive the benefits of their land." Even though this would burden the company, "[i]t's something that can be lived with."[15]

Indeed: because the BOS had failed to place a *minimum* bond requirement on mining operations. Nor did the supervisors impose the Planning Commission's minimal reclamation requirements. Rae Ely quipped that their decision "and a dime will buy you a cup of coffee." Grace was delighted to withdraw its original application for rezoning and reapply under the new ordinance. Calling it "a sad day for Louisa," the *Daily Progress* argued that the BOS had "enacted an amendment to the county zoning ordinance which in its vacuity, will probably be remembered as something of a landmark in the exercise of local government, something the Louisa Board is supposed to be very 'big' on." The requirements were so minimal that "the ordinance might just as well have been written by the mining interests themselves." Grace would now have a license to plunder.[16]

By the fall of 1973, even picnics had been weaponized. "While the Louisa County Sheriff's Office kept a wary eye on them, more than 200 Green Springs residents and sympathizers picnicked, chatted and sang away Saturday afternoon on a farm next to the site of the state's prison facility." The deputy sheriff said that he was just "making sure that nobody gets on the prison site." "Here we're having a neighborhood picnic," Rae responded, "and now we find the sheriff hiding in the bushes." Though nobody breached the prison site perimeter, the protesters did mobilize some weaponry of their own. The picnic's centerpiece was a bulldozer sporting a straw figure with a strong resemblance to Governor Holton at the wheel.[17]

That driver's seat was getting hotter for the governor. A few weeks before the picnic/protest, Republican Secretary of the Interior Rogers C. B. Morton publicly released a letter to Governor Linwood Holton blasting his decision to site the diagnostic center in Green Springs. The backstory reveals Rae's handiwork that tapped the preservation network, prep school ties, and class privilege.[18]

Morton replaced Nixon's first secretary of the Interior, Walter Hickel, in January 1971, after the president fired the former Alaska governor for his opposition to the Vietnam War. U.S. Representative Morton had wanted the Interior job in 1969, but settled for Republican National Committee chair instead. As it turned out, Morton was even more critical of Vietnam than Hickel—at least "Holton's Vietnam." Morton led the parade of agencies that chastised the Commonwealth for its failure to conduct a proper environmental review of the diagnostic center, forcing the governor of Virginia to forgo Federal funding for the project.[19]

Morton's letter to Holton made the fight public and personal. Bureaucratic infighting was one thing; a former Republic National Committee chair criticizing a fellow Republican elevated the national visibility of the conflict. So too growing concern that Vice President Agnew might have to resign in the wake of corruption charges dating back to his stint as governor of Maryland, thrusting Holton into the national spotlight as a possible replacement for Agnew. Though the Virginia governor never made it that far, he was generally viewed as an up-and-comer in the Republican Party—certainly not somebody a former RNC chair should publicly embarrass.[20]

Morton's letter reiterated Interior's now-familiar reasons that Green Springs was "unique and irreplaceable." Morton then urged "Lin" to reconsider the location for the diagnostic center. The secretary leavened his criticism with well-deserved praise, citing Holton's accomplishments in "environmental quality, historic preservation, land use planning, and penal reform." The secretary then warned that the diagnostic center created "an unnecessary conflict between . . . [Holton's] penal reform and environmental goals."[21]

Rogers Morton followed a long line of patrician Republican public servants who cherished nature and conservation. Born into wealth in Kentucky in 1914, Morton graduated from Yale and served in the Army during World War II before returning home to run his family's flour-milling business. When the company merged with the Pillsbury Corporation in 1951, Morton moved to a house on Maryland's Eastern Shore once owned by Francis Scott Key. "Rog" pursued his passion for farming and sailing at Presqu'ile.[22]

Morton might easily have assumed his brother Thurston's open congressional seat in Kentucky in 1963, but by then he had established ties to the Eastern Shore so strong that he liked to say that the initials C. B. in his name stood for Chesapeake Bay. He ran for the Eastern Shore's congressional seat because he "wanted to get inside and see what went on." He also "really got hipped on this bay, this shore, these marshes." Morton served as the congressman from Maryland's 1st District from 1963 to 1971.[23]

Bruce Blanchard explained that Morton would never have intervened if he had been a westerner like Hickel. "It wouldn't have gone anywhere. . . . [Green Springs] was not a big thing to us at the beginning. . . . I'm not sure it ever became a big thing in the Department of the Interior: it just hit the right people at the right time." Morton was definitely the right person. Another right person was Assistant Secretary of Interior for Fish and Wildlife and Parks Nathaniel Reed. Blanchard, the Army brat, and Reed, the patrician, appealed to Morton's sense of noblesse oblige, his love of eastern landscapes, and his sense of history to press the Green Springs case.[24]

Rae played another class-inflected card with the secretary. Morton had prepped at the Woodberry Forest School in Orange, Virginia, just up the road from Green Springs, and his family had deep ties to the Richard S. Reynolds family. Both Major Reynolds and his brother Sarge attended Woodberry. When Reynolds Aluminum moved its administrative headquarters from New York City to Richmond in 1938, the Reynoldses purchased Hawkwood. Like many of the old houses in Green Springs, it had seen better times. Hawkwood had stood vacant for forty years, and at times was even used to store grain. Secretary Morton had visited Hawkwood on several occasions after the Reynoldses restored it to its antebellum glory. Rae informed Nat Reed about Morton's friendship with the Reynolds family and his visits to Hawkwood. Knowing of Secretary Morton's knowledge of the area, the former family ownership, and family involvement, Nat Reed kept Morton informed about the proposal.[25]

Class ties hardly moved the man from Big Stone Gap and may have even soured his impression of the Green Springs crowd. On August 23, 1973, an aide to Holton announced that the "governor has no intention of stopping or delaying the project at this late date." "Heavy equipment roared into action" a few days later as work began on the facility's water and sewer system. Chick Larsen captured Holton's dogged commitment in a cartoon headlined "City Hall Wins Again?" It portrayed a hand-hewn Green Springs sign surrounded by a pile of tattered handbills marked "NO" littering the ground. A building permit signed by Governor Holton was tacked to the signpost, dwarfed by gigantic sewer pipes.[26]

Morton doubled down on his opposition in a second letter. He conceded that because Virginia was no longer using Federal funds for the prison, Interior's formal authority over the matter was limited. "However, there is no question as to my responsibility to do what I can to maintain the integrity and cultural values of our national historic districts." Publicly releasing both letters underscored that determination.[27]

Labeling the Green Springs standoff a matter of "major national importance," the *Washington Post* insisted that this "was not the typical case of residents fearing crime and resisting progress with the familiar cry, 'Put it anywhere but here.' " The area's unique history distinguished it from more appropriate sites, as Morton's public rebuke of Holton underscored. As for the effort by Green Springs residents to preserve that history through the donation of private easements, no less a figure than Russel Train, chair of the President's Council on Environmental Quality, termed the grassroots effort "an unprecedented action" and singled it out as "a possible model for private citizen initiative in cooperation with local and state authorities." This could lead to the "preservation of valuable natural areas and rural landscapes from undesirable development at little or no public cost."[28]

Richmond Mercury reporter Mary Edwards covered prison reform, and her interest in the plan to dismantle the Virginia State Penitentiary in the wake of the Attica Prison uprising in New York soon led her to the Green Springs saga. Her story pitted a beleaguered group of citizens against powerful establishment forces led by the governor. Its central question, however, was why Holton refused to budge.[29]

"The mystery behind the Green Springs fight has been the motive of Gov. Holton in so adamantly standing behind his original decision." The most widely held view was that Holton was "simply 'bullheaded' and reacts badly to citizen pressure." Another theory offered by Edwards was that local government was sacrosanct in Virginia, and Holton was not about to defy the unanimous support of every local official in Louisa County. A third theory turned on the Purcell family's windfall profit from the land Dickie sold to the Commonwealth. Yet, there was no evidence that Governor Holton would personally profit financially from this transaction. Vermiculite offered another explanation for Holton's behavior. "Some observers contend that the prison is the key to strip mining coming into Green Springs because it creates a change in the character of the area and thus allows for rezoning."

Chick Larsen's "All Out of Step But Linwood" cartoon opted for "bullheaded," displaying the proud governor carrying a "BUILD IT!" sign, striding in the opposite direction of a line of prison opponents.[30]

The latest round of criticism prompted Governor Holton's letter to the *Washington Post*. He insisted that the crux of his decision rested on the Virginia Historic Landmarks Commission's determination that the easements Green Springs residents had collected did not "ensure the preservation of the Green Springs area." Holton also was convinced that claims about the facility disrupting the historic character of the area were greatly exaggerated and that Green Springs faced many other pressures that would likely change its character whether the diagnostic center was built or not. One of those "pressures" was the likelihood that vermiculite would soon be mined in Green Springs.[31]

Change was coming to Green Springs, Holton insisted. Combined with the unanimous support of Louisa's elected officials and reports that landowners in Green Springs were divided among themselves, there was every reason to stay the course. He regretted that the *Post* had chosen to view such a complex issue through a lens that pitted "black hats versus white hats." Appealing to popular culture, Governor Holton hoped "that just as the cowboy movies became more sophisticated so will our discussion of environmental issues."[32]

Holton's letter probably did not change many minds, but it did reinforce a growing consensus among opponents: with the gubernatorial election just a few months away, it was best simply to wait out Virginia's term-limited governor. "For reasons best known to himself," the *Daily Progress* editorialized, "the Governor is determined to build his prison, and no amount of logic seems likely to prevail to the contrary while he still holds office."[33]

The war was not going well for Historic Green Springs, Inc. at the end of 1973. Despite Morton's politically unorthodox intervention, construction equipment could be heard from Hawkwood. Nor did Rae Ely and Angus Murdock's stealthy surveillance of the enemy in South Carolina repulse the mining forces in Louisa County. The Planning Commission voted, albeit in a divided fashion, to recommend rezoning more than 3,000 acres from agricultural to industrial. While the Board of Supervisors had not yet rubber-stamped this recommendation, it did gut minimal reclamation requirements, crippling local government oversight.

The Fourth Circuit slap-down of Merhige's first decision regarding *Ely v. Velde* (*Ely 1*) had stripped the Commonwealth of $1 million in Federal funding and established a national precedent when it came to the application of environmental impact statements for projects that were born Federal. But when Merhige ruled on *Ely v. Velde* after being overruled by the Fourth Circuit (*Ely 2*), he again ruled against HGSI and allowed the Commonwealth to repurpose those "lost" Federal dollars toward other state projects—in essence ruling that the money was fungible. Although Manny Emroch appealed, nobody could predict the outcome. No wonder the October 28, 1973 semiannual meeting of HGSI was a gloomy affair. "There are many difficult questions facing our organization," Elisabeth Nolting told the members. "In fact," she continued, "we are probably in the most critical phase of our existence."[34]

As Rae took over the fight against the prison, then vermiculite mining, Hiram grew increasingly resentful of the time she spent on these causes as well as the expense. Eventually Rae consulted a divorce lawyer. The journal that Hiram began in September 1973 suggests that he did as well. Each voiced anger, despair, and, in Rae's case, genuine grief about the deteriorating relationship. On November 13 Rae wrote to Hiram, "You have broken my heart. It's hard for me to believe that after all these years of closeness and concern for one another, that you would turn on me the way you have." She had devoted eleven years of her life to him and had "borne you happy, healthy children." For the first nine years, she wrote, "I was literally in your presence 24 hours a day, seven days a week." Of course, there had been problems from time to time, but "considering that half a century separates our ages, our problems have been fewer than might have been expected." Now, Rae continued, "you seem willing if not eager to toss it all aside, and have taken steps to facilitate the ends."[35]

Hiram focused on highly gendered pop-psychological explanations for behavior that he deemed emotional, irrational, and hysterical, offering evidence to support his perspective. For instance, when he climbed into the couple's Mercedes to drive into town, Rae threw herself against the open door and would not let him leave until he handed over the keys to the other car. The standoff continued until he finally gave up and went back into the house. "This of course is a . . . type of action taken for emotional reasons best known to the actor," Hiram wrote in his journal.[36]

When he tried to leave an hour later, "[s]he flew out of the kitchen and again propped herself against the open forward door." This time Rae drew blood, according to Hiram, gouging his hand in two places. "I gave up the ship." In December, after he chastised Rae for sending the boys to school "looking like 2 little tramps," she flew into a rage. Rae "picked up the . . . Register of Historical Places and threw it at me hitting me on the head." The bickering continued with the occasional physical tussle, all initiated by Rae, according to Hiram. The arguments were over money and Rae's access to what an increasing number of American women in her position considered basic rights in a marriage: cars, bank accounts, credit. From Hiram's perspective, Rae's requests were always "emotional," while his responses were reasoned, experienced, and well informed.[37]

Rae told Hiram that she had married him, "a man a half century older than myself, and have stayed with you because I wanted to, not because I thought you were the only man who would ever have me." She had "paid dearly for that decision in 1962," in ways that Hiram could never understand. Still, Rae insisted, she had never faltered in her resolve to stay with him always—until November 1973. Hiram was changing from the man she had "always adored so dearly into one I do not recognize." Rae was still willing to try to restore the relationship, but things would have to change.[38]

15
Genteel Civility

"RAE ELY WAS THE RIGHT PERSON in the right place at the right time," Clare White reported in the *Roanoke Times* shortly after Governor Mills Godwin announced in the spring of 1974 that he would not build the diagnostic center in Green Springs. Rae was "an inexperienced, publicity-shy 28-year-old when she was catapulted into a situation that eventually would make her name known across the state and in much of the nation." Underscoring women's hidden work—a pattern that White experienced first-hand in the newspaper business—HGSI President Hiram Ely's wife "became his assistant, the only title she ever held." After describing the battle as "textbook" for environmental conflicts, White delivered the punchline: "The leader of the battle *was* the assistant to the president."[1]

It was a full-time job, Ely told White: "more than full-time." The article described how the challenge of raising three kids while fighting the prison required homegrown management techniques—like connecting the phone to a fire bell. Instead of playing cops and robbers, Rae's boys Addison and Todd (ages nine and seven, respectively) played "Green Springs and Virginia Government." Upon his mother's return from the press conference that ended the struggle, a "beaming Todd" greeted his mom by sticking out his hand. "Put 'er there."[2]

The final six months of the battle was no easier than the first three years. Mills Godwin, Linwood Holton's successor, gyrated from one position on the prison to the next, but in the end, the Democrat-turned-Republican political survivor deftly unloaded this no-win issue without suffering much collateral damage. Godwin did not "undiplomatically axe" the facility "in the messy way a city-slicker might chop an old hen's head off," *Daily Progress* reporter Peter Bacque instructed. Instead, the governor used Virginia's tradition of genteel civility to deliver the message in a fashion that allowed the polite conversation to continue. "If the governor had wanted to say that the Green Springs prison was the wrong type of facility, designed for the wrong purpose and located in the wrong place he could not have said it more clearly than that and still be able to drink a quiet bourbon in the evening with his Republican predecessor and colleague, Linwood Holton."[3]

Genteel civility precluded any acknowledgment that a political novice had humiliated the courthouse crowd and Godwin's predecessor. Yet Rae Ely's fingerprints were all over the final decision. To be sure, there were events beyond anybody's control, like the raging inflation that quadrupled the estimated cost of the diagnostic center over the course of the dispute. Yet there was also the Fourth Circuit Court of Appeals decision in *Ely 2* just days before Godwin's decision that once again reversed Judge Merhige—this time costing the Commonwealth close to $1 million should it continue with Holton's plans for Green Springs. Simultaneously, Holton's nemesis, Secretary of the Interior Rogers Morton, accepted his advisory committee's recommendation—teed up by Rae Ely and Bruce Blanchard—designating Green Springs the first rural national historic landmark district. These long-term investments paid dividends at the same time that the Charlottesville *Daily Progress*, the *Richmond Times-Dispatch*, and the *Washington Post* delivered a steady stream of antiprison editorial advice to Governor Godwin.

When Mills Godwin was elected in 1973, Linwood Holton became the only Virginia governor to be succeeded by the man he had replaced. Godwin embodied the complex state of partisan politics in the mid-1970s. A long-serving state delegate, then senator from rural southeast Virginia, he climbed the political ladder as a loyal lieutenant in the fiercely Democratic Byrd organization. When Federal courts ordered a handful of schools integrated by a small number of Black students in 1958, Godwin led the organization's "massive resistance" to these minimal reforms—nine Virginia schools closed rather than integrate. As recently as his successful race for lieutenant governor in 1961, Godwin had found it politically expedient to label his opponent with a term that was still a pejorative for many Virginians: "integrationist."[4]

The political winds, however, shifted quickly in the Commonwealth, and Mills Godwin was a veritable weathervane when it came to discerning their direction. He moderated his positions on race and several other issues by 1965, when he won the race for governor, astutely adjusting to the economic development and population growth that reshaped Virginia's political map. Godwin even tapped portions of the growing Black electorate by moderating his statements on race and promising to increase support for education and mental health—pledges he eventually fulfilled.[5]

By 1969, even Godwin's political agility and acumen could not hold the Virginia Democratic Party together in the face of two powerful forces: the disintegrating grip of the Byrd organization and the fractious emergence of progressive opposition to national Democratic leadership epitomized by the contentious 1968 Chicago convention. Adapting yet again, Godwin chaired an advisory committee to reelect Republican President Nixon in 1972, and in 1973 accepted the Republican Party's nomination for governor. Asked shortly before the election if his victory might revive the old Byrd organization under the GOP banner, the former governor initially rebutted the idea. "Now that's not it at all: it would be a regrouping of people who think alike and want to act together." Smiling, he added: "Well, that's what the Byrd organization was after all."[6]

Just as rare as a second-term Virginia governor or a lifelong Democrat running as a Republican was the absence of any Democratic opponent in 1973. Godwin's long-time nemesis, Henry Howell, was "commended to the voters" by the Virginia Democratic Party, which had balked at officially nominating him. Howell, the former Independent, was difficult to pigeonhole. He had once worked as a "water boy" for a construction company and burnished genuine populist roots. Howell rose to statewide prominence as a state senator from Norfolk when he attacked Governor Godwin's sales tax as regressive.[7]

Godwin won by a whisker in 1973, tallying 15,000 more votes than his opponent out of one million cast. The race was close in Louisa County as well, where Howell bested Godwin by less than fifty votes out of 3,200 cast. Helen Dewar and Paul G. Edwards of the *Washington Post* characterized the voters who narrowly elected Godwin as "overwhelmingly affluent, white, conservative—but apparently not much concerned with building a new Republican Party on that base."[8]

Neither candidate went near the prickly issue of the diagnostic center or W. R. Grace's plans to mine vermiculite in Green Springs, but those reading tea leaves quickly discerned a shift in the attitude of at least one key state lawmaker. Soon after the election State Senator Edward E. Willey, the powerful chair of the Finance Committee, announced that he was no longer committed to building the diagnostic center. Willey cited the forthcoming recommendation of consultants working for the State Crime Commission who believed that the project should be scrapped. Their reason for pulling the plug on the project had little to do with its location. Rather, the consultants found the very concept of a reception and diagnostic center to be "obsolete, poor penology," one that was "being phased out in other states." A few weeks later Governor-elect Godwin broke his silence on the topic and offered another ray of hope to opponents. Godwin claimed that he would devote his immediate attention to penal reform and promised to listen to both proponents and opponents of the Green Springs facility.[9]

Historic Green Springs, Inc.'s day in court appealing Judge Merhige's decision in *Ely 2* could not have come at a better time as it provided yet another opportunity to remind the new governor that he should ditch the Green Springs diagnostic center. Arguing before the Fourth Circuit Court of Appeals on January 8, 1974, Manny Emroch charged that the Department of Welfare and Institutions had failed to comply with the provisions of the National Environmental Policy Act and the National Historic Preservation Act. Money that the Commonwealth was now counting on to fund other prison projects was at stake. Emroch pressed a claim that had failed in Merhige's courtroom: the Commonwealth had used a "mere bookkeeping shift" to evade the two acts, defying Merhige's ruling in *Ely 1*. Prison opponents also underscored how costly the project had grown. The Commonwealth argued that the size and cost of the Green Springs facility had been reduced due to the loss of Federal funds. Emroch refuted that claim, introducing testimony from state officials confirming that the facility had not been scaled back. He then dwelled on the cost, which had ballooned to almost $19 million.[10]

The *Daily Progress* published a sketch of the gargantuan facility drawn to scale that underscored its sheer size. Thomas Jefferson's seventy-seven-foot-wide Rotunda at the University of Virginia cowered in the lower left-hand corner. Eight such Rotundas would fit across the front of the monster looming behind it. HGSI quickly reprinted the sketch and used the back of the handout to list a parade of prison horribles (see Fig. 2). The poured concrete exterior would be painted " 'dead gray' in color"; the "gun tower" would be sixty feet high.[11]

The sketch appeared next to a lead editorial aimed directly at Governor Godwin headlined "Time to Correct an Error." It explained why the facility would be "outmoded . . . before its construction is even begun," standing as a "hulking monument to the inability of government to place practicality and rationality above politics." The *Progress* was confident that Governor Godwin would order "the construction of a properly conceived facility in a well considered location." Godwin was in "an excellent position to take a fresh, objective look at all the evidence," a *Richmond Times-Dispatch* editorial chimed in.[12]

On February 7, 1974, Governor Godwin warned that inflation would require substantial cuts in the capital budget. Coming soon after Senate Finance Committee Chair Willey expressed misgivings and on the same day that the Crime Commission's out-of-state experts testified that a centralized diagnostic facility in Green Springs was an outmoded concept, the delay offered Godwin a convenient excuse to scrap the project entirely. He soon informed the House Appropriations Committee that he was deferring construction on all major projects due to the "massive dislocation" of the economy caused by the energy crisis.[13]

As for the diagnostic center itself, Godwin stated we "find ourselves in a position at the present time in which these facilities which have been recommended have taken over themselves a cloud placed there by the consultants who have looked at these projects." It might be best to study further "just exactly the kind of facility, the place for the facility and how many facilities we may need." Seizing the moment, two Department of the Interior officials visited the governor's office to reiterate the secretary's opposition to the Green Springs site.[14]

The *Daily Progress* wasted no time deciphering the governor's words. An editorial titled "A Corner Gently Turned" concluded that Godwin "seemed to be taking the first tentative steps toward disengaging his administration from the legal and political morass." The governor "was clearly telling the lawmakers—as well as everyone else—that his administration is not wedded to the idea of building the prison facility in Green Springs." Without the stubborn support of Holton, the threat of building there "can now be expected to recede with quietness and grace, buried in the classic manner in which Virginia inters its official blunders, without fanfare, apologies or mourning."[15]

An unnamed "Capitol denizen, long wise in the ways of legislative politics" explained, "You couldn't expect Mills to run up a white flag and surrender. . . . [H]e has knocked the legs out from under the Green Springs location by withdrawing not only the money, but his positive commitment to the site. That's all it will take. It's all over." Peter Bacque offered readers a political grammar lesson. "That tortured circumlocution, those vague prepositional phrases that the governor of the Commonwealth spoke Monday to the General Assembly's House appropriations committee were the bureaucratic eulogy for the state's unloved Frankenstein."[16]

Like the final shot of a horror film scanning the gravesite while the credits roll just to ensure that a hand doesn't pop out of the ground, Bacque quoted a "well-informed Richmond source" who assured him that the prison would never be built. Still not convinced, the *Progress* headline asked "RIP: Has Green Springs Prison Been Laid to Rest?" Eleven days later the newspaper was more confident: "After Four Years a Small Woman Wins Giant Battle."[17]

If the *Daily Progress* believed that the prison was dead, supporters were certain it was just napping. The Louisa County Board of Supervisors was eager to wake it up. At its March 5, 1974 meeting the BOS voted 4–1 for a resolution urging the governor to proceed with the Green Springs site. The *Central Virginian* reported that since the project was well underway the supervisors were merely asking that it be completed. The following week the paper ran a large photo spread of the completed construction. "I believe they are more worried about the W. R. Grace mining plans than they are about the prison," a construction worker observed. Underscoring the article's theme of progress, the photo of the prison was flanked by another that showed construction at Louisa's nuclear power plant. The headline above the nuclear facility punned, "Building Today for Tomorrow's Generation."[18]

The House of Delegates Appropriations Committee, encouraged by Governor Godwin's requested delay, had stripped funding for the Green Springs facility from the budget. The full House, however, left the door open, again at the behest of Godwin, to fund the project in the 1975–77 budget. Before the session concluded on March 10, the House revisited its decision on funding the diagnostic center. It inserted over $8 million into the final budget for a facility, to be spent at the governor's discretion—provided that it was located in Louisa County. When the *Richmond Times-Dispatch* labeled the final days of the legislative session a "carnival," exhibit A was the diagnostic center. "How many [legislators]," the paper asked, "knew that they were voting to give Gov. Mills E. Godwin Jr. money that he had said he did not want this year for a proposed state prison facility in the Green Springs section of Louisa County?" The governor easily could have quashed speculation. Rather than splash "the end" across the screen, however, it was Godwin's hand that shot up from the grave. After a month of silence, the governor announced that he was "leaning strongly" toward building the diagnostic center in Green Springs.[19]

Although Godwin did not believe its environmental impact on Green Springs would be sufficient grounds to move or cancel the diagnostic center, the appropriation allowed him to select a site other than Green Springs in Louisa County. The governor would not commit himself to completing the diagnostic center in Green Springs, the *Daily Progress* reported, but "virtually everything he said indicated a strong leaning in that direction." The one thing that both sides could agree on as the battle entered its fifth year was that the fight was not over.[20]

On May 3 Governor Godwin announced that he would soon hold a hearing at the state capitol that provided each side in the prison dispute an hour to make their case. Several days later the Fourth Circuit Court of Appeals again quashed a Merhige Green Springs decision. Judge Merhige had ruled in *Ely 2* that the Commonwealth could repurpose roughly $1 million in federal funds originally allocated to the Green Springs diagnostic center despite that facility's failure to comply with Federal environmental and preservation requirements. The appeals court disagreed. It ruled that Virginia could build at the proposed site, but only if it returned the Federal funds that had since been allocated to other projects. Virginia could not "have its Green Springs prison cake and eat it too."[21]

In the short term, the appeals court decision in *Ely 2* was a victory for HGSI because of those costs. In the long run, however, the decision clawed back some of the precedent-setting power of its earlier ruling in *Ely 1*. As a 1974 comment in the *Iowa Law Review* argued, because the appeals court failed to issue an injunction in *Ely 1*—which would have prohibited construction until Virginia complied with NEPA—that straightforward option was not available to the court in *Ely 2*. Rather than enjoin construction, the court was forced into vague language about returning Federal funds should the Commonwealth build in Green Springs, which is exactly what Governor Holton chose to do. Faced with a similar situation, nothing would prevent other states (or for that matter Virginia) from *reapplying* for those Federal funds in the next cycle, simply recording them as reimbursement for some other state project that complied with the requisite Federal statutes. Although the timing of the *Ely 2* decision helped HGSI, it offered a virtual road map to those seeking to evade the broader objectives of statutes like NEPA or NHPA without sacrificing block grant and revenue sharing funds from the Federal government.[22]

On the eve of the governor's hearing, the *Washington Post* took its best shot at convincing him to move the diagnostic center or kill it. The *Post*'s editorial praised Godwin for listening to both sides, cited the increased costs imposed by *Ely 2*, and noted the landmark recommendation. The *Post* also focused on Secretary Rogers Morton. The governor's decision could be "greatly facilitated" if the secretary "would take action today on still another level." Morton's signature on his advisory board's recommendation would "pave the way for a decision by the governor that the tract should be protected."[23]

In fact, Morton designated Green Springs a national historic landmark the same day the *Post* editorial appeared. Straddling a fine line between insisting that landmark status did not deprive landowners of their private property rights and assuring Federal protection for national treasures, an Interior official told the *Post* that while the action would not likely provide any new legal protections against development in the area, the department hoped it would persuade the governor. Secretary Morton phoned Governor Godwin the next morning to press his case.[24]

Godwin heard prison supporters in the morning and opponents in the afternoon of May 14, 1974. The hearing offered a snapshot of the political, cultural, and, in some instances, social gulf between advocates and opponents—"a study in contrast," the *Richmond Times-Dispatch* reported. Columnist Shelley Rolfe provided the color commentary through an extended series of baseball metaphors. He described Governor Godwin's uniform—a conservative gray suit and white shirt, highlighted by a "not so conservative wide red and off white striped tie." By the time the "first game" of what future historians might call the "double-header" ended, the old Senate chamber of the Capitol had grown hot under the glare of television lights. Godwin confessed that he had heard a great deal about the controversy second-hand, but explained that this was his first opportunity to hear about Green Springs directly. He patiently took notes on his legal pad well into the second game of the double-header.[25]

Prison advocates, largely local elected officials, stressed that the poor county needed the jobs—claiming that 90 percent of the graduates from the local high school had to go outside the county to find one. There was plenty of discussion about representation as well. Advocates argued that elected officials knew best what the people of Louisa County wanted, and the BOS, the Planning Commission, the mayors of Louisa and Mineral, as well as Louisa County's state delegate and senator all supported the facility. The Louisa County administrator criticized a process that privileged a small minority of citizens. Dean Agee was amazed that the local governing body was not consulted before Green Springs was declared a landmark. Many people "are becoming fed up with a small segment of residents who are trying to run roughshod over the local governing body." A. D. Peers, M. F.'s brother, simply called them "a bunch of retirees, living on pensions and watching the world go by."[26]

Green Springs' alleged history took a beating. Several county officials wondered why there had not been any effort to declare Green Springs a landmark until the prison was announced. "I was born in Green Springs," Supervisor A. D. (Sambo) Johnson testified, "but did not know of any historic value until after the prison project was announced." Johnson preferred the kind of history that increasingly was dismissed in the academy. "Lafayette may have had a drink of brandy in Green Springs," Johnson quipped, "but no governor, no senators, no great men ever lived there." Completing the caricature of history-as-famous-white-males, Johnson pointed out that Green Springs did not have one place "that can even claim that George Washington even slept here."[27]

During their hour with the governor, prison opponents presented a petition signed by 13,000 people supporting their position. Their testimony leaned heavily on the expertise of those who deemed the district a unique national resource. Assistant Secretary of the Interior Nat Reed flew down from Washington to underscore Morton's support, and the dean of the University of Virginia School of Architecture testified to Green Springs' unique architectural qualities. Opponents also disparaged the facility's approach to rehabilitation. The director of Action Services of the National Council on Crime and Delinquency and the associate director of the National Clearinghouse for Criminal Justice Planning and Architecture testified that the whole concept of a reception and diagnostic center was outdated. Opponents reiterated their support for penal reform—just somewhere else. As Rae Ely put it, "there are numerous documented sites without the adverse impact [of the present proposed location]." Ending the hearing, Governor Godwin promised to make a decision "shortly."[28]

The final editorial word on the hearing was offered by the Richmond *News Leader*, which had consistently supported building the facility in Green Springs. The paper noted that the governor's two-hour session was "perhaps the first development in the Green Springs Thing that nobody could criticize." The *News Leader* argued that even if the area was historic, this should not immunize it from development. It also claimed that if Godwin moved the prison, "then some other facility . . . ought to be constructed on the Green Springs site." Louisa's leadership should be forgiven "if it is growing exasperated by the obstructionism of a small percentage of county residents—aided by many outsiders with free advice as to how the county should be developed." Whatever the governor decided, the editorial concluded, "let us support it—and be done with the nigglings in which the Green Springs facility has been mired for too long."[29]

In June, Godwin made up his mind. In a "measured voice," he "declared a halt to the hostilities which have raged over the rolling hills of Green Springs." Godwin was abandoning the facility in Green Springs, persuaded by the likelihood of litigation-related delays, the possible loss of Federal aid, and "concern for the historic value of the area," the *Washington Post* reported. His decision "ends a four-year battle that brought national attention . . . to a section of Louisa County described by conservation groups as a 'unique outdoor museum of rural American life largely undisturbed by modern institutions.' "[30]

Godwin's tone was infused with "mutual forgiveness and weariness with the struggle." "I don't fault anybody for selecting the Green Springs site. Very few people recognized that it was an historic site," he told reporters. "I might say the present governor did not realize it." In a direct rebuke of HGSI, Godwin claimed that "the judgment was made upon factors that had nothing to do with the opposition."[31]

Nonetheless, Godwin concluded, we "have to be practical about these things." Observing that endless delays and litigation were likely should the project continue in Green Springs, the prison could probably be completed more quickly elsewhere. The most recent round of litigation loomed large: by abandoning the Green Springs site, the Commonwealth could keep $870,00 in Federal funds. Retaining that revenue would offset the $1.5 million that had already been spent at the Green Springs site, as would the supposed $900,000 that the state could "salvage" by selling the land and reusing architectural plans at the new site.³²

Overjoyed, Rae Ely rushed up to thank the governor. "Don't thank me," Godwin responded. "We were just doing what was right." He insisted that a diagnostic center would be built, but refused to specify where that would be, or promise that it would be built in Louisa County. Carson Winston expressed "shock" at the decision: "Everyone in Louisa County is going to pay the penalty." Even Winston, however, acknowledged that the fight was over, as the empty field that currently occupies the former prison site confirms. Nor was the diagnostic center ever built elsewhere—those professionals who asserted that the idea was now outdated carried the day.³³

The *Richmond Times-Dispatch* called it a "wise business decision." It credited the prison opponents and cited the recent appeals court decision. More than money and litigation were at stake. The decision was "justified purely on aesthetic grounds, as well." The *Daily Progress* labeled Godwin's deft maneuvering an "example of government decision making at its finest." Even though Holton sought "to tie the hands of the incoming administration," Godwin refused to be "mousetrapped." Demonstrating "political courage as well as strong personal character, the governor based his decision on the evidence, understanding well that many of his close political and personal friends strongly supported siting the prison in Green Springs." That's "just how Mills Godwin is."³⁴

Perhaps because there were a few other things going on in Washington, D.C., during the Watergate hearings, the *Post* editorial board was the last to weigh in. "After four years of stormy controversy that engaged federal, state, local and court officials in rounds of litigation over the fate of this historic area the citizenry has fought off plans that would have brought irredeemable blight and desecration to a valuable cultural heritage." Both Morton and Godwin deserved credit for saving this resource, the paper said. There should be quite a celebration in Green Springs this weekend, and the *Post* was "happy to join in it by hailing the outcome of this struggle as well as congratulating all of the people of the area who fought the odds to bring it about."[35]

Rae Ely captured the moment: "It's over. We've won. It's unbelievable." Ely, "more than any other one person," Peter Bacque concluded, "was responsible for the environmentalist victory." Green Springs "cast its shadow to the state and the nation, attracting the attention of environmentalists, lawyers, penologists, architects, historians, corporations, politicians and countless citizens." The controversy over the prison and mining polarized the county, dividing the local political establishment and preservationists. The stakes were high, threatening "homes, jobs, incomes, friendships and pride, a great deal of pride."[36]

County Administrator Dean Agee believed that the battles would leave a lasting residue. "I'd say the split'll stay here till the people leave . . . because there are people mad at each other who've been friends for life." The bitterness was palpable far beyond Louisa County. One top Virginia official insisted it "was one of the most frustrating things I've ever been involved with. . . . I've never been involved in locating a facility that had so much support from local officials and citizens. . . . Usually local officials are against them."[37]

The *Roanoke Times*'s summary illuminated rapidly changing conceptions of gender, even in small-town newspapers. Just a year earlier it had condescendingly conceded that home-grown hero Linwood Holton was outmatched by a bunch of amateurs in the Battle of Green Springs, "done in, if not by editorial pages, then by the women's pages." Now, both the article's protagonist and author were women, reflecting rapidly shifting media attitudes toward gender. "Rae Fought the Prison and Won," published in June 1974, was written by "Tempo" section editor Clare White. "Tempo" had recently replaced the "women's page," and picked up the pace in 1977, transitioning to "Extra." Sandra Kelly, who edited "Extra" for almost a decade, noted that the so-called women's department covered stories like gay culture and abortion that eventually would become "hard news."[38]

White touched upon Rae's move from New Jersey and Hawkwood's décor, quickly returning to politics. "From a volatile girl whose emotions were perilously near the surface, she has developed into a poised advocate who can cite legal opinions as smoothly as . . . a recipe." Was that description limited to

Rae Ely, or did it also capture the evolution from the "women's pages" into the "Tempo" sections across America?[39]

As usual, Rae had the last word. "There were no guidebooks; we had to devise strategy as we went along. It was almost an instinctive thing." Instinct, the right people in the right places at the right time, the rapidly changing relationship between lived experience and what constituted "politics," or simply identifying the malleable nature of the line between novices and experts at a time when the vast majority of women engaged in politics were labeled "amateurs," Rae Ely, Clare White, and the "Tempo" pacesetters were reshaping the agendas and tactics of American politics.[40]

As Rae was the first to acknowledge, HGSI was a team effort, a female-powered squad. Elisabeth Nolting, Doris Krahenbill, Deborah Murdock ("assistant to the president"), Rae Ely, and many others subtly underscored this in "A Love Letter from Green Springs." Thursday, June 13, 1974, the letter began, was "a bright and sunny afternoon." That is when the governor, in "an admirable display of courage and statesmanship," brought a sudden end to "one of the most prolonged and significant battles ever fought in historic preservation." The fairy-tale ending proved that "you can fight city hall." Only one thing had made this possible: "that was You." The letter thanked financial supporters, lawyers, journalists, and the many garden clubs and women's clubs and other citizens' groups that had advanced the cause.[41]

Ultimately, it was the people of Green Springs who made this possible. By "people," Nolting and Ely meant women. "You have welcomed countless visitors, you opened your homes seven days a week at all hours. You canned and pickled and baked. You addressed and licked thousands of envelopes. You babysat for one another's children while others attended meetings and hearings." The letter had a kind word for *"The Husbands"* as well, whom it described as those "long-suffering tolerant and generous dears! What can we say but we love you? Just think how much your cooking improved all that time the girls were away working for Green Springs."[42]

A few months later the Elys were sitting on their veranda when they heard the deep rumble of an approaching helicopter. They rushed outside to get a better view of the "Huey-sized" copter lugging a water tower from the prison site, legs and all. It carried its cargo right over Hawkwood's nineteenth-century tower. The Elys waved goodbye as the aircraft and the tallest remnant of the diagnostic center disappeared into the northwestern sky.[43]

PART THREE

PRESERVING HISTORY

16

Guys and Dames

HISTORIC GREEN SPRING, INC.'S SUCCESS would not have been possible without the efforts of all those women. But there were plenty of men in the National Park Service who did not want to administer the Green Springs easements. Ernest Connally and Robert Utley believed that staking the reputations of the Park Service and its parent, the Department of the Interior, on a patchwork of easements in a district under intense development pressure was a bad idea. Although the naysayers lost the early rounds, they had just begun to fight. Connally and Utley joined forces with the "property guys" responsible for land acquisition and management in the NPS to strike back with a vengeance.[1]

Their weapon of choice was not the shovel or land-surveying tripod but the memorandum, and Philip O. Stewart, chief of the National Park Service's Land Acquisition Division, knew how to write a good one. His May 9, 1974 seven-page, single-spaced memo to the associate director of park system management spelled out the risks entailed in accepting easements. He also knew that the best time to kill a bad idea was during gestation.[2]

One experience cast a long shadow over any plan for the Federal government to accept donated easements to protect scenic views rather than buying the land outright. Recalling his experience with the Mount Vernon Ladies' Association, Stewart stated that it would be one thing if the NPS had to file a suit to enforce easements against a "private" property owner, "but a suit against the Dames of Mount Vernon . . . is quite another." Those "Dames" had played an active role in the preservation effort that created Piscataway

Park along the banks of the Potomac River. Not only was this association a citizens' group, like HGSI, it was one led by a former housewife turned powerful political operative.[3]

There was no need for Stewart to tell Washington insiders the details of the Ladies' Association campaign because his colleagues had followed it in the pages of *Washington Post* over the past two decades. They were acutely aware of the trouble it had caused NPS administrators. For Stewart, the parallel between Rae Ely and the leader of the "Dames" was as obvious as it was alarming. What had begun in the 1950s as a well-intentioned, low-cost effort to protect the view from Mount Vernon using the same kind of scenic easements that HGSI now wanted to donate to Interior embroiled the Park Service in over a decade of wrangling, ending in a $10 million appropriation to purchase the land outright.[4]

The Mount Vernon Ladies' Association was led by Congresswoman Frances Payne Bolton (R-Ohio). She started her campaign to protect the view in 1955, when a facility that would house large oil-holding tanks was proposed for a site directly across the Potomac from George Washington's estate. Representative Bolton stepped in personally and purchased the threatened tract. Bolton could afford it because she was one of the richest women in America. There was poetic justice behind her efforts to stop the unsightly oil tanks—her wealth came from a trust supported by Standard Oil profits. As vice regent of Mount Vernon, Bolton's interest in preserving its view was more than a passing fancy.[5]

Frances Bolton was the wife of prominent Ohio politician Chester Bolton. When he died in office in 1939, Frances ran for his congressional seat, harvesting more votes than any other candidate in Ohio. She was also the first woman elected to Congress in Ohio and served there until 1969. Promoting the careers of women in Congress across partisan lines became a passion for one of the institution's longest-serving women.[6]

In 1957 Bolton jump-started a broader effort to preserve Mount Vernon's viewshed by donating 485 acres she owned along the Potomac to the Accokeek Foundation, a coalition of individual property owners, a real estate firm dedicated to preserving the "rural character" of the area through easements, and the Mount Vernon Ladies' Association. Public and semipublic agencies, like the National Park Service and the Smithsonian Institution, also supported the coalition.[7]

Representative Bolton came to the rescue again in 1960, when the Washington Suburban Sanitary Commission (WSSC) announced plans to build a three-story sewage treatment plant across from Mount Vernon, deploying its power of eminent domain to acquire the necessary land. In response to mounting opposition, WSSC tried to mollify opposition by designing the plant as a replica of Mount Vernon. Visitors to each would be able to see the mirror image across the river. Bolton ultimately used her congressional clout to defeat the WSSC initiative.[8]

Soon after, the National Park Service's property guys were drawn into the effort to permanently protect Mount Vernon's viewshed. President Kennedy signed authorizing legislation in 1961 that created Piscataway Park to preserve and protect "the view enjoyed by George Washington." More patchwork than park, it included land purchased outright by the National Park Service, donated land (from the Accokeek Foundation, for instance), and land protected by scenic easements. By the early 1970s, the government owned roughly 1,000 acres outright; the rest of the 2,500 acres were knit together by donated easements from 180 landowners that restricted any use that interfered with the view from Mount Vernon. For good reason, the mix of private easements, a nonprofit foundation, and NPS oversight in the service of protecting viewsheds reminded NPS officials of the proposed Green Springs initiative.[9]

There was even a man who owned property along the Potomac, who, much like some in Green Springs, bridled at the prospect of placing his land under easement. Much to the chagrin of the preservationists and self-interested landowners eager to protect the value of their property across from Mount Vernon, Joseph I. Goldstein was not very charitable, and since he had been negotiating with the National Park Service for over a decade, that was not likely to change. The *Post*'s Ken Ringle called him a "wheeler dealer extraordinary" in a 1971 article that quoted Goldstein as saying, "I'm just a little country Jew boy trying to make a buck." An exasperated NPS official told a congressional hearing, "The original assumption that everybody was altruistic and philanthropic in here was just a false premise. They are not. They want money. . . . There are many wonderful, generous people who have given great value. But that is no longer the situation out there."[10]

Much as the neighbors despised Goldstein personally, it was his amusement park that was the real problem. Though not as "historic" as Mount

Vernon, Marshall Hall was much older than the surrounding homes that had sprouted up as Washington, D.C., expanded after World War II. Parts of Marshall Hall, on the other hand, had been built as far back as the 1880s. Goldstein purchased Marshall Hall's concessions in 1958 and the land itself in 1966. Through 1971, plans to include Goldstein's property in Piscataway Park were sidelined as the NPS negotiated with him over a scenic easement. By then, Marshall Hall faced two lawsuits, one from the neighbors and one filed by the Department of the Interior, which saw the amusement park as a "garish, honky-tonk" intrusion into the view enjoyed by the nation's first president. While neighbors no doubt shared this assessment, Marshall Hall was a more immediate threat to their property values than the view that George Washington had enjoyed.[11]

Goldstein saw things differently. "What they don't like," he told Ringle, "is that I bring inner-city blacks downriver. . . . They don't want them at Mount Vernon and they don't like them being at Marshall Hall." When Goldstein urged the *Post* reporter to visit Mount Vernon and see how "many blacks . . . you see there," the newspaper sent an observer who counted twenty-two African Americans out of 5,800 visitors that day. More damning than the headcount was resident director Cecil Wall's response when confronted with the numbers: "Mount Vernon is color blind my good man." He insisted that Mount Vernon's visitors were a "representative cross-section in the Washington area." When pressed, the director added, "A Marshall Hall type amusement park is not a credit to any community because of the clientele it attracts. I just wouldn't care to have them near my home."[12]

At one point it looked like Goldstein was close to an agreement with the Department of the Interior to purchase an easement that would allow him to continue his operation if adequately screened by a bank of trees. When the deal fell apart, Goldstein upped the pressure, threatening to cut down five trees a day and acting on that threat intermittently. He also pursued plans to develop the "Spirit of America Center," a 150-acre enterprise that would replace Marshall Hall's decrepit rides with a regional amusement complex. Given the long slog to protect one view, not to mention the embarrassment to the Federally maintained park that was literally located in the nation's backyard, Stewart urged caution about an easement acceptance program— especially one engineered by a determined, politically connected woman.[13]

The guidance system for Stewart's 1974 memo was embedded in the "subject" line. "Unanticipated Ramifications" targeted the proposed program's soft underbelly—implementation. Implementation required money to administer programs properly, which in turn required congressional approval. Stewart recited examples of Congress admonishing the NPS for unauthorized actions from the Eisenhower through the Johnson administrations, criticizing and revising executive actions that bordered on abuse of authority. The common thread was neglecting subsequent costs. A new easement program, the property guy argued, would meet the same fate.

Those who placed scenic easements on their property were usually well intentioned—they would not have placed voluntary restrictions on their right to subdivide their property if they were not already "conservation-minded." The problem, Stewart warned, "arises from their heirs or from subsequent purchasers." Stewart also worried about the public relations nightmare that an easements program might trigger. Suing an individual of means or a company for intentionally violating an easement's restrictions was not the same as suing the "penniless nonprofit organization, church or just a citizen of ordinary means." What do we do then? Stewart asked. Do we just stand by and watch the landmark fall into ruins? Or would the NPS have to step in? "It would be almost like Vietnam." Stewart feared a preservation quagmire, with the NPS owning the historic district, or at least thousands of acres essential to protecting it. "We could become by degree responsible for the whole ball of wax."[14]

The ideological implications of an easements program also bothered Stewart. As some of his colleagues had already pointed out, the proposed easements program was at odds with President Nixon's New Federalism. Dismissing advocates' claims that the program would honor Nixon's commitment to place "responsibility at the level of government nearest to the affected citizens," Stewart insisted that it would instead be seen as a "new federalistic invasion and the opening of a Pandora's Box."[15]

In a July 1974 memo Ernest Connally took his best shot at killing the Green Springs initiative, or at least slowing it down. Capitalizing on the news that Governor Godwin had nixed the Green Springs prison, Connally carefully probed to see if it was now okay to reject the proffered easements. He converted Stewart's broadside at the ideological heresy of such a program into a question. "Would the public be likely to regard such a program favorably or as an example of federal domination of local and private concerns?" That rhetorical question produced a deafening silence.[16]

Landowners in Louisa County were fighting back as well, challenging the Commonwealth's historic designation. In July 1974, the Board of Supervisors, joined by sixteen landowners, finally got their day in circuit court. The landowners charged that their property had been included in the historic district against their will, without proper notice and due process. They demanded that the court overturn the district's historic designation, or at least remove their properties from it. Like HGSI's complaints about the BOS and Governor Holton, the plaintiffs charged that the Virginia Historic Landmarks Commission had acted arbitrarily and capriciously.[17]

At the end of the oral argument Circuit Court Judge David F. Berry signaled his likely decision, finding no indication that the VHLC's historic designation placed a "legal encumbrance of any kind" on landowners. Regardless of Berry's ruling, the plaintiffs' written arguments distilled years of pent-up hostility toward the litigious "newcomers" in Green Springs, even as the BOS and the other sixteen petitioners now used some of the very same tactics and arguments that had roiled the courthouse crowd in the first place.[18]

BOS counsel W. W. Whitlock's "Petitioner Memorandum of Fact and Law" provided more insight into deeply held political and cultural values than the law. Because the VHLC empowered individuals who would probably be called "experts," Whitlock speculated that it must be difficult to find people to serve on the commission "except those who have but one primary objective in life"—the field they have devoted their life to. "Because of the limited experience, the sheltered lives, the restricted interest, the unobjective analysis," their background "should make these people cautious about the methods they use, instead of recklessly proceeding to ignore the rights of property owners." Whitlock charged that HGSI members appeared to "think they have the inherent right to prevent their neighbors from using the property owned by the neighbors for any purpose that would interfere with the plantation type effect" of their views.[19]

W. W. pined for the days when farmers used to help each other. However, "many of the residents of short-term in the area have not chosen to work with their neighboring farmers and the people in the community to find reasonable solutions to their problems. They have consistently and constantly subjected these parties ... to continuous litigation community pressures and press ridicule, and pseudo-intellectual bombardment." Offering a backhanded compliment to Rae Ely, Whitlock conceded that "she has been able to accomplish more than anyone could imagine possible because of her persistent efforts and dedication to this cause. It would be commendable if it did not jeopardize the property interests of others."[20]

The Green Springs activists were a symptom of a larger problem, Whitlock concluded. "Governmental interference with property rights has become so predominant that it is endangering the future welfare of the country." Free enterprise was becoming so jeopardized by "the various crusaders expounding one cause or another in litigation, by public pressure politically and otherwise ... that working and productive members of our society are fast becoming [sic] to accept the attitude of 'what is the use of struggling or fighting, we may as well join the great society and all become wards of the state?' " Views like Whitlock's were not new. What had changed was the need to articulate them, even defend them in court. Also different was the degree to which that perspective began to resonate with constituencies far beyond Louisa County. Easily dismissed by progressives as "backwards," Whitlock's world view proved to be a remarkably accurate guide to some of the major political currents that would roil politics over the next fifty years.[21]

In mid-August, Ernest Connally pinged the NPS director, stating bluntly, "I would like to back out of the easements proposal if possible, I think the time is not right." The firm answer from Nat Reed was not the one that Connally or Stewart sought. In fact, Reed called in the official preparing materials for the October Advisory Board meeting and "scolded him because we were not doing anything about Green Springs."[22]

From the Advisory Board's report to Secretary Rogers Morton, one might assume that the discussion of an easements program was moving along at a predictable bureaucratic pace: it required further study. In other words, the program was still alive, but Stewart and Connally had succeeded in slowing its pace to a crawl, with plenty of opportunities to kill it on the horizon. The summary minutes of the History Areas Committee discussion captured a bit more detail. It reported that Connally directed the discussion, noting that the previous experience with easements in the NPS had "not been encouraging."[23]

The first-hand accounts of two bureaucratic enemies, one contemporaneous, the other retrospective, narrated a far more complicated story. Writing the day after the meeting, Philip Stewart unburdened himself, acknowledging that Connally had generally followed the script laid out in the briefing materials prepared by the NPS. That "presentation was perhaps a little less forceful than it otherwise might have been because of the presence of Mrs. Ely of Greensprings who came into the meeting with Bruce Blanchard." Stewart also offered the committee a summary of the Park Service's experience with easements and the pitfalls that could be expected if a broader program were adopted. He summarized the attitude of the field managers as "[g]eneral disillusionment with scenic easements and a firm belief that this is merely a foretaste of things to come." Stewart was able to deliver additional warnings and to insist on an outright prohibition on accepting easements from landmark historic districts "before being usurped by Mr. Blanchard."[24]

Blanchard "presented a very glowing and encouraging picture about the subject." In Stewart's telling, the committee was confused about what to do in response to the sharp disagreement in a setting that generally required little more than a rubber stamp. Then Lady Bird Johnson "expressed the opinion that she was not prepared to vote for such a program at this time." Stewart described Mrs. Ely's comments about collecting easements on thousands of acres in Green Springs and why those donated easements were worth several million dollars. He was not impressed.[25]

With 6,000 unprotected acres in the district, there was no guarantee that scenic vistas or historic values would be preserved. Should W. R. Grace proceed with its plans to strip mine vermiculite, an easement program "would only guarantee the miners a protected view of the remaining valley." Stewart would "have liked very much to query Mrs. Ely about some specifics," but "did not deem it appropriate." He was particularly peeved that he did not have the chance to ask Ely just how many "man-years" had gone into collecting those easements and how expensive it was to do so. "I have a pretty good idea in my own mind considering what the Accokeek Foundation . . . encountered at Piscataway."[26]

Thirty-five years later Bruce Blanchard provided additional information. "The Department, historically, didn't like to accept easements; specifically, the realty people don't like easements." Over time, the land acquisition bureaucracy "had concluded that easements just weren't worth it." They would have preferred to spend 25 percent more and buy the whole piece of property.²⁷

Blanchard recounted that the NPS preservation people made a good case for accepting the easements, and "then the chief land acquisition person said he opposed the idea." After all, his voice was important, as he would be the one to implement and administer the program. Blanchard recalled that "the position of the chief land acquisition specialist would clearly have killed accepting donations." That's when Blanchard spoke up. He stressed that these easements were being *donated*. He underscored that it shouldn't cost that much to visit the properties, just as the NPS did with other historic districts. At that point in the meeting, however, he was not optimistic. Connally and Stewart were the experts and they carried a lot of weight. Bruce presumed that the proposal for the donations "was dead."²⁸

"Then Lady Bird spoke up." She didn't say very much, she didn't expound on anything, according to Blanchard, she simply said: "I think this is [accepting the donations] is a good idea." Blanchard recalled, "on that committee, if Lady Bird was going to take a position, no one was going to oppose her. That was the end of the discussion." The result was to accept the donated easements.²⁹

Although we may never know which account is accurate, it is reasonable to assume that if Rae Ely and Bruce Blanchard had not been at the meeting, and had Lady Bird Johnson not voiced support for a broader easements program, the matter would have died in that room. The plan to protect historic Green Springs from mining vermiculite by donating easements to the Department of the Interior lived to fight another day.

Whether in a courtroom, the Virginia Capitol hearing room, or a conference room, those pushing back against the historic district had gotten off to a halting start: momentum was on HGSI's side. On New Year's Day 1975, Green Springs claimed the number four spot in the *Progress* poll of the most important news stories of the year. It had been a successful year for the embattled preservationists: Rae Ely was even named the *Daily Progress* Citizen of the Year.³⁰

Ely recounted her unlikely path to activism in a feature interview with *Richmond Times-Dispatch* reporter Bill McKelway in February 1975. Over the past couple of years Rae had become "somewhat of a folk hero among advocates of environmental causes and . . . a speaker on what might be called a nationwide ecology circuit." Ely impressed even her staunchest opponents.

One prison advocate stated that she "probably has more guts and fewer friends in certain areas of the commonwealth's government structure than any person living today and most of the dead ones." Although it was not likely that "in its own context the name Green Springs connotes as deep a meaning as Watergate," as Rae claimed, it was plausible that four years into the battle, "[p]eople can no longer hear the name Green Springs and not associate it with the environment."[31]

Rae was in demand around the country because, as she put it, there "is no longer the feeling of earlier years that one should accept governmental decisions as being correct and altruistic just because that's the way it's supposed to be." She embodied the broad, often highly localized impulse to engage in politics through matters that directly influenced the quality of life for white middle-class citizens, especially women. Though marginalized politically, not to mention socially and economically, some of these women turned sexism to their advantage. As Rae put it, "many people never took us seriously until it was too late." Lynn Darling, a Radcliffe-educated reporter for the iconoclastic *Richmond Mercury* in the early 1970s, believed that her gender provided an edge with some of the men she interviewed because "being female, and especially a young female, was an asset in . . . these worlds. No one took you very seriously, which meant sources tended to reveal a whole lot more than they realized."[32]

Ely also viewed moderation as central to her success at the very moment that the women's movement and demands for racial equality grew more strident. McKelway pointed out that Rae was "as wary of the crazy females with 'wild ideas' " as she was of "the government officials who said that the prison facility would blend with its surroundings." Yet Ely also appreciated the deeper connections to social movements that laid the groundwork for many of her strategies. Comparing the state of environmental concern to the civil rights movement of the 1960s, Ely pointed out that "there are the initial successes and then a period of long, hard battles."[33]

Sitting in her living room, McKelway reported, "chatting glibly, almost coquettishly," Ely exuded a "sort of cocktail party-like familiarity with the subject she knows best." That, however, belied the "tenacity and thoroughness of her knowledge," observing that the Book-of-the-Month Club selections that dotted Hawkwood's bookshelves were interspersed with far more serious volumes about the environment and politics. "I know so much about government and how it works it almost scares me," Ely told McKelway. And then she laughed.[34]

Rae and Hiram no longer shared much laughter. Nineteen seventy-four had begun with a battle over the alleged damage that Rae had caused when the family car rammed the garage door. Hiram took disciplinary action. "I . . . told her no more telephone, no more Green Springs, no more discussion until she returned the key." By his own admission, he then "discontinued all the tel. service. Turned off electric power. Let the air out of Mercedes left front tire." His journal also recorded that Rae asked the boys whether they would like to live in Washington, D.C. In November, Hiram documented "[e]xamples of venting hostility in verbal abuse on family." Analysis soon overtook observation. "An outward expression of inner turmoil and desires—free floating hostility and impatience toward family." And "she pictures her family as a restraint in keeping her from doing the things she wants to do, frustrating her guilt complex." By the end of the year Hiram devoted an entire journal entry exclusively to a list of symptoms:

"Frustration—giving way to anger."
"Restraint—no respect for law and order"
"Need for attention—publicity"
"Have own way—bossiness"
"Short attention span"
"Guilt complex—husband, family responsibilities, household, animals, etc"[35]

Hiram finally named the diagnosis under the heading "Type A Personality." He was referring to the blockbuster book written by two cardiologists, Meyer Friedman and Ray Rosenman—*Type A Behavior and Your Heart*. As the *New York Times* reported, "Type A quickly became a household phrase, a convenient label for people who blew up at slow sales clerks, pounded their horns in traffic and generally lived their lives in double time." Hiram believed that this explained Rae's behavior, quoting: "the really high risk individual is habitually impatient, constantly under stress from an urgent pressing feeling that he hasn't enough time," and underscoring two of the classic characteristics—"hurry sickness, and free-floating hostility."[36]

Without question, Hiram concluded, "Rae is filled with inner turmoil and stress which keep her in a chronic continuous struggle. The stress comes from many desires to do and accomplish, well beyond her capabilities and limitations." He ticked through the evidence. She could not abide any restraint—like driving at the speed limit. She had a consuming desire to be in the limelight. Her "bossiness" and desire to run the show were further indications of the type. Her lack of any college training galled her. She felt guilty, especially about ignoring her responsibilities toward her children, which probably explained why she took any opportunity to escape from family responsibilities. Rae had "an overwhelming feeling of urgency to get to the telephone, to read the list of all who called (generally none), to get at the important letters (most of the time junk mail)."[37]

There was a glaring flaw with Hiram's theory: Type A behavior was supposed to be *male* behavior. Virtually every example cited in the book was about a man. Stumped by the question of why the women in the San Francisco Junior League had far lower rates of heart attacks than their husbands, Friedman and Rosenman originally hypothesized that diet explained the difference. As it turned out, however, the diets of those men and their wives were the same. The authors asked the president of the Junior League for her explanation. "It's stress," she answered, "the stress men receive in their work, that's what's doing it." A new theory was born, one that put the two men on the best-seller list.[38]

Would Hiram have complained about any of these qualities, or even noticed, if Rae had been a man? Did she have "hurry sickness," or was Rae simply leading a political battle against a series of formidable opponents? Did she have "free-floating hostility," or was Rae expressing herself about matters that she considered to be basic rights, fundamental to an egalitarian marriage? Was Hiram accusing Rae of acting like a man rather than acting the way women, especially wives, were supposed to? Rae Ely was not only a "woman out of place" with the property guys at the NPS, she was out of place in her own home as well—at least from Hiram's perspective.

17

Repurposing Civil Rights Strategies

WHILE GOVERNOR GODWIN CRAFTED ONE SURPRISE coda to the prison saga after another, W. R. Grace & Co. continued to press for rezoning that would enable vermiculite mining. It certainly appeared that the Board of Supervisors was ready to rubber-stamp yet another opportunity to develop and "modernize" the county's economic base. Then something quite extraordinary happened: the board split 3–3, placing the fate of vermiculite mining in the hands of a public official whose duties were parochial, even by Louisa County standards. He was the "tie-breaker."[1]

Ironically, this was one local practice that initially worked against the home team. Because Louisa County's tie-breaker refused to cast his vote, he stymied vermiculite mining for almost a year. Home cooking proved more successful in nearby kitchens, however. Although Judge Harold Purcell recused himself from most mining matters, the colleague in Purcell's circuit who presided over the case filed by the Niningers against the stalemated BOS shared Purcell's perspective on property rights.

When Louisa's tie-breaker finally resigned in disgust, Harold Purcell chose his temporary replacement and the voters of Louisa County soon overwhelmingly elected a pro-mining tie-breaker to a full term. Once again, Louisans' ballots seconded the courthouse crowd's quest for economic development.

And once again HGSI turned to Federal courts for relief. The plaintiffs argued that the BOS had violated the Voting Rights Act of 1965 when it appointed a temporary tie-breaker without first clearing that move with the U.S. Department of Justice. This time the Fourth Circuit rejected the claim. Even though the ploy did not work, it illuminated the ways in which Louisa's preservationists repurposed some of the civil rights movement's strategies toward very different ends.[2]

In a move that stunned everybody, John Q. Butler, James King, and A. R. Lassiter refused to approve W. R. Grace & Co.'s rezoning request. King was the only supervisor who explained his position, complaining that he had been "a little bit left out on a number of things in the county.... Now this doesn't set too good with me when I have people in all areas of the County calling and telling their Supervisor of a district what is to be brought before the governing body of this County." King demanded that the vote be delayed.[3]

Scrambling to resolve the deadlock, board Chair Carson S. Winston temporarily joined the nay-casting trio to comply with King's request. At the next BOS meeting Winston tested the waters by reading a letter from Thomas Lyall requesting that the BOS discuss the matter with Grace officials. The motion failed to garner a second. Winston then abandoned any pretense of neutrality: "sooner or later we are going to mine vermiculite in Louisa County. The question this Board has to deal with is whether they will accept their responsibility and control the mining companies." In case anybody missed his use of the plural, Winston revealed that a second company was now interested in mining.[4]

Any possibility for reconciliation was dashed when the question of rezoning agricultural land to industrial—a crucial prerequisite to mining—was debated at the April BOS meeting and the board deadlocked again. Both sides of the mining question had been running paid advertisements in local newspapers for weeks. A half-page advertisement in the *Central Virginian* touted the wonders of reclaimed strip mines. The photo-spread and question-and-answer format were designed to reassure Louisans, especially farmers. One photograph portrayed an eerily symmetrical pond that had once served as a sand and gravel pit; another featured a gigantic harvester operating on a farm that previously had been a nickel mine. The text quoted Pennsylvania governor Milton Shapp bragging that "companies are on their way to making a garden of Eden out of strip-mined land in Western Pennsylvania." The ad asked, if reclamation was so common, "how come the public was not aware of it?" The answer: reclaimed mine sites blended into the landscape so well that they were not obvious, "even to those people living on or using the site."[5]

Strip mining opponents matched Grace's hyperbole. A full-page advertisement in the *Central Virginian* asked, "A Choice ... Production or Destruction?" Photos of horses, hay barns, and fields were displayed under the word "production." "Destruction" featured the scarred landscape of Grace's vermiculite mining in South Carolina. "Concerned Citizens of Louisa County asked: "How Can W. R. Grace and Co. Justify the Rape of Prime Agricultural Land for the Sake of Short Term Profit in the Face of Imminent Food Shortage?"[6]

Dr. Griffith B. Daniel was the unfortunate appointed official charged with breaking ties on the six-member Board of Supervisors. Tie-breakers had up to thirty days to study the disputed matter and cast their vote. In the past, Daniel had taken the entire period to cast his vote, and most assumed that he would weigh in by May. After using the entire allotted time, Daniel refused to cast his vote because he believed that he had a conflict of interest. Because he owned property in Louisa County that had been "surface mined" in the past—and he hoped it would be mined again—Daniel could not "separate what I'd like for my interests versus other considerations."[7]

Rae pounced: Daniel's abstention meant that the motion to rezone failed. It would be "highly improper," Ely continued, to appoint a replacement for the tie-breaker. Carson Winston disagreed, suggesting that the matter should be resolved by Circuit Court Judge Harold Purcell or the Commonwealth's attorney general. Matters devolved from there. Contacted by the county's attorney, Purcell asked the BOS to request an opinion from the attorney general, simultaneously commenting that he might not wait to hear that opinion, or be bound by it.[8]

On cue, the BOS split 3–3 on a vote to ask County Administrator Dean Agee to request an opinion from the attorney general. After a convoluted series of maneuvers that included another recusal—county attorney W. W. Whitlock could not extend this request because he had been charged with his own conflict of interest—and parliamentary moves, a spokesperson for the attorney general's office ruled that only a state representative or local Commonwealth's attorney could request a legal ruling from the attorney general. Louisans, and anybody else, had good reason to be perplexed.[9]

Grace and the three supervisors who favored the rezoning ordinance fought furiously to break the tie. Their frustration only grew when Daniel intimated that if he *did* vote, he would favor rezoning the property. Even when the Louisa Commonwealth attorney ruled that Daniel did not have a conflict, the tie-breaker refused to vote. Daniel's principled behavior triggered a last-minute court battle in Charlottesville circuit court, where W. R. Grace and five Louisa landholders filed a petition requesting the judge to force Daniel to vote.[10]

Judge George M. Coles agreed with Grace's attorney, the ubiquitous William Perkins, that Daniel's situation did not violate the letter of the Commonwealth's conflict of interest law. The judge then proceeded to lecture the petitioners. "[T]he whole purpose" of the law, Coles instructed, "is to prevent an official from making a decision improperly." The judge praised Daniel for going above and beyond to ensure that personal interest did not bias his decision. He "acted under great pressure with dignity, sincerity and honesty." "Forcing him to make that decision would set a terrible precedent," Coles continued. "I can't sit here and tell a man he's got to vote."[11]

In June, John Butler introduced a resolution to eliminate the tie-breaker position altogether. Nobody was surprised when the vote ended in a tie. Nor was there any suspense about Daniel's response: silence. The normally humorless *Central Virginian* summed up months of frustration in county government with the headline "Tie Breaker Fails to Break Tie on Tie Breaker Resolution." One important variable did change: Daniel announced that he planned to step down, explaining, "The way board members are acting towards each other right now, well, I just don't think it's right." He was uncertain, however, about the exact date of his departure. Few expected him to make a quick decision.[12]

Mining advocates turned to other venues and made steady progress in local courts. Betty and Elgin Nininger's case against the BOS for failing to act on zoning legislation was heard by Judge Vance Fry of Orange in March 1975. In closing arguments their attorney, S. Page Higginbotham, charged that HGSI was made up of the idle rich who controlled the fate of the county with their "tentacles," reaching into the "governor's office, the federal government and the Attorney General's office." These people in Green Springs "ought to stay at home and tend to their own business."[13]

Judge Fry ruled definitively in favor of the Niningers, finding that the BOS did not act reasonably when it failed to grant their rezoning request. "Unlike most uses, mining can only be done where there is something of value to mine," he opined. "To prevent the operation of a mine at a particular location is to deny the landowner the value of the mineral which is in or upon his land." Fry invalidated the board's nondecision that had derailed rezoning; he sent the matter back to the BOS, which had thirty days to correct its error or else the rezoning resolution would go into effect under court order.[14]

"Having survived the threat of a mammoth prison in their midst and having apparently defeated the efforts of a giant corporation to 'desecrate' their countryside," the Waynesboro *News Virginian* editorialized, "the people of Green Springs in nearby Louisa County had begun at long last to embrace the theory that right eventually will prevail." That confidence was shaken, however, by Judge Fry's decision, the editorial continued, which cast a shadow "far more severe than any prison." The *Daily Progress* could not resist taunting, "If a vein of vermiculite—or gold—ran through Monticello mountain, or the University's Rotunda, would we unleash the bulldozers?" For HGSI, it was "back to the trenches."[15]

After Fry's ruling a deadlock that previously had served HGSI's purposes now favored mining advocates. Because Daniel still refused to break the BOS tie, Fry's decision meant that the BOS stalemate now enabled mining. Supervisor Butler summed things up: "I don't know where we stand. I'm just as confused as a little girl in a chicken house who dropped her chewing gum. I don't know what to pick up."[16]

R. H. Deeds was not the least bit confused. He applauded Fry's decision, calling the ruling a shot in the arm for constitutional protections of property and "equal justice for all." As for Butler's dilemma, Deeds suggested that retrieving chewing gum was the least of the supervisor's problems. The real issue was that the chickens had come home to roost. Blocked by their own Board of Supervisors, the Niningers and other property owners turned to litigation, just as HGSI had. *Home,* not poultry, was the key word in Deeds's clever rejoinder to Butler. A local legal venue yielded that crucial victory.[17]

When mining opponents tried to appeal, the ensuing shenanigans reinforced the local advantage. To initiate that appeal, HGSI had to submit a transcript of Fry's decision, but the judge who had to sign off on this routine matter was none other than Harold Purcell. He refused to sign the order even though HGSI obtained a writ of mandamus ordering him to do so. Sheriff Henry Kennon refused to force the issue and would not accept the "improper" papers. Kennon complained that "Mr. Emroch and them are trying to use me as a back door to get what they can't get through the front door." Judge Purcell was more succinct, if not any more legally sound: "the suit is concluded."[18]

There was also a parochial tinge to Higginbotham's rhetoric as he fought the appeal. Labeling HGSI a "troublemaker" supported by "foreign interests" resonated with similar accusations, like "outside agitators," that had been leveled at civil rights activists. Who is Henry J. Vor, Higginbotham asked, and why did he pay for an ad in the *New York Times* criticizing strip mining vermiculite? Presumably Higginbotham was referring to Henry Javor, a successful real estate developer who had restored Grassdale Plantation to its original 1860 condition. Javor emigrated from Hungry when he was five years old, served in the U.S. army during World War II, and attended the University of Virginia on the G.I. Bill. Was Javor "foreign" because he did not live in the United States before he turned five? Or because he had once lived in New York City and Los Angeles?[19]

On July 16, 1975, while HGSI battled through the appeals process, tie-breaker Griffith Daniel finally resigned, triggering a battle that pitted local against national jurisdiction and minority rights against majoritarian rule—a struggle that reclaimed, quite literally, some of the ground that Louisa County's courthouse crowd had ceded in the previous five years. It was too late to save the prison, but there was still time to encourage companies like Grace to create the kind of jobs that would boost the local economy. Wearing the white trunks in the courthouse crowd's corner was Judge Harold Purcell. Until now, the man who governed Louisa County had stepped outside the ring, at least in his formal role of circuit court judge, recusing himself, for instance, on the rezoning lawsuit. The Purcell family's extensive land holdings had eliminated him from several rounds up to this point.[20]

Citing the Commonwealth's tie-breaker statute, Judge Purcell gave the BOS five days to decide between two options. They could select a tie-breaker by a countywide referendum. Alternatively, Purcell decreed, a "tiebreaker shall be appointed by the court." When the Judge referred to "the court," he meant himself. Rubbing salt into the wound, he chided, "As you know, the board of supervisors has been having difficulty agreeing on anything." The BOS chose both options. It passed a resolution that called for the tie-breaker to be chosen in the November general election. Concerned that there might not be sufficient time to file the names of candidates on the ballot, the BOS passed a second resolution, asking Judge Purcell to appoint an interim tie-breaker who would serve until that election.[21]

Harold Purcell was happy to oblige. Although the order appointing Jesse Martin interim tie-breaker was signed by all of the judges of the 16th Judicial Circuit, there was little doubt that it was Louisa County's Purcell who selected Martin. The new tie-breaker managed the Ragland Pulpwood Company, where he had worked for several decades. He was also the vice president of Mineral Trailer Park and a deacon and board member of the Louisa Christian Church—Harold Purcell's church.[22]

Wearing the black trunks in this bout, Rae Ely punched back, stating that there "is a distinct likelihood the propriety of this appointment will be challenged in court." She soon made good on that threat. As Clyde Gouldman, the self-described "low man on the totem pole" in the small firm that represented HGSI in the ensuing litigation, put it, "Rae arrived . . . with a lot of fire and heat . . . and a timeframe that, in retrospect, was unbelievable." Gouldman crafted the complaint within days. The reason for the haste was that those supervisors who supported mining were now armed with a tie-breaker who was actually prepared to break the tie in their favor.[23]

On August 1, 1975, Gouldman filed a complaint in Lynchburg Circuit Court. Challenging the state and Federal constitutionality of the tie-breaker system in Virginia, HGSI asked for a temporary injunction that would prevent Jesse Martin from voting on the mining issue scheduled for the following Tuesday. Besides claiming that the statute "disenfranchises" voters, the complaint charged Martin with bias because he had lobbied board members in the past in favor of mining.[24]

Nor did the complaint ignore the alleged bias of the man who appointed Martin, arguing that Judge Purcell and his family "hold extensive tracts of land in and around the Green Springs area," and Martin's votes on zoning would "substantially affect the value" of that real estate. In a hastily called hearing, Lynchburg Circuit Court Judge William Sweeny refused to issue the injunction. There simply was not sufficient urgency to justify "interference by a Lynchburg Court in the legislative affairs of Louisa County."[25]

"I vote for the hearing," Jesse Martin declared the next day, breaking the 3–3 year-long tie among Louisa's supervisors and reviving efforts to rezone the contested land from agricultural to industrial use. HGSI was soon back in court, where it requested that the Virginia Supreme Court enjoin the

Board of Supervisors from holding the public hearing in September. Request denied.²⁶

Each time one of Purcell's colleagues in a neighboring county deferred to local prerogatives, news accounts reported that HGSI was considering Federal action. In the wake of interim tie-breaker Martin's vote, Rae Ely left little to the imagination: there was "a strong probability we will pursue the matter in the federal courts now." After losing at the local and state levels, Ely pointed to an argument that was particularly resonant at the Federal level: "personal and civil rights."²⁷

On August 29, 1975, HGSI was back in Judge Robert Merhige's Federal district courtroom. Its suit against the BOS charged that the manner in which the tie-breaker had been appointed deprived voters of the due process guaranteed by the Fourteenth Amendment by denying their participation in the electoral process. HGSI asked Merhige to enjoin Martin from voting until the court could issue an opinion. Gouldman, who had served as an attorney for the City of Charlottesville and knew a thing or two about Federal oversight of local matters, included a far more provocative charge: the Louisa County Board of Supervisors had violated the 1965 Voting Rights Act by failing to seek the approval of the U.S. Department of Justice for a change in voting laws.²⁸

The Voting Rights Act (VRA) covered eleven southern states and was aimed at ensuring the right of Blacks to register to vote. It explicitly ended devices that had long been used to suppress Black registration, like the literacy test. In a move that fanned the flames of southern white resentment, it sent Federal personnel to oversee the registration process and combat threats of violence against Blacks who dared to register. The initial results were dramatic. In the region covered by the VRA, over a million new Black voters registered in the next three years bringing overall African American registration to 62 percent. The most dramatic increases were in the deep south—in Mississippi, for example, from less than 10 percent in 1964 to almost 60 percent by 1968. Because of long-standing Black-led voter registration efforts, 38 percent of Virginia's eligible African American population was already registered to vote when the VRA passed. Within two years of passage that number rose to 56 percent. Many southern jurisdictions responded by attempting to dilute the *impact* of that Black vote.²⁹

It was "subtle actions" like Purcell's appointment of Martin, designed to "debase" voting rights, Gouldman argued, that the VRA sought to prevent.

Gouldman's plaintiffs claimed VRA protection at the height of the legislation's impact on the Federal judiciary. Both substantively and procedurally, the U.S. Supreme Court systematically expanded the VRA's coverage. Yet, when Chief Justice Earl Warren ruled in *Allen v. State Board of Elections* (1969) that "[a]ll changes, no matter how small, shall be subjected to Section 5 scrutiny," he probably did not have Rae Ely, the tie-breaker statute, or preserving a historic plantation community in mind. Nevertheless, the court did call upon citizens to help litigate possible violations because the Department of Justice simply did not have the resources or the staff to handle the massive challenge on its own.[30]

HGSI was pleased to answer the call. Because the Commonwealth's tie-breaker statute had never been submitted for review by the Department of Justice, Gouldman contended that the Supreme Court decision invalidated both the legislation and Martin's appointment. Given the long-standing deadlock, it was clear that "three of the six elected members of the board have had their votes nullified by one man who was appointed by the judge of the Circuit Court of the county."[31]

Chief Commonwealth Deputy Attorney General Anthony Troy was outraged. He accused HGSI of "abusing" the Voting Rights Act for the sole purpose of stopping a local action it disagreed with. Mining opponents were simply "bootstrapping" themselves to the VRA in order to get into Federal court, Troy told Judge Merhige, once again the gatekeeper to the Federal judiciary. They just want to stop the tie-breaker from voting, Troy continued. "They'll go to any extreme to achieve that goal." Merhige was not persuaded. "I think the big issue here is whether the Voting Rights Act has been complied with," the judge who had presided over mountains of civil rights litigation proclaimed. As for gaming the system, Merhige remained agnostic. Noting that violations of the VRA had not yet been vetted, he told Troy, "I can't be critical of people using the courts."[32]

On Friday, August 29, Judge Merhige announced that he would decide on the request for an injunction the following Wednesday, immediately before the BOS hearing on zoning. He demanded briefs from both sides by Tuesday morning. It was not going to be a festive Labor Day weekend for Clyde Gouldman. Just hours before the BOS meeting, Merhige ruled against an injunction, although he did ask the Fourth Circuit to appoint a three-judge panel to hear the merits of the case. He could not resist commenting that the suit was "a local political hassle" and that the Federal government should not concern itself with "exhaustive review of local controversies."[33]

W. W. Whitlock was "sorry to see" the Voting Rights Act invoked, because "[w]e don't have any racial problems in Louisa County. We never had any." Inviting the National Park Service, the Department of the Interior, and the Environmental Protection Agency to override local officials touched a raw nerve because it undoubtedly reminded the courthouse crowd of the "troublemakers" in the civil rights movement who encouraged Federal judges, marshals, and a host of other Feds to meddle in local affairs. Yet the courthouse crowd never drew a direct parallel between HGSI and the struggle to dismantle Jim Crow. How could they? That would have required acknowledging that in fact there had been racial problems in Louisa County and still were.[34]

The Louisa Branch of the National Association for the Advancement of Colored People disputed W. W. Whitlock's history of race relations in Louisa County. In April 1964 it had presented a petition signed by 185 citizens, insisting that the Louisa County School Board develop a desegregation plan; it threatened litigation. From the segregationists' perspective, the school board was between a rock and a hard place. As the Commonwealth attorney spelled out, it could opt to close public schools, as Prince Edward County had infamously done, or it could ask Black students to submit applications to the Commonwealth's "Pupil Placement Board" as part of a "freedom of choice" plan. Should Louisa choose the latter, "we might be in a better position regardless of whether a suit is filed or not."[35]

Louisa opted for "some integration," which the school board interpreted to mean as little as legally permissible until the Supreme Court got serious about enforcing the decade-old *Brown v. Board of Education* decisions. Even when it did, in 1968, Louisa County continued to stall, prompting the U.S. Department of Health, Education, and Welfare to move toward cutting off desperately needed Federal funding for education. Despite the threats, the Louisa school board stuck with what was now a clearly unconstitutional freedom of choice plan. Although lower grades had been integrated, the high school remained segregated, citing budgetary cutbacks as the reason it backed away from its earlier commitment to desegregate fully by the start of the 1969 school year.[36]

Frank Drumheller was the man tasked with administering Federal programs for the school board. He arrived in Louisa County in 1967 and watched as Federal funding appropriated to equalize education between Black and white students was used to buy new tires for the entire fleet of Louisa County's school buses. There surely were more appropriate uses, Drumheller thought, as many of the Black schools labored with antiquated or nonexistent materials; some did not even have cafeterias. Drumheller, who was white, attended every school board meeting between the fall of 1967 and 1971. He noted that the all-white elected officials wanted "to drag out noncompliance just as long as they could." After a summer of haggling, the school board finally agreed to desegregate Louisa County High School.[37]

Rolling in roughly a dozen mobile units that served as classrooms, an integrated Louisa County High School opened its doors in August 1970, with Frank Drumheller as its new principal. He claimed that he had never called upon God as many times as during his two years as principal. There were no major in-school racial incidents, for which he credited his Black assistant principal, Harry Nuckols, who defused daily near-misses. When a violent conflict almost broke out over the demand by African American students that a Black band play at the prom, Nuckols brokered a deal to let the Black band play, whispering to Drumheller, "Got to do it, Frank."[38]

Avoiding violent conflicts inside the high school did not mean that race relations had improved in Louisa County. Lewis Stephens, a Black teacher who moved to Louisa County the year that the middle school desegregated (1969), was born in 1945 on a farm in Halifax County, Virginia. He was taught from an early age that "when you went into a drug store or a local store, you knew not to touch anything or pick up anything . . . because people expected you to steal." After graduating from Virginia State University and working in Indiana steel mills, Stephens interviewed for a teaching position back in Halifax County. When he did not get any of the three open jobs and inquired about the reason, Stephens was told by the assistant principal: "we got enough n***** teachers." Louisa County looked good by comparison. Stephens was hired to teach "agriculture" to eighth- and ninth-graders. He recalled that his job interview focused on whether he had played college football.[39]

He also recalled feeling ill while driving to a teachers' meeting near Charlottesville. Stephens stepped into a local convenience store and asked the white woman behind the counter for a cup of water. "The lady looked at me—and I mean, I'm fully dressed with a necktie and everything—[and she said to me,] 'You'll get no water here. If you want some water in the creek . . . go over there and get you some.'" Stephens never experienced anything quite like that closer to home, where people knew he was a local teacher. Still, he was always a simple request away from racism's raw edge in central Virginia. This was especially true when it came to financial resources widely available to Louisa's white citizens. When Stephens applied for a home construction loan at a local bank that was virtually handing out money to white people, the banker advised, "The only thing I can tell you to do is to go back home and save some more money."[40]

Stephens went on to a long, distinguished career as an educator, serving as a consultant to Virginia Commonwealth University on hiring practices for school principals. He claims that he was always treated with respect by his Louisa students—both Black and white. But when he oversaw curriculum during the late 1970s and into the 1980s and insisted on including Black history, white parents called to ask for the specific dates it would be taught so they could keep their kids out of school those days.[41]

Greg Jones, an African American student in the middle school when it was integrated, described the tortured nature of Louisa County's race relations at the time. It wasn't pretty, Jones recalled. "White boys: they didn't like us; and we didn't like them." School buses were particularly volatile turf. Both Jones and Stephens recalled the final day of each school year as particularly fraught, so much so that teachers were assigned to bus routes. Nothing triggered greater tension than interracial dating. Both Jones and Stephens recounted instances of violence, even a mysterious drowning, triggered by white girls dating Black boys.[42]

Stephens did not support Historic Green Springs, Inc.'s political agenda. Most of the local jobs for Black men were on farms or in sawmills, lumbering, and the pulpwood business. Like lower-middle-class whites, many African Americans traveled as far as Washington, D.C., daily for employment. In Stephens's opinion, most Blacks in Louisa believed that both the prison, and then vermiculite mining, would bring far better paying jobs closer to home. White politicians did not benefit from this potential support, however, because Black opinion didn't matter to the political establishment. Had Louisa's race relations resembled anything like W. W. Whitlock's description, countywide support for the prison and mining might have been even stronger—and articulated more forcefully.[43]

Yet, Louisa's Black population and Green Springs' privileged preservationists did share a powerful interest when it came to local governance. Both groups readily turned to the Federal government to ensure that their rights were protected on matters previously the exclusive domain of a tight-knit governing establishment that controlled local politics. While HEW administrators threatened to send Louisa County officials to jail for resisting school desegregation in the summer of 1970, preservationists invited Federal courts and agencies to intervene in land-use decisions—a matter that previously had been left to local government.

In the interregnum between Daniel's resignation and interim tie-breaker Martin's appointment, the sliver of shared interest between those who opposed mining vermiculite and the Black community was briefly exposed in a maneuver that must have seemed odd at the time. In July 1975 the *Daily Progress* reported that Supervisor John Q. Butler, a mining opponent, had backed John Thomasson for the temporary tie-breaker position. The *Progress* described Thomasson as "a black who operates a Louisa funeral home." (Neither Daniel nor Martin was ever described by his race.) Appointing Thomasson would have made him the first Black to serve in any major appointed or elected countywide capacity.[44]

Thomasson was an influential spokesperson for Louisa's Black community and a strong advocate for any development that might create jobs. That Butler, the leading mining opponent, recommended Thomasson suggests that the antimining forces were already considering using the Voting Rights Act as their ticket into Federal court long before they appeared before Judge Merhige. HGSI sought to use the VRA for a very different kind of minority —middle-class and wealthy white landowners whom the courthouse crowd also excluded from the decision-making.

At the September BOS public hearing, Mrs. J. W. Hill, one of the landowners who hoped to profit from mining, urged the board to stand up to "people from out of state . . . and foreign countries" who felt "they could come in and tell us what to do." William Perkins stated that the landowners objecting to the historic designation "are tired of having it rammed down their throats." The *Washington Post*'s Megan Rosenfeld reported that the hearing "turned farmers, housewives, shopkeepers and students into eloquent orators." Among the people and documents invoked by the speakers were the Bible, the Constitution, Thomas Jefferson, and Abraham Lincoln. At 12:45 a.m. the next morning, Jesse Martin cast the deciding vote to permit strip mining on 1,000 acres in Green Springs. To Martin and the supervisors who joined him, it was the Niningers, Peerses, and several other long-time Louisa residents who were the oppressed minority—drowned out by recently arrived foreigners like Rae Ely. "We've got a few landowners no one is speaking up for," Martin explained.[45]

Both sides immediately turned their attention to the upcoming elections and the two candidates running for tie-breaker. It was not hard to discern how Robert L. Lloyd would vote, since he had recently testified that mining would not have any negative consequences for the value of historic properties that surrounded the mine site. While Lloyd openly supported mining, Earl Poore, the HGSI-backed opponent, was more cautious, perhaps because he understood that mining was popular with the county's voters. Poore stated, "I suppose I'm running because I think it's about time that both sides of the issues be heard by the board."[46]

On November 4, the voters chose Lloyd over Poore and mining over historic preservation. The *Richmond Times-Dispatch* reported that advocates for strip mining "scored a resounding victory Tuesday . . . capturing five of six seats." The handwriting was on the wall long before the election, when antimining leader John Q. Butler announced that he was not running for reelection. A. R. Lassiter, another mining foe, was trounced. Perhaps the most embarrassing tally for HGSI came in its own magisterial district, where incumbent supervisor and fierce advocate for both the prison and mining Earl Ogg won handily, 392–232. The only antimining supervisor who survived, James King, ran unopposed. The victorious Lloyd had the last word: "I think the people were simply saying they didn't want Historic Green Springs to run the County."[47]

A month later, locally owned startup Virginia Vermiculite, Inc. (VVI) assessed the situation in its loan application to finance mining in Green Springs. The company noted that three property owners and W. R. Grace had overcome "extensive litigation" by HGSI to rezone their property for mining. "Most importantly on November 4, 1975, a new Board of Supervisors was elected which overwhelmingly favors vermiculite mining." VVI planned to apply for rezoning as soon as the new board members were installed in January.[48]

In the wake of the election and a series of legal setbacks in local and state courts, Rae Ely did some polling of her own. HGSI gathered fifty property owners and asked whether the citizens' group should continue the fight against strip mining. A near-unanimous tally said yes. Putting the best spin possible on the crushing recent events, Ely observed that "there was no place to go but up."[49]

The newly formed BOS majority moved quickly. With litigation pending in the Federal courts that disputed the process by which Jesse Martin had initially broken the deadlock, the supervisors voted 5–1 on a series of measures to confirm the earlier vote, specifying that they wanted the Federal appeals court panel to get the message. At the January 1976 Fourth Circuit hearing, William Perkins reinforced that message, asking the judges to dismiss the suit because the recent BOS vote rendered it "pointless."[50]

That the tie-breaker appointment violated the Voting Rights Act remained the foundation of the case before the Fourth Circuit. HGSI notes confirm that the antimining supervisors had indeed sought to bolster—some would say manufacture—evidence for its case by urging Purcell "to appoint a black." The three-judge panel ultimately dismissed the case, because it was "not persuaded that the rezoning procedures were in any way illegal or unconstitutional."[51]

HGSI's record of success in Federal venues ended when it repurposed a powerful tool designed to address southern racial injustice into a gimmick to protect history and its environs. While HGSI's agenda was very different from that of Lewis Stephens, Greg Jones, and many other Black residents in Louisa County, the battle for racial equity and historic preservation *did* share a common enemy. That enemy was the Louisa County governing establishment. Like the civil rights movement, HGSI used a combination of citizen activism networked to allies in the Federal government to challenge the same tight-knit governing class that had presided over Jim Crow segregation. HGSI's setback in the Fourth Circuit hardly deterred the citizens' group from inviting Federal partners to intervene, even as it enraged many Louisa voters who opposed desegregation *and* HGSI's preservationist agenda. Most of those voters were just fine with the home cooking that they had feasted on for decades.

18

The Problem of Asbestos

RAE ELY WAS USUALLY THE "bad cop," litigating, investigating, testifying at the Board of Supervisors or the state legislature, and forever sounding the alarm to a stable of assiduously cultivated reporters. In 1976, however, Rae played the "good cop" when she appeared at the W. R. Grace & Co. shareholders' meeting in Boston to tell Peter Grace in front of the assembled crowd how grateful the people of Green Springs were "for the efforts that this fine company is making to preserve the beautiful historic Green Springs." An unlikely "bad cop" gave her that opportunity when Gerald Ford's Interior secretary, Thomas Kleppe, sought to publicly shame Grace into abandoning its plans to mine in the Green Springs Historic District.

At the same time a number of regulatory agencies, newly sensitized to the growing list of toxic hazards threating the health of workers, began to police, or at least surveil, the link between vermiculite and asbestos. The media had been asleep on the vermiculite/asbestos beat until an intrepid reporter at the *Richmond Times-Dispatch* sounded the alarm with a series of stories on the topic in 1976. Tragically, it would take several more decades before the national press exposed the slow-moving disaster at Grace's vermiculite mine in Libby, Montana—too late to save the many victims who died or suffered disabling illness.

None of the growing concerns about safety slowed the momentum for mining vermiculite in Louisa County in spite of HGSI's best efforts to highlight the issue in the litigation it filed to challenge rezoning from agricultural to industrial use. Nor did it deter a new entrant into the vermiculite sweepstakes: Virginia Vermiculite, Inc., headed by a former EPA administrator. VVI, not W. R. Grace & Co., was the first company to apply for a conditional use permit to mine in Green Springs.

Secretary Thomas Kleppe wrote to Peter Grace on March 1, 1976. A former mayor of Bismarck and Republican congressman from North Dakota, Kleppe headed Interior from October 1975 until the Carter administration took office in January 1977. The secretary let Grace know that Interior was actively considering accepting thousands of acres of Green Springs easements, warning that "mining in the National Landmark . . . is incompatible with the cultural and scenic values of the area which our designation was intended to protect." Grace should consider mining elsewhere; it had the large vermiculite reserves to do so.[1]

Kleppe even invited Grace to join forces with HGSI by placing its Green Springs vermiculite reserves under easement. This was a bold request, proffered, as Kleppe put it, "to protect the country's national heritage for future generations of Americans." The prompt was all the more remarkable because *asking* was all he could do—at least until his department actually held Green Springs' easements. Even then, it was not clear that Interior could prevent mining, although it surely could slow it down through mechanisms like the environmental impact statement.[2]

Rae Ely made sure that Kleppe's letter found its way to *New York Times* reporter Ben A. Franklin. His March 10, 1976 article emphasized the unusual nature of Kleppe's request, reporting that the secretary had asked the "top executive of one of the nation's largest mineral and chemical conglomerates" to abandon plans to strip mine. Kleppe's letter was surprising, coming from an "administration pledged to clear environmental and regulatory obstacles from the path of the mineral industry." The Federal government had no legal leverage, the article emphasized. "We can only appeal to the Grace Company's conscience," an Interior official noted. Kleppe's bold request fit squarely into his department's exceptional past actions regarding Green Springs. This was the second time that a Republican secretary of the Interior had publicly defended the historic district.[3]

Grace's vice president for corporate communications, Richard L. Moore, responded publicly that "considerable study" would be required. In a surprisingly candid aside for a communications professional, he then warned that there was "no way we're going to say, 'Oh sure, we'll just bow to your request.'" Kleppe was asking for a "momentous thing" from a company that had already invested a great deal in the project, saying to Grace, "'Don't do it fellas, be one of the boys.'" Moore told Kleppe, "afraid it is not that simple."[4]

Sambo Johnson, now chair of the Louisa Board of Supervisors, was blunter: "I think the Secretary of the Interior should take care of things in Washington and let [the] governing body of Louisa County take care of things here." A follow-up letter slammed Interior for having "too much money and its officials too much time to spend on matters that can and should properly be handled by local governing bodies." James King, now the lone mining opponent on the BOS, shot back: "I mean, we criticize on one end and look for hand-outs on the other." As a minority of one, King could not do much about the board's stance on mining, but exposing hypocrisy was another matter. "I know we don't like federal control," he observed, "but when there is a grant available we sure are quick to grab at it."[5]

If Peter Grace was surprised that the secretary of the Interior would bother to write to him about a small project in the middle of nowhere, and angered when the *New York Times* drew national attention to it, he must have been shocked by a lead *Times* editorial on March 22, 1976. It applauded Kleppe's intervention, which promised "to save a thousand acres of farmland from being strip-mined for vermiculite." Adding insult to injury, the *Times* reminded its readers that vermiculite was used for "insulation and cat litter." Grace could not ignore such a prominent editorial, even if it had no intention of sacrificing its mining profits. The company would "reassess its plans under pressure from U.S. Interior Secretary Thomas Kleppe" and claimed that it would reach a decision in a matter of weeks.[6]

Central Virginian columnist H. D. N. Hill spoke for those Louisans who bridled at Federal intervention in local affairs, labeling Kleppe's actions "astonishing!! . . . Perhaps the time has come . . . to establish a commission to regulate and restrict the regulators!!" Initially, Rae held her fire, although not for long. She scoffed at the company's offer to consider a meeting between HGSI and Grace's construction products division. "That would be like telling someone to go to Lucky Luciano to complain about the Mafia."[7]

Although Rae spent a lovely afternoon with Peter Grace after she elicited a standing ovation for him at W. R. Grace's shareholders' meeting and cemented a relationship that would pay dividends down the road, neither Ely nor Kleppe altered the company's plans to mine vermiculite in Green Springs. In fact, the rezoning frenzy intensified in June, when the Board of Supervisors voted to permit mining on 97 percent of Louisa County's land by eliminating a requirement that mined land first be zoned industrial. Rae Ely charged that it would turn Louisa County into "little Appalachia"—an "unconscionable and irresponsible act," throwing the county into "a state of siege." The *Daily Progress* labeled the day "Black Wednesday" and savaged the supervisors' justification for this action. "While the board of supervisors filled the air with damp phrases about letting a landowner 'harvest his vermiculite just like he harvests his timber,' the plain fact is that trees grow and land does not." It mocked values that placed "the present exploitive worth of the land above the less tangible but more enduring aesthetic and historic considerations."[8]

The growing divide between those who insisted upon the productive use of natural resources and their opponents who advocated for preserving those resources in order to enhance their quality of life was hardly limited to Louisa County. By the mid-1970s, real wage growth stagnated while unemployment and energy prices rose. Simultaneously, the quest for beauty, health, and permanence intensified, making even more contentious the choice between advancing economic opportunity for those who had not yet arrived in the middle class and preserving, even enhancing life, for citizens who were already there.

Even zoned industrial, land could not be mined before the BOS approved a conditional use permit specifying details of operation. It was local upstart Virginia Vermiculite, Inc., owned by former Environmental Protection Agency Deputy Administrator Robert Sansom, that was first cleared to mine vermiculite. While Grace's Thomas Lyall and William Perkins watched from the audience, Sansom announced that his company would begin mining forty acres of Francis H. and Fredericka S. Purcell's (no relation to Harold) 459-acre tract in the fall. VVI promised to employ roughly thirty Louisans and pump half a million dollars into the local economy annually. Predictably, Historic Green Springs, Inc. filed a suit in Louisa circuit court charging the BOS with "spot zoning," a practice that distinguished zoning for specific properties from the zoning regulations applied to surrounding property. Given the string of losses in local courts, its prospects were not promising.[9]

Greater recognition of vermiculite mining and processing's potential health hazards offered a new path of resistance. On September 3, 1976, the front-page headline "Louisa May Feel Montana Problem" kicked off *Times-Dispatch* reporter Allen Short's series. Short's impressive reporting turned out to be just another dot in a larger pattern that would not come into focus for decades. The dot was large enough, however, for HGSI to raise health concerns about mining vermiculite, especially after news that Grace's Montana mine had been cited for excessive concentrations of airborne asbestos fibers.[10]

Grace officials countered Short's charges, citing the recent changes in the way that the mineral was processed; the plant now sprayed water to reduce dust and fibers in the air. Six million dollars, Grace pointed out, would be spent on a similar wet-processing plant in Louisa County. Although he refused to rule out the possibility of health-threatening asbestos, a spokesperson said that the firm was "not aware" of any. Thomas Lyall also hit back hard in a letter to the *Central Virginian* disparaging any comparison to the Montana reserves. "I wish to repeat that we have consistently stated that the Green Springs deposit is similar geologically to the South Carolina vermiculite deposit, and it is not accurate to liken it to Libby [Montana]." Lyall insisted that Short's reference to asbestos in Green Springs was "misleading" because the mineral in question in Libby "is called tremolite, and it does not have the characteristics of commercial asbestos."[11]

The misleading statement was Lyall's. He chastised Short's reporting just as Grace's sales of its popular product Monokote were taking off. Builders switched to Monokote for insulation precisely because Grace claimed that its wonder product did *not* contain asbestos. "When asbestos was labeled a killer 30 years ago," the *New York Times* wrote in 2001, "one company moved to cash in. As competitors phased out asbestos because its fibers could lodge in the lungs and cause cancer, Grace reported a 'research breakthrough,' a completely asbestos-free spray." Grace's new product was not completely asbestos-free, however. The *Times* exposé revealed that a "little-known kind of asbestos, tremolite, laced the ore" in the spray that Grace advertised as asbestos-free.[12]

Short's sequel, "Problem of Asbestos Comes with Vermiculite," placed Louisa County in the easternmost "asbestos belt" in the United States. The article quoted Dr. Irving J. Selikoff, professor of environmental medicine at Mount Sinai Medical School, who warned of dangers from asbestos in vermiculite, including the dust that seeped out of processing plants, clung to the clothes of workers, and blew off trucks transporting the mineral.[13]

Growing concerns about the safety of vermiculite mining were first aired publicly in Louisa at a September 20, 1976 BOS meeting. Hanne Heimer read a letter from the Mount Sinai team warning that there was "cause for considerable concern." On September 26, the *Times-Dispatch* reported the preliminary findings from two samples taken in Louisa County. Tremolite asbestos was detected in both. One of the samples was located just a few hundred yards from the proposed Virginia Vermiculite, Inc. mining site. Although VVI claimed that it did not find asbestos in its own sampling, Robert Sansom was quick to throw W. R. Grace under the bus. He announced that test borings drilled several years earlier on property that Grace was considering had tested positive for asbestos.[14]

Sambo Johnson, one of vermiculite mining's staunchest supporters, expressed concern and hoped "to come up with some information within several weeks." Claiming that the presence of asbestos posed a serious threat to public health, HGSI promptly asked Judge Vance Fry to order testing. Fry granted that request, but not the time needed to ensure that the test results were completed by the scheduled November trial date. W. W. Whitlock, representing the BOS, dismissed the newfound concern about asbestos as "obviously another delaying tactic."[15]

Other mining advocates sought to block or at least slow down the citizens' group's efforts to obtain test results. William Perkins conceded that he had called the National Institute of Occupational Safety and Health (NIOSH), the EPA, and James Madison and Mary Washington Colleges to "express surprise" that these publicly funded institutions offered to test at no fee for HGSI. Manny Emroch claimed that NIOSH had backed off its agreement to test after Perkins called. Rae Ely also charged that Robert Sansom personally phoned several testing facilities. Nonetheless, Judge Fry refused to delay the hearing, conceding that it "would have been nicer had this not happened" and instructing both sides not to contact the other's testing facilities.[16]

On November 16 Fry ruled that the BOS had acted properly because plaintiffs failed to prove arbitrary, unreasonable, or capricious actions. The judge explicitly rejected the public-health challenge mounted by HGSI because it had not introduced any evidence that mining "would adversely affect the ecology, would create any health hazards, or would fail to promote the general welfare of the public." Even if there was asbestos, Fry added, potential health hazards could easily be mitigated, citing Grace's mine in Montana as just such an example. After all, "there are many elements in our environment dangerous to mankind" if used without proper safeguards.[17]

In December 1976 Robert Sansom filed an application for a mining permit with the Virginia Department of Conservation and Economic Development. The department's director, Marvin M. Sutherland, stated publicly that he saw no reason for further study and expected to issue the permit by the end of the year. Asbestos was not his department—health-related issues were not covered by the regulations governing the issuance of permits.[18]

W. R. Grace & Co.'s image today is inextricably linked to toxic threats to health and the environment, but this was not the case in the mid-1970s. Most Americans were introduced to Grace because it was responsible for a disaster that polluted the water supply of Woburn, Massachusetts, in the 1980s. The saga was popularized in the book *A Civil Action*, published in 1995, and the subsequent film. Even deadlier consequences of mining asbestos-laden vermiculite in Montana were not widely known until 1999, when Andrew Schneider, an investigative reporter for the *Seattle Post-Intelligencer*, and his editor/coauthor, David McCumber, published a series of articles propelling Grace and Libby, Montana, into national headlines. Both "Woburn" and "Libby" were indelibly linked to environmental health disasters. A combination of negative publicity and legal liability pushed Grace into bankruptcy in 2001.[19]

In 1976, Woburn, Libby, and Love Canal, New York, were just towns or neighborhoods, not iconic labels for toxic pollution. Even before these dramatic examples, however, the environmental movement had raised public concerns about health threats from industrial chemicals. A wave of new regulatory agencies quickly targeted asbestos as one of these threats. Created in 1970, the Occupational Safety and Health Administration immediately issued a workplace guidance, and by 1972 the agency promulgated a permanent standard governing the use of asbestos, albeit one constrained by the "technical feasibility" of implementing it for employers. In 1971, the newly created Environmental Protection Agency considered an outright ban on asbestos, ultimately limiting its amount in spray applications to 1 percent in 1973. Though schools were not systematically protected against flaking asbestos, some cities did place restrictions on using asbestos in building materials in the early 1970s. In October 1974, a *Washington Post* editorial labeled asbestos, along with other commonly used substances like vinyl chloride and mercury, "time bombs." Dr. Selikoff led the charge to restrict the use of asbestos, warning that "[s]trong and healthy young men enter the construction trades at 18 or 20. Asbestos lung cancer and mesothelioma will not cause their death until 50 or 55."[20]

Exposing the hazardous links between mining and processing vermiculite and asbestos took even longer. Virtually all paths led to the mine in Libby, Montana, purchased by Grace in 1963 from the Zonolite Company. A state public health official raised concerns as early as 1956, subsequently filing five reports, all suppressed by Zonolite or Grace. When a local doctor brought his concerns to Zonolite, the company dismissed the issue as "nuisance dust." If Grace was not aware of the asbestos problem before it bought the company, its executives soon found out that they had purchased trouble.[21]

Even litigation failed to sound the alarm. In 1966, Lilas Welch became the first Grace worker to file a disability claim based upon respiratory problems related to dust in the air. Grace settled for $10,000 rather than risk a trial that might provide opportunities for legal "discovery." It was not until 1973 that the first plaintiff won a case that went to trial, yet the company did not inform its workers until 1979 that the tremolite asbestos–laced vermiculite they were processing could be hazardous to their health.[22]

Grace closed its Libby operation in 1990, long before regulators or journalists definitively linked the asbestos mined there to disease and death. Roger Morris, the editor of Libby's newspaper, blamed the limited resources and parochial perspective of his small-town newspaper for failing to report on the problem. "There's no way we could cover it all. We're an 8-to 12-page paper that comes out twice a week. People want us to cover the high schools, sports, churches and the bridge club. They don't want to read court reports," Morris told the *Missoula News* in 2000. By that time more than 200 residents of Libby had died of asbestosis or mesothelioma.[23]

No definitive link between the vermiculite that eventually was mined in Louisa County and life-threatening disease among the workers was ever proven. Nevertheless, Allen Short's series in the *Richmond Times-Dispatch* about vermiculite's potential dangers might have saved lives in Libby had it gained national traction. HGSI did its best to encourage just that, but like so much when it came to asbestos, it took a long time to connect the dots.

19

A Formidable New Foe

UNTIL ROBERT SANSOM ROLLED INTO LOUISA COUNTY, Rae had never faced opposition from an adversary who was comfortable on both sides of the D.C. beltway. The quintessential Washington insider, Sansom came from a mining background and had extensive experience in the private sector. His academic and political pedigrees, combined with deep ties to rural resource extraction, made Sansom a formidable foe. So too his determination to mine in Louisa—a stubborn streak that rivaled similar qualities in Governor Linwood Holton and Rae Ely.

Mining was in Sansom's blood. "I remember playing in vermiculite when I was a kid," he recalled in 1979. "We had a bag of it around." Sansom's brother, John C. Sansom, eventually joined Bob at Virginia Vermiculite. Their father had been president of American Zinc Co. and American Limestone Co. in Knoxville, Tennessee. He also ran a small vermiculite mine. After graduating from West Knoxville High School, Bob entered the U.S. Air Force Academy, where he was a varsity football player, golfer, and wrestler. More than a jock, Sansom was honored for his academic performance in the social sciences and economics and graduated first in his class in 1964. Commissioned as a captain, Sansom completed a master's program in the School of International Affairs at Georgetown, traveled to Argentina on a Fulbright scholarship, then enrolled in New College, Oxford on a Rhodes scholarship.[1]

Sansom served for two years as an "economic consultant" to the U.S. Mission in South Vietnam, where he conducted field research in the Mekong

Delta, often working in "less-than secure rural areas." Bob returned to Oxford after his stint in Vietnam (Nuffield College), where he wrote a Ph.D. dissertation titled "The Economics of Insurgency in South Vietnam." MIT Press published it in 1970 under the title *The Economics of Insurgency*. The tragedy of Vietnam, Sansom argued, was that peasants had no clear choice because "the good and the bad were so evenly divided": neutrality was the best choice, but that "was seldom an option."[2]

Frank Gannon, who befriended Bob at Oxford in the mid-1960s, recalled that Sansom "was like the Arrow Collar Man," meaning the model featured in advertisements for Arrow dress shirts. Standing over six feet tall and built like an athlete, "he was just a strapping physical specimen with a . . . rock stone-cut jaw and just very impressive . . . physically. . . . One word described Bob's character: 'winner.' " Gannon coined the nickname for Bob that stuck: "The King." Gannon was quick to explain that this was a term of endearment: "because of the easy way Bob wore his many accomplishments," it "was entirely a term of affectionate respect."[3]

Robert Sansom joined the 1968–69 class of White House Fellows, a program that produced many illustrious alums, ranging from Doris Kearns Goodwin to Colin Powell. Bob was assigned to work with the architect of the nation's economic policy for developing nations, Walt Rostow. His other boss was National Security Council Director Henry Kissinger. Sansom's stature in the White House rose quickly, as did his reputation for being a straight shooter. Sansom served as the Environmental Protection Agency's assistant administrator for air and water programs from 1972 through early 1974. He left the EPA to cofound Energy and Environmental Analysis, Inc., a consulting firm that contracted with government agencies—especially the Department of Energy—and private firms like Shell Oil and Exxon.[4]

In 1978, Sansom was targeted in a muckraking series in the *New Republic* as one of the "New American Hustlers" who traded upon his insider EPA connections to procure lucrative contracts. The *Richmond Times-Dispatch* offered a more charitable description, reporting that Sansom was accustomed to stepping carefully as he tacked between government work and private clients. "Government contracting specialists say that Sansom apparently walks the thin line with agility." In 1981 the company was split into two parts, with Sansom serving as president of the portion that concentrated on private-sector clients—Energy Ventures Analysis.[5]

Sansom's second book, *The New American Dream Machine: Toward a Simpler Lifestyle in an Environmental Age* (1976), tackled the complex relationship between economic development and environmental protection. He was no friend of those he considered to be radical environmentalists, especially advocates for a "no growth" policy. He also chastised "the fuzziness of environmental thinking on the subject of economic growth" and saved some of his harshest criticism for the "difficult alliance of environmentalists with the most elite and conservative elements of our society."[6]

Yet, Sansom's book supported the kind of progressive thinking that characterized the Ruckelshaus EPA. For instance, Sansom regretted the demise of national land-use legislation in 1974 and bitterly denounced Nixon for withdrawing his prior support for the bill after intense lobbying by conservative Republicans. The central argument of *Dream Machine*—that only a lifestyle change by millions would protect the environment—soon became a mantra for some environmentalists. Reviewing the book for the *New York Times,* Deborah Shapley described Sansom as "one of William D. Ruckelshaus's brightest lieutenants during the formative years of the Environmental Protection Agency," even though the book was a "disappointment."[7]

Given the epic battle with Rae Ely and Historic Green Springs, Inc. that ensued, Sansom's affection for grassroots citizens who mobilized against the toxic hazards of mining was surprising. For instance, the book praised Arlene Lekto, a Duluth, Minnesota, hairdresser, for organizing the Save Lake Superior Association. That citizens' group advocated for stricter regulation of a taconite mine that threatened the downstream water supply with a submicroscopic asbestos-like substance shown to cause cancer. Enforcing existing laws was essential, Sansom argued. Lekto's kind of "citizen action" was crucial to achieving that and the best balance between economic development and environmental protection.[8]

With his impressive resume and high-level connections in Republican administrations, Bob soon turned to the Federal government to dismiss the pesky preservationists who threatened his mining operation in Louisa County. In March 1976 Sansom drafted a letter to President Gerald Ford, charging that Interior Secretary Kleppe's letter to Peter Grace was not "consistent with individual rights as guaranteed by the Constitution, energy conservation, environmental preservation, nor with the aspirations of the citizens of Louisa County, Virginia." The country "desperately needs more vermiculite."[9]

He also argued that the creation of a historic district ran roughshod over the rights of Louisa's citizens. "Elected supervisors, the public, and affected property owners, were not given the opportunity to participate in the proceeding as required by Federal and State law." Noting that citizens of Louisa had rejected the "no growth" agenda in the November 1975 election, choosing instead supervisors who were "committed to the economic revival of Louisa County through vermiculite mining," he argued that Kleppe's pressure defied "the political will of the people." Bob was far too savvy to send the letter to Ford directly; rather, he consulted with his White House Fellow friend James E. Connor, now secretary to the cabinet. Sansom mailed the letter to Connor with a "Dear Jim" cover note and Connor sent both to Kleppe, asking him to draft a response for President Ford's signature.[10]

The message to the secretary was clear: back off. Kleppe's reply sent its own message. He reinforced his contention that there was a surfeit of vermiculite and alternative materials available, more than enough to avoid mining in a historic district. According to reporting by the *Times-Dispatch*'s peripatetic Allen Short, the matter settled into a stalemate when Connor sent the response back to Interior for a do-over, labeling Kleppe's draft "too bureaucratic."[11]

Perhaps the nationally syndicated political gossip columnist Jack Anderson picked up on Short's story, or possibly Rae's friends in Interior or Ely herself provided the backstory to Anderson and his partner Les Whitten. Whatever the column's genealogy, their exposé of Sansom bristled with post-Watergate "gotcha" style. Headlined "White House Aide Intervenes" in the *Post,* but in less restrained language in other newspapers—like "White House Okays Ex-EPA Man's Mining"—the column charged Sansom and Connor with conspiring to impose their pro-development views on the Ford administration.[12]

"A White House official intervened with the Interior Department earlier this year in an effort to gain permission for a friend to dig pit mines in a national historic landmark," the column began. The former EPA administrator was now "more interested in mining than in protecting the environment." The columnists charged that Sansom schemed "to put profit ahead of history." They also reported that Connor simply deep-sixed Kleppe's draft response (and accompanying report on vermiculite reserves) so that it never reached the president. Anderson and Whitten praised Kleppe for resisting this "pressure to spoil the site."[13]

The version of the column that ran in the *Post* ended with a mea culpa from Connor, who wished he had told Sansom to send the letter directly to Kleppe. Other outlets carried an additional paragraph that quoted Bob Sansom: "I would do it again.... There's nothing of historical value within five miles." The man who had quietly interviewed besieged farmers in the Mekong Delta, and remained behind the scenes at the White House and Nixon's EPA, now saw his name splashed across newspapers around the country. His first attempt to solicit assistance from the Federal government while wearing his miner's hard hat ended in embarrassment and another triumph for local preservationists in a national arena.[14]

On the very day that Anderson and Whitten exposed Sansom's lobbying efforts, Congress enacted legislation that raised additional barriers to mining in Green Springs. The original objective of the Mining in the Parks Act was to "prevent or minimize damage to the environment and other resource values." When Rae learned about the pending legislation, she reached out to its sponsors and convinced them to add an amendment that would protect Green Springs. Although it did not outlaw surface mining in historic districts outright, it required the secretary of the Interior to report to the President's Council on Historic Preservation all activities that might destroy or do irreparable damage to them. *Preservation News* reported that the "only case the bill appears to be applicable to currently is the historic Green Springs area of Louisa County, Va." Members of the Senate and House Interior Committees aptly dubbed the amendment the "Ely Rider."[15]

The *Washington Post* focused on that provision crafted to protect Green Springs from strip mining. Allen Short's reporting stressed that the legislation gave Interior officials "unprecedented statutory authority" to take actions to " 'abate or mitigate' activities such as the vermiculite mining." When asked about the legislation, Rae responded, "It's a whole new ballgame now." Although she warned that the game was not over, the legislation "gives us a boost ... a really useful tool that will lead, I believe, to the ultimate banning of strip mining in or upon national historic landmark areas."[16]

Bob Sansom countered by putting the best face possible on the situation, stating that the law did not "empower Kleppe to intervene in the Green Springs controversy," which was technically true, since the secretary could only ask the President's Council to investigate. Besides, Sansom added, the matter had "already been resolved.... We've got a conditional use permit and zoning." Louisa's congressman, J. Kenneth Robinson, had little to say about the Ely Rider, although his aide claimed that the long-time mining advocate had been aware of the provision. Rae disagreed: "Robinson did not know what he was voting for ... because the amendment went through in the middle of the night," adding, "that's how I learned how these things were done."[17]

The one-two punch of negative national publicity and the Ely Rider paled in comparison to the next body blow to mining advocates. On October 3, the entire cover of the *Washington Post*'s "Potomac" section was devoted to a drawing of one of Green Springs' most iconic historic houses, white columns and all, sitting in a box of kitty litter. The headline atop the roof of Westend Plantation read, "Old Virginia's Cat Litter War." "O Louisa!" informed readers in bold letters that "Louisa County, Virginia's historic plantation paradise may be gone ... as a new Civil War rages over strip-mining for cat litter."[18]

The multipage spread was festooned with photographs of unspoiled vistas, country lanes, Rae in front of Hawkwood, and moonscape-like views of Grace's vermiculite operations in Montana and South Carolina. The whole mess would never have happened if "it hadn't been for the volcano that blew up ... millions of years ago." Meandering from the volcanic bowl that made Green Springs green, to the vermiculite that contributed to this fertility, winding through the poverty that ensued after the "War Between the States," and pausing at the slave quarters that were turned into hen houses, the article eventually settled into its theme of paradise lost.

Green Springs was a "super-fertile bowl of paradise" that once drew nineteenth-century visitors to its "health spring in the center." Connections to Richmond through canals, then railroads, carried wheat from Green Springs' verdant fields to a hungry world, fueling the profits that financed huge mansions and villas. A century later it was declared a national historic landmark, a "unique assemblage of rural architecture" and "textbook of Virginia architecture." Paradise, however, was now threatened by "large deposits of a flaky mineral which scientists would name vermiculite from the Latin *vermis*, meaning worm ... the worm in the perfect apple."

This was a "textbook conflict in a textbook area: the Haves vs. the Have-nots. The Keepers of the Land vs. the Breakers of the Land." To mine or not was the question that divided "even families and church congregations into bitter warring factions." Changing scripts to "some absurdist way-off-Broadway" playwright's "comically ridiculous" theater, the article swung wildly between underscoring the tragedy of citizen fighting fellow citizen to the bizarre prize they fought over—kitty litter.

When reporter Gordon Chaplin asked for directions to Green Springs, he was told, "Take my advice, boy, and you get on back to Washington because that just isn't *any* business of yours." Gladys Kennon, the sheriff's wife, spoke for a lot of Louisa's residents when she told Chaplin that the preservationists "think they're better than we are. They think they can tell us what to do." According to Mrs. Kennon, "they're all a bunch of dam-yankees up there anyway. They don't even belong here."

Dean Agee told the *Post*, "Why they're nothing but a bunch of frustrated women. Historical Society now? I call it the Hysterical Society. They're against progress up there. Zero progress. They want to keep everything like it was 500 years ago. They're against jobs. Progress, as I define it, is full employment." Nor was Agee pleased with HGSI's methods. "We can't even conduct a meeting down here anymore without them and their tape recorders and their yak yak yak."

Mining opponents were happy to detail the "unvarnished pure hatred" they had endured. Hanne Heimer told Chaplin that she believed "the whole mining thing is an act of vengeance on the part of the county." Because Green Springs defeated the prison, she reasoned, "they figure we deserve the mining. There's a viciousness down there, a shrewd cunningness." The Louisa political establishment "hang out down there in the courthouse like bats. They fly by night."

Building to its grand conclusion, the article returned to Gladys Kennon, who insisted that if "they took a vote as to whether to throw the Queen out of the county, she'd be gone so fast it would make your head spin." "The Queen," Chaplin noted, was old-timers' nickname for Rae Ely. Hardly endearing herself to many Virginians, Rae shot back, "Outsiders are responsible for all the preservation in this state. Williamsburg. Mount Vernon. All of it. Virginians just don't care at all about historic preservation." Ely then compared her cause to the civil rights struggle. "As far as voting to throw me out of the county is concerned," she continued, "why back in the '60s if they could have taken that kind of vote, they would have thrown all the black people out."

This time, Millard Filmore Peers, not Rae, got the last word. Describing Peers as a short, solidly built man with thinning hair and "wary" eyes, Chaplin quoted him extensively. Peers explained that he simply wanted to make a buck off the land he owned, but had been prevented from doing so by "outsiders" who used "high-handed tactics" to create the historic district "without our consent," imposing the will of a minority on the majority. Peers was worried that HGSI's machinations would convince Grace to walk away from mining his land. The article ended with M. F.'s observations about history. "They talk about historic preservation. . . . We've been here for 200 years and if cat litter is going to help preserve us, then let's bring on the cat litter." In a battle over historic preservation, those who disparaged the importance of Green Springs' alleged history were, for the most part, the same citizens whose histories there went back the farthest.

20
Local Affairs and the Law of the Land

THE QUEST FOR RACIAL EQUALITY HAD dramatically tilted the balance between local and national government. By the mid-1970s, a broad national consensus supporting the rights of Blacks—to vote, attend the school of their choice, and compete for employment—superseded many local and private preferences. That stunning victory opened the way for other groups, like HGSI, to advocate for *their own* Federally protected rights. Whether preserving history, the environment, and scenic views merited the same weight as protecting the civil and political rights of Blacks, however, was a contentious question—and not just in Louisa County.

The debate about who would hold and enforce Green Springs' easements turned on the very meaning of federalism in the last third of the twentieth century. Did HGSI, which represented a minority view in Louisa County, deserve the protection of Federal laws that preserved the environment and cultural resources, regardless of how their Louisa County neighbors voted? Or should the proper arbiter of such questions be Louisa's Board of Supervisors, elected by a majority of county voters? M. F. Peers posed the question bluntly after asbestos was found on farmland laced with vermiculite. Would every farmer in Louisa County now be required to don proper safety gear and conduct an environmental impact study before they planted crops?[1]

As President Jimmy Carter's Department of the Interior moved toward accepting Green Springs' donated easements, it was advocates for mining who now demanded due process and attention to grassroots participation. Louisa County Supervisor Sambo Johnson wrote to the new secretary of the Interior, quoting President Carter's pledge to "return the government to the people." After all, Carter had carried his own garment bag when traveling and quashed the obligatory round of "Hail to the Chief." Johnson fumed at the elitist nature of Interior's past actions: "a small group within your department chose to meet with a small, private group in Louisa County rather than the governing body who represents the views of the people." This was "just the kind of behavior on the part of the Federal government that President Carter was elected to reverse."[2]

At a public hearing in Green Springs, Interior's chief preservation officer, Jerry Rogers, acknowledged the dilemma that federalism posed: to some in the audience, the mere presence of the NPS and Interior officials represented "Federal meddling in local affairs." Others saw the federal presence as an obligation to follow up on a national commitment. "We are not insensitive to local democracy," Rogers insisted, "but we must also be responsive to the national obligations as expressed in the law of the land."[3]

Rumors circulated in September 1976 that the Department of the Interior would soon accept Historic Green Springs, Inc.'s easements as a "hedge against proposed strip mining." Holding the easements would move the department beyond mere jawboning; it provided a powerful lever that could be deployed to defend the historic district. Referring specifically to pending litigation, an unnamed Interior source said it "will allow us to participate in anything that affects that interest." Nature Conservancy head Tom Richards labeled Interior ownership "the most useful means of actual preservation the government has ever gotten into," because unlike the Nature Conservancy, Interior would be impervious to the threat of eminent domain. Manny Emroch underscored Interior's direct access to the Federal courts—"a definite advantage in our situation."[4]

Louisa County Supervisor R. E. Curtis's angry response invoked that year's popular Bicentennial theme: "200 years ago we signed a Declaration of Independence . . . and I am ready to sign another one." Sambo Johnson warned that Rae Ely would use the Federal courts to shift what should be a local decision to the national government: HGSI "sues us every time we rezone property in that part of the county," Johnson complained. "This is going to give them a crutch to bring in federal help in those suits."[5]

More bad news dribbled in for staunch advocates of "local control" in October. President Ford signed legislation requiring Interior to step up its monitoring of national landmarks. It now had to report any incompatible activities—like surface mining. Deputy Assistant Secretary for Fish and Wildlife and Parks Doug Wheeler explained that the recent passage of the Ely Rider, coupled with the Parklands Enforcement Act, required that his department "keep a much closer watch" on scenic and historic sites. Speaking on behalf of the cost-sensitive Ford administration, Wheeler quickly added that no additional Federal funds would be required because compliance depended on the vigilance of "active civic groups such as . . . Historic Green Springs." From Wheeler's perspective, this epitomized the kind of partnership between the public and voluntary sectors that allowed Interior to achieve its mission during fiscally challenging times.[6]

On November 23, the National Park Service circulated the Green Springs easements study that would endorse or quash the budding partnership. Authored by Senior Historian Benjamin Levy, the report was an exercise in thinking out loud. Although it recommended accepting the Green Springs easements, Levy struggled with the fact that key parcels of land were not protected and could well be subjected to subdivision, strip mining, or other industrial uses. That was precisely the problem that another staunch advocate for preservation—the Virginia Historic Landmarks Commission—had run into a few years before. Its determination that the pattern of easements would *not* guarantee preservation provided Governor Holton the opportunity to rule that Green Springs could not withstand development, prison or not. Answering its own question about sufficient coverage, Levy's report stated that "the only fair answer is that it is not," because unprotected tracts constituted a "critical focal belt through the mid-section of the district." Delicately summing up the potential consequences, the report conceded that "the landmark could become severed with incompatible uses." Expert historians at both the VHLC and the NPS now agreed on this crucial point.[7]

Levy's report, however, went beyond assessing whether coverage was *currently* sufficient, venturing into the realm of incentivizing *future* protection. Interior's acceptance of the easements, though it would not guarantee preservation, might "itself become a catalyst for perfecting easement coverage." In other words, accepting the donated easements, though it failed to guarantee preservation, was an important step toward achieving that end. The question really came down to a matter of "public policy"; the case for accepting easements should be seen as "initiating a preservation action rather than consummating one." Levy's report was "good enough for government work," as the phrase goes. A handwritten note from Doug Wheeler to Rae Ely attached to Levy's report captured the view at the top of the department: "A souvenir of your herculean effort; may it come to a successful conclusion."[8]

On the last day of the Ford administration, outgoing Assistant Interior Secretary Nat Reed wrote to HGSI President Elisabeth Nolting to inform her that he was instructing the National Park Service to accept the easements by May 1, 1977. He also acknowledged that the Louisa County Board of Supervisors opposed the donation and instructed the Park Service to hold a public hearing in Louisa County. Ely, Blanchard, Wheeler, and Reed had come a long way toward adding yet another layer of Federal protection. Rae applauded the decision; Sambo Johnson cited the upcoming public hearing as an opportunity to push back.[9]

Bob Sansom took a page out of the HGSI playbook and sought a Federal ally of his own. In February 1977 Virginia Vermiculite asked the Farmers Home Administration (FmHA) to guarantee $900,000 of a $1 million loan to finance mining. A federal guarantee would allow VVI to procure a loan from Virginia United Bank at a reduced interest rate. While the Department of the Interior sought to preserve Green Springs' historical assets, the FmHA's objective was job creation in rural areas. With an anticipated payroll of half a million dollars annually spread across forty-five new jobs, Sansom claimed that VVI was an ideal candidate.[10]

The Louisa County Board of Supervisors had no problem with *this* kind of Federal intervention, voting 5–1 to support the request. The Louisa Chamber of Commerce and the Louisa and Mineral Industrial Development Corporation soon backed the proposal. The only local public official who opposed the loan request was James King, who remarked that there were far better ways to use federal dollars, starting with aid to farmers suffering from a tough winter.[11]

Former EPA Administrator Bob Sansom surely knew that Federal aid might trigger an environmental impact statement, especially now that the potential asbestos hazard had surfaced. Given the history of its fight against the prison and its precedent-setting litigation in *Ely v. Velde*, no preservation group in the country was more attuned to that requirement than HGSI. An unnamed spokesperson for the Department of the Interior (most likely Bruce Blanchard) predicted that the request for a Federally subsidized loan would be subjected not only to the provisions of the National Environmental

Policy Act, but to the National Historic Preservation Act as well. That Congress had recently enhanced Interior's power to review potentially negative activities in national parks and historic landmark districts only increased the likelihood. FmHA would reverse its position about the need for an environmental impact statement multiple times over the coming year.[12]

News about Interior's opposition to the loan was soon drowned out when its new head, Cecil D. Andrus, announced that the department would accept the easements. Andrus's actions fit perfectly with Jimmy Carter's "environmental message" to Congress that made preserving the nation's history a priority. Carter called for a comprehensive National Heritage Trust that would preserve places that have "special natural, historical, cultural and scientific value." Under the direction of the secretary of the Interior, the National Heritage Trust would coordinate Federal programs "within states and private citizens more effectively." Task force membership reflected this emphasis on partnership, bringing together the voluntary sector's National Trust for Historic Preservation and public officials like the National Conference of State Historic Preservation Officers. What better example of such coordination than the partnership in Green Springs?[13]

Sambo Johnson soon wrote to the new secretary, demanding that Interior terminate its plans to accept easements. Only then could it assess legitimate historic sites "from the grassroots" by "consult[ing] with the people and the government." Interior should draft a full environmental impact statement that establishes the minimum acreage required to protect legitimate historic sites and assesses the "adverse health and economic impacts to the nation if the country is denied the insulation materials through easements accepted in areas having vermiculite." Much of Johnson's letter echoed Robert Sansom's previous correspondence with the White House. Andrus's perfunctory response assured that environmental matters would be considered, but the secretary promised little more.[14]

A day before the Department of the Interior hearing in Louisa County, a *Central Virginian* headline announced that Dickie Purcell had recorded at the county clerk's office a subdivision with eighty-six lots in the Green Springs Historic District. Purcell claimed that he had been working on the project for a year. Whether the timing was a coincidence or not, it was a stark reminder of Interior's and the VHLC's greatest concern—hundreds of acres in the heart of the historic district that were not protected by easements and were owned by a Louisan who planned to develop them.[15]

On the morning of April 22, seated behind a table covered in a checked blue and white tablecloth, Department of the Interior administrative law judge Franklin P. Michels presided over the public hearing at Will's Chapel Meeting House. The small white clapboard building owned by HGSI was located close to property targeted for mining. Neither the home touch of the tablecloth nor the scent of crops (and perhaps other agricultural smells) wafting through the open windows soothed the charged atmosphere of the packed chapel. "It was an unruly mob—screaming, calling everything a communist plot." Everybody who signed up in advance got their say and the judge went out of his way to accommodate those whose participation was confined to their lunch break. The hearing's lunch break was just half an hour long—not enough time to get to Louisa's only restaurant, but sufficient to dash to the general store for canned sausages, saltines, and a Coke.[16]

Jerry Rogers read an opening statement that provided a brief history of the process leading to Green Springs' national landmark status and offered a lucid explanation of what easements were, the process for considering their donation, and the legal implications of Interior holding easements. Sidestepping the most important consequence of Federal acceptance—standing in Federal courts—Rogers did acknowledge that owning the easements would provide the Department of the Interior the "rights of a private landowner." Interior's chief preservation officer also deftly synthesized some of the key fault lines in the longstanding battle. "We are keenly aware that there are those of you who see the threat of a disintegrating environment. We are equally aware," Rogers continued, "that there are those of you who feel your economic well-being is being jeopardized by what is perceived to be an excessive zeal to preserve the environment." He insisted that "[o]ur minds are not made up."[17]

Rogers then addressed another fault line: some in the audience were passionately committed to preserving the area as an important historic and architectural site. Others, he countered, "are puzzled that anyone could find anything of historical or scenic merit here." There was one more fissure: was Federal presence in Green Springs an overreach by a national government meddling in local affairs? Or was the Federal government intervening to protect the rights of all American citizens, regardless of the county or state that they happened to live in?[18]

Grace's local counsel Bill Perkins immediately asked that the public hearing be adjourned. Interior had "the cart before the horse," since there was not any plan to administer the easements should they be accepted. The advocate for one of the world's largest natural resource extraction companies also complained that the hearings should not begin until an environmental analysis was completed. Commonwealth Attorney Stephen C. Harris, representing the Louisa Board of Supervisors, seconded these objections: interested parties had been denied due process. The claim was familiar, but it now came from the courthouse crowd and Grace rather than a tiny citizens' group.[19]

After the administrative law judge denied Perkins's postponement request, Grace's counsel drilled into the issue that Rogers had sidestepped. Would the Federal government intervene in litigation on behalf of HGSI? Would it take matters out of the hands of state courts? It was no secret that Historic Green Springs, Inc. had filed over twenty lawsuits since 1970. Would the federal government add to this list by joining these litigious citizens? Thomas Lyall, now a Grace consultant, cited a treasure trove of internal memoranda that featured complaints about donated easements by Interior's internal critic, Philip Stewart. This showcased a valuable asset should mining advocates decide to litigate. Rae Ely was not the only stakeholder who had friends deep within the Park Service.[20]

Lyall also attacked the preservationists' motives, insisting that their cause had little to do with preserving history. Rather, it was "part of a concerted effort to stop legitimate economic development in a rural county which desires such development." The former Grace vice president repeated the elitism charge, citing a clause contained in every donated easement: nothing "herein shall be construed to convey a right to the public of access or use of the property." He charged that this directly violated the "public use" and "public benefit" requirements of the Historic Sites Act of 1935.[21]

Samuel P. Higginbotham II strayed from narrow legal explication to political philosophy, stating that the "greatness of America is not the product of the government but the product of its people." If you "take away the property rights of individuals . . . this republic will fall," he warned. When land could be designated historic without consent of the landowner, M. F. Peers testified, it was "time for a change."[22]

Robert Sansom hammered away at the flawed process through which the Department of the Interior had arrived at this juncture. Why no environmental impact statement, for instance? Sansom also charged Bruce Blanchard with "silencing Philip Stewart." Claiming that Interior officials had conspired with Green Springs' elite, Sansom stated that the conflict in Green Springs was all about the "landed gentry vs. the poor."[23]

Keeping big government out of local affairs was a common theme. Leroy Chisolm, who owned a 500-acre farm, stated that "we can look after our own affairs without the government [involved] in it." Dickie Purcell insisted that there "was no way you can farm this land with Uncle Sam looking over your shoulder." Dean Agee, now circuit court clerk, asked, "Who is to govern Louisa County?" Just "how far will the arm of the federal government reach?"[24]

The majority of those who spoke in favor of easements were members of Historic Green Springs, Inc. Cast in the unusual position of defending the status quo, they reiterated the importance of history and preserving the area's cultural heritage. They also featured members like "farmer's wife" Eunice Fisher, who had lived in Louisa County for seventy-two years. "I'm not the idle rich," Fisher testified. "I truly believe I can trust the Department of the Interior more than I can the board of supervisors down in Louisa." Some of HGSI's national allies, like the National Trust for Historic Preservation, also weighed in. Perhaps unaware of Stewart's memos about the decade-long negotiation with amusement park owner Joseph Goldstein, Samuel N. Stokes cited the fight to save Mount Vernon's viewshed as a model. Others who supported donating easements ticked off familiar arguments rehearsed since Governor Holton had proposed building the diagnostic center in 1970: preserving vanishing farmland and a rural way of life; saving a habitat for wildlife.[25]

While Bruce Blanchard kept the momentum going from one administration to the next, Robert L. Herbst, who replaced Nat Reed as assistant secretary for fish and wildlife and parks in the Carter administration, picked up the pace. Somebody in Interior had been listening at Will's Chapel, however, because Herbst's instructions to NPS Director Gary Everhardt emphasized that rules for administering easements should only apply to "*offered* easements," exempting "properties not covered by easements but included in the historic district." Herbst hoped to make a final determination by June 15.[26]

Shortly after the public hearing at Will's Chapel, the building was torched. Firefighters from three companies were able to bring the fire under control in less than an hour, but not before the building was destroyed. Sheriff

Henry A. Kennon quickly concluded that there was "no way to know" what started the fire. HGSI members immediately suspected arson; Rae Ely recalled that she was "almost expecting" the phone call that alerted her to the blaze. Not only had opposition to the historic district spread to the grass roots, many believed that somebody felt strongly enough about "outsiders" running things to express that opposition violently.[27]

The group's worst fears were confirmed by the ensuing investigation when the state arson investigation unit announced that the blaze was indeed the work of an arsonist. Sheriff Kennon disagreed, calling it "a very controversial fire," adding that the "pros and cons of the fire are no different from the pros and cons of the mining [controversy]." The debate continued for months, with each side replicating the mining-antimining divide. In November, the arson unit reported that it had identified a suspect in the crime, although it refused to release the name to the public. Not surprisingly, since Kennon flatly denied that the fire had been set, the suspect was never arrested. "No one found an oil can or anything piled up in the corner," the sheriff explained. He labeled the arson finding "one man's opinion," calling that opinion "garbage."[28]

Interior was not the only agency wrestling with citizen input. Back at the Farmers Home Administration, the on-again, off-again requirement for an environmental impact statement was batted around like a ping-pong ball. Knocking the decision back to the Virginia office of the FmHA seemingly resolved the matter. Its director, B. B. Brown, certainly did not invoke science when he explained why his office waived the requirement. "The information that we received," Brown explained, "indicated that everyone, including the state and the county, wanted the mining to proceed. We saw no reason to hold it up."[29]

"Everybody" apparently did not include Historic Green Springs, Inc. Rae Ely labeled the action a "blatant violation" of environmental laws. "If an environmental impact statement isn't required in this case," she fumed, "I can't think of anywhere it would be." Two days later HGSI was back in front of their old nemesis, U.S. District Court Judge Robert R. Merhige. Because the FmHA was part of the Department of Agriculture, the suit named Agriculture Secretary Bob Bergland and Virginia Vermiculite, among others. HGSI sought an injunction prohibiting the FmHA from approving a loan to

VVI before an environmental impact statement was filed. As with *Ely v. Velde*, the preservationists also cited violations of the National Historic Preservation Act.[30]

Although Judge Merhige refused to issue the injunction, he scheduled a full hearing for the following week and cautioned the FmHA and VVI that any action taken before then "will be at their own risk. . . . If I thought they were going to start digging tomorrow," Merhige told the plaintiffs, "I would give you a [temporary restraining] order." Perhaps recalling the two reversals by the Fourth Circuit in the *Ely v. Velde* cases, the judge added: "If you see them digging out there, let me know."[31]

On May 1, Allen Short stepped back to assess where things stood in a story headlined "Zoning, Mining Confrontations Create Louisa's Second Civil War." Short distilled a "classic confrontation between would-be strip miners and history-conscious conservationists that threatens to linger indefinitely." These skirmishes, however, did not take place in pastureland or wilderness. Rather, they unfolded in courtrooms "with mahogany benches periodically filled with executives of one of the nation's largest business conglomerates, owners of two dozen antebellum estates, and adjoining landowners, beneath whose properties lie vast deposits of a mineral valued in building, insulation and construction."[32]

Short never mentioned kitty litter. He did portray the frustration of some of Louisa's elected officials, quoting Dean Agee's complaint about the Federal government's long reach into Louisa County. Agee did not complain about the Federally subsidized North Anna nuclear generating station, which the administrator believed was the only employer that "could make or break the County." In the two months that followed Short's article, the Board of Supervisors looked into Federal grants to build an airport in Louisa, approved a Federal revenue sharing budget of over $1 million, and asked the governor to request Federal disaster aid for drought relief.[33]

PART FOUR

HISTORY RHYMES

21
Preservationists as Lobbyists

WHEN THE DEPARTMENT OF THE INTERIOR accepted Green Springs' 8,000 acres of easements, it looked like the district's historic landmark status had permanently been secured and, with that protection, its history and environment preserved. "What a Partnership!" the HGSI newsletter proclaimed. "Never before had there been such an alliance. . . . Never before has the power of the United States been placed squarely in a position to protect for the future irreplaceable cultural resources not owned outright by the government." Less than two years later, however, in August 1980, Federal District Court Judge Robert Merhige ruled that the Department of the Interior had acted improperly in establishing the Green Springs National Historic Landmark District. "I just saw my whole life flashing before my eyes. . . . For a moment I didn't even care. . . . It was a terrible moment of despair," Rae Ely recalled.[1]

The architect of that legal victory was Robert Sansom, who had emerged as the undisputed leader of pro-development advocates in Louisa County. He used HGSI's own federal lawsuit that sought to impose an environmental impact statement on his mining firm to turn the tables on his bitter opponents. The courthouse crowd remained important allies, as did the property owners who stood to make a fortune mining vermiculite. Nor was there reason to believe that support for any initiative promising jobs had waned since Louisans overwhelmingly elected a mining advocate as the county tie-breaker. If anything, economic hard times likely intensified this support.

Although Circuit Court Judge Harold Purcell had once effectively directed the courthouse crowd from atop the political hierarchy, there was a new kind of field general in town—one who could match Rae Ely strategy for strategy, whatever the venue or jurisdiction. Robert Sansom was that man. Like the Air Force he once served, Sansom was prepared to fight in a variety of theaters, especially federal ones like Judge Merhige's courtroom. And like Rae Ely, he took no prisoners.

A decade after the *Bergland* decision Sansom asked why Green Springs had been designated historic in the first place. His answer was that "a local NIMBY transplanted from New Jersey, opposed a Virginia Governor's decision to fund the construction of a State prison across from her big house." Although the acronym NIMBY was not coined until the mid-1980s, by 1990 everybody knew what that pejorative meant.[2]

Weighing whether to give up and get on with her life or deal with "what was truly the greatest crisis ever to hit us" in the wake of the *Bergland* ruling, Ely decided that "I've gotta go fix it, but I'm gonna fix it in about five minutes . . . that's all the time I have to deal with it." She was also convinced that it "had to be done with great stealth—sleight of hand." It was. The midnight amendment she added to one of the last pieces of legislation signed during the Carter administration restored Green Springs' landmark status. One Justice Department attorney quoted in the *New York Times* could not recall a "legislative reversal of a judicial judgment as total or as quick. These preservationists are good lobbyists."[3]

In May 1977, Virginia Vermiculite, Inc. filed a counterclaim in the *Bergland* litigation, challenging HGSI's listing on the National Register of Historical Places and subsequent designation as a national historic landmark. Sansom's suit also asked Judge Merhige to restrain other Federal agencies from recognizing the landmark status when they reviewed VVI's loan request. Those Federal agencies—the Department of the Interior and the president's Advisory Council on Historic Preservation—were HGSI's staunch allies.[4]

The counterclaim blasted the Farmers Home Administration director for treating the landmark designation "as if it was valid," when FmHA yet again reconsidered requiring an environmental impact statement. One Louisa supervisor quipped that the trial was "like watching summer re-runs." Even Robert Merhige was growing weary. During a debate over the district's historic significance, the judge suggested that it was the amount of litigation generated that might "turn out to be the most significant fact of Green Springs."[5]

As they prepared to accept the easements, Interior officials continued to shore up their position in the wake of the April public hearing and the VVI litigation. For instance, Interior made amends for its failure to solicit public comment during the rush to put Green Springs on the National Register of Historic Places and designate it a national landmark. Bowing to the pressure to invite "citizen input" from the likes of Robert Sansom and the Louisa County establishment, Robert Herbst, assistant secretary for fish and wildlife and parks, issued a statement on June 24 declaring that Interior would "reconsider" Green Springs' designation as a national historic landmark and its listing on the National Register. Critics were understandably skeptical.[6]

The unenviable task of explaining all this backtracking fell to the National Park Service's leading easements advocate, Ben Levy. Reconsideration was "not an admission that the department had done anything wrong," Levy insisted. It simply was "part of the new Administration's commitment to openness." When pressed, Levy conceded that should the reconsideration reverse Green Springs' landmark status, Interior's plans to accept easements would "probably be jeopardized." The quest for "openness" was announced the same day that HGSI, FmHA, and Robert Sansom were back in court, prompting Judge Merhige to ask whether the injunctive relief that VVI sought was still necessary since the department already planned to reconsider the district's listing.[7]

VVI's counsel, Carl Eardley, had plenty of answers. He characterized HGSI's agenda as self-serving and parochial. The preservationists "wanted roads but didn't want a quarry" near them; they wanted "electric power, but they don't want electric power plants." Eardley also accused those who had imposed landmark status on Green Springs of acting "deceitfully" to obfuscate their unpopular move. Judge Merhige was not convinced. He denied VVI's request for an injunction to suspend the district's landmark status and bar it from consideration as part of FmHA's loan review process.[8]

On July 27 officials from the Department of the Interior once again visited Louisa County for a day of public commentary. Top brass for VVI and W. R. Grace & Co. again drew upon criticism from inside the bureaucracy, quoting NPS Director Everhardt's warning that without sufficient staff it would not be possible to execute the easement program. Although Sansom vigorously opposed a VVI environmental impact statement, he insisted that Interior produce one before accepting scenic easements. Citing a departmental manual that required consideration of Federal actions affecting the "human environment," Sansom argued that the "viability of such basic human institutions such as the constitution, [and] property rights," would be affected by the easement program. He also argued that using vermiculite for insulation would lower the demand growth rate for energy—a *positive* environmental contribution.⁹

Critics forced Interior to clarify two crucial matters. Department attorney Lars Hanslin admitted that even if Secretary Cecil Andrus determined that the landmark nomination was flawed, the secretary could simply designate Green Springs a national historic landmark *without* a nomination. Sansom charged that this bait-and-switch was "dramatically misleading." What was the point of the current hearing about the state designation nomination process for national landmark consideration if Andrus could uphold the status quo by unilaterally "re-designating" the district a national landmark? Interior's attorneys also acknowledged that incompatible activities, including mining by landowners adjacent to properties covered by easements, "would probably be challenged in federal court if the easements are accepted." Both state and Federal administrators had consistently maintained that landmark status did not threaten property rights—you could even dynamite your landmark property if you wanted to. They now admitted that should Interior accept the easements it could intervene in Federal courts to protect the historic and environmental integrity of the landmark. That protection might well extend to threats like mining outside the district itself.¹⁰

Central Virginian columnist H. D. N. Hill articulated the local pro-development sentiment. Involving the Federal Department of the Interior was "a ploy." Green Springs did not merit the "historic" label any more than other parts of Louisa County and "all the other Virginia counties that for some two hundred years have remained rural." The "great and important objection," however, was "involving the Federal government in the strictly local affairs of a small . . . county."¹¹

Hill did not convince the Feds: one day after the public meeting in Louisa, the FmHA announced that a full-scale environmental impact study would be required before it could guarantee the VVI loan. It was now estimated that this could delay mining for two years. Agency officials advised that the Federal government could save "considerable time and expense" if VVI withdrew its loan application. When asked what prompted the decision, the FmHA spokesperson cited comments from several federal agencies, including the Department of the Interior.[12]

Interior also followed up its investigation into mining vermiculite in a historic district. A cautious National Park Service official underscored the legal risks entailed for his agency: "I understand that this will be the first such study on non-federal lands to be undertaken under the Mining in the Parks Act." The study was bound to stir up controversy, and if it concluded that irreparable damage would result, "the mining interests in Green Springs will most certainly challenge us in court to prove our findings." His colleague was not deterred, noting that the higher-ups in Interior expected the study to be carried out.[13]

Acting NPS Director Ira J. Hutchinson knew when to give up. Although the property guys had dragged their feet and delayed the final decision on accepting easements, it was apparent that incoming Secretary Andrus backed his predecessors Rogers Morton and Thomas Kleppe. Skilled infighters like Bruce Blanchard, Nat Reed, and Doug Wheeler had successfully sustained the pressure between administrations. On November 25, Hutchinson wrote to the incoming assistant secretary for fish and wildlife and parks. He began by granting critics of the landmark district a huge win: Virginia's original nomination to the National Register was defective because it failed to give landowners adequate notice. Based upon this finding, the keeper had already removed historic Green Springs from the register as a state nomination.[14]

He then eviscerated that momentary victory by recommending that the district be maintained on the National Register because his department's extensive review confirmed that Green Springs met the criteria for national landmark status. Hutchinson based his recommendation on many of the same factors enumerated in the Commonwealth of Virginia's original nomination. Hutchinson also recommended that the secretary accept the easements. Although this would not provide a "total solution" to preserving the district and there were advocates on both sides, Hutchinson relied upon the judgment of "individuals with professional expertise [who] are very supportive of the historic values of the Green Springs area."

Robert Herbst wasted no time passing along the recommendation to Secretary Andrus, who ruled on December 13 to maintain the district's landmark status and accepted the easements on behalf of the Department of the Interior. Formally, at least, the four-year saga that began with HGSI inviting the Federal government into the neighborhood had finally come to an end. Andrus's press release offered some hints about what kind of neighbor Uncle Sam would be. Congratulating the easement donors for voluntarily "binding themselves to preserve an important part of the Nation's cultural legacy," the secretary underscored that "some residents of the area rallied their forces against efforts to strip mine vermiculite in the historic district." The shout-out to citizen action, combined with the term "strip mine"—Grace and VVI preferred "open pit mining"—signaled that Interior planned to be a vocal neighbor.[15]

Ben Franklin of the *New York Times* interpreted Interior's move as a clear indication that it planned to defend its newly acquired property rights aggressively. Headlined "U.S Joins Preservationist's Fight," the *Times* article reprised the long history of support for HGSI from past Interior secretaries, even though the preservation group had "lost scores of battles at the state and local levels." Accepting the easements would change that calculus, Franklin observed, because Interior could now go into Federal court to defend its "ownership" interest. An Interior spokesperson even told the *Times* that if the donated easements proved successful, "the new concept would probably be used to benefit other preservation efforts around the country."[16]

Inside the Park Service, historian Ben Levy pressed his colleagues to maintain the momentum. The first order of business, Levy advised his boss, Jerry Rogers, was to carry out the study required under the Mining in the Parks Act. It was "now more urgent than ever," Levy insisted, following up with a list of matters that required "immediate attention," including the possibility of strengthening the existing easements and obtaining additional easements. It was "especially important at a time when all involved in this easements venture might want to relax and breath [sic] a sigh of relief." Reminding Rogers that this was essentially a pilot program, Levy asked, "Should we not use our best offices to encourage, indeed, at the very least, test, the effectiveness of this idea about which there has been so much controversy?"[17]

Others in the NPS continued to fight a rearguard action when it came to administering the easements that Interior now owned. Acting NPS Director of Cultural Resources Ross Holland warned that managing the Green Springs easements would embroil his agency "in a celebrated preservation case of considerable litigation and the likelihood of more. . . . Make no mistake about it. Historic Green Springs Inc . . . will not rest in its efforts to see that the managing agency fulfills its obligations," because it was "a vigorous organization under tireless and persistent leadership." That organization—HGSI—and its leadership—Rae Ely—were essential to an effective public-private partnership, yet, from the perspective of those NPS bureaucrats now stuck with administering the easement program, they were also the greatest liabilities.[18]

Interior's move to the neighborhood was indeed precedent-setting. The *Richmond Times-Dispatch* characterized its arrival as "the first time in the department's 128-year history that it has become a caretaker of privately owned land deemed to be of significant historical value." Interior's Lars Hanslin explained that it would "make us landowners in the area. We will have the same rights as any other property owner," including "the right to attempt to ward off nuisances." Rae Ely welcomed her new neighbor, calling the decision "the best Christmas present we could have hoped for." BOS Chair Sambo Johnson shunned his new neighbor: the whole thing was "a sham."[19]

A few weeks before the announcement, Robert Sansom withdrew VVI's request for an FmHA loan guarantee. He used the mineral rights to the land he planned to mine, some personal property, and a percentage of his future mining revenue as collateral to secure an agreement in principle with the National Bank of Detroit for the loan. Even though the bank's vice president acknowledged that Sansom's application disclosed "myriads of problems," VVI forged ahead without the Federal subsidy.[20]

With a Democrat in the White House, Sansom also changed his lobbying strategy. He likely drafted William A. Strong's letter to Senator Dale Bumpers (D-Arkansas), who sat on a key Department of the Interior oversight committee. Strong, whose Strong-Lite Products Corporation was located in Pine Bluff, Arkansas, warned that his company "desperately needed vermiculite" and that supply problems could easily be resolved by the discovery of new reserves in Virginia. There was "just one hitch. . . . The Department of Interior is attempting to block mining through a complex series of maneuvers that the layman and taxpayer could hardly unravel." Interior was the "agent of a few wealthy landowners against the interest of the working people," even though nothing "of national historic (or even state) importance has ever taken place in this Manhattan-sized area."[21]

Bumpers wrote to Secretary Andrus in November 1977 and asked him to consider his constituent's request carefully. Was there some way to mine "without impairing the historical value of the area"? Though polite, Assistant Secretary Richard Myshak's response was resolute. The issues raised in Strong's letter (and the senator's) had been fully vetted at a series of public hearings; the secretary stood behind his decision to relist Green Springs as a landmark and accept the donated easements.[22]

Undeterred, Sansom informed the Louisa Board of Supervisors in February 1978 that Virginia Vermiculite would begin constructing its processing plant "within a matter of days." Mining by Virginia Vermiculite, Inc.—now Virginia Vermiculite, Ltd. (VVL)—"could begin at any time." Starting slowly in November 1978, operations soon ramped up to more than 60 percent capacity. By April 1979 the *Central Virginian* proudly announced, "Richest Vermiculite Deposit in World Being Mined in Green Springs."[23]

On August 11, 1980, Judge Merhige invalidated Green Springs' landmark status. He based his opinion on violations of due process as guaranteed by the Fifth Amendment and the Administrative Procedures Act. Echoing criticism leveled by Sansom and Thomas Lyall in public hearings, the judge found that Interior had failed to follow its own guidelines, that the criteria used were vague, and that the department had failed to inform the public of the criteria being used to establish landmark status before holding hearings. Ironically, the basis for Merhige's decision rested on the same charge that HGSI had leveled at Louisa's courthouse crowd for a decade—excluding the voices of affected parties. This time, however, those affected parties were Robert Sansom, VVL, and vermiculite-rich Green Springs landowners.[24]

Rubbing salt into the wound, Judge Merhige relied upon a series of precedents brought by citizens' groups like the Environmental Defense Fund. Rejecting Interior's defense that Virginia Vermiculite had not actually been harmed by the district's landmark status, the judge cited the Fourth Circuit's decision (overturning his own decision) in *Ely v. Velde* as an example of the federal government's extensive reach. VVL "need not speculate about the Department's intentions to utilize the protective measures available to it," the opinion underscored, "after having experienced the Department's effort at preventing vermiculite mining in the District, coupled with those aimed at blocking the construction of the state prison facility." The judge ordered Secretary Andrus to promulgate substantive and procedural regulations that would "articulate meaningful standards" for reviewing landmark candidates.[25]

Judge Merhige did reject VVL's claim that there was no history in Green Springs, but could not resist stating that the court was "troubled ... by the Department's assertion that a 'district' the size of Manhattan can be a historic 'site' in spite of the absence of any significant commemorative event or historical person associated with it." Evidently the growing appreciation within the academic and historic preservation community of the relationship between architecture and its surrounding landscape as a valuable lens through which to interpret the nation's history had not yet penetrated Judge Merhige's courtroom.[26]

The *Bergland* decision had national implications. The *New York Times* stated that the decision threatened "efforts to preserve thousands of historic sites and buildings across the country." Rae Ely was more colorful, telling Ben Franklin that the decision would "bastardize retroactively every historic landmark designation in the country. Not one of them is now safe from challenge." As one legal journal put it, albeit a bit less dramatically, the decision exposed "preservation actions to invalidation on procedural grounds," posing "a significant threat to the success of historic preservation regulation."[27]

Advocates for a broad range of facilities and activities, some in the private sector like Sansom, some charged with building roads and airports or disposing of waste in the public sector, and some in the voluntary sector who sought to site facilities that were considered "undesirable," like homeless shelters and drug treatment centers, were beginning to push back against neighborhood-based citizen activists. A few months before the *Bergland* decision, the Newport News *Daily Press* used an acronym that labeled this pattern. Buried on page 23 of this local newspaper, the article quoted a retired Atomic Energy Commission official discussing the technical likelihood of an effective solution to the nuclear waste challenge. The prospects were good, as long as the "nimby (not in my backyard)" syndrome was eliminated. Though this was one of the first times the acronym appeared in print, it would soon be deployed to disparage a broad swath of political engagement as self-interested.[28]

Rae Ely's first response to the *Bergland* decision was damage control—a "great big showy press conference.... I did exactly what I've always done. I said . . . we're going to appeal this, I was extremely self-confident and everybody believed me, what they always do. And I knew that we had zero chance of success on appeal—I knew we were dead! But nobody else did."[29]

Rae also knew that HGSI had to avoid a public legislative battle because the Virginia congressional delegation would block her efforts. She soon met with an ally in the Department of the Interior counsel's office who convened a "pow wow." Somebody at the meeting pointed out that a related bill was already moving through Congress—President Carter's National Heritage Policy Act. The minute he mentioned it, there was a collective sigh of relief. "It was like a miracle," Rae recalled. "Everybody immediately recognized that an amendment reversing Merhige's decision could be yoked to the pending legislation."[30]

Rae's allies also agreed that the amendment should not come to the floor. It had to be introduced "at the very last minute, at midnight, in conference," just like the Ely Rider to the Mining in the Parks Act four years earlier. The bill now targeted for midnight conference treatment had encountered several obstacles since its introduction, especially at the April 1980 Senate hearings. By that time, Representative John Seiberling (D-Ohio), who had visited Hawkwood on several occasions, had introduced a House bill that sought similar ends by focusing on private ownership and restoration of historic properties.[31]

The phrase " 'historic preservation' has a musty elitist ring, conjuring images of well-meaning dowagers engaged in a white-glove cause," Merilyn Bethany wrote in the *New York Times Magazine*. However, Bethany believed that both bills embraced a kind of history that went "beyond the preoccupation with the scenes of American political history to include properties of importance to cultural, social and natural history." As Nellie Longsworth, president of Preservation Action, told the *Times*, "More people in this country have their roots in the industrial revolution than the Revolutionary War."[32]

The Senate quickly passed legislation by unanimous consent that contained the Green Springs midnight amendment. The Conference Committee's report made clear that its purpose was "to assure the continued validity of all National Historic Landmarks designated by the Secretary prior to the effective date of the legislation." The amendment addressed Judge Merhige's concerns about adequate notice and public participation in the approval process going forward. It also included language promoted by Representative Dick Cheney (R-Wyoming) requiring the consent of landowners before their property could be listed as a national historic landmark. Cheney's measures, however, did not apply to existing landmarks—like the Green Springs Historic District.[33]

Even potential allies were kept in the dark during the sausage-making. Although Rae was a member of Preservation Action, she was terrified that its young group of activist preservationists, who updated the status of the historic preservation bills daily, would discover plans for the midnight amendment. They would have supported the amendment, but Rae worried that "[i]f word had leaked out, [about] what we were doing, it would have spread like wildfire." Consequently, she was "tiptoeing around in the Capitol building" to avoid them.[34]

Jimmy Carter signed the legislation on December 12, 1980. Ben Franklin's story reported that the legislation "overcame a Federal Court decision regarded as a threat to hundreds of existing 'historic landmark' designations." Once again, HGSI overturned Judge Merhige's interpretation of the law—this time via congressional legislation rather than the Fourth Circuit Court of Appeals. Bob Sansom, who at the time was part of President-elect Ronald Reagan's transition team, called the action "a travesty of justice," complaining to the *Times* that neither he nor others who fought this through the courts had even known that Congress was considering this matter. The final chapter of the saga was written by Judge Merhige himself, who ruled that the new law made it "plain" that Congress had acted legitimately to "shelter landmarks." The Green Springs Historic District once again was a national historic landmark.[35]

For Rae, the episode ended with a compliment from an unanticipated source. She reported to a friend that "[m]y little ole bill that sailed through Congress . . . may prove to be one of the great coups of my life." Even Judge Merhige acknowledged her successful coup when she ran into him at UVa Law School a few months later. She was "bopping along and here comes Merhige—he always dressed like a peacock, you know. He'd wear teal blue trousers and a turquoise shirt." The judge looked up and said, "Rae Ely!" He then laughed out loud and told Rae, "I've got one thing to say to you: I want you to know that I'm saving my seat for you, I'm gonna keep it warm for you whenever you are ready to come up here and get on the bench."[36]

Robert Sansom wrote his own postscript a decade later in a pamphlet that seethed at the injustice he had endured. *US vs. NPS* charged that the

"National Park Service has mounted an attack on Virginians; not a frontal assault, but a cancer that is eating at the life, liberty and pursuit of happiness Thomas Jefferson proclaimed." Among other overheated claims, the pamphlet charged that the Advisory Council on Historic Preservation wanted to herd "housing into trailer camp-like concentrations . . . which would make Joseph Stalin proud."[37]

A case study that documented NPS's strong-arm tactics purportedly written by Sansom was titled "Historic Green Springs: Where Preservationists Cut Their Teeth." Property owners, the Board of Supervisors, and the mining companies "thought they had won" after Merhige's ruling in *Bergland,* Sansom recounted. "But in secret, without hearings or even notice, the lame duck 1980 Congress put 14,000 acres of Green Springs back on the National Landmarks list in December 1980 using the phony argument that . . . [the] decision might lead to the undoing of all the NPS's procedurally flawed designations nationwide." Even though Congressman Dick Cheney believed that he had headed off prospective "frivolous area designations" in 1980, by 1991, Sansom warned Secretary of Defense Cheney that Saddam Hussein was a "conquerable foe of individual rights compared to the NPS and the preservationists."[38]

By then NIMBYs were everywhere. Self-described housewife Lois Marie Gibbs's campaign to spotlight the toxic calamity at Love Canal—in Niagara Springs, New York—in the late 1970s often served as the model for citizen activists in the 1980s. The *New York Times* first used the phrase "NIMBY syndrome" in a 1983 article about hazardous waste sites. That syndrome grew into a "movement" in William Glaberson's 1988 feature story in the *Times.* Glaberson, for instance, described a thirty-eight-year-old small business owner who believed that a trucking company planned to start dumping toxic waste across the road from her. The first thing that went through her mind when she heard that the company had purchased the land were "images of the poison leaching out of the ground at Love Canal." Glaberson did not limit NIMBYism to the "NIMBY movement." He explored the NIMBY "mood . . . syndrome, and gridlock," amounting to the "age of the NIMBY." In Green Springs, citizen activists battled Robert Sansom long before NIMBY was a syndrome, movement, or even an acronym.[39]

Whatever such groups were called, cooperating with the NPS, Sansom warned, would lead to control by "national government bureaucrats who are managed by national pressure groups financed by rich people whose motives are to lock up large areas and deny economic opportunity to others who: (a) have not inherited their wealth, and (b) are part of the tax-paying (as opposed to the not-for-profit) enterprises and families that make America free and productive." Working with elite insiders, pulling strings, denying due process, and operating behind the scenes were some of the very charges that HGSI had leveled at the county and state officials they originally challenged. The citizens' group had forged alliances at the national level and beaten a highly skilled Washington insider at his own game. Sansom sought to even the playing field with litigation, only to be caught flat-footed again by Ely—a replay of the Mining in the Parks legislation. Sansom, who earlier in his career had backed progressive land-use legislation and conducted business around the world, was now defending the kind of "local control" that Richard Nixon envisioned when he advocated a "New Federalism." Like Nixon, Sansom was also tapping genuine grassroots class antagonism toward outsiders who meddled with long-standing local prerogatives, from land use to public education. And like Nixon and Reagan after him, political momentum was on his side, in spite of Ely's midnight amendment.[40]

Fifteen years after that amendment, Sansom wrote to Congressman Don Young (R-Alaska), chair of the House Committee on Resources. "I read with interest the article about you in *Beef Today*," the letter began, endorsing Young's concerns about the Endangered Species Act. He then abruptly transitioned to the 1980 Historic Preservation Act amendment, which, as he explained, overturned a decision by a Federal district court judge and violated the property rights of landowners. Whatever this had to do with endangered species, it did demonstrate that Bob Sansom, like Rae Ely, was tenacious. Like Ely, Sansom was not bashful about litigating, even if his successful legal assault on historic Green Springs had been overturned by an act of Congress. And like Ely, Sansom understood that no matter how local the dispute, success at the Federal level was often the key to victory. Whether 14,000 acres of history or a few dozen acres of vermiculite, the distinction between neighborhood and nation was increasingly difficult to discern.[41]

22

Wife or Environmentalist?

MOMENTARILY ENSNARING PETER GRACE, consummating Green Springs' easement donation to the Department of the Interior, and besting Robert Sansom in multiple Federal arenas occurred against the backdrop of the deteriorating relationship between Rae and Hiram Ely. They continued living at Hawkwood, with the bickering mitigated to some extent by Hiram's long visits to his daughter in Florida and Rae's busy schedule. However, In May 1976, shortly after the W. R. Grace & Co. shareholders' meeting in Boston, Rae told Hiram that they could either resolve their differences and live in the same household or separate. Rae wrote to Hiram again in June. "As I have watched this ship of ours crashing on the rocks, I have known that my story of why it foundered, would have to be told. . . . Like a dying suffering animal, the great union that was Hiram and Rae needs now to be put to as painless a death as possible."[1]

Rae was no feminist, if that meant participating actively in the second-wave feminist movement that publicly fought sexist institutions. Nor were her views shaped, like those of so many other white middle-class women at the time, by participating in consciousness-raising groups, transforming what previously had been categorized as personal shortcomings into broader critiques of the gendered way in which power was structured in society. Nevertheless, she *was* becoming a "liberated woman": actively engaged as an equal (in her own mind) in many male-dominated worlds; balancing her work with child care; and demanding equality in her marriage. As Rae imbibed many of the liberating influences from the 1970s, Hiram doubled down on his vision of the relationship he believed he had consummated when he married Rae in 1962, in which, to use the military jargon Hiram preferred, the wife reported to her commanding officer—the husband.

A good example of Rae's "liberation" was the decision to apply to the University of Virginia School of Law in 1980, when women were still a distinct minority of the student body. Not many of the women who applied were Rae's age, and no student, male or female, had been accepted for years without a college degree. Rae's application summed up in one sentence the reasons she applied: in May 1970, "everything was instantly rearranged. . . . I found myself where I always longed to be—out of the kitchen and into the courtroom."[2]

At 6 a.m. on January 28, 1982, as her second term in law school began, the phone rang in Rae's Charlottesville apartment. "The house is on fire," the Louisa County dispatcher told her. Rae collapsed on the floor but soon headed to Green Springs. From I-64, a good fifteen minutes before reaching Hawkwood, she could see "a funnel of pitch-black smoke going way up into the sky; it was the most sickening sight. And I started just praying that the tower would still be standing." It was.[3]

Rae's 1976 ship-crashing-on-rocks letter to Hiram attached a four-page "story" of Rae's evolution as a woman—a narrative separate and independent from Hiram. Even though Rae was sorry that their marriage did not work out, she was not sorry "that I grew up. Grew into an individual, thinking person who wanted a little more out of life than just whatever reward might have been mine for having devoted my entire being and existence to trying to please an octogenarian friend." Besides raising their children and becoming an accomplished "hostess," Rae had become "a competent and highly respected woman, known for dedication and integrity." She achieved this "without the benefit of an 'education' " or "cashing in" on Hiram's position.[4]

Nor were her accomplishments purely civic: she had significantly contributed to the "family fortune." Finding Hawkwood, "accepting a greatly reduced standard of living" to improve it, "working successfully to maintain the integrity of . . . the whole neighborhood where it is situated and researching and promoting the property so that it is now recognized as being one of the most important country houses in America and of immense value, have caused the family's net worth to be increased several times over."[5]

Over the past decade, millions of women had begun to question their status and, by the mid-1970s, demand an equal partnership in relationships and full citizenship outside the home. They demanded recognition for the financial contributions they made to their families whether they held "paying jobs" or not. They challenged long-standing hierarchical gendered relations. As Rae wrote Hiram, "You constantly accuse me of being 'bossy' if I dare open my mouth to indicate what I would like or what my opinion is, or God Forbid, I dare take issue with you. 'Bossy' is a joke! What the children and I live under in this family, is *tyranny!*"[6]

In August 1976, a few months after the Louisa County BOS rezoned a large portion of the county's agricultural land "industrial," Hiram informed Rae that he was ending "the whole arrangement as rapidly as possible." His "decision to terminate this unhappy and unnatural business permanently ... is the kindest thing you could ever do for us," she responded. "This ain't the Army, you know. You may think you are 'more equal' than the others in your family, but no one else does. ... We will grow and flourish and find a new life where we can breathe free and be who we are."[7]

The battle would now be prosecuted through lawyers and the courts. Hiram filed for divorce in November 1976 but quickly withdrew this complaint. Over the next couple of years both parties would file for divorce, only to withdraw the motion or in one instance endorse the court's stay of a divorce decree. Although that stay was lifted in October 1980 when Rae and Hiram were finally divorced, legally severing the bond of marriage was but a small part of the tortured relationship that endured for years.[8]

The divorce did not settle who owned jointly held property, nor how to divide their most valuable asset—Hawkwood—which in 1980 was assessed at over $1 million. It did not settle who would manage the historic house and the rental properties on the estate. Like it or not, Rae and Hiram were business partners. Neither could afford to buy out the other; neither partner trusted the other to manage their jointly owned property.

Another unsettled question was Hiram's obligation to Rae for "separate maintenance" of her and the kids. Even though Hiram withdrew his initial petition for a divorce, the couple continued to live separately, prompting Rae to petition for financial compensation. The court issued a decree of separate maintenance in July 1977 and adjusted that decree over the years in response to changing circumstances. Each adjustment was contested.[9]

In September, Judge Vance Fry, the same man who had approved vermiculite mining in Green Springs ten months earlier, issued a revised decree of separate maintenance that awarded Rae custody of the three children and specified Hiram's monthly financial maintenance obligation. The judge also declared that Hiram was responsible for managing Hawkwood and was entitled to keep the net profits from it. Fry also decreed the parties would "attempt to agree on a division of all the personal property in the residence at 'Hawkwood.'" Trusting Rae and Hiram to agree on anything proved to be a mistake; dividing personal property, managing Hawkwood, and partitioning their joint equity in Hawkwood roiled the relationship and the Louisa County court system for years. Rae summed up the situation elegantly: "I am in an interesting state of limbo. I am the *undivorced*; the divorced-undivorced."[10]

Soon after Rae and the children moved from Hawkwood to a small furnished house in Charlottesville, Hiram's attorney charged that Rae was still "occupying space" at Hawkwood that "interfered with Colonel Ely's use and enjoyment of the premises." On December 1, 1977, Rae was arrested, fingerprinted, and booked by the Louisa County sheriff for what she claimed was simply attempting to oversee the care of her own property. And so it went regarding personal property and management of Hawkwood—for a decade.[11]

Five months after the arrest Rae charged that Hiram was using his discretion over Hawkwood's management to force a settlement about their personal property. "What will be next?" Would he threaten to paint the parlor in red enamel unless Rae forfeited monthly support? "Perhaps he will threaten to burn down one of our fine ... buildings if I keep sending him the children's medical and dental bills."[12]

Rae then claimed that Hiram rented out the main villa to unsavory tenants. "I will not stand by while you allow strangers and particularly unmarried ones to shack-up in my house, use my furniture, dishes and personal belongings ... and fornicate in my bed." The next day Rae informed Hiram that she and the kids would be moving back to the main house at Hawkwood. As threatened, Rae took Hiram to court, adding several other claims, including the charge that Hiram's "disposal" of nine purebred Shetland ponies owned by the children "caused them worry, sorrow and anguish and is a breach of ... responsibility as a parent." Those ponies, Rae informed the court, had been pets. Yet Hiram "did dispose of his children's beloved pet ponies in an unknown and secretive manner." On June 22 the renters called the sheriff to remove Rae and her kids from Hawkwood. In fear of "bodily harm and physical removal from their home," Rae claimed that she and the kids "were required to call neighbors to the home and remain barricaded in defendant and cross-complainant's bedroom for more than twenty-four hours."[13]

On August 21 Hiram wrote to Rae to end the "flibber-de-jibbity atmosphere" once and for all. A divorce, which Hiram insisted Rae had often talked about, would allow her to become a completely "separate individual," to "gain the freedom to go your own way which you have seemed so anxious for, independent of me and able to develop your own individuality to the utmost." He insisted that "the emotional bangle we have been through had had so many trying times that as two separate and untied persons we can proceed our own ways." Rae had neglected her wifely responsibilities. "When I married you," Hiram confessed, "I wanted a wife, not an environmentalist. A wife has enough to do to look after her husband's needs and those of the family."[14]

He also charged that Rae had not followed the rules established by the head of the household—the man. Hiram explained his own responsibilities in an extended naval metaphor. "As Captain of the Ship I have many times—in the Ordnance Corps, in the Bell Labs, in my families—had to establish the rules; anyone who cannot follow the rules can get off the ship, but I cannot have aboard those who pull in opposite directions to the ship's course." Hiram would continue sailing the ship according to his principles. Sadly, Rae had "developed into a person not capable of being the wife that I hoped I was getting in 1962."[15]

Rae responded that she was not interested in developing her "individuality —it has been [developed] for a long time." Perhaps Hiram was reading too many "women's" magazines. Instead, he should admit that "you simply want to dump your family because you're bored with us and are tired of the financial responsibility since you have been unsuccessful in your efforts to bend and intimidate us into a submissive and subservient role, and have us pretend that you are doing an adequate and competent job as you play your game of Household Lord and Master." Rae refused to be dismissed, "like you discarded our ponies without a flicker of conscience."[16]

Still, she balked, asking Hiram to "get rid of your destructive bill of divorce. . . . Let your heart soften and start learning to love again." She backed up this appeal in court, albeit with less florid language. Even though Rae had never gone to college, she served as her own defense attorney. The first line of her trial memorandum stated that "complainant Rae H. Ely does not wish or desire a divorce and has . . . requested that this Court not grant a divorce."[17]

The court ultimately did issue a divorce decree, but simultaneously stayed its implementation until further notice. According to Rae, Hiram agreed to stay the decree because after the judge calculated the percentage of Hiram's income that Rae would receive, "it was almost laughable . . . [H]e realized he couldn't afford to get rid of me." Suddenly, Rae recalled, Hiram's lawyer decided that maintaining the status quo was not such a bad idea after all. Besides the continued support under the separate maintenance decree, Rae surmised, "what I also get is my husband back. He now doesn't want a divorce."[18]

Rae agreed to the stay, in part, because a divorce would have deprived her of the military benefits to which she was entitled through her marriage to Hiram. More significantly, implementing the order would have required the sale of Hawkwood. While she undoubtedly would have benefited financially from her share of such a sale, "the *last* thing I need, given the posture of the Green Springs situation, is for Hawkwood to be sold."[19]

Indeed, Rae did her best to keep the proceedings confidential. Whatever her other reasons, political opponents would have feasted on the portion of her legal memo that articulated Rae's financial contributions to the value of Hawkwood. It stated that the property was worth many times the original purchase price thanks to Rae's work to "preserve the integrity of the immediate neighborhood and protect Hawkwood from incompatible encroachment," which had increased its value between six- and eightfold.[20]

In the midst of public battles and her collapsing marriage, Rae took the first step toward realizing a dream she had harbored for some time: going to law school. For a woman thirty-seven years old, the mother of three, without a single college credit to her name, it would not be an easy journey. Rae, however, relished climbing steep paths. As the property guys in the National Park Service were fighting a rear-guard action to forestall administering the Green Springs easements, in the midst of a messy divorce, Rae applied to St. John's, the "great books" college in Annapolis, Maryland.

One recommender, Rich Collins, chair of the Division of Urban and Environmental Planning in the UVa School of Architecture, asked: "Have you ever known anyone who you felt might be an attorney, or have an advanced degree in the humanities or the arts, or possibly in government or economics reveal to you that she only had a high school education?" Ben Franklin stated that in a struggle "won by the underdog preservationists, she learned quickly, acquiring such a grasp of environmental law that corporate counsel came to regard her as a nimble and awesome adversary and universities and law schools sought her widely as a lecturer." Calling her a "doyen of pioneering environmental and preservation law," Franklin noted that landmark cases bore her name, adding that important provisions of state and Federal law "ought to, because she put them there." The reporter even invented a word to describe Rae—"striven." All this drive, talent, and accomplishment "comes in a high-voltage container. Altogether, quite a bundle." Rae was accepted at St. John's and joined the small group of other students who enrolled in the winter term of 1979.[21]

With Sherri off to Friends World College on Long Island, Addison, fourteen, went back to live with Hiram at Hawkwood and attended a private school in Charlottesville. Eleven-year-old Todd moved to Annapolis with Rae, where he attended public school. They lived in an apartment on the top floor of a historic three-story building, a block and half from the St. John's campus. Todd's transition was not easy. Already skilled at multitasking, Rae balanced full immersion in Greek with calls from school about her son shooting peas across the cafeteria. In an era before grade inflation, facing stiff competition from talented classmates, Rae's GPA at the end of three semesters was a respectable 3.17. No number could capture what St. John's meant to her. "It was another world." Rae "was just picked up and dropped into a warm and happy environment. . . . It was an adventure."[22]

Even without an education in classics, Rae had long ago mastered quid pro quos. The one that proved most valuable to both partners grew out of her friendship with Joel Weingarten. Rae described him as "a chubby, nineteen-year-old very Jewish chap" who looked at her "through squinty eyes." Rae assumed that to a dedicated Zionist like Joel, her "fancy jewelry and white Mercedes . . . represented everything that was wrong with the world."[23]

As it turned out, "we each had what the other needed." Joel remembered that their close relationship was built upon complementary skills and talents. "We, basically together, were able to fill each other's gaps." Rae was struggling with Euclidian equations and Joel, whose father was a mathematician, had inherited a gift for the subject. Rae had the contacts that "such a Zionist as he needed." After a word to the wise from an assistant dean who informed Joel that Rae could use a little help with math, he delivered the quid, spending long hours preparing Rae to present propositions in "Euclid"—the freshman math class. Rae feared she would never get it. "[D]on't worry," Joel assured her, "I've worked in the past with the developmentally disabled." Just as he realized how that sounded, Rae cackled, "Joel, you will be perfect for this."[24]

The quo also began during those sessions. Joel knew that "when you were around Rae, you know, she'd be getting phone calls . . . telling me about some of her adventures in Virginia . . . lobbying and trying to push litigation." Rae also introduced Joel to Ben Franklin. The undergrad had never met a journalist before, let alone a reporter of Franklin's stature. Joel was captivated by this rumpled, hard-boiled, fifty-something man of the world. "He truly fit the stereotype of an old-fashioned newspaper man," Joel recalled. "Could belt down a drink, could tell you an off-color joke, didn't put up with any B.S., had seen it all . . . great at telling a story, very down to earth." Plus, he was a wordsmith. Before Franklin headed out to cover the nuclear reactor meltdown at Three Mile Island in Pennsylvania, he wrote on the white board at the *Times*'s Washington bureau, "not here, gone fission."[25]

At Rae's urging, Joel drafted a letter to the *Times* reporter about Israel's proposed peace accord with Egypt. Rae "had it vetted in advance, as we lobbyists do." One Sunday morning, she heard thunderous knocking at her door. Answering, Rae thought Joel was having a heart attack. Ashen-faced, he stood there with the newspaper in his hand. The *New York Times* had published his letter under the headline "Prelude to the Destruction of Israel," a week after the signing of the Camp David Peace Accords.[26]

What began as a transactional relationship soon blossomed into a warm friendship that paid pragmatic dividends. Six months after Joel's letter to the *Times*, he alerted Rae to the recently established Truman Scholarship Program passed by Congress to award individuals who demonstrated outstanding potential for public service. Joel and Rae both applied for and received this prestigious scholarship. A recommendation letter from Patrick Conklin, acting director of the Federal Executive Institute and president-elect of the American Society for Public Administration, called Rae one of the nation's "hidden resources." And one of the two best students of "applied democracy" that he had worked with in his thirty-year career. Conklin recounted his discussions with Rae about ways in which citizens' groups could "battle with city hall." He was particularly impressed with Rae's grasp of "our complex intergovernmental policy system."[27]

The way that Joel learned that he received a Truman Scholarship confirmed that Rae deserved one as well. Even though nobody knew he was lobbying in D.C., a Senate page announced that there was a call for a Mr. Weingarten. Surprised, Joel picked up the Senate phone to hear Rae's voice. "Joelie, are you sitting down?" she asked. "I'm not, but how did you find me?" "That doesn't matter," she continued. "Are you sitting down?" Finally, she told him that they both had won Truman Scholarships. Forty years later, Joel seemed more impressed that Rae had tracked him down in a Senate cloakroom than by the exciting news she delivered.[28]

Rae raced toward a career in law. In a move that Hiram might have viewed as more evidence of "hurry sickness," she capitalized on the Truman Scholarship to apply to the University of Virginia School of Law. Collapsing the standard Truman timetable, she skipped her last two years of college along with the undergraduate degree that came with them. Rae explained to the admissions committee why she was applying under the Law School's rarely used "special student" procedures. "There comes a time in the life of everyone when those dreams long-held . . . must be either brought to fruition or forever laid aside." Growing up in the South in the 1940s and 1950s, she had been discouraged from going beyond high school. Marriage at eighteen, raising three children—they take a long time to grow up—and managing a large farm all but ended the dream. The battle against the prison, then mining, changed that. From that point on her life had been "devoted to learning the law through practical means—in the courtroom, at the side of capable lawyers, in the role of litigant in issues of public interest." At the time Rae was actively engaged in three cases. Not sure she was "special," she was certainly different.[29]

Rae's appeal was directed toward a distinguished jury—the entire Law School faculty—and she mounted a full-scale lobbying campaign. Law School Professor A. E. Dick Howard was the self-acknowledged "spear-carrier" for the operation. Howard joined the faculty in 1964 and could not recall any other special students being accepted between that time and 1980. Although the number of women enrolled at UVa began to rise in the 1970s, climbing to roughly one-third of the 1980 entering class shortly after the *Virginia Law Review* named its first female editor in chief, letters supporting Rae reflected some of the obstacles that women faced at the time. Emeritus Professor T. Munford "Munny" Boyd offered a sobering glimpse when he wrote that he considered Rae to be "one of the smartest, as well as one of the most attractive women I have ever known," adding for good measure that he had been "fortunate in knowing a number of ladies who would deserve those two adjectives." Other supporters chose their compliments more carefully but clearly believed that Rae's reputation for being a tenacious advocate for causes needed a bit of polishing.[30]

Admissions Committee Chair Tom Bergin was Rae's strongest advocate after Howard. Professor Bergin had met Rae when she asked him for advice on drafting easements during the prison fight. He was a persuasive ally, citing extensive evidence supporting his assessment that Rae would be a "corking-good" law student. Bergin felt compelled, however, to address the fact that Rae could come on very strong; she "somehow has gotten the reputation of being the Tigress of Green Springs." He then devoted the rest of the paragraph to a tortured defense of what might have served as compliments for a male candidate—save the suffix attached to tiger. "She is not a timid creature. Nor is she a diffident one. The word 'aggressive' is, I think, too strong a word to use to describe her; yet, 'forceful' is bit too week [sic]." Summing up, Bergin stated, "Rae Ely, it must be said, has the heart of a battler. She is not all daisies and ladylike gentleness. But who in hell cares about that?" It is difficult to imagine that so much effort had ever been devoted to parsing the distinctions between aggressive and forceful for male candidates.[31]

Professor Howard did not need to throw his spear at the faculty meeting. Bergin strongly endorsed admitting Rae, as did all the faculty on the committee. The sentiment outside the committee was not unanimous, however. Charles Goetz was one professor who spoke and voted against admitting Rae. "I thought that it was the classical case of somebody who might have been meritorious but was just well-connected," Goetz explained. "She had letters from . . . big-wigs all around the state of Virginia." Others were opposed as well, but the faculty ultimately decided that admitting Rae was a good bet. She entered law school in August 1980.[32]

Rae did not impress anybody as the best student in her classes. But Howard, the most complimentary of her instructors, reported that she was "never over her head." Rae was in his constitutional law class, and perhaps because there was a significant public policy component, she was more attuned to the material compared to torts or contracts. Howard recalled that "she was quick to speak up . . . She seemed to love it, she had an obvious passion for the . . . law, certainly for public law."[33]

While Rae's advocacy fueled and schooled that passion, her preservation battles undoubtedly took time she might otherwise have devoted to her studies. Rae's first semester in law school coincided with her successful lobbying effort to restore Green Springs' landmark status after Judge Merhige overturned it—that's why she had to solve the problem in "five minutes." There were also maternal responsibilities. The Truman Scholarship subsidized a three-bedroom apartment down the block from the Law School where she lived with Addison, Todd, Sherri (when she was home from college), and Zeke the ferret. Living next to the Law School meant frequent half-hour drives to Hawkwood to ensure it was being properly maintained. Professor Goetz recalled seeing Rae at the Law School one day in boots and mud-splattered jeans. She had just birthed a lamb. In fact, she might have brought the lamb to his class.[34]

A bitterly cold day had followed a blizzard the night before the fire at Hawkwood, making it difficult even to get in the driveway. Rae never forgot the vision of Hawkwood as the truck struggled up the driveway: the villa was "wrapped in bright orange flames." The fire had probably burned for hours before it was reported. Motorists who saw the flames from Route 15 assumed that the firefighters were already on the scene. Colonel Ely, who had been asleep upstairs, was awakened by the smoke in his room around 5 a.m. He could not get out of his bedroom door but was spotted leaning out of his window by alert drivers who found a ladder, climbed up, and pulled Hiram to safety. Had they gotten there fifteen minutes later, Colonel Ely probably would have died that morning.[35]

The fifty firefighters were handicapped by the elements as well as the blaze's head start. Although some of the local volunteers knew that there was a large pond on the property, they couldn't find it because it was covered by snow and ice. Once they located this source of water, they had to use chain saws to cut through the ice before they could tap into it. Ice was not the only element that snarled the long hoses. Rae's beloved Newfoundlands decided that this was the perfect time to play "tug-of-war."[36]

Still wearing his one-piece long underwear, Hiram was sequestered in one of the cottages. A few weeks later he moved to Tampa to live near his daughter and eventually bought a condo there. Writing to Addison on February 17, Hiram apologized for having left "without seeing you and the others for a better farewell," explaining that he "had to conform somewhat to the needs of others and to the legal situation." Hiram assured his son that he was very fond of him, his brother, and Sherri, but he "had to leave Hawkwood like an old Indian moving to a new site with his possessions in a small bundle." Rae never saw him again.[37]

When Rae called the insurance company, she learned that Hiram had canceled the insurance on the estate five months earlier. Still, she went back to Charlottesville later that morning, missing only one class that day. "When your life is hanging in the breach you get very focused because I began to realize that it was all going to be up to me now and that having this opportunity at a law school was the biggest opportunity in the world." After attending class she returned to stand guard over the still-smoking ruins of the villa. Rae believed that one of her enemies might come with a bulldozer to get rid of the villa, and presumably Rae, once and for all. She set up a vigil in a cottage devoid of furniture and slept on the floor—with a gun and her Newfoundlands at her side. Preserving what was left of the villa turned out to be more than a full-time job. Several months after the fire, Rae took a year's leave of absence from law school.[38]

It was lawyers, not bulldozers, who soon arrived. Even though the estate lost more than half its value in the fire, neither Rae nor Hiram could afford to buy out their former spouse. When the judge ordered the property sold, Rae delayed the sale by charging Hiram with negligence. Hiram countersued, leveling the same charge against Rae. Ultimately those claims were dismissed or withdrawn.[39]

As the divorce proceedings and property settlement headed toward their second decade, there were more detours. For instance, Rae filed a motion demanding that Judge Harold Purcell and his son Charles, who was representing Hiram in the battle over Hawkwood, show why they should not be disbarred or disciplined for "dishonest, improper and unlawful conduct."

She also insisted that Judge Edward D. Berry disqualify himself because he let retired Judge Harold Purcell sit in the courtroom and pass notes to Charles. Her charges did not gain legal traction but did prolong the epic battle.[40]

Four years after the fire, Judge Berry was ready to end the litigation by auctioning Hawkwood. There were several problems, however. Public notice yielded just one offer, which was only half of the appraiser's assessed value. There was also the question of the sole bidder's identity: all of the board members and the sole shareholder of the Green Springs Cattle & Grain Farm were named Purcell. Charles Purcell, who had served for years as Colonel Ely's lawyer in the settlement litigation, had presided over the bid solicitation process as special commissioner. Green Springs Cattle & Grain's agent was Judge Harold Purcell.[41]

The single bid, if not the composition of Green Springs Cattle and Grain, was too much, even for Judge Berry. Rae told the judge that if the court was going to accept such a low bid, she wanted an opportunity to bid herself. After an eight-hour hearing in February 1986, the judge ruled that both Rae and Hiram had a week to submit bids, stipulating that the offers had to be at least 5 percent over the $305,000 offered by Green Springs Cattle. Berry also accepted Charles Purcell's explanation of why there was only one bid and why it was so low. Fear of litigation—a reasonable concern given Rae's reputation—was one factor. Continued deterioration of the property after the fire was another. The main culprits, according to a parade of neighbors, were the scenic easements and historical preservation restrictions on the villa and the land that encumbered its value. "And I'm thinking," Rae recalled, "good: let's have it worth nothing." They were "walking right into the trap. . . . Come on here, Brer Rabbit."[42]

As though scripted by Verdi or Puccini, the final act of the operatic love triangle featuring Rae, Hiram, and Hawkwood came down to a battle between those who claimed to be advancing a public good by improving the quality of life for many, and those who claimed to be advancing the interests of many by profiting from their property. In one aria, Rae explained that there were actually *two* markets in play. "One . . . is simply people who buy up land in Louisa County and aren't concerned about the property," she told the court. "The second are those handful of people who will make an attempt not to deprive the people of the United States of a unique piece of architecture, who are willing to spend the money to put a roof on the house and protect it."[43]

A March 2, 1986 *Richmond Times-Dispatch* article provided the libretto, describing Hawkwood's owners as "a feeble and bedridden Army colonel and inventor and his ex-wife, a tough-minded, sharp-tongued preservationist more than 40 years his junior." The couple was "embroiled in a messy divorce when, on January 27, 1982, the villa was destroyed by fire." The battle would end the next day, the deadline for each Ely to submit a bid on Hawkwood. Rae had submitted hers long before the deadline. It was exactly 5 percent higher than Green Springs Cattle's bid. Fifteen minutes before the court-ordered deadline, Hiram weighed in with a bid that topped Rae's by $5,000. Waiting offstage, Warner Granade, a neighbor of Rae's, spotted Hiram's bid and entered stage right to submit a new bid on behalf of Rae that topped Hiram's as the legal curtain fell.[44]

Berry had not only presided over years of the divorce case—he starred in some of the legal battles over land use in the historic district. The rest of the veteran Louisa cast was on stage as well. Richard Purcell momentarily occupied center-stage to plead that Judge Berry had erred in allowing additional bids after Green Springs Cattle submitted its offer. In a cameo appearance, W. W. Whitlock, who had opposed HGSI at every turn, appeared briefly to claw back $1,925 in appraisal and legal fees for the Purcells. In her swan song, Rae vowed to "have the roof on the house by the fall," belting out, "Hawkwood is a great American house. . . . By God, it's going back up, even if it takes me the rest of my life, and it probably will."[45]

The spotlight illuminated the now-charred Tuscan-style tower that captivated Rae Ely in 1967, reminding her of George Engel's villa on Bayshore Drive—a sanctuary that offered occasional relief from an abusive father. Hawkwood would remain Rae's sanctuary for the next four decades. That George Engel's house now serves as the clubhouse for the Coral Reef Yacht club in a Coconut Grove neighborhood overshadowed by high-rise luxury condominium buildings, while Hawkwood's reconstructed tower sits at the center of a national historic landmark district, speaks volumes about Rae Ely's determination to secure a home of her own and her dedication to preserving history.

23

A Silk Jungle

RAE ELY EVENTUALLY ESTABLISHED A LAW practice in the town of Louisa that was a "go-to" resource for citizens' groups. Those cases often entailed zoning controversies over siting unwanted facilities, from jails to power plants. She also handled a good number of domestic relations cases, representing women in the vast majority of them. She charged those clients who could pay, but her assistant could not recall Rae ever turning away a case if the client could not. One connection between both kinds of cases, he noted, was that "everything was a fight. . . . We didn't do contract work, we didn't do transactional work except maybe on the side as a way of generating some revenue. . . . The purpose of the firm was not to become a profit center; it was to battle the demons."[1]

In May 1991, fifteen years after Rae spent the day with Peter Grace in Boston, she decided "the time to move was at hand." She would go to the annual Grace shareholders' meeting. "Sitting at my desk at 4:00 in the afternoon and something said to me, 'Just get in your car and drive to Greenville, South Carolina.'" Rae asked herself, "[What] am I wearing? Cause I knew I had to pull it off. I knew today was the day I had to go get this couple thousand acres of land back." Fortunately, she was dressed for the occasion; she did go to Greenville; and she did pull it off.[2]

Rae believed that her personal appearance was a potent weapon. At shareholders' meetings, she "was always dressed very, very tastefully. Whereas the other women would be dressed . . . in plain suits, I would come in a *beautiful* silk dress that would stand out and have people say, 'oh, who is that?'" Referring to her meetings on Capitol Hill, for instance, Rae believed that there "was always this problem" of a young woman going in and expecting to be taken seriously, "when they weren't used to dealing with women, much less young women. So I had to dress and convey a sense of power . . . and presence, and kind of a 'don't mess with me.'" The trick "was to make people believe that you had power and wealth, simply by your very physical appearance. And this was all smoke and mirrors."[3]

Since Rae's last meeting with Peter Grace, Virginia Vermiculite, Ltd. had started mining in Green Springs. In the epic legal and legislative battles of the past two decades, the national landmark status of the historic district had been revoked and restored. Interior had accepted thousands of acres of donated conservation easements and the National Park Service was now administering them. One thing had not changed however: Grace still had not started mining vermiculite in Green Springs despite controlling more than 1,000 acres of land with the capacity to produce roughly 1.5 million tons of vermiculite concentrate.[4]

Sitting on all that Green Springs vermiculite was expensive. By 1990, Grace had paid over $1 million in advance royalties and estimated it would have to pay at least another $1 million over the next twenty years. Up to this point the executives at Grace had calculated that this investment was worth it since it might well drive VVL out of business. They had good reason to believe that the time was near: in the late 1980s, according to mine manager Ned Gumble, VVL was "running out of reserves" and could only find "bits and pieces" available for mining.[5]

Gumble approached Greg Poling, the general manager of Grace's specialty vermiculite unit, to let him know that Bob Sansom wanted to discuss "options for accessing Grace's vermiculite reserves in Virginia." Poling exhaled a sigh of relief in his confidential memo. "It appears that the long anticipated 'lease on life' of Virginia's [VVL's] reserves is finally running out." Still, Poling warned that VVL might acquire other properties, negating its need for Grace's reserves. Should VVL fail to find other reserves, however, Poling believed that Grace's competitor "could be forced to cease operations."[6]

The first meeting between Grace and VVL occurred on April 25, 1991, a month before Rae's last-minute decision to attend the shareholders' meeting in South Carolina. Bob Sansom was there along with Poling and Grace's manager of strategic planning. They discussed options that included an offer to buy all of Grace's Louisa reserves for $1.75 million or lease Grace's reserves for roughly $250,000 annually. Grace promised to take the options under advisement and set up a subsequent meeting to discuss its response.[7]

On the afternoon before the South Carolina shareholders' meeting, Rae drove the Mercedes straight to Greenville. Arriving at the meeting hotel at roughly 10 p.m. and figuring that Peter Grace would be out on the town, Rae told the bellhop she was supposed to meet Mr. Grace. After Ely described him, the bellhop confirmed that just such a man had gone out several hours earlier and had not yet returned. Rae positioned herself between the front door and the elevators. She only had to wait about a half an hour. Sure enough, several big cars pulled up and, as Rae had surmised, Peter Grace rolled in surrounded by women. Rae walked from couch to reception desk and smacked right into Peter, exclaiming, "*Well*, Mr. Grace, my goodness!" Flashing her most radiant southern gentlewoman smile, Rae continued, "I'll bet you don't remember me." Did he have "just a *little* minute" to talk to her? He sure did: "Why for you, honey, I *have* a little minute."[8]

"There's something you need to do," Ely told Grace. "'What is that, honey?'" (or it might have been "darling," Rae recalled). "You know all that land up in Green Springs we've been fussin' over all these years? . . . You need to just give it to my little group up in Green Springs; you need to just go ahead and give it to us. It's the only right thing to do." Peter Grace pondered and then said, "You know something? You are right! You are absolutely right. It's the thing we need to do." Incredibly, Rae then told the chairman of W. R. Grace & Co. that they didn't want to waste any more time—they should do it right then and there. Grace agreed: his "boys" were over in the bar. "You come on with me."[9]

Rae described the scene when she walked in with Peter. "There's these guys sittin' with their ties all undone hanging around their necks. . . . And he goes charging up to them—scared them to death—calls them by name and said, 'You all come on over here.' " Peter asked if they knew this lady. They did not. "This here is Rae Ely from Green Springs," he told them. "We've got some land up there in Green Springs in Virginia and I want you all to get busy and give it to her!" Stunned, one of the men blurted out that they did not know anything about Green Springs. That did not deter Peter Grace. "Well, she'll tell you about it . . . you just get together with her." At which point Rae told Peter Grace he was just the sweetest man. They kissed and hugged, and before he told everybody he was going to turn in for the night, he took aside two of his employees and told them: "You take care of this for her."[10]

Even the most aggressive activist would have declared victory and left well enough alone at this point, but Rae Ely knew better. "Come on, gentlemen," she said, "I've got the maps in my car." Rae went over the parcels that their boss had just asked them to give to the citizens' group that Grace had battled for two decades. One of the "boys" Grace tasked with the project, Executive Vice President Donald Kohnken, dutifully looked at the maps and told Ely that he would get back to her.[11]

Rae insisted appearances were a vital contributing factor to this victory. "That night in Greenville, where he was just falling all over himself? That's only because I was a really pretty girl, all dressed up." The pale green sueded silk dress with a fairly full skirt and the contrasting silk sash combined with the high-heeled sandals were very smart—perfect for a spring evening. "And of course," she added, "I always had my big, long red hair, all fluffed up."[12]

A long-term strategy, an ability to size up the individuals essential to achieving it, and the discipline to play the long game were crucial to Rae Ely's success. But those prerequisites also required an agent skilled at forging relationships and the performative elements that cemented those relationships. Before Rae's "hunch" about driving to Greenville, she had welcomed Grace's benign neglect of its holdings in Green Springs—especially since their approach implicitly denied over a million tons of vermiculite reserves to VVL. As Rae put it, "Grace is so huge, it's like a government. Somebody, somewhere, was just writing a check [for royalties] every . . . year. . . . It just went on automatic pilot. That was fine with me. Cause I knew one day I'd see the opening and I'd slide through it."[13]

That "opening"—W. R. Grace & Co. donating its land to HGSI—seemed like a moonshot, even after the secretary of the Interior publicly promoted the idea back in 1976. By then, Rae was used to biding her time. "Once Grace got hold of the land, what's the ultimate solution? I've got to get it. How am I going to get it? I can't buy it, I've got no money. So, they're going to have to give it to us." Rae believed that she was good at sizing up people. "It was very simple. Mr. Grace was a jovial, sweet—he didn't look sweet—but he was a sweet old Catholic. I understand the personality." There was hope.[14]

Grace counsel Mario Favorito had not thought about Green Springs for a long time before Kohnken's May 24, 1991 memo informed him about the Peter Grace–Rae Ely conversation. Based on his previous dealings with Rae, however, Favorito advised his colleague to proceed cautiously; the company should "politely declin[e] any invitation to place preservation easements on the Green Springs property at this time." Grace was now considering divergent options—one was doubling down on a decades-old request from the secretary of the Interior that Grace donate its land to HGSI; the other, selling their reserves to a competitor.[15]

On July 8, Grace officials offered to sell its Green Springs property and reserves to VVL for roughly $3.5 million, revealing at the same time that Rae Ely had approached Grace with the donation alternative. Poling's internal memo, drafted before the VVL meeting, made it clear that Grace's staff did not view Peter Grace's hotel lobby conversation as an iron-clad pledge. Although Poling mentioned that "Peter Grace received pressure from Mrs. Ely in recent months regarding Grace's properties in Virginia," donating reserves to HGSI was not listed as one of several options outlined by Poling.[16]

A third meeting between the competitors in September did not go well. Sansom refused to budge from his $1.75 million initial offer. Both parties left the final meeting believing that their adversary had negotiated in bad faith. Grace executives were miffed that Sansom essentially lowered his offer by adding new conditions to his original offer. By now, Sansom believed that Grace was merely going through the motions of a negotiation with VVL to establish a price that could be used for tax deduction purposes if the land was donated to HGSI.[17]

Grace's 1992 shareholders' meeting in Boca Raton, Florida, provided the ideal opportunity for Rae Ely to follow up on Peter Grace's pledge from a year earlier. There are no records of communications between Rae and the Grace executives before that meeting. It is likely that she recognized by May 1992 what Grace and VVL had long since understood. As a district court subsequently concluded: "The conjunction of VVL's depleting reserve situation with Grace's newfound interest in donating its properties presented, for the first time, the real possibility that Grace would leave Virginia and that VVL could run out of reserves." Although Grace's team hadn't gotten back to her over the course of the year, Rae was certain that they would meet with her because they believed she could pick up the phone and talk to Peter Grace. Rae could not recall exactly how she set up the meeting—it would not have been unusual for her simply to walk into an executive's office unannounced.[18]

She did recall in vivid detail the outfit she wore for the meeting. It was "a silk jungle of a wrap-around skirt, orange and gold and black—with a little bit of green. It had big cats peering out from its folds, right out of the Florida jungle—it was so perfect." Complementing the skirt was a brilliant orange and gold blouse. Black patent leather high heels and a bright white blazer finished it off. Though she had spent a career explaining the damage from mining, not to mention the asbestos sometimes contained in it, Rae greeted the men "like my dearest friends." We will never know if the jungle cats enhanced Rae Ely's cause, but the upshot of the meeting was to move the initiative forward by assigning it to Robert Walsh, a senior Grace official. In follow-up letters thanking Walsh and Kohnken, Rae congratulated Grace on its "snazzy new location," calling its move to Boca Raton "a masterstroke." She also invited both men to visit Green Springs.[19]

The donation option was gaining momentum inside W. R. Grace & Co. because selling its holdings to VVL at an acceptable price now seemed unlikely. A July 27, 1992 memo even estimated the value of a tax deduction for gifting land to HGSI and considered ways to maximize it. "Satisfies Ms. Ely and the local Historic Green Springs preservation society" was now listed in the "Advantages" column. Grace executives also kept a close eye on alternatives that Sansom's VVL might pursue in lieu of purchasing Grace's reserves. Rae Ely was watching as well. On August 2 she reported to the HGSI board that VVL had recently been seen at the county courthouse picking up an application for a conditional use permit to expand their operation. Although the portion of "Brandy Farm" that VVL was rumored to have procured was only twelve acres, Rae was afraid that mining Brandy would allow VVL to jump across the road to the Nininger property containing 1,457 acres. Combined, those vermiculite reserves would last up to eighty years.[20]

On September 2, VVL confirmed the rumors when it filed an application to mine on the Brandy property, located across the South Anna River from VVL's current operations. Bob Sansom had procured the vermiculite reserves that VVL desperately needed to stay in business in Green Springs. Denying a conditional use permit, or severely restricting the amount of vermiculite that could be mined on Brandy Farm, was the last line of defense for both HGSI and Grace.[21]

That is why Robert Walsh visited Green Springs the first week in September 1992. The tall, middle-aged executive with grey-streaked dark hair was a pleasant man with a good sense of humor, according to Rae. HGSI put him up at the Prospect Hill Inn, one of the few commercial businesses in Green Springs, housed in a plantation that had turned some of the old quarters of enslaved people into guest rooms. "We just wined him and dined him," Rae recalled, "and he was the happiest man in the world." Pausing, she added, "Unfortunately, he's the one who took all these notes."[22]

Walsh's notes summarized Grace's goals: 1) eliminating $1 million of future operating costs; 2) maximizing benefits from past expenditures; 3) keeping VVL from improving its competitive position; and 4) cooperating with HGSI. The corporate language about "keeping VVL from improving its competitive position," understated the crucial bond between the two frenemies: driving Sansom's company out of Green Springs. That is why Walsh was eager to find out just where "things stand on ... Green Springs attempts to stop Virginia [Vermiculite]."[23]

No wonder Rae found him to be pleasant—Grace now shared an agenda that she had pursued over two decades. Besides the favorable public relations and tax advantages that Grace might receive by donating its land to HGSI, Ely could be counted on to aid Grace's quest to prevent its competitor from mining. If a preservation group like Historic Green Springs, Inc. had not existed, the corporation might have invented one.

Things moved quickly on both sides of the budding alliance after Walsh's visit. "I believe we should get the long-standing issue behind us," Walsh urged in mid-September, "avoid the future expenses, and get the favorable P.R. value." Donating the land would generate "favorable publicity for Grace as a responsible citizen and friend of the environment and cultural history of Virginia." Because the vermiculite business was now less important to Grace strategically, it was "extremely unlikely that Grace will ever mine vermiculite in Virginia." Walsh recognized that "keeping the reserves out of the hands of an adjacent competitor" was now the objective. Doing so by doing nothing, however, would cost more than $1 million in pre-tax advance royalty payments over the next twenty years. "Rae Ely's pitch for twenty-years has been for Grace to donate its owned land and leased vermiculite rights to Green

Springs Historical Inc. [sic] and take a charitable donation." Walsh also believed that HGSI would likely be willing to assume the company's obligations, "including the future annual payments (thereby keeping the reserves off the market)." HGSI might prove crucial to defeating VVL's conditional use permit. "Rae Ely and friends are determined to take on Virginia Vermiculite in what she labels . . . 'the war of all holy wars.' Their war with Virginia Vermiculite and its owner, Robert Sansom, has been going on for years." Grace's own experience with HGSI had already demonstrated that the citizens' group could be a formidable opponent.[24]

The opening salvo in Rae's battle would be fired when HGSI reported some chemical spills at the VVL processing plant. "She intends to bring the State down on them," Walsh reported to his colleagues. In a reference to Grace's delicate position when it came to deploying the threat of toxic hazards as a tactic, he was quick to note that "[i]n past conversations, she has talked about bringing the issue of asbestos contamination of vermiculite in Virginia into this arsenal of arguments. I think I have convinced her that that is not a good idea."[25]

Walsh dutifully reminded his readers of the possible negative consequences, noting that there were property owners "who consider Ely to be a meddling devil." Although potential legal liability was never mentioned, he noted that "Virginia Vermiculite may argue that Grace and Green Springs have cooperated to their detriment." Taking warnings about meddling devils and collusion to heart, public relations staff excised from the press release a paragraph praising Rae Ely's multiple amicable meetings with Grace executives.[26]

Bob Sansom was no pushover. He "has some money in his family," Walsh cautioned, was a Rhodes Scholar, a White House Fellow, and "claims political connections." On balance, however, Walsh concluded, "the positive will far outweigh the negative": he recommended that Grace make an announcement the following week and clean up the details later.[27]

This left HGSI with a long to-do list. The day after Walsh sent his memo, Rae faxed him a list of chemicals purportedly used by VVL in its processing operations. Presumably "the world's largest specialty chemicals company"—Grace's tagline—would be able to identify violations of EPA rules. The *Central Virginian*'s headline captured the paradoxical nature of Grace's gift: "Company That Fought to Mine Gives Land, Rights to Opponent." Rae told the newspaper, "we are like old soldiers who have become friends since the battle is over." Peter Grace, in turn, expressed his happiness "to be in a position to protect our national heritage for future generations of Americans."[28]

The *Central Virginian*'s editorial page was less flattering, charging that the landowners "who put their trust in W. R. Grace have been betrayed, and so has Louisa County." It asked why Grace had announced the gift "just a week prior to the time its main competitor is coming before the Louisa County Planning Commission seeking a permit to expand its operation." Coverage in the *Richmond Times-Dispatch* and *Washington Post* quoted Rae praising Grace as "a company that puts its money where its mouth is." The PR team must have been pleased with the positive publicity surrounding the donation, although they probably winced when the *Post,* once again, mentioned that vermiculite was used in cat litter.[29]

VVL's prospects looked grim in the winter of 1992. At a February board meeting in Hot Springs, Virginia, Ned Gumble reported depleting reserves and declining profitability. Nor did things look promising with the Louisa County Board of Supervisors. Gumble's recent conversation with County administrator Bill Porter had not ended well. Porter was tired of the sniping between VVL and the National Park Service. "You fucked up," Porter told Gumble, by not allowing the NPS to visit because it conveyed the impression that there was something to hide. VVL and the NPS were "acting like the PLO and the Israelis shooting missiles at each other. . . . [I]f the Supervisors were voting on something today, you don't stand a chance in hell." Gumble claimed that the problem was Bob Sansom: he "wanted the [historic] district to be gone."[30]

Ned Gumble's pessimistic assessment confirmed just how close Grace came to successfully executing its starve-them-out strategy. He later acknowledged that his company purchased its holdings in South Carolina around this time because "if we run out of reserves in Virginia . . . we at least have some means of staying employed." Even though strangling VVL meant that Historic Green Springs, Inc. and the Department of the Interior might finally realize their goal of eliminating mining in the historic district, there was a gap in Grace's defensive perimeter that Robert Sansom ultimately drove a dump truck through: "Brandy B."[31]

During Grace's 1970s acquisition spree, the company leased Brandy Farm with a standard clause to pay royalties to the owners for any vermiculite mined. To seal the deal, Grace also agreed to maintain the buildings on a thirty-seven-acre portion of the land designated "Brandy B" as long as the owners lived there. Should Ann Hill Granger, who owned Brandy Farm, Ltd., move out, however, nobody else could occupy Brandy B without the explicit permission of Grace. When the Grangers moved to Williamsburg in 1984, Grace reduced its operating costs by permitting Brandy Farm, Ltd. to lease the entire farm (Brandy A + B) to a third party, which the Grangers soon did.[32]

Ned approached the Grangers in 1992 and told them: "we are running out of vermiculite." When he added that he was aware of the agreement with Grace, it "cracked the door open." On April 25, 1992, much to the consternation of W. R. Grace and Rae Ely, Virginia Vermiculite, Ltd. leased Brandy B and immediately began test drilling. VVL found the vermiculite reserves it had desperately been searching for; it now had to procure a permit from the BOS to mine them.[33]

With Grace's donation, the battle shifted to the Louisa County BOS, who by now, according to Rae, looked at her as though she "had some magical powers." Ned Gumble had very different memories. He was literally waking up with nightmares during the approval process. "I was responsible for twenty-five employees, and we were running out of material." Ned would send out the crew to mine in the recurring nightmare and they would come back and say, "There's nothing left."[34]

Rae was working hard to "provide the BOS with evidence of 'adverse [impact] to the health, safety and welfare of the adjacent properties.' " There was a problem, however. "This argument will be for naught," Ely insisted, "if we don't even have standing to raise the issue in the first place."[35] Public announcements were nice, but Grace better deed the property in a hurry. Grace agreed and began transferring property on November 30. Favorito might have been one of the few executives at Grace who could recall a similar moment in 1972, when W. R. Grace had stood before the BOS requesting that the very same land be rezoned to allow mining. Grace's property transfer allowed Rae to announce to the BOS: "I'm now [representing] the landowner of both properties between [VVL's] two operations—HGSI."[36]

Predictably, negotiations between HGSI and VVL to allow its dump trucks to rumble over land that lay between the mining company's newfound reserves and its old processing plant soon broke down. Two days before the BOS vote on a conditional use permit, W. W. Whitlock wrote to County administrator Porter informing him that it would obviously "be some time" before negotiations were concluded. He then asked the county to authorize up to thirty-five daily dump truck round trips along Route 22. The BOS complied, voting unanimously in January to grant VVL a conditional use permit that allowed thousands of dump truck trips annually.[37]

It was time for W. R. Grace & Co. to cut its losses. A February 23, 1993 memo from Greg Poling to Bob Walsh acknowledged that Grace's strategy had failed. The remaining property that Grace had not yet deeded to HGSI "was deemed significant only if Virginia Vermiculite's efforts to open a new mine on the adjacent . . . property was severely restricted by the pending use permit": it was time for Grace to withdraw as gracefully as possible.[38]

Not only had HGSI lost the battle to deny vermiculite reserves to VVL, the conditional use permit had imposed an easily avoidable burden on the historic district by routing dump trucks along a public road. VVL had been prepared, at significant cost, to construct a private road and bridge between its processing plant and its new source of raw material. That road, however, would have crossed the property that Grace deeded to HGSI in a last-ditch effort to strangle VVL. It was a bridge too far for Rae Ely, who refused to negotiate in good faith to allow this alternative route across property that the citizens' group now owned. Historic preservation proved to be a two-way street. Ely's all-or-nothing strategy in this case failed to drive VVL from Green Springs and, at least in the short-term, imposed additional burdens on the national landmark.

This did not mean she failed to appreciate the value of compromise, especially when it came to HGSI's relationship with W. R. Grace. In December 1993, the HGSI Board considered asking Congress to condemn VVL's mining "because of asbestos," citing the Mining in the Parks Act. The option was raised again at the January board meeting and the minutes capture HGSI's delicate relationship with its newfound patron, W. R. Grace. "Rae noted that at the time we had agreed with Grace that we would go easy on the asbestos problem. Yet asbestos is our best bet." Going easy on the potential health threat of asbestos was one of those difficult tradeoffs that HGSI endorsed as it pursued its long-term strategy of preserving the landmark district.[39]

On June 17, 1993 HGSI sought an injunction from the circuit court in Louisa to prevent VVL from mining Brandy B, claiming rights recently gifted by Grace. Sansom had begun test drilling without informing Grace, and Ely contended this violated Grace's (now HGSI's) agreement with Brandy Farm.

She cited evidence in the form of a 1984 Favorito letter to prove that mining by a third party was *not* permitted. Shortly after the HGSI Board met, Rae received an updated assessment of the lease from Favorito. Grace's counsel, who had no love for long-time competitor VVL, warned Rae that "although the position raised can be argued, it has a very slim chance of success." Grace never presumed to have any rights to the contested property, Favorito continued, "and I do not believe that the lease gives Grace or HGSI any rights to control what happens on the property." Years later Rae acknowledged that the *Historic Green Springs Inc. v. Brandy Farm, Ltd.* litigation was "Ely's folly," pursued out of sheer anger. "It was me having a fit of pique."[40]

VVL soon took advantage of other opportunities to ensure a steady supply of vermiculite. M. F. Peers's brother, A. D. (Icky) Peers, held an option to buy back, at essentially the 1973 price, a portion of the land he had once owned should Grace decide to sell or donate it. Because the land likely contained rich reserves of vermiculite that both HGSI and Grace hoped to keep out of VVL's hands, Grace had withheld the Icky Peers parcel when it donated the rest of its holdings to HGSI. With potentially millions of dollars of vermiculite reserves sitting under that land, Icky was understandably eager to exercise his option. Grace had been happy to keep him waiting on the chance that the BOS would restrict mining on Brandy B.[41]

Perhaps because HGSI was still litigating to stop VVL from mining on Brandy, Grace had not yet transferred this remaining Green Springs property. M. F., however, was not willing to wait any longer. "Here in Virginia," he wrote to Peter Grace on August 16, 1993, "we were raised to speak bluntly.... You and your company have done a horrible thing." W. R. Grace was killing his brother, M. F. explained. Icky had recently suffered a massive stroke and was now in a nursing home. This was the third time that he had been hospitalized "since your employee Greg Poling came here late last year to inform us that W. R. Grace was giving *our land* . . . to Historic Green Springs." Icky's first trip to the hospital was on the very day that Poling informed him of Grace's "gift" to HGSI. If anything happened to Icky, M. F. warned, it would be Grace's fault.[42]

Noting that he had worked for Grace for two decades and that he had borne the brunt of multiple lawsuits on Grace's behalf so the corporation could maintain a "low profile," M. F. told Peter Grace that his company was *"giving away our homeplace to a group we have fought for 20 years."* After informing

Peter Grace that "your people have stepped in it," M. F. asked him "to help save my brother's life. . . . *Please let us buy back his property, all of it.*" "Icky, you, and I are not young men," M. F. concluded. "We have seen a lot. You should know as we do, a betrayal when you see one."[43]

Once again, a direct appeal to Peter Grace produced results. But not before HGSI lost its suit to prevent VVL from mining the Brandy property. Nor was Grace able to avoid another round of damaging publicity about a donation designed to improve its image. "In Louisa, the Gift Is Bittersweet," the *Richmond Times-Dispatch* headline announced in late November 1993. The article recounted Icky's deteriorating health and the millions of dollars in royalties that had evaporated due to Grace's gift to HGSI. As Grace's beleaguered spokesman bemoaned, "For 20 years we caught it from the preservationists. . . . But making them happy made some other people unhappy."[44]

Things moved more quickly after the *Times-Dispatch* article. On December 18, W. R. Grace notified the Peerses that it intended to donate the property once owned by Icky Peers to HGSI. Icky immediately informed Grace that he planned to exercise his option to buy back the land, and on January 3, 1994, Icky and Elizabeth Peers mailed a certified check for $36,241 to buy back the thirty-seven vermiculite-laden acres (which were worth many times that amount in future royalties). When the Virginia Supreme Court turned down HGSI's *Brandy Farm* appeal, even Rae Ely acknowledged that her efforts to drive vermiculite mining out of Green Springs had failed. As she wrote to Mario Favorito in August 1994, the reserves on Brandy Farm, combined with those which Icky was about to lease to VVL, were sufficient to keep Sansom's company supplied for many years.[45]

Virginia Vermiculite had scored its biggest political and economic victory since the rezoning battles in the late 1970s. VVL's only corporate competitor in Green Springs had retired from the field, and HGSI had lost in Louisa County and in the state's highest court. Why Robert Sansom chose that moment to intensify the battle may never be known, but on February 21, 1995, he filed a complaint in the Federal District Court for the Western District of Virginia, alleging that W. R. Grace and HGSI had conspired to monopolize the vermiculite market.[46]

24

"A Female in Your Face"

VIRGINIA VERMICULITE, LTD. ALLEGED THAT GRACE'S decision to donate its holdings and constrict land use by placing no-mining provisions on it rather than selling it to VVL removed more than 80 percent of the vermiculite from the Louisa mining rights market in violation of the Sherman Antitrust Act. VVL also alleged that HGSI and Grace had conspired to injure VVL in trade, business, or profession—a violation of Virginia law. Robert Sansom's company sued to nullify the HGSI–Grace agreement and claimed $20 million in damages.[1]

The litigation, which paired Historic Green Springs, Inc. and W. R. Grace & Co. against VVL and two property owners who had leased mining rights to Grace, lasted for eight years, ending only when the U.S. Supreme Court declined to review the case. As U.S. District Court Judge James H. Michael stated, "The court is presented with the novel argument that the federal antitrust laws require nullification of a donation to a nonprofit preservation organization. . . . The unique circumstances in this case, to this court's knowledge never encountered by any other court, force one to reason by analogy."[2]

It was not every day, as Francis Clines of the *New York Times* pointed out, that a mining company sued a nonprofit citizens' group for colluding to monopolize anything, let alone vermiculite. "The suit involves a group of preservationists in a rustic, antebellum enclave of Louisa County and two strip mining companies, but not in the usual configuration. . . . This time it is Historic Green Springs Inc . . . that is being sued, after decades of aggressively using the courts to help create an 11,000-acre land trust." Although enigmatic, the litigation was nonetheless nationally significant. "Preservationists fear that the suit, if successful, could chill future donations under federal programs that currently protect over 700,000 acres of historic areas across the nation from industrial development by the use of conservation easements and pledges to keep the land configured for agriculture." Judge Michael trumped Clines' description of the litigation's "curious mix": "a scarce, valuable resource donated to an entity which vows never to use it; a corporation whose profits are, in part, derived from exploitation of the resource it has permanently surrendered; and a rival which resolves to reverse the transaction in order to extract the resource. All the makings of a mystery novel are contained in this strange brew."[3]

To Charles Montange, the attorney Rae Ely eventually engaged, there was nothing mysterious about Sansom's motivations: "I thought the antitrust case with which she was threatened was a classic kind of SLAPP." That acronym stood for "Strategic Lawsuit Against Public Participation," and as Montagne explained, "It's hard to get those cases dismissed . . . hard to get summary judgment in them." SLAPPs became an acronym in the late 1980s—less than a decade after those seeking to impugn the motivation of neighborhood activists tarred *their* opponents with the pejorative NIMBY. The scholars who coined the term SLAPP described it as a nefarious type of civil action. The prototypical example pitted real estate moguls against citizen activists opposed to rezoning and development. As soon as the activists made their voices heard—in a petition to local officials, a public hearing, or some other form of protected speech—deep-pocketed opponents "SLAPPed" them into silence by initiating lawsuits that threatened hefty damages. The core strategy was to overwhelm the nonprofit group with seemingly unlimited legal resources.[4]

SLAPPers used a range of charges: defamation, conspiracy, tort, and antitrust. The specific charge mattered little because the simple threat of damages sufficed to silence defendants. As one of the environmental groups that had been SLAPPed put it in 1991, "we haven't said anything at a public meeting . . . and we are struggling financially, trying to pay our attorney bill." SLAPPs had all the trappings of permissible civil actions, creating a conundrum for any judge who cared to ferret out legitimate legal actions from frivolous ones. What to do about this was not always clear. Consumer advocate Ralph Nader advocated free counsel to SLAPP victims so that they could "SLAPP back."[5]

There was every reason for Bob Sansom to use this legal device to silence a citizens' group that had been nothing but trouble. Yet the eight-year lawsuit was likely more than a tactic: it was payback for decades of Ely's success in Federal venues. Whether Jack Anderson's exposure of the former White House Fellow's failed lobbying efforts or midnight legislation that caught the former EPA administrator flat-footed, Sansom had suffered embarrassing defeats at the hands of his crafty foe. That the victor was a woman may well have added insult to injury.

"Robert Sansom was the angriest man I ever knew," Rae Ely explained years later. He was furious when he learned that in the midst of his negotiations to buy Grace's holdings in Green Springs, she had met with Peter Grace. "What does he do? . . . He lowers his bid." Predictably, Grace ended negotiations, and then, "when he finds out that I, in fact, got it, he goes berserk, and decides to file this lawsuit." Sansom is so smart, Rae conceded, "but he does the strangest things." She then drew a parallel to Governor Holton to explain why both men dug in their heels when they might more easily have moved on. "I don't understand it unless it's just a female in your face." This SLAPP could only be explained by understanding the relationship between the SLAPPing man and the woman being SLAPPed.[6]

Ned Gumble claimed that he did not fully understand the relationship between Sansom and Ely. Bob didn't spend a lot of time talking about Rae, Gumble reported, but "I think there was basically mutual hatred there." Gumble quickly added that perhaps hatred was too strong a word and that there was an element of respect "in terms . . . of how long Rae's tentacles were, and her ability to reach out to different areas." Leri Thomas, another Sansom ally, believed that Sansom and Ely "had their teeth sunk into each other and they were *not* going to let go." Thomas confirmed that Bob rarely talked about Rae: "He just fought her." Sansom's antitrust attorney, David Izakowitz, described Bob and Rae as "larger-than-life characters." At least around his attorney and in the presence of others, Sansom did not hesitate to offer his opinion of Rae. He depicted her as a "complete fraud," according to Izakowitz. He viewed Rae as an elitist and, even worse, a phony—"someone who tried to be of the patrician class and was acting as though she belonged to old Virginia." Rae, despite her 400-acre estate and wardrobe, saw herself, and especially her law practice, Izakowitz believed, as somebody who was "just sort of a fighter," advocating for common folks, especially abused women. "She did not see herself as a member of any sort of elite." Both she and Sansom "claimed the common touch and saw the other as not."[7]

Izakowitz acknowledged that gender was a factor. "Bob lived in a very male world." There might have been a woman in the VVL office, but the rest of the operation was entirely male. Bob was a gruff, plainspoken man who spoke a few decibels too loudly: "he was an imposing guy, he liked spending a lot of time outdoors." Izakowitz recalled that Sansom "was happiest when he was out in a rural setting, with quite physical activities." To Professor Charles Goetz, who had voted against Rae's admission to law school and as part of the HGSI defense team only saw Sansom in the courtroom, Bob "looked like a well-kept older guy who probably came from a good family and voted Republican." Yet, according to Izakowitz, Sansom "never looked like he was comfortable in a suit." Despite his Oxford education, Bob "was very much sort of salt of the earth, working class, 'Hi, how are you,' slap you on the back" in his manner.[8]

Bob "sexualized" Rae and portrayed her "as a seductress. . . . He would use some rather unflattering terms about her," Izakowitz recalled, words like "whore, bitch—things of that nature." Sansom did not use these words regularly, "but he would definitely often insinuate that she, you know, slept her way to power and wonder how she got into UVa Law School. . . . It always seemed to relate back to her sexuality—and that was sort of odd." Izakowitz concluded, "I think [the fact] that Rae was such a formidable foe and was female did bother him in one sense." Sansom's attorney quickly pointed out, however, that Bob "very much respected" the opinion of Jane Champion, David's colleague on the legal team. As for Rae, who was well over fifty years old at the time, Izakowitz recalled—she "was a bit of a flirt. She would even flirt, I mean, she would even flirt with me."[9]

Sansom and Ely were also on opposite sides of an ideological battle that increasingly divided the nation. According to Ned Gumble, "Bob very much believed in a free enterprise. He believed in creating jobs. He had a relationship, of sorts, with all the employees here. . . . it wasn't specifically about making money . . . it was about creating an opportunity." Bob Sansom claimed that he cared about preservation, according to Gumble, and was not simply an advocate for development at all costs. He "really thought that they were being responsible about what they were doing, they were providing jobs for an area that badly needed them." Like many of Rae's opponents, and most of the residents of Louisa County, Sansom always felt that Green Springs was no more historic than some place twenty miles down the road—this was Virginia.[10]

Attitudes toward gender and conflicting views on how to square economic development and quality of life issues collided in the term that Sansom sometimes used to characterize Historic Green Springs, Inc.: NIMBY. By 1995 that term was bandied about freely by pro-development advocates. Yet Sansom did not shoehorn Rae into this category: "It's not as if he brought that notion and then found Rae. . . . It's more the opposite: he focused on Rae," Izakowitz said. His favorite term for Rae was "newbie," meaning "someone who had no real stake in this." She acted as though "she was always a part of this old South and using it, this pretext, when all she really wanted was a nice quiet neighborhood to live in."[11]

"In a way, Rae was very important to him," Izakowitz concluded. Sansom almost embodied her with certain god-like qualities. The obsession was mutual. "I think they both . . . were a bit infatuated with the other person." Izakowitz believed that one of Sansom's "great desires" was defeating Rae Ely: he saw this "as a lifelong battle in which she won some of the times and he won some of the times." Both Rae and Bob imbued their life's work, which clearly was motved to some degree by self-interest, with a larger, public-serving meaning. For Rae, it was identifying, and in many ways creating, a national treasure that just happened to preserve Hawkwood's view and enhance its value. For Sansom, it was providing jobs in an economically challenged rural county that just happened to improve his bottom line.[12]

Mutual obsession forged an unlikely bond between the two mortal enemies. "On the surface of it they kind of hated each other, they couldn't stand the other one being even mentioned. But there was on both sides, there really was a grudging amount of admiration for the other because these were two tenacious fighters like I have never seen in my life." Izakowitz got that right. Rae still keeps Robert Sansom's obituary on her bedside table.[13]

By 1995, W. R. Grace was used to being sued. It quickly procured legal representation with a top Manhattan law firm—Kaye, Scholer. HGSI, on the other hand, was used to being the plaintiff in Federal court. Saddled with debt from previous litigation, HGSI faced the daunting task of locating a lawyer with expertise in both environmental and antitrust matters, and the even greater challenge of paying for this legal expertise. They eventually got "a real find" in Charles H. Montange, according to Charles Goetz.[14]

Rae Ely discovered Montange when she represented a client who sought to block construction of a cogeneration power plant just north of Louisa County. Though small, those plants were noisy. Legally, they were difficult to stop precisely because of their size—too small for the courts to care. With a difficult fight ahead, Rae cast about for a world-class litigator. She asked Karl Bausch, who worked at the President's Council on Environmental Quality, to recommend the best environmental lawyer in the country. The answer was easy, Bausch replied: Charles Montange.[15]

Montange, who grew up on a farm in Iowa, attributed his interest in the environment to his love of the outdoors as a kid. Charles had majored in math and economics at the University of Iowa and took the LSAT on a whim. When the house he was living in was condemned, he figured, "What the hell; I had gotten into Yale Law School, so I went there." After graduating in 1975, he clerked for the chief judge of the Ninth Circuit Court of Appeals. Montange then joined Covington and Burling in Washington, D.C. He worked there for seven years but left because some people "enjoy defending the position of something that is fundamentally wrong. It's kind of a contest to see how much you can get away with. . . . I did not relish that feeling." Montange partnered with a friend at the National Wildlife Federation to help create the Rails to Trails Conservancy. He also began to take on public interest environmental law cases. He did not know Rae personally but knew the name because he was familiar with *Ely v. Velde*. When she called, his reaction was, "Oh . . . *that* Ely!"[16]

Montange and Ely took on the big law firm that represented the power plant. "I have never seen anything like it," she recalled. "We filed the most impressive Federal suit I have seen since the early days of Emanuel Emroch." Not only did the electric company agree to forgo cogeneration in the surrounding one hundred miles, according to Rae the firm "asked us to sign an agreement that we would never sue them again." Rae suddenly could see her career flourishing—that together, they were "now on a roll." Then Montange moved to Seattle. It was "a terrible, terrible day when he moved to Seattle."[17]

Faced with VVL's lawsuit, Rae asked Montange, "how would you like to visit the Northeast more often?" She then faxed him the complaint and also sent it to her old nemesis, Charles Goetz, an authority on law and economics. Goetz was no fan of HGSI. "My honest opinion ... was that it was a bunch of well-to-do people in Green Springs, who were, under the rubric of environmentalism, creating a nonprofit organization that was basically serving more their private interests than the public interest." He agreed to help them because he believed they were entitled to good representation. Goetz faxed back, "Your friendly neighborhood economist can help you." Rae quickly shared that information with Montange, which may have convinced him to say yes. "I think Charles Montange must be kind of like an old nineteenth-century fire horse," Rae concluded. "You know, he heard the fire bells ringing, so he agreed to do this."[18]

To Montange, it "seemed like it was a righteous cause from the beginning." It was a national landmark: "why *wouldn't* you try to preserve it?" On cases like this one, Montange explained, he usually told people to get local counsel. He assumed, however, that she could not find anybody to do it "because an antitrust case is a phenomenally hard thing to take on." It is not clear if he ever visited the burnt remains of Hawkwood, but he had a strong interest in the mercenary John Hawkwood, for whom the villa was named. Describing the legendary knight, Montagne compared John Hawkwood and Rae Ely: "Don't mess with Sir John and don't mess with Lady Rae."[19]

Lady Rae got a promotion when Montange compared her to Queen Isabella of Spain, whom Montange described as "Admin. General for the Spanish Army. Ferdinand got the glory of leading the army, but the ammunition, the troops, the logistics, making sure he got there 'firstest with the mostest,' that was Isabella. She was commissariat, she was the treasury, she was the nervous system. . . . You need to have that behind you if you are going to battle on the public interest side. . . . You need someone who's dedicated and wants to win and . . . understands the drudgery and time that it will take." Rae Ely, Montange summed up, was "someone that if she asked you to do something, and you went to battle for it, she would be there with you."[20]

Montange told the HGSI Board that there was no basis in law for VVL's claims. Nonetheless, it was going to be expensive to mount a defense. Montange noted that it was possible that VVL was just bluffing and suggested that a "tough response" might be enough to convince them to abandon the suit. The board agreed upon this plan and also stipulated that Charles would represent them if the case did move forward. He estimated that it would cost $50,000—$60,000 should that occur and advised the organization to set aside an additional $10,000 in a reserve fund. Though in the end HGSI only shouldered a small portion, Ely estimated that litigation cost the parties $8 million.[21]

The idea of suing Grace and HGSI for antitrust was Sansom's and once the case moved forward, he "very much micromanaged the case. . . . He wanted to see everything and had comments about it and . . . was actively involved in whatever strategizing we did," Izakowitz recalled. Bob was smart and came up with good ideas. But it took Izakowitz's firm a lot of time to educate him on some of the differences between an economic perspective and the law.[22]

More problematic was Sansom's role in strategy, according to Izakowitz. "That's when his personal grudge with Rae sometimes got to be a problem." "Too much would be read as a personal vendetta," Izakowitz feared. "We didn't want to try the case as *Rae Ely vs. Bob Sansom*." Nor could you be subtle with Bob, Izakowitz reported, you had to be confrontational. Although Sansom often got mad at his legal allies, he did not hold a grudge and usually came around.[23]

Both Grace and HGSI moved to dismiss the case. On September 19, 1995, Magistrate Judge B. Waugh Crigler issued a report that recommended dismissing all the Federal charges and declined to exercise jurisdiction over the alleged violations of state law. VVL objected.[24]

There were multiple delays, but on April 22, 1997 Judge Michael dismissed all of the charges against HGSI. The "threshold question" regarding the nonprofit group was "whether Section 1 of the Sherman Antitrust Act can be used as a tool against HGSI or whether these 'facts have been forced into an antitrust mold to achieve federal jurisdiction.' " Although the irony was likely lost on Judge Michael, the question he raised about VVL stretching its interpretation of the law to bludgeon its way into the Federal court system echoed the very criticism that had been leveled at HGSI in *Ely v. Velde*, not to mention the tie-breaker challenge it brought in Federal court under cover of the Voting Rights Act.[25]

Federal antitrust legislation and jurisprudence should *not* apply to the facts in the case before him, Michael ruled. The legislative history of the

Sherman Act suggested that the statute did not apply to an "eleemosynary"—was a pun intended?—"organization pursuing primarily political or social objectives, from which it does not receive pecuniary gain." The judge dismissed the charges against HGSI, ruling that "like the participants in the temperance movement and anti-abortion movement, HGSI is not engaged in commercial activities and should not be exposed to antitrust liability."[26]

It was a different story for W. R. Grace. Although Judge Michael dismissed some of the Federal charges against Grace under Section 1 of the Sherman Act (conspiracy in restraint of trade), he refused to dismiss charges that Grace had violated Section 2 of the Sherman Act (attempt to monopolize, monopolization, and conspiracy to monopolize) or comparable state law. Surprisingly, VVL appealed the decision to the Fourth Circuit, in part to contest Judge Michael's decision about HGSI—just one more indication that Sansom was determined to SLAPP Rae Ely.[27]

On September 1, 1998, a three-judge panel for the Fourth Circuit reversed Judge Michael's ruling and remanded the case to the district court. Writing for the panel, Judge Michael Luttig ruled that HGSI was indeed subject to antitrust scrutiny: the district court had erred when it dismissed the nonprofit group from the suit. Judge Luttig's opinion rejected Michael's claim that "HGSI is exempt from the antitrust laws because it is a nonprofit organization pursuing noncommercial, sociopolitical objectives." Whether HGSI was or was not exempt due to its nonprofit status, Luttig concluded, the transaction between the nonprofit organization and Grace was "fundamentally commercial." Acknowledging that a number of sister circuits had provided exemptions for nonprofit organizations, Luttig distinguished this case from the others. "We emphasize," the opinion underscored, "that the dispositive inquiry is whether the *transaction* is commercial, not [whether] the *entity* engaging in the transaction is commercial." The Fourth Circuit found ample evidence that Grace's donation, combined with restrictive covenants on the use of the donated land and assigned leases, was indeed commercial.[28]

By now the National Trust for Historic Preservation and the Land Trust Alliance had joined HGSI and Grace as *amici curiae,* or friends of the court, with a leading preservation newsletter warning that the case "may have repercussions on easements and land donations for years to come." Citing costs of up to $1 million, Ely told *Preservation News* that "we think this [suit was filed] to put us out of business. . . . [A] little outfit like us can get dragged into a Bill Gates–type litigation, just for pursuing its mission of preserving an historic district." This did not deter the Fourth Circuit which ruled that nonprofit status did not provide a free pass for voluntary organizations. HGSI would have to defend its actions in costly litigation. Losing would mean that even more citizens' groups would get SLAPPed.[29]

HGSI was back to square one. Once again, it sought a summary judgment from the district court. This time, however, it did so after extensive discovery and expert depositions. On February 11, 2000, less than a week before the latest summary judgment hearing was scheduled to begin, HGSI filed a motion to exclude the market analysis and the testimony of a key VVL expert witness, Seth Schwartz.[30]

Although clearly irritated by the last-minute interruption, Judge Michael scheduled a so-called *Daubert* hearing to vet the qualifications of VVL's expert witness. The first sentence of Michael's opinion began promisingly enough for the expert witness. "Mr. Schwartz attained a bachelor's degree in geological engineering at Princeton University." Any reader expecting the next sentence to name the university where Schwartz got his Ph.D., or at least an M.A. degree in economics, however, would have been disappointed. Instead, Michael continued: "Upon earning this degree, Schwartz began working for Robert Sansom (the President of VVL) at Sansom's then consulting firm, Energy and Environmental Analysis ('EEA'). When Sansom formed another consulting group, Energy Ventures Analysis ('EVA') four years later, Schwartz followed Sansom to EVA. Schwartz is currently the co-owner of EVA with Sansom; and together the pair own over 50% of the company's stock."[31]

The judge required relatively few additional words to underscore the potential for bias in Schwartz's analysis. Michael also eviscerated Sansom's partner's qualifications as an expert. "Schwartz lacks the minimal requirements of education, training, experience, and knowledge to qualify him as an expert in antitrust economics." Goetz's research also exposed flaws in Schwartz's methods. Goetz used an exhibit crafted to appeal to Michael "because I knew that he had gone through one of the 'economics for judges courses.' " That work proved essential, as the court deemed the methodology "unreliable." The court granted the defendants' motion to exclude Seth Schwartz as an expert witness, leaving VVL with a crater at the heart of its case on the eve of the trial.[32]

Charles Montange's strategy when the odds were bad was to "develop a[n] approach where you kind of fight the battle on the field you are best able to defend." In the field of economic expertise, for example, HGSI's resources were formidable. Montange himself was trained in economics and Professor Goetz was a renowned expert in the economics of antitrust. "We were well-equipped on the market thing," Montange noted.[33]

Montange, also understood that sometimes the best defense was a good offense, which in this case meant attacking VVL's economic expert. "The one truly new legal development in the United States that you can attribute to that antitrust case," Montange said later, "was that Goetz and I . . . knocked out VVL's economics expert as incompetent." In a precedent-setting gambit, Montange and Goetz applied a set of laws derived from medical malpractice litigation to the Green Springs case. Goetz really thought that "when Schwartz got knocked out that that was going to be the end of the case." Obviously, he was not well versed in the history of anything having to do with Rae Ely and Robert Sansom.[34]

Rae bolstered the team's expertise in an age before "google" was a verb when she discovered and procured the services of the world's leading expert on vermiculite markets, Graham Ellicott. A member of the Royal Society of Chemists in Great Britain, he had twenty years of experience in the global vermiculite business. When Rae made one of her patented cold calls, much to her surprise, Ellicott answered the phone. Rae delicately outlined the case and Ellicott exclaimed, "My, my, that's an unusual situation." After describing her "lovely historic district," she told Ellicott, "It's so curious, because Virginia Vermiculite is claiming that by our accepting this gift of this beautiful land, that we are monopolizing the world's supplies. And he laughed out loud. And I thought, well, that's a good sign." It was. "That would be delightful, delightful," he responded. When Montange informed VVL that Graham Ellicott, the handsome tall, distinguished Englishman in his late forties and secretary general of the Vermiculite Association would be testifying, "you could almost hear them peeing in their shoes. They never had *anybody* to counter Graham Ellicott."[35]

If overwhelming your opponent with unlimited resources was essential to SLAPPing successfully, VVL did not hold a strong hand. Izakowitz explained that Bob Sansom had chosen his small Charlottesville law firm because he "probably didn't want to pay one of those big urban center [law firms]. . . . Bob kept wanting to do the economic analysis himself [to reduce expenses], and I kept explaining to him why that's a terrible idea." It was also Bob's decision to have his colleague Seth Schwartz testify as an economics expert on the vermiculite market, ignoring Izakowitz's objections.[36]

On July 27, 2000, Judge Michael ruled on the request for summary judgment. To sustain its charges that HGSI and Grace violated Section 1 of the Sherman Antitrust Act, the plaintiffs had to present sufficient evidence to demonstrate that the defendants "restrained trade in a relevant market." That carried the burden of providing sufficient evidence to establish the relevant product and geographic markets. Acknowledging that there was no rule that mandated expert testimony on this complex matter, Michael noted that "as a practical matter . . . the plaintiff's lack of a witness to testify about antitrust economics, or to rebut the defendants' economists, proves fatal."[37]

When the dust settled from the fifty-page ruling, the only charges that survived as worthy of going to trial were VVL's conspiracy-to-monopolize claims under Section 2 of the Sherman Antitrust Act and corresponding state laws. As Judge Michael put it, a conspiracy claim "is a different offense from the crime that is the object of the conspiracy," and one that did *not* require a "rigorous definition" of the relevant market. There was ample evidence that HGSI and Grace had conspired to monopolize. Accordingly, Judge Michael denied the defendants' request for summary-judgment dismissal of that claim. The case would finally go to trial, albeit on far narrower grounds than the plaintiff's original complaint.[38]

The HGSI team prepared for the trial with the wind at their back. They had knocked out VVL's expert witness on the shape of the market, enjoyed the resources of codefendant like W. R. Grace, and the original charges had been reduced to conspiracy. Even though Rae believed that Judge Michael did not like her personally, Charles Goetz convinced her to opt for the bench trial because "with a jury, you just never know." Goetz believed that he had a good feel for Judge Michael, whom the law professor had seen up close in his continuing education class for judges. Goetz was convinced they could win on the merits "if the right arguments were made to him."[39]

Appointed to the Western District of Virginia by Jimmy Carter in 1980, James Henry Michael graduated in 1940 from the University of Virginia with a B.S., and from UVa Law School in 1942. Serving as a state senator for twelve years, Michael was known as "the Silver Fox" for his thick shock of hair, and also for his long black cigarette holder. "He looked like a thinner, taller clean-shaven Colonel Sanders." Five years into the litigation, Francis Clines portrayed Michael as a combination of "Virginia courtliness" and the last hope that the court would survive the deluge of pretrial litigation that had already produced depositions "growing in Dickensian stacks dense enough to make the judge cry out, 'This court has been submerged.' " When "courtly" did not suffice, the judge turned to southern mule driver-talk that got asses moving in the right direction: "You all aren't doing very much in the way of 'geein' and hawin',' " he told the litigants.[40]

Montange described Judge Michael as a very polite man who ran a tight courtroom. Montange learned the hard way that Michael would not abide cell phones. "You were better off, whether you thought you had turned it off or not, don't bring it in." Except when interrupted by cell phones or in mule driver mode, Judge Michael was a "Virginia gentleman" who "believed in the prerogatives of the establishment."[41]

Judge Michael's commentary, interspersed throughout the direct and cross-examinations, surely kept both sides entertained. When David Izakowitz asked if the judge wanted to examine the site of a VVL processing plant, Michael reminded counsel, "I [am] about 50 years older than the Commonwealth and I know Louisa County very well indeed. I think I probably could walk down Route 22 there to the appropriate spot and within ten feet spot exactly where you were planning to put in the new plant." Michael told Izakowitz that he would get back to him on the proposed field trip. "Right now," the judge continued, "you all have mapped me to death."[42]

The day before the trial W. R. Grace settled out of court. Goetz recalled that it was almost like "a knife in our hearts. . . . All hell broke loose." The HGSI team did not need the Grace-funded Kaye, Scholer law firm for research or the strategy behind its case. Professor Goetz and other scholars donated their services—legal work that would have cost hundreds of thousands of dollars—and Montange billed at a deeply discounted rate. Those "Dickensian stacks" of documents, however, were costly and the HGSI team depended upon Grace's lawyers for "paralegals, taking care of the document photocopying—all that stuff is really very expensive, and takes people."[43]

Rae Ely was stunned by Grace's decision. "They had all the trial notebooks and they had all the exhibits prepared," she recounted. "It was immense, it was overwhelming. . . . We felt, initially, like they were forcing us to settle.

It was the most stress-filled period of my life." So Rae called in the cavalry. She rented a gigantic Xerox machine—"the biggest thing I've ever seen"—and literally moved into Charlie Goetz's Charlottesville house to reproduce thousands of documents around the clock with a team comprising Rae's trusted friend and associate, Robin Patton, Rae's secretary, and her secretary's daughter.[44]

Ely also recounted a meeting with District Court Magistrate Waugh Crigler, who called her and Goetz into his office to encourage HGSI to settle on the eve of the trial. Montange's response, Rae thought, was very Old Testament. "Our cause is righteous," he told Crigler. "We will not be intimidated." Montange continued. "We will not back down. We will go forward. We will not settle any element of this. And we will try this case."[45]

Onlookers and participants alike were surprised that HGSI did not settle at that point. Rae suspected that "Mr. Sansom was especially astounded." As for Grace, the terms of its settlement were confidential, but estimates by informed observers ranged between one and two million dollars. It is likely that Grace calculated the cost of a two-week trial might well be higher.[46]

The trial began on September 11, 2000. Montange described it as "intense [and] exhausting." Although both sides used examination and cross-examination of witnesses to distill the economic arguments at the heart of this antitrust case, the attorneys for both VVL and HGSI underscored the long-standing animosity that infused virtually every interaction between Rae Ely and Bob Sansom. After a lengthy effort by Charles Montange to press Robert Sansom on his campaign to rescind Green Springs' national historic landmark status—a journey that wound through the *Bergland* litigation in 1980 and continued through Sansom's more recent efforts to have the IRS look into tax deductions for Grace's gift to HGSI—an exasperated Judge Michael finally put his foot down. "This Court is absolutely in no doubt about the fact that this witness perceives Green Springs as not being a friendly entity. Similarly, the Court is under no doubt at all that Green Springs perceives Mr. Sansom as not being friendly. If that's what you are undertaking to prove, you don't need to. I've already concluded that and I don't think it took a genius to figure it out. . . . They've been at war for ten years and it looks like it's going on another ten." An hour later, Judge Michael intervened again. "When I spoke earlier . . . I did refrain from using a phrase that came to mind. I'm going to use it now. The Court does not perceive anything in this case—anything in this case—that would indicate either that VVL regards Historic Green Springs or Green Springs regards VVL as, in any sense, a warm and cuddly entity."[47]

As long days ended for Charles with a bourbon, the nights began with more work to prepare for the next day. Describing how it felt while VVL argued its case, Montange confessed: "I know it's going to be bad—there's nothing we can do about it.... OK: you're going to take a lot of bullets. You just say those are not the mortal parts of us. Let them vent their steam.... In the end, we prevailed."[48]

Before Judge Michael handed down his opinion, however, Andrew Schneider, the *Seattle Post-Intelligencer*'s senior national correspondent who had doggedly exposed W. R. Grace's cover-up of mounting evidence about the link between asbestos and vermiculite in Libby, Montana, used the antitrust case to tie that health hazard to Green Springs. His vehicle was an apparently irresistible caricature of HGSI—the discovery of asbestos a "vindication for a group of silver-haired Southern belles who have fought for 30 years to save their historic land." Most likely unaware of Rae Ely's decision to play down the asbestos issue after receiving a generous donation from Grace, not to mention pandering to stereotypes about women in politics that differed little from those found in Virginia's conservative press in the 1970s, Schneider described the "Ladies of Green Springs" as "fewer than a dozen widows and 'maiden ladies,' the descendants of families" who lived on their "18th and 19th century farms ... that have remained virtually untouched since the Civil War."[49]

Between descriptions of these "feisty women," many in their "golden years," and accounts of the "band of belles" digging in, Schneider laced a far more authoritative account of Grace's troubles in Montana and hopes for new reserves in Green Springs. He also reported that the same kind of asbestos found in Libby's vermiculite was present in Grace's early Green Springs samples. This, of course, was old news. Nor was HGSI ever able to demonstrate that, given proper processing, those traces of asbestos in Green Springs vermiculite posed a health threat to VVL's miners.

What had changed, however, was national awareness of the environmental damage that W. R. Grace had wrought in Libby. Schneider and his colleagues at the *Post-Intelligencer* deserve a great deal of credit for exposing them, along with Montana's *Daily Inter Lake*, Colorado's *High Country News*, and the *New York Times*. Still, nine months after Schneider's article about asbestos in

Green Springs, Senator Patty Murray (D-Washington), who presided over the Committee on Health, Education, Labor, and Pensions' Hearing on Workplace Safety and Asbestos Contamination, could say, "Like many Americans, I thought asbestos was banned many years ago."[50]

Judge Michael did not admit evidence related to this hazard. Although he acknowledged that the information might have some relevance to the question at hand—the marketability of Green Springs vermiculite—he ruled that the "Court will not serve as a sounding board for marginally probative evidence that likely would harm VVL if aired in the public arena." Montange agreed, at least in retrospect. "It's an antitrust case . . . . The government doesn't care if you get mesothelioma. . . . The government cares about the market." Whether introducing evidence about asbestos would have hurt Grace (if it had not settled) more than VVL is hard to know. Judge Michael was not going down that mine shaft.[51]

In May 2001, six years into the litigation, the concluding paragraphs of Judge Michael's decision in favor of HGSI captured the nature of the journey. "On reading the Findings of Fact for the case," Michael summed up, "one develops an intuitive conclusion that the plaintiff will prevail. It is only upon a consideration of the relevant statutes, and of the cases which have interpreted and applied those statutes, that the conclusion set out herein in favor of the defendant is properly reached, contrary to that intuitive though the result may be." Even though "Grace and HGSI acted in concert to injure VVL in its reputation, trade, business, and profession, VVL did not satisfy its burdens of proving that Grace intended to monopolize a discernable part of interstate commerce, or that Grace's and HGSI's concerted actions injured VVL or harmed competition."[52]

Rae told the *Richmond Times-Dispatch* that she was pleased the ordeal was over. It was not; VVL immediately appealed. Although their purported expert on vermiculite markets had been knocked out in the *Daubert* hearing, Bob Sansom, who had hoped to limit expenses, opened his wallet and brought in one of the world's top experts on antitrust, Harvard Law School Professor Einer R. Elhauge (who would go on to chair President Barack Obama's Antitrust Advisory Committee).[53]

The Fourth Circuit scheduled oral arguments for the morning of May 6, 2002. The session quickly turned into a two-hour drama in the packed courtroom. When asked to describe his opponent years later, the only thing Montange could remember was that Elhauge "had really scruffy shoes." Montange also recalled the rivalry he and Goetz felt when going up against the star: "I was from Yale," Montange told me, "Goetz was University of Virginia. We are bringing this guy down, man." Montange, who was not given to self-congratulation, labeled his own performance "the finest oral argument I ever gave."[54]

In an opinion delivered by Judge Michael Luttig, the Fourth Circuit upheld the district court's decision, although it disagreed with Judge Michael's reasoning. Rather than affirming Michael's dismissal of Section 1 Sherman Antitrust claims against HGSI because VVL had failed to prove unreasonable restraint of trade, the appeals court based its decision on its finding that Grace's gift to HGSI was a unilateral act that did not rise to a concerted action "in which multiple parties join their resources, rights, or economic power together in order to achieve an out-come that, but for the concert, would naturally be frustrated."[55]

The bottom line remained the same: HGSI was exonerated. On April 28, 2003, the Supreme Court of the United States unanimously denied VVL's petition for writ of certiorari. The eight-year saga was finally over. By some estimates, it had cost HGSI close to half a million dollars, even with all the pro bono work and reduced legal fees. They retained the land that Grace had donated to them—at least those portions that had not been sold to pay the legal fees. And most important, they had survived an intense counterattack from a determined foe.[56]

Rae Ely claims she never doubted the outcome. "There were a number of times when reasonable people believed that the case was over," she told a reporter, "only to have Virginia Vermiculite appeal yet again. This has been a costly and tiring experience for Historic Green Springs, but we would do it again in a minute if we had to." A "Case Comment" in the *Yale Law Journal* did not take issue with the appeals court ruling, but excoriated Judge Luttig's reasoning. Labeling it a "missed opportunity," Olivia S. Choe chastised the formulaic approach that defined "concerted action" in cookie-cutter fashion. Had the court grappled with the complex question of what constituted a "concerted action," rather than taking the easy way out and "focusing on a formal category ('gift')," it might have addressed more directly "whether and how nonprofits may be liable under the antitrust laws." Of course, Choe argued, if the appeals court was determined to avoid that question, it simply should have confirmed the ample evidence presented at the district court level that VVL failed to prove "anticompetitive effect" or "antitrust injury." In a parting shot, Choe wondered out loud whether given "the unusual facts about the case, the Fourth Circuit's decision may have been driven less by a desire to narrow the scope of concerted activity and more by a desire to avoid exposing a nonprofit to antitrust liability."[57]

"Realize," Montange concluded, "that I did not ask for that kind of an opinion. Neither I nor Goetz anticipated it at all." Goetz confirmed this. He was in London when he heard that an opinion had been issued, so he looked it up on the internet and recalled his reaction years later. "You could have knocked me over with a feather." Both men agreed, however, that "you take whatever you can get."[58]

Taking whatever she could get had characterized Rae's approach to politics since the moment she asked Hiram, "What are you going to do about *this*?" When it came to stopping the prison, donating thousands of acres of privately held easements was not the perfect way to preserve the historic district, but, with constant vigilance, it turned out that it was good enough. Accepting Grace's donation was not sufficient to prevent its competitor and HGSI's foe from mining in the historic district, but it did limit the operation and ensured that the property originally mined by VVL was eventually restored to look the way it had before mining began. If muting concerns about the dangers of asbestos was part of the bargain with Grace to achieve that end, ultimately, Rae took what she could get.

None of this would have occurred if Rae had not devoted her considerable talents, and much of her life, to the cause of finding and restoring Green Springs' history. Among her most valuable skills was an ability to pursue a long-term strategy and a talent for seizing the moment when an opportunity arose. She did this from the time she read the *Life* magazine article about the Nature Conservancy and easements. She pursued her political agenda at a time when women who did so were automatically labeled "amateurs." She kept alive, for several decades, the unlikely prospect that W. R. Grace would donate the very land it had planned to mine. She recognized long before many scholars that what constituted history was changing, and that these new understandings of what was historical would, quite literally, put Green Springs on the map. And she ensured that the refuge she found as a child in George Engel's stucco, tile-topped tower could be replicated, made her own, and preserved at Hawkwood.

Epilogue

RAE ELY LOOKED OUT AT THE residents gathered in May 2012 who were waiting to hear from their elected representatives. The homeowners were there to stop the latest threat to their neighborhood. Louisa County was considering rezoning land that would authorize a new subdivision—"The Ridges"—300 apartments built on land flatter than the Wal-Mart parking lot next to the proposed development. "We are your neighbor," Rae told the gathering, and "we are concerned. . . . You have a LUV-lee community here."[1]

The term "neighbor" only applied loosely. These were not residents of the historic homes in the landmark district that Rae had forged and defended for half a century. Rather, this was a meeting of the Spring Creek Homeowners Association, and nobody had fought harder to stop the construction of *their* gated community built around an "award-winning" golf course located on the edge of historic Green Springs than Rae Ely.

Since I had just started the research for this book and had not yet discovered Rae's tactical flexibility, I was amazed to hear her praising the hundreds of homes that had recently sprouted in Spring Creek. When I pressed her after the meeting, she explained, "This latest offers a rare opportunity to form an alliance with the 500-plus votes of Spring Creek." That voting base "could have significant political ramifications." The next day, she e-mailed, "Can you imagine what it is doing to me to have to traffic with them?" Ten minutes later Rae sent another series of e-mails updating me on her decade-long litigation against Spring Creek, Louisa County, and the Louisa County Water Authority.[2]

By the time I had completed my research, none of this surprised me: this was the same woman who publicly praised Peter Grace for backing off from mining when, in fact, he had no intention of doing so. This was one political activist who knew when to threaten, when to litigate, which outfit to wear for the right effect, when to charm the opposition with a mere wiggle of her finger, and, if necessary, when to turn a blind eye. Even if Spring Creek's homeowners were draining water from the springs that fed the historic district, why not consider them part of the "hood" and call those landscaped cul-de-sacs "luv-lee" if an alliance might stop the next thirsty development?

Louisa's Board of Supervisors had long searched for a reliable source of water to develop Zion Crossroads. That this prime real estate sat empty at the intersection of Interstate 64—a major east-west thoroughfare—and Route 15—a north-south connector—gnawed at pro-development advocates. Richmond's spread westward and Charlottesville's eastward expansion made the I-64 Zion Crossroads exit an ideal site for light industry, retail, or even a gated golf course subdivision—*if* anybody could find water. Zion Crossroads was dry as a bone. Piping in water might one day allow developers to include nouns like springs, creeks, or, better yet, both in their branding. Louisa County's elected officials believed that a reliable source of water surely would turn a generic term like "light industry" into a Walmart distribution center, and "retail," into a companion Supercenter.

By 1995 Louisa County looked to the James River, just twenty-three miles south of Zion Crossroads. The problem was that virtually all the territory between the river and Louisa County, including the bank of the James River that might serve as the site for a pumping station, was located in neighboring Fluvanna County, which was in no hurry to fund a pipeline. Meanwhile, Louisa County spent almost $10 million on water infrastructure over the next decade.[3]

Frustrated by the delay, Louisa County ultimately tapped water that bubbled up from Green Springs. When the Commonwealth of Virginia pulled the plug on the diagnostic center, it capped the wells that had been drilled to serve the anticipated prison, and in February 1999 the Board of Supervisors created a public utility that would draw water from them. The county's budget was being squeezed from both the revenue and expenditure ends.

Dominion Power's North Anna nuclear power plant—which had been paying over $11 million a year in property tax—slashed payments by a third. Simultaneously, residential growth exploded and the property taxes these new residents paid fell far short of new services like schools that they required. Desperate to develop a new commercial tax base, the county supervisors claimed that more water for light industry and retail, not subdivisions, was the solution.[4]

Rae Ely soon reminded the BOS that the county did not own the wells it expected to water Zion Crossroads. Several other citizens raised concerns, noting that tapping the water from these wells might dangerously lower the water table in Green Springs. The county addressed the first concern by purchasing the state-owned wells in 2000. They soon began pumping water to a new Wal-Mart distribution center in Zion Crossroads that employed 500 workers—the very kind of light industry the county hoped to attract. "WAL-MART'S HERE!!" the banner *Central Virginian* headline boasted on March 13, 2003. A 135-foot-high water tower emblazoned (aspirationally) "Louisa County Zion Crossroads Business Park" hovered over the landscape, even as the usually optimistic local newspaper sheepishly acknowledged that "a business park does not exist . . . presently."[5]

Surprisingly, given its long history of opposition to any intrusions into the historic district, HGSI did not formally oppose using the wells to serve commercial needs in Zion Crossroads. It is possible, as some members subsequently claimed, that HGSI genuinely supported economic development outside of Green Springs. Whatever the group's attitude about commercial development on its borders, the organization had its hands full with the antitrust suit and a host of other challenges.[6]

County Administrator Ed Kube underscored that the supervisors were looking to diversify the county's tax base—"taking the initiative ourselves in order to make ourselves more visible to get industries." As HGSI member Amanda Welch put it several years later, "water was touted as the county's golden egg to spur the kind of development needed in Zion Crossroads to offset the rampant residential development." When developer Charles D. Kincannon proposed Spring Creek, he stipulated that he would find the water required to service all those homes and amenities. A land-use planner vowed: "If we don't find it [water] then we don't build it. That's the bottom line."[7]

A native of Louisa County who had worked on farms in Green Springs as a boy, Kincannon did find water; but not in Zion Crossroads. In October 2001 Kincannon purchased the remaining 140 acres of the original prison site abutting the county wells. Notably, the Commonwealth of Virginia limited development on the 140 acres to no more than "10 detached single family dwellings." Since the land would not support septic systems even for ten houses, Kincannon was then limited to "no more than three." Ultimately, this land in the heart of the national historic landmark district would supply water to Kincannon's 1,200-home golf course development in Zion Crossroads.[8]

Rae learned of the sale in late March 2002 and immediately asked Governor Mark Warner to prevent the closing and consider a competing offer from HGSI. If there was any doubt about Kincannon's intent, it evaporated a week later when a landowner in Green Springs spotted drilling equipment on the 140 acres. Asked what was going on, a drilling company employee revealed that his team had been tasked with finding three wells "as deep as 600 feet. . . . Someone must be planning to build one heck of a lot of houses on this land."[9]

HGSI filed a bill of complaint in Louisa County Circuit Court, asking for an injunction. Among other charges, their attorney, David S. Bailey, argued that because Kincannon had never revealed his intent to mine water, the Commonwealth "was led to believe that the developer had negotiated with them in good faith to preserve the historic property [and] cause no harm to the District." In truth, this "national treasure . . . didn't get any more consideration than a vacant lot next to the . . . dump."[10]

Labeling it an "outrageous violation of the public trust," Rae predicted that exporting Green Springs' water to the Spring Creek subdivision would have a catastrophic impact on the historic district, changing its character, which in turn might undo the coveted historic landmark designation. Testifying in Judge F. Ward Harkrader, Jr.'s court, she noted that for "33 years the landowners in the area have banded together to protect [it] from intrusions." But the landmark designation is "kind of a house of cards." Once you started "nibbling" at that, "you risk losing all designations."[11]

In weighing the request for injunctive relief, Judge Harkrader acknowledged that the plaintiff's arguments were "innovative and address the cutting edge of land and water rights." He was "both surprised and deeply concerned by the apparent caustic and cavalier interaction of State agencies." The bottom line, however, was that HGSI had failed to present sufficient evidence to overturn Kincannon's contract: the court would not interfere. The judge stressed that his decree did not abolish any of the rights of the landowners in the aquifer, inviting them to present evidence of harm in future litigation. They did.[12]

On May 3, 2004, the Louisa County Board of Supervisors formally accepted easements that conveyed the water from Kincannon's Green Springs wells. There was no public notice prior to this action, nor was it listed on the board's agenda. The BOS accepted the easements with no discussion immediately upon returning from a closed executive session. A month later HGSI was back in court, and this time both Louisa County and the Louisa County Water Authority were the target of its litigation, along with Kincannon's Spring Creek Land Development LLC. The suit claimed that acceptance of the water from these Green Springs wells and its use for Spring Creek violated Kincannon's original proffer to find his own water for his subdivision.[13]

At a joint meeting of the Louisa County Planning Commission and the Board of Supervisors, Rex Murphy, a long-time HGSI supporter who lived between the new wells and Zion Crossroads, called it "a devious way to legislate county business." The county was draining precious water needed for agriculture in order to serve frivolous purposes such as "watering golf greens." What could be more basic to protecting Louisa's farming communities than safeguarding the water that supplied them? Instead of doing that "the County wants to line the pockets of developers at the expense of farmers."[14]

Under the irresistible headline "At a Crossroads," the "business journal" pullout section of the *Daily Progress* offered a snapshot of just where development stood in June 2005. "Zion Crossroads still may be a bit sleepy but the community is poised to wake up in a big way," reporter David Hendrick wrote. He then quoted Louisa County Executive Lee Lintecum's gleeful summary: "We think commercially it's going to be the fastest growing area, and probably with the Spring Creek [residential community] it will be the fastest growing residential area." Wal-Mart was poised to build a Supercenter. Best Western was constructing a hotel. Lowe's soon announced that it would be opening a big box across the parking lot from the Supercenter.[15]

Even though the original rationale for pumping Green Springs water to Zion Crossroads was to promote commercial development to mitigate the cost of burgeoning residential growth, by 2006 the logic had been turned on its head. Louisa County planner Darren Coffey summed up the new thinking: "That's the key—rooftops. As more people move in [to Zion Crossroads], it will raise the comfort level for a national retailer."[16]

The legal status of the water remained cloudy until December 2006, when Louisa County Circuit Court Judge Timothy Sanner ruled that the water authority could continue pumping. The news was not all bad for Historic Green Springs, Inc., however, as Sanner also determined that if adjoining landowners could demonstrate injury from the county's water use, they would be entitled to injunctive relief.[17]

Although HGSI's attorney tried to spin the decision in positive fashion, the group appealed the decision to the Virginia Supreme Court in May 2007. It sought to reverse the original sale of the wells by the state, the use of that water to serve Spring Creek, and the county's failure to implement a monitoring plan. The appeal was denied on September 24, 2007.[18]

Fifteen years later, Spring Creek residents were still using water from Green Springs and HGSI was still monitoring water levels, poised to litigate should the water table drop. The residents of "Stonegate," the 155-apartment complex located on the site originally proposed for The Ridges, also use that water, no doubt ready to oppose any developer who threatens to build near them. The votes that Rae sought from homeowners in 2012 did not stop the county from approving this successor to The Ridges. But they might help block the next development in Zion Crossroads—unless those voters calculate that more rooftops will lure an Olive Garden restaurant and a grocery store a notch above Food Lion to the neighborhood.[19]

On April 21, 2005, Devin Nunes, chair of the U.S. House of Representatives' Parks Subcommittee, who was presiding over hearings to amend the Historic Preservation Act of 1966, charged that the historic review process was being used by cities and some agencies to stop development. Nunes queried witnesses like the general counsel for the wireless communications trade association, prompting horror stories of delays as long as three years to locate a cell phone tower. Peter F. Blackman was another star witness. He testified that the "National Park Service and others will use the National Register as a bludgeon against the property owner and trample his property rights if they can. To them, your property, once listed, is just a 'resource'; to them, it is not a home."[20]

Blackman's "resource" or "home" in Green Springs—depending on who was telling the story—was the very one that Angus and Deborah Murdock had rented three decades earlier—Eastern View. D. L and Frances Atkins sold that 250-acre property to Blackman in 2002, and it came with the scenic easement that the Atkinses had placed on it in 1973. That easement was first held by Historic Green Springs, Inc., which conveyed it to the National Park Service. The Atkinses were founding members of the group that battled the diagnostic center and the largest easement donors during the prison fight.[21]

Blackman claimed that he too cared about history and sought to renovate and rehabilitate the house, which clearly needed care, even when the Murdocks lived there. A graduate of Yale, Columbia Law School, and the Wharton School of Business, Blackman had worked for the international financial advisory and asset management firm Lazard and also served as an editor at the *New York Law Journal*. When it came to property rights and National Park Service administration of national landmarks, the views of Blackman and Rhodes Scholar Bob Sansom were no different than those of less educated Louisans like Millard Filmore Peers and Dean Agee.[22]

Blackman soon ran afoul of the Federal official administering the Eastern View easements. In January 2004 Blackman's attorney informed the NPS that his client would "commence the Rehabilitation at a time of his choosing without further notice." Blackman subsequently removed Eastern View's front porch. The NPS responded by filing *U.S. v. Blackman* in Federal district court. Two days later the judge issued an order temporarily restraining Blackman from "commencing and/or continuing renovation work to the manor house."[23]

That more than a front porch was at stake became apparent when Blackman challenged the validity of the 1973 easement on his property, and implicitly, the legality of a broad range of easements in the Commonwealth of Virginia and beyond. Because this question had never formally been settled, the Federal district court asked the Supreme Court of Virginia to opine. Citing the *amici curiae* brief filed by seven other preservation-oriented organizations, including the National Trust for Historic Preservation and the Nature Conservancy along with HGSI, Supreme Court Justice Lawrence L. Koontz noted in his June 2005 opinion that "the issue is of considerable significance beyond the specific historic district involved." His opinion on behalf of a unanimous court was unequivocal: Virginia law in 1973 did in fact recognize easements for "the purpose of land conservation and historic preservation" as valid. Even the *Central Virginian,* no friend of HGSI, labeled the ruling a "landmark decision." Rae Ely called it a "stunning victory" that validated "all conservation and historic easements donated prior to 1988, not only in Green Springs but across Virginia."[24]

One sentence from Judge Koontz's opinion resonated more than Rae's hyperbole. In refuting Blackman's contention that the 1973 easements were invalid when issued, the judge emphasized that "the granting of conservation easements by the landowners in the Historic Green Springs District was the direct result of the encouragement of the Governor for the express purpose of preserving the historic and natural beauty of a unique area." Holton's clever trap, inviting easements only to declare that they failed to assure Green Springs' preservation, had yielded a short-term victory for the governor. In the long run, however, those easements were the gift to HGSI that kept giving.[25]

As the Nunes hearings suggested, the "property rights" counterattack previewed in Robert Sansom's libertarian screed a decade earlier in *U.S. v. NPS* had by now gained momentum nationally. At the hearings, Blackman charged that the Historic Preservation Act of 1966 allowed the Department of the Interior and the NPS "to run roughshod over the property rights" of an owner. Speaking in October 2005 to the Ninth Annual National Conference on Private Property Rights of the Property Rights Foundation of America, Blackman argued that most Americans "had no illusions" about the threat from communism to private property. He compared that past vigilance to the stealthy approach of Federal bureaucrats, noting that "it may not occur to most Americans that a milder subversion on property rights has gone on in our own backyard."[26]

Blackman's relationship with the NPS had only deteriorated over the past year. In September 2004 the court reinforced its temporary restraining order, issuing an injunction that enjoined him from any renovation without prior approval from the NPS, although it did provide an exception for "basic maintenance and preservation of the manor house in its present state."

Blackman interpreted that exception broadly. Without obtaining permission, he removed the siding from large portions of the house. Refusing to back down, the NPS filed a motion for the defendant to "show cause" why he should not be held in criminal contempt of the injunction. On October 19, 2005, District Court Judge Norman K. Moon found Blackman guilty of criminal contempt and fined him $4,000. The crime was also punishable by up to six months in prison, but the judge chose to waive that option. Blackman's appeal failed when the Fourth Circuit determined that he had "willfully violated" the district court's order.[27]

The Virginia Land Rights Coalition (VLRC), whose purpose was to "provide information to Americans about the protection, ownership and wise use of private property and natural resources, and the core principles of our American Constitutional Republic," was Blackman's most vocal supporter. "Private Property is the cornerstone of our Constitutional Republic," the group's website proclaimed in 2021, "one of the three inseparable, unalienable, God-given Rights conveyed to man in the original Covenant." To preserve these rights local government should "control . . . local affairs, by consent of the governed and free of consolidated or centralized power."[28]

VLRC Chair L. M. Schwartz put the Blackman case in historical context. Characterizing the struggle against the prison, vermiculite mining, and housing development as "the efforts of a group of environmentalist and preservationist 'come-here NIMBYs' to run roughshod over the Property Rights of local landowners and businesses, and to undermine the decisions and authority of the Louisa County Board of Supervisors," Schwartz zeroed in on "Rea" [sic] Ely. He described HGSI as the asbestos-bashing reporter Schneider had portrayed them—" 'Ladies of Green Springs' . . . widows and 'maiden ladies' . . . silver-haired Southern belles who have fought for 30 years to save their historic land." Schwartz quoted another unnamed source who described Rae Ely as one of the "wackos and crazies and part of a fringe element."[29]

When I first looked into those rumors about Rae, I mistakenly assumed that the fiercest local advocates for property rights and local control—Judge Harold Purcell, County administrator Dean Agee, vermiculite-laden property owner M. F. Peers—were merely the parochial remnants of a regime forged in the Jim Crow South. Like Jim Crow itself, they would soon be overwhelmed by the more cosmopolitan, progressive tendencies afoot during the 1970s, often enforced by the federal government's intervention into local affairs. I began to question that assumption when I recognized how the courthouse crowd adapted its tactics to a more participatory style of politics—and a more litigious one as well.

These embers, like others smoldering in rural communities across America, ignited a powerful social movement that propelled a New Yorker, who could not have been more different from those rural citizens, into the White House. In Green Springs, the coals grew into part of a national conflagration through the efforts of cosmopolitan and highly educated men such as Bob Sansom and Peter Blackman, men who shared attitudes about property, economic growth, and federal meddling and railed against what President Donald Trump would call the "deep state."

Schwartz's article quoted some of those Green Springs easement holders who had also appealed to the Nunes subcommittee. D. L. Atkins carried the most clout since he had placed the easement on Eastern View in the first place. "I love Green Springs and its beautiful farmland, and I wanted to preserve that for my children and grandchildren," Atkins testified. "I contributed well over 1,500 acres [of easements] and did not receive any tax credits." In return, Atkins continued, "I have been treated with suspicion and like an adversary." He claimed that "the Park Service led us to believe that our easements . . . would allow us to manage our properties just like we had been doing before," but once the NPS controlled the easements, "they changed their tune. . . . If people knew what I and others have been through, they would run from any property over which the Park service has a say."[30]

D. L. Atkins was correct when he noted that he had not received any tax benefits. Neither had any of the other original easement donors who sought to stop the diagnostic center and then W. R. Grace & Co. Over the years, however, the number of acres protected by easements had grown significantly, from roughly 7,000 to 11,000. Many of those newer easement-holders *did* benefit from both state and Federal tax deductions. The "checkerboard" pattern of easements had been strategically filled out and now provided better protection from development—even if that coverage still contained gaps. The easements offered impressive scenic views to property owners and the public who found their way out to the dirt roads that crisscross the landmark district. Joggers still drive from Charlottesville to enjoy those vistas as they run. Those with access can gaze out upon "A Tapestry of Rural Landscapes and Architecture," as the NPS website describes it.[31]

Yet, as Robert Sansom pointed out decades earlier, there is no public access to any of the properties whose views are protected. Nor are there publicly accessible trails; not even a visitor center. Just those bullet-pocked brown signs marking the boundaries of the landmark district and a website. Between the cost of administering the district and the taxes forgone on the more recent easements, it is fair to ask if Americans got their money's worth from this public-private partnership forged in the 1970s. Were the National Park Service property guys right when they insisted that protecting Green Springs with easements was a mistake?

In 1973, the *Roanoke Times* editorialized that it was time to "bury the tomahawks dug up from Indian mounds in Louisa County" and get on with the critical business of constructing a diagnostic center in Green Springs. The offensive comment disparaged more than Native Americans; it poked fun at newly minted history that seemed to grow in proportion to the size of the threat to Green Springs' property owners. This was faux history, skeptics claimed, because nobody had cared about it before property values were threatened. Critics also charged that it was not "real" history because it did not address subjects that "serious" historians wrote about, like American presidents or Civil War battles.[32]

When Monacan chief Kenneth Branham addressed the James River Water Authority at a public meeting held at the Spring Creek Golf Course clubhouse in August 2019, he evoked the memory of his ancestors, whose remains were threatened by a proposed pumping station that would suck water from the James River to keep fairways green and ensure that Spring Creek homes and Zion Crossroads businesses had adequate water. "I don't think any of you gentleman would like to see your grandparents and great-grandparents dug up and removed," he told the meeting. "So I'm asking you to do the same thing that you would do if you were in my place, you would fight it. That's why we're here." Fifty years after Governor Holton announced his plans for the prison, a new battle pitted history and Indian artifacts against development.[33]

If the James River pipeline fight did not repeat Green Springs' history, it certainly rhymed with it. Planning the precise path of the pipeline and squabbling about who would pay for the on-again, off-again project stretched over a decade. The Fluvanna County Board of Supervisors finally issued the required permits in January 2016—but only after Louisa County threatened litigation. In July, their jointly formed utility, the James River Water Authority (JRWA), purchased land at the confluence of the James and Rivanna Rivers, a spot known as Point of Fork. This appeared to clear the way for construction.[34]

History soon intervened. The JRWA had ignored that history for some of the same reasons that the Commonwealth ignored Green Springs' history in 1970. Like Holton's Vietnam, the history grew richer and better documented over the course of the battle. Everybody knew that the pumping station site enjoyed its share of well-documented histories of white men, or at least the property they had owned: Thomas Jefferson's visit to the spot; the British capture of an American arsenal during the Revolution; and Point of Fork's namesake, a plantation occupied by federal troops during the Civil War.[35]

The history of Virginia's Indians? Not so much. As *Washington Post* reporter Gregory S. Schneider noted in 2020, "In a state that prides itself on preserving history, Native American heritage has long been overlooked." The very existence of Native Americans was nearly erased by the eugenics movement in the first half of the twentieth century when public officials insisted on a rigid binary to categorize race—"white" or "colored." Tireless work by archeologists dating back a century proved to be the exception to the studied neglect of Native American history. A recent example, and one directly "on point," was that of Professor L. Daniel Mouer, director of the Virginia Commonwealth University Archeological Research Center. In 1980 Mouer was working on a dig at Elk Island in the James River when he noticed construction at Point of Fork. When Mouer and his students examined the work site for the Colonial Pipeline, they discovered rich deposits of Native artifacts. The Virginia Department of Historic Resources subsequently identified human remains on the site. This did not spare those artifacts: they were bulldozed to complete the pipeline after a brief construction delay.[36]

As with HGSI's fight to stop the prison and vermiculite mining, what counted as "real" history continued to evolve, driven by another confluence— social and political trends. During the first two decades of the twenty-first century, historical scholarship began to address its centuries-long neglect and worse when it came to Native American history. Public historians did as well. As the director of the Virginia Department of Historic Resources told Schneider in 2020, "documenting and preserving Native American sites . . . was an important part of Virginia history and it was not as well understood or documented."[37]

The James River Water Authority did not inform the Monacans about its plans to build the pumping station until May 2017, almost a year after it purchased the Point of Fork land. Yet, even the JRWA recognized the need to go through the motions when it came to digging up what by 2017 was likely to be deemed a culturally sensitive site. A few weeks before informing Monacan leadership of its plans to construct the pumping station, the JRWA hired consultants to begin archeological probing on the site. The notice, however, did not invite the representatives of the tribe to observe or comment. Even though there was plenty of evidence to suggest that the Monacan ancestral capital, Rassawek (translated as "people who dwell at the fork"), lay beneath the site chosen for the pumping station, the Monacan Indian Nation initially only expressed "its concern and a desire to be consulted."[38]

Federal intervention proved to be a game changer, and it arrived via two routes. The first was regulatory. The JRWA required approval from the Army Corps of Engineers to draw water from the James, and that approval came with requirements reinforced by court cases like *Ely v. Velde*. The decision in that case and its successors underscored that an applicant to one Federal agency was subject to rules and regulations enforced by a host of others. For the history of the Monacans, a key voice was the Advisory Council on Historic Preservation—the same body that proved instrumental to HGSI's success.

The Monacan Nation used the Federal approval process as a lever to expose questionable archeological practices by the JRWA and introduce historical evidence supporting their claim that the pumping station would desecrate their ancestral capital. This, in turn, strengthened their hand at the negotiating table. Less than a month after the JRWA informed the Monacans of its plans for the pumping station, the Army Corps of Engineers invited the Nation to consult in the approval process. By the end of 2017, Preservation Virginia, also brought in by the Corps, raised concerns about the methods used by the JRWA's archeological and historical consultants.[39]

At this point Federal reinforcements arrived via the second route: tribal recognition. Congress passed the Indian Tribes of Virginia Recognition Act, signed into law in January 2018. The Monacans soon tested the power of their newfound federal recognition. "The eyes of everybody were on the project once we were federally recognized," Chief Branham noted. As with the discovery of Green Springs' history, Rassawek's past took on new life, energized by the tribe defending its *ancestral* backyard.[40]

To navigate these two powerful Federal streams the Monacan Nation engaged Cultural Heritage Partners as legal counsel. Their managing partner, Marion Werkheiser, appeared alongside Chief Branham at that 2019 Spring Creek Golf Course public meeting of the James River Water Authority. Less emotionally, but more legally fraught, Werkheiser's comments to the taxpayers of Fluvanna and Louisa Counties explained why the JRWA found itself embroiled in a dispute with the Monacan Nation and its allies. The Monacans now were demanding that the pumping station be moved to another site—one originally proposed by the JRWA but ultimately rejected as too costly. Werkheiser wanted taxpayers to know that "when the bill comes due for the additional money it costs to move this project, those extra dollars are the result of bad choices that YOU [the JRWA] made—not the fault of Native Americans or others who are simply exercising their right to oppose the destruction of their history and the disturbance of their ancestors."[41]

She then enumerated six mistakes made by the JRWA. Even before the Monacan Nation had been informed of the site, Preservation Virginia, the Virginia Department of Historic Resources, and prominent archeologists had told the JRWA that "you could not choose a worse location along the James River on which to site your project." Mistake number one was ignoring this advice. Federal law required the Army Corps of Engineers to consult with "community groups and impacted Tribes on the design of the project." Yet the JRWA had not engaged with the Monacan tribe until a year after purchasing the property for the site. Other items on the list included "playing games with the permitting system"; hiring "a vastly underqualified consultant because they were the lowest bid"; and "approving development that you expect to rely on this water source before you have approval to build it. You are bootstrapping yourself into a crisis of your own making."[42]

Werkheiser concluded her presentation with some advice to the Water Authority. "Be honest with your constituents about what you have done to create this problem and stop attacking the tribes for speaking up to defend their ancestors' burials and their heritage. Be assured that we will be taking that message directly to your constituents in the weeks ahead. The sooner you recognize that this dog won't hunt and move the location, the better. Save Rassawek."[43]

Rae was watching (Fig. 7).

Figure 7. Rae Ely in front of St. John's Chapel in Green Springs, February 2000. (Shana Raab/*The New York Times*/Redux)

NOTES

Abbreviations

CV   *The Central Virginian*
DP   *The Daily Progress*
NYT *The New York Times*
RTD *The Richmond Times-Dispatch*
WAPO *The Washington Post*

Introduction

1. Rae Ely interview, February 1, 2011. Unless otherwise noted, all interviews were conducted by the author.
2. Rae Ely, e-mails to author, June 7, 2020; Rae Ely interview, February 1, 2011.
3. T. M. D. to Peter Grace, March 4, 1974, attached to September 14, 1992, Bona to Walsh, Plaintiff's Trial Exhibit [hereafter, PTX] 319, Civil Action No. 3:95CV 0015, Ely Office Files, Antitrust Collection [hereafter, Antitrust Collection].
4. Rae Ely interviews, February 1 and March 17, 2011.
5. Bill McKelway and Allen Short, "Amateur Cockfight Was a Real Bust," *RTD*, May 11, 1976; Allen Short, "Six Acquitted in Albemarle Cockfight Case," *RTD*, August 20, 1976; "Uproar Over Cockfight Ruffles Virginia Gentry," *NYT*, August 1, 1976.
6. Rae Ely interview, February 1, 2011.
7. Rae Ely interview, February 1, 2011.
8. Rae Ely interview, February 1, 2011.
9. Rae Ely interview, February 1, 2011.
10. Rae Ely interviews, July 13 and August 10, 2010, March 22, 2014; Mrs. Hiram Ely Dead," *NYT*, February 17, 1962; Rae Ely interview, August 5, 2010.
11. Rae Ely interview, August 5, 2010; Megan Rosenfeld, "Historic-Area Strip Mining Triggers a Fight in Louisa," *WAPO*, September 5, 1975.

12. Helen Dewar, "Virginia Prison Site Decided," *WAPO*, March 31, 1973.
13. "Saving Green Springs," *Time* 100, no. 17 (October 23, 1972).
14. Bill Wayson interview, August 5, 2010. I have capitalized federal when it refers to the national (as opposed to state and local) government to distinguish between the level of government and the federal system of governance embedded in the United States Constitution.
15. Martha Derthick, *Keeping the Compound Republic: Essays on American Federalism* (Washington, D.C.: Brookings Institution Press, 2001), 138.
16. John Darnton, "Many Big Projects Near City Stymied by Public Protests," *NYT*, July 18, 1970.
17. Richard Nixon, "Statement About the General Revenue Sharing Bill, 1972," Gerhard Peters and John T. Woolley, *The American Presidency* Project, accessed September 13, 2022, https://www.presidency.ucsb.edu/documents/statement-about-the-general-revenue-sharing-bill.
18. Ric Stephens, "From NIMBYs to DUDEs: The Wacky World of Plannerese," *Planetizen*, July 26, 2005, https://www.planetizen.com/node/152; Wyatt Gordon, "Governor Glenn Younkin: YIMBY-in-chief?" *Virginia Mercury*, November 21, 2022, accessed November 24, 2022, https://www.virginiamercury.com/2022/11/21/governor-glenn-youngkin-yimby-in-chief/.

Chapter 1. A Reform-Minded Republican

1. Ray L. Garland to Linwood Holton, December 8, 1969; Holton to Garland, December 12, 1969, Environmental Affairs Folder, box 127, A. Linwood Holton Papers, 1968–1974, Library of Virginia [hereafter, Holton Papers].
2. Linwood Holton, *Opportunity Time* (Charlottesville, VA: University of Virginia Press, 2008), ch. 1.
3. Holton, *Opportunity Time*, 36.
4. James H. Hershman, Jr., "Holton, A. Linwood (1923–2021)," *Encyclopedia Virginia*, March 24, 2014, accessed September 15, 2020, https://encyclopediavirginia.org/entries/holton-a-linwood-1923/.
5. Reuben Fischer-Baum and Kim Soffen, "How Virginia Went from Blue to Red and Back Again," *WAPO*, November 6, 2017, accessed September 15, 2020, https://www.washingtonpost.com/graphics/2017/politics/virginia-election-history/; Holton, *Opportunity Time*, ch. 7 and p. 3.
6. James T. Wooten, "South Peaceful and Many Schools Are Integrated," *NYT*, September 1, 1970; Jon Nordheimer, "Richmond's Black Pupils Want Whites to Feel at Home," *NYT*, September 1, 1970.
7. Garland to Holton, December 8, 1969; Holton to Garland, December 12, 1969, Holton Papers; Adam Rome, *The Genius of Earth Day: How a 1970 Teach-in Unexpectedly Made the First Green Generation* (New York: Hill and Wang, 2013), 2; Holton, *Opportunity Time*, 100; "Environmental Awareness Week," *RTD*, April 21, 1970; Linwood Holton interview, August 10, 2010.
8. Linwood Holton interview.

9. "The Gallup Poll: Crime Tops Domestic List," *WAPO*, February 28, 1968; Marie Gottschalk, *The Prison and the Gallows* (Cambridge, UK: Cambridge University Press, 2006), 172–73 for quotation and 37; Eric Cummins, *The Rise and Fall of California's Radical Prison Movement* (Palo Alto, CA: Stanford University Press, 1994); Elizabeth Hinton, *From the War on Poverty to the War on Crime* (Cambridge, MA: Harvard University Press, 2016), 55–57.
10. Woody Holton interview; "Feasibility Study for the Virginia Division of Corrections," September 8, 1969, box 201, Welfare and Institutions folder, Holton Papers.
11. "Feasibility Study"; "Our Jails and Prisons," *DP*, March 15, 1970, 4.
12. Otis L. Brown, "Personal Data Statement," box 201, Holton Papers; *Richmond Mercury*, September 5, 1973, 5 for quotation; Brian Balogh, *Chain Reaction* (New York: Cambridge University Press, 1991), ch. 8.
13. *CV*, April 11, 1968, and "So Here We Are Forum," April 16, 1970; for quotation, see *CV*, December 11, 1969; Balogh, *Chain Reaction*, ch. 8.
14. Beverly Roger, "Penal Flap Meeting in Louisa Next Week," *DP*, June 3, 1970.
15. Woody Holton interview; *CV*, April 16, 1970.
16. Dorothy Mench, "Western Louisa Citizens Oppose Penal Facility," *DP*, June 2, 1970; "Brief Summary, Diagnostic Center," May 28, 1970, box 201, Holton Papers; "Louisa County Virginia, An Economic Study," VEPCO, Louisa County Historical Society Archives; U.S. Census Bureau, Census 1970 Survey, Table NT1, generated by Hamilton Lombard, Weldon Cooper Center for Public Service, University of Virginia, using Minnesota Population Center; National Historical Geographic Information; Frank R. Blackford, "Prison Proposal Unlocked Dispute," *Virginian-Pilot*, November 14, 1971; John Stanley Mahoney, Jr., "For Principle or Profit: Ideology and Interests in Historic Preservation" (Ph.D. diss., University of Virginia, 1983), 8; Dean Agee interview, December 2, 2010.
17. "Louisa Site Eyed for 3.7 Million State Prison Unit," *DP*, May 30, 1970; Jerry Simpson, "Brown: Penal Center to 'Fit In,'" *DP*, March 18, 1971.
18. "Louisa Site Eyed," *WAPO*, May 30, 1970; Jerry Simpson, "Brown: Penal Center to 'Fit In'"; Simpson, "Art Unit Okays Louisa Facility," *DP*, April 4, 1971; Claire White, "Green Springs," unpublished manuscript in author's possession; "Virginia's Correctional and Medical Center: A Giant Step Toward Effective Correctional Treatment," DWI, 9–10, Rae Ely Office Files [hereafter, EOF].
19. Otis Brown interview, December 13, 2010.

Chapter 2. Escaping Cul-de-sacs

1. Hiram Ely to Hope Ely, November 5, 1963, EOF.
2. Rae Ely interview, August 5, 2010; Rae Ely, e-mails to author, July 13, 2010, March 18 and 19, 2014, July 21, 2019; Facebook web page accessed September 16, 2022, https://www.facebook.com/Dade-County-Childrens-Home-in-KendallFlorida-DCCH-706216756100204/; Rae Ely interview, July 13, 2010.
3. Rae Ely interview, August 5, 2010.

4. Cliff Corcoran, "99 Cool Facts About Babe Ruth," *Sports Illustrated*, July 12, 2013, https://www.si.com/mlb/2013/07/12/99-cool-facts-about-babe-ruth; "Divorce Is Granted to New York Broker," *Miami Herald*, January 14, 1925; Hatfield Marriage Certificate, December 15, 1939, Florida Central Bureau of Vital Statistics; Rae Ely interview, July 13, 2010; *Miami News*, September 22, 1939; Bert Collier, "40-Foot Yacht Burns and Sinks," *Miami Herald*, May 28, 1958.
5. Rae Ely interview, July 13, 2010; "Woman Killed by Car on Bridge," *Miami News*, December 1, 1946.
6. Rae Ely interview, July 13, 2010.
7. Rae Ely interview, July 13, 2010.
8. Rae Ely interviews, July 13, 2010, and March 22, 2014.
9. Rae Ely interview, July 13, 2010.
10. Barbara Savidge, e-mail to author, September 17, 2022; Rae Ely interview, August 10, 2010; Dade County Children's Home, 1935 photograph, Florida State Archives, 1935, https://www.pbase.com/image/80258569.
11. Rae Ely interview, March 22, 2014; Rae Ely, e-mails to author, July 13, 2010, March 18 and 19, 2014.
12. "Grove Passes Test," *Miami News*, January 11, 1964; "Billy Graham's Beginnings with Youth for Christ," Billy Graham Library, https://billygrahamlibrary.org/yfc-billygraham/, accessed March 26, 2014; Richard Evans, "Reverent Teen-Agers Have Answers to Your Worries," *Miami Herald*, March 23, 1952.
13. Rae Ely interview, August 10, 2010; Barbara Moore-Savidge interview, May 19, 2014.
14. Rae Ely interviews, March 22, 2014, and July 20, 2010.
15. Rae Ely interviews, July 13 and March 22, 2010; "Mrs. Hiram Ely Dead," *NYT*, February 17, 1962; Chris Ely interview, May 12, 2014.
16. Rae Ely interview, March 22, 2014; Ely Prenuptial Agreement, October 18, 1962, EOF.
17. Rae Ely interview, August 5, 2010.
18. http://www.google.com/patents/US1758393; http://www.google.com/patents/US1939675, both accessed July 19, 2015; Rae Ely, interview, August 5, 2010; Chris Ely interview, May 12, 2014.
19. Rae Ely interview, August 5, 2010.
20. Rae Ely interviews, August 5 and July 20, 2010.
21. Chris Ely interview; Hope Ely to Dad, October 5, 1962; Coby to Hiram, October 7, 1962, EOF.
22. Rae and Hiram Ely Prenuptial Agreement.
23. Hiram to Hope, November 5, 1963, EOF.
24. Chris Ely interview; photo of "No Trespassing" sign and locked gate outside of ham-shaped pool, July 8, 1966 (in author's possession).
25. Rae Ely interviews, July 20 and August 5, 2010.
26. Christopher C. Sellers, *Crabgrass Crucible* (Chapel Hill, NC: University of North Carolina Press, 2012), 3; "RAPE" from a photograph in Adam Rome, *The Bulldozer in the Countryside: Suburban Sprawl and the Rise of American Environmentalism* (New York: Cambridge University Press, 2001), 152–53.

27. Rae Ely interviews, March 22 and August 5, 2010.
28. Rae Ely interviews, March 22 and August 5, 2010.
29. Rae Ely interview, August 5, 2010.
30. Rae Ely interview, August 5, 2010; George Gilliam and Mason Mills, interview with D. Barry Marshall, 2001, *The Ground Beneath Our Feet,* Virginia Center for Digital History, University of Virginia, accessed November 4, 2022, http://www2.vcdh.virginia.edu/xslt/servlet/XSLTServlet?xml=/xml_docs/modernva/modernva_transcripts.xml&xsl=/xml_docs/modernva/interview_modernva.xsl&level=single&id=Barry_Marshall.
31. Steve Suitts, "Segregationists, Libertarians, and the Modern 'School Choice' Movement," *Southern Spaces,* June 4, 2019, https://southernspaces.org/2019/segregationists-libertarians-and-modern-school-choice-movement/, accessed September 25, 2020.
32. Rae Ely interview, August 5, 2010.
33. Rae Ely interview, August 5, 2010.

Chapter 3. Competing Histories

1. Rae Ely interview, October 25, 2010; Angus Murdock, "A Private Opinion of the Future of the Green Springs," June 2, 1970, attached to John Askew to Holton, June 2, 1970, Holton Papers.
2. Murdock, "Private Opinion."
3. Meade Palmer, "Green Springs: A Land Use Study," December 1973, 10; Joseph Martin, *Virginia Gazetteer,* 1835, quoted in Benjamin Levy and Katherine Cole, "Report on Green Springs," 4–5, April 1974, NARA Green Springs File; Claire White, "Green Springs," unpublished manuscript in author's possession, 4, 114; "Green Springs Historic Landmark District, Statement for Management," May 1987, 2, National Park Service, EOF.
4. White, "Green Springs," 2–3, 186.
5. White, "Green Springs," 191, 186.
6. Rae Ely interview, October 25, 2010; Rae Ely interview, August 5, 2010 for quotation.
7. "Large Turnout Opposes Green Springs Site," *CV,* June 4, 1970; Dorothy Mench, "Western Louisa Citizens Oppose Penal Facility," *DP,* June 2, 1970; Jean Purcell, "Louisa Foes," *RTD,* June 3, 1970.
8. Mench, "Western Louisa Citizens."
9. "Penal Flap Meeting in Louisa Next Week," *DP,* June 3, 1970; "Green Springs' Fate," *DP,* June 9, 1970; quotation from Purcell, "Louisa Foes."
10. Beverly Roger, "Green Springs Area Is Promised," *DP,* June 12, 1970; "Green Springs Citizens Question Brown," *CV,* June 18, 1970; "Green Springs Area Is Promised" for Virginia Sargeant Reynolds quotation; Brown to Holton, January 28, 1970, Holton Papers.
11. "Large Turnout"; Mrs. John Askew to Holton, June 4, 1970, Mrs. D. L. Atkins to Holton, June 5, 1970, Krahenbills to Holton, June 1, 1970, box 201, Holton Papers.

12. Chris Dovi, "Elisabeth Nolting Dies at Age 94—She Helped Preserve Green Springs," *RTD*, August 14, 2000; "Carl Henry Nolting" obituary, *CV*, April 11, 1958; Nolting to Holton, June 2, 1970, Papers of the Nolting Family of Bracketts Farm, Louisa County, VA, Accession #13944, Special Collections, University of Virginia Library, Charlottesville; Elisabeth Nolting to Holton, June 2, 1970, box 201, Holton Papers.
13. Krahenbills to Holton, June 1, 1970; John Askew to Holton, June 2, 1970, box 201, Holton Papers.
14. *Kenyon Collegian*, October 25, 1957; Angus Murdock, e-mail correspondence with author, March 28, 2017; Angus Murdock interview, June 28, 2011; Deborah Murdock interview, December 31, 2015.
15. Joseph E. Illick, *At Liberty: The Story of a Community and a Generation* (Knoxville, TN: University of Tennessee Press, 1989), xvi.
16. Angus Murdock, e-mail to author, March 30, 2017; Deborah Murdock interview; K. Edward Lay, *History of the A School* (Charlottesville, VA: University of Virginia School of Architecture, 2013), 62.
17. Lay, *History*, 57; Deborah Murdock interview; William Frazier interview, April 18, 2018; Angus Murdock, e-mail to author, March 28, 2017.
18. Angus Murdock, e-mail to author, March 28, 2017; Deborah Murdock interview.
19. Angus Murdock, e-mail to author, March 28, 2017; Deborah Murdock interview.
20. Rae Ely interview, November 3, 2010; Deborah Murdock interview.
21. Deborah Murdock interview; Rae Ely interview, November 3, 2010.
22. Murdock, "Private Opinion."
23. Murdock, "Private Opinion."
24. Murdock, "Private Opinion."
25. Murdock, "Private Opinion"; underlining is Murdock's.
26. Murdock, "Private Opinion."
27. Beverly Roger, "What Is Now at Stake in the Green Springs Area," *DP*, June 18, 1970.
28. Rae Ely interview, November 3, 2010.
29. Rae Ely interview, November 3, 2010.
30. Samuel P. Hays, *Beauty, Health and Permanence* (Cambridge, UK: Cambridge University Press, 1987).

Chapter 4. "He Was Not Always Right—But He Was Never Wrong"

1. Bill Wayson interview; W. W. Whitlock, "Fact and Law," August 8, 1974, 25, attached to Whitlock to Judge Edward D. Berry, Legal Memorandum, August 8, 1974, Bracketts Archive; *WAPO*, October 3, 1976.
2. Eugenia T. Bumpass, *Portraits of Louisa County* (Charlottesville, VA: Bailey Printing, 1998), 168.
3. Otis Brown interview; Robert Whitlock interview.
4. Dean Levi, "Green Springs Battle Lines," *News Leader*, November 17, 1972, Department of Historical Resources Green Springs Collection [hereafter, DHR]; "Saving Green Springs," *Time* 100, no. 17 (October 23, 1972).

5. Levi, "Battle Lines"; Peter C. Luebke, "Battle of Trevilian Station," *Encyclopedia Virginia*, October 31, 2012, accessed March 8, 2023, http://www.EncyclopediaVirginia.org/The_Battle_of_Trevilian_Station_June_11-12_1864.
6. Holton to Scott, June 23, 1970, box 201, Holton Papers; Dean Agee interview.
7. Brent Cebul, "Creative Competition: Georgia Power, the Tennessee Valley Authority, and the Creation of a Rural Consumer Economy, 1934–1955," *Journal of American History*, June 2019: 45–70, esp. 54–55; see also Cebul, *Illusions of Progress Business, Poverty, and Liberalism in the American Century* (Philadelphia: University of Pennsylvania Press, 2023).
8. Cebul, "Creative Competition," 54–55.
9. Franklin D. Roosevelt, "Remarks to Directors of the National Emergency Council," February 2, 1934, American Presidency Project, accessed September 21, 2022, https://www.presidency.ucsb.edu/documents/remarks-directors-the-national-emergency-council, quoted in Cebul, *Illusions of Progress*, 35; Roosevelt: "Message to Congress Recommending Legislation," November 5, 1937, American Presidency Project, accessed September 21, 2022, https://www.presidency.ucsb.edu/documents/message-congress-recommending-legislation.
10. Brent Cebul, "Supply-Side Liberalism: Fiscal Crisis, Post-Industrial Policy, and the Rise of the New Democrats," *Modern American History* 2019: 139–64, esp. 145–46.
11. Ronald L. Heinemann, "Harry F. Byrd, 1887–1966," *Encyclopedia Virginia*, accessed December 22, 2021, https://encyclopediavirginia.org/entries/byrd-harry-f-1887–1966; and Heinemann, *Harry Byrd of Virginia* (Charlottesville, VA: University of Virginia Press, 1996), ch. 9, quotation at 170.
12. On "Little Harry," see William Yardly obituary, *NYT*, July 30, 2013, accessed November 25, 2021, https://www.nytimes.com/2013/07/31/us/harry-f-byrd-virginia-senator-dies-at-98.html; on his father, see Heinemann, "Byrd."
13. *Time*, September 28, 1958: 16, quoted in J. Harvie Wilkinson III, *Harry Byrd and the Changing Face of Virginia Politics, 1945–1966* (Charlottesville, VA: University of Virginia Press, 1968), 6; *WAPO*, July 18, 1965, quoted in Wilkinson, *Harry Byrd and the Changing Face*, 35.
14. Heinemann, *Harry Byrd*, 270, 8, 16, 128–30, 171, quotation at 10.
15. Wilkinson, *Harry Byrd and the Changing Face*, 33, 60; Heinemann, *Byrd*, 12; Bill Wayson interview, August 5, 2010.
16. "Judge Harold Purcell," accessed September 21, 2022, https://woodwardfuneral.com/obituaries/judge-harold-purcell/; Bumpass, *Portraits*,168; Earl Poore interview, December 29, 2014; Virginia Senate Resolution No. 266, 2008 Session, March 3, 2008, https://leg1.state.va.us/cgi-bin/legp504.exe?081+ful+SJ266+pdf; "Harold Purcell; Democratic Va. Legislator for 17 Years," obituary, *WAPO*, July 21, 2007; Purcell obituary, *RTD*, July 16, 2007.
17. Bumpass, *Portraits*, 168.
18. Earl Poore interview.
19. Earl Poore interview; Dockside Realty, e-mail to author, February 19, 2018.
20. Dean Agee interview.
21. Whitlock interview.

22. Dean Agee interview.
23. Dean Agee interview.
24. Lewis Stephens interview, November 27, 2019.

Chapter 5. Peppery Women

1. Terry H. Anderson, *The Movement and the Sixties: Protest in America from Greensboro to Wounded Knee* (New York: Oxford University Press, 1995); Sarah Evans, *Personal Politics: The Roots of Women's Liberation in the Civil Rights Movement and the New Left* (New York: Vintage Books, 1979); on Black women specifically, see Rhonda Williams, *The Politics of Public Housing: Black Women's Struggles against Urban Inequality* (New York: Oxford University Press, 2005); quotation in Paul Sabin, *Public Citizens: The Attack on Big Government and the Remaking of American Liberalism* (New York: W. W. Norton, 2021), 51; Michell M. Nickerson, *Mothers of Conservatism: Women and the Postwar Right* (Princeton, NJ: Princeton University Press, 2014).
2. Rome, *Bulldozer*; Lily Geismer, *Don't Blame Us: Suburban Liberals and the Transformation of the Democratic Party* (Princeton, NJ: Princeton University Press, 2015), ch. 4 and p. 97 for Concord quotation; Darnton, "Many Big Projects"; James Longhurst, *Citizen Environmentalists* (Medford, MA: Tufts University Press, 2010), 72.
3. Minutes, Green Springs Association, June 28, 1970, Amanda Welch Papers (in author's possession); Rae Ely interview, October 25, 2010; Sherri Ely to Holton, June 13, 1970, box 201, Holton Papers.
4. Rae Ely interview, November 3, 2010.
5. Rae Ely interview, November 3, 2010.
6. Emanuel Emroch File: R 28 L 31, University of Richmond Alumni Files; "Emanuel Emroch, Richmond, Va.: Man of the Month," *American Jewish Times-Outlook*, Greensboro, NC, September 1962.
7. Rae Ely interview, November 3, 2010.
8. Rae Ely interview, November 3, 2010.
9. Doris Krahenbill interview, January 19, 2015; Poore interview.
10. Krahenbill interview; Mr. and Mrs. Chauncey Krahenbill, "Penal Site Opposed," *DP*, July 3, 1970.
11. Krahenbill interview.
12. "Protest From Green Springs," *DP*, July 5, 1970.
13. Rae Ely interview, October 25, 2010; Roger Beverly, "Save Green Springs," *DP*, June 18, 1970; sign in author's possession with misspelling; Krahenbill interview.
14. Deborah Murdock interview.
15. Deborah Murdock interview; Richard Evans, "Reverent Teen-Agers Have Answers to Your Worries," *Miami Herald*, March 22, 1952; for a brief history of the mission, see Miami Rescue Mission, accessed September 23, 2022, http://www.miamirescuemission.com/about.php; Rae Ely interview, July 20, 2010.
16. Rae Ely interview, November 3, 2010; as of November 30, 2020, there were only seven Henrys—Jay Taylor's son is the seventh (e-mail from Jay Taylor to author, November 30, 2021).

17. Bumpass, *Portraits*, 148–49; "Cobham Park," Cvillepedia, accessed October 6, 2020, https://www.cvillepedia.org/Cobham_Park; "Tudor Place," accessed September 23, 2022, http://www.tudorplace.org/; "Elisabeth Aiken Nolting," obituary, *CV*, August 17, 2000; "Elisabeth Aiken Nolting," accessed September 23, 2022, http://bracketts.org/obituaries.htm; Chris Dovi. "Elisabeth Nolting Dies at Age 94—She Helped Preserve Green Springs," *RTD*, August 14, 2000.

18. Deborah Murdock interview, December 31, 2015; Rae Ely interview, November 3, 2010.

19. Deborah Murdock interview; Rae Ely interview, November 3, 2010.

20. Rae Ely interview, November 10, 2010; Deborah Murdock interview.

21. Carolyn Welton, "Leisurely Style of Life Flows from Green Springs," *Richmond News Leader*, September 30, 1970: 33.

22. Rae Ely interview, November 10, 2010.

23. Green Springs Association, October 28, 1970, Welch Papers; Rae Ely interview, November 10, 2010.

24. Rae Ely interview, November 10, 2010.

25. Rae Ely interview, November 10, 2010.

26. Deborah Murdock interview.

27. Deborah Murdock interview; Edward Lay interview, March 29, 2017.

28. Rae Ely unrecorded interview with author, July 8, 2021, documented in notes dated July 9, 2021, copied in July 11, 2021 e-mail (in author's possession).

29. Elizabeth Blum, *Love Canal Revisited: Race, Class, and Gender in Environmental Activism* (Lawrence, KS: University Press of Kansas, 2008), chs. 2 and 5, esp. pp. 31–35; Carolyn Merchant, "Women of the Progressive Conservation Movement, 1900–1916," *Environmental Review* 8, no. 1 (Spring 1974): 57–85, accessed July 18, 2022, http://www.jstor.org/stable/3984521?origin=JSTOR-pdf.

30. Bob Wimer, "State Panel Hears Plea to Save Green Springs," *DP*, January 30, 1971; Rae Ely, speech to Governor's Council on the Environment, Newcomb Hall, University of Virginia, January 29, 1971, 1, 3, Welch Papers.

31. Ely speech, 3–4; Wimer, "State Panel."

32. Jerry Simpson, "Art Commission Okays Green Springs Prison Plan," *DP*, April 4, 1971.

33. Rae Ely interview, November 24, 2010.

34. James Patterson, *Grand Expectations: The United States, 1945–1974* (New York: Oxford University Press, 1996), 562–69.

35. Lyndon B. Johnson, "Remarks" at the University of Michigan Online, Gerhard Peters and John T. Woolley, eds., American Presidency Project, accessed September 29, 2022, https://www.presidency.ucsb.edu/node/239689; Brian Balogh, "Making Pluralism 'Great': Beyond a Recycled History of the Great Society," in Sidney Milkis and Jerry Mileur, eds., *The Great Society and the High Tide of Liberalism* (Amherst, MA: University of Massachusetts Press, 2005), 145–82; Patterson, *Grand Expectations*, 569.

36. United States Conference of Mayors, Special Committee on Historic Preservation, *With Heritage So Rich: A Report* (New York: Random House, 1966); Ronald D. Anzalone, "A 'New Preservation': Creation of the National Historic Preservation

Act," in Virginia Department of Historic Resources, *Notes on Virginia* 54 (2016): 10, https://www.dhr.virginia.gov/pdf_files/Notes_on_Va_54_web.pdf; John M. Fowler, "Federal Historic Preservation Law: National Historic Preservation Act, Executive Order 11593, and Other Recent Developments in Federal Law," *Wake Forest Law Review* 12, no. 31 (1976): 40–41.
37. Bart Barnes and Joe Holley, "Neal Potter, 93; Montgomery Leader Stood for Slow Growth," obituary, *WAPO*, May 30, 2008, accessed September 28, 2022, http://www.washingtonpost.com/wp-dyn/content/article/2008/05/29/AR2008052903682.html; Rome, *Bulldozer*; Sellers, *Crabgrass Crucible*.
38. Barnes and Holley, "Potter"; Darnton, "Many Big Projects."
39. Darnton, "Many Big Projects."
40. Longhurst, *Citizen Environmentalists*, 72; Sarah Milov, *The Cigarette: A Political History* (Cambridge, MA: Harvard University Press, 2019), quotation at 176.
41. Hays, *Beauty*; Geismer, *Don't Blame Us*.
42. Nancy Talmont, *DP*, October 6, 1970.
43. Bryce Loving, "Three Score and Eleven," *DP*, October 25, 2011.

Chapter 6. Federalism's Fissures

1. Richard Nixon, "Address to the Nation on Domestic Programs," American Presidency Project, accessed September 30, 2022, https://www.presidency.ucsb.edu/node/239998.
2. Nixon, "Address."
3. James Cannon, "Federal Revenue-Sharing: Born 1972. Died 1986. RIP," *NYT*, October 10, 1986, accessed September 30, 2022, https://www.nytimes.com/1986/10/10/opinion/federal-revenue-sharing-born-1972-died-1986-rip.html.
4. Richard Nixon, "Annual Message to the Congress on the State of the Union, January 22, 1971," American Presidency Project, accessed September 30, 2022, https://www.presidency.ucsb.edu/documents/annual-message-the-congress-the-state-the-union-1; White House Press Release, March 5, 1971, 4, Nixon Move 2010, SFSM Colson, 108, White House Special Files, National Archives and Records Administration.
5. Press release, March 5, 1971.
6. Nixon, State of the Union, January 22, 1971; Richard Nixon, "Address to the Nation"; "Statement About the General Revenue Sharing Bill, 1972," American Presidency Project, accessed September 30, 2022, https://www.presidency.ucsb.edu/documents/statement-about-the-general-revenue-sharing-bill.
7. Hinton, *From the War on Poverty*, 14–15.
8. Nixon, "Statement About the General Revenue Sharing Bill."
9. Robert C. Lieberman, "Weak State, Strong Policy: Paradoxes of Race Policy in the United States, Great Britain, and France," *Studies in American Political Development* 16, no. 2: 138–61, at 148; Abourezk quoted in Sean Farhang, *The Litigation State: Public Regulation and Private Lawsuits in the U.S.* (Princeton, NJ: Princeton University Press, 2010), 4.

10. Paul Sabin, *Public Citizen*; for EDF and NRDC, see 43–45; Quinn Mulroy, *Litigation: How the American Bureaucracy Leverages Private Legal Power to Make Policy Work* (New York: Oxford University Press, forthcoming), ch. 2.
11. Rae Ely interview, November 10, 2010.
12. Rae Ely interview, November 10, 2010.
13. Rae Ely interviews, November 3 and 10, 2010.
14. Hinton, *From the War on Poverty*, 2.
15. "Prison Site Is Settled, Officials Say," *DP*, August 19, 1970; *Hiram B. Ely et al. v. Richard W. Velde et al.*, Civ. A. No. 459-70-R., 321 F. Supp.1088 (U.S. District Court, Eastern District of Virginia, Richmond Division, 1971) [hereafter, *Ely v. Velde 1*], quotations at 1–2; "Suit Seeks to Block Location of Prison Center in Louisa," *RTD*, August 22, 1970; "Green Springs Suit Cites Constitution Amendments and National Public Laws," *CV*, August 27, 1970; *Preservation News* 10, no. 10 (October 1970); James Taranto, "Roman Hruska Lives!" *Wall Street Journal*, May 4, 2009, accessed July 25, 2022, https://www.wsj.com/articles/SB124145651417883981; Hinton, *From the War on Poverty*, 144–45.
16. "Prison Site Settled"; *Ely v. Velde 1*, 1–2; "Suit Seeks to Block Location"; "Green Springs Suit."
17. Rae Ely interview, November 18, 2010.
18. Fowler, "Federal Historic Preservation Law," 42–43.
19. "Decision of Judge Merhige Awaiting Results of Tests," unlabeled newspaper article in Welch Papers, ca. November 11, 1970; Harry S. Raleigh, Jr., "Case Comments," *Notre Dame Lawyer* 47 (1972): 1042–77, at 1049.
20. Rae Ely interview, November 18, 2010.

Chapter 7. Virginia's Preservation Network

1. H. Bryan Mitchell, "The Virginia Historic Landmarks Commission: The State's Preservation Agency," *University of Virginia News Letter* 56, no. 11 (July 1980); 41–44. On picket fence federalism see Terry Sanford, *Storm Over the States* (New York: McGraw-Hill, 1967).
2. James Moody to Edward Alexander, September 18, 1970, DHR.
3. Henry Taylor to Linwood Holton, June 5, 1970; Taylor to John W. Riely, June 9, 1970; Junius Fishburne to Taylor, June 17, 1970, DHR.
4. Jane B. Davies to Fishburne, June 30, 1970, attached to Fishburne to Davies, July 8, 1970, DHR.
5. Angus Murdock, e-mail to author, March 18, 2018; Murdock to Riley, June 10, 1970, DHR.
6. "Sequential Calendar: National Trust and Green Springs," February 1, 1971; James Biddle to Otis Brown, July 8, 1970; Alexander to Brown, July 13, 1970, DHR.
7. Susan Peters interview, January 15, 2015; Boswell's Tavern Description, Virginia Department of Historic Resources, Historic Registers, Louisa County, accessed January 26, 2021, https://www.dhr.virginia.gov/historic-registers/054-0007/.
8. Calder Loth interview, January 15, 2015; James Moody to Alexander, July 9, 1970, DHR.

9. Virginia Historic Landmarks Commission [hereafter, VHLC], "Green Springs, Louisa County," July 28, 1970, DHR.
10. "Green Springs Suit."
11. Brown to Alexander, July 28, 1970, DHR.
12. Composite of VHLC minutes, October 6, 1970, August 4, 1970 excerpt; Fishburne to Frisbee, July 28, 1970, DHR.
13. Moody to Garvey, August 18, 1970, DHR.
14. DHR Historic Register, accessed October 1, 2022, https://www.dhr.virginia.gov/historic-registers/louisa-county/.
15. Moody to Alexander, September 18, 1970; Moody to Elys, September 17, 1970; Moody to Taylors, September 17, 1970, DHR.
16. Holton to Hartt, September 3, 1971, Welch Papers.
17. Hartt to Holton, September 13, 1971, Holton Papers.
18. Hartt to Holton, September 13, 1971, Welch Papers.
19. Biddle to Holton, September 8, 1970, Holton Papers; Biddle to Brown, September 8, 1970, DHR; Ed Temple to Brown, August 26, 1970, Holton Papers; handwritten note from Moody to Holton, July 24, 1970, attached to Temple to Brown, August 26, 1970.

Chapter 8. Federal Court

1. Moody to Biddle, January 21, 1972, DHR.
2. Ronald Bacigal, interview with Robert Merhige, November 25, 1985, downloaded from University of Richmond Library; Ellen Kehril-Steinberg, "Taking a Tour through Merick's Unique Neighborhoods," *Patch,* March 20, 2010, accessed October 2, 2022, https://patch.com/new-york/merrick/taking-a-tour-through-merricks-unique-neighborhoods; Robert E. Payne, "The Honorable Robert R. Merhige, Jr.," *University of Richmond Law Review* 40, no. 23 (2005): 23.
3. Payne, "Honorable," 24; Bacigal, Merhige interview.
4. Robert R. Merhige, Jr., "A Judge Remembers Richmond in the Post-Brown Years," *Washington and Lee Law Review* 49, no. 1 (1992): 26, 23; Payne, "Honorable," 25; Robert B. Fitzpatrick, "Stories of a Judge: Remembering Robert Merhige Jr.," *Legal Times* 27, no. 9 (February 28, 2005).
5. Robert A. Pratt, "The Conscience of Virginia: Judge Robert R. Merhige Jr. and the Politics of School Desegregation," *University of Richmond Law Review* 52, no. 29 (2022): 29–37, at 36; Merhige, "A Judge Remembers," 29.
6. Rae Ely interview, November 18, 2010; Ronald Bacigal interview, May 8, 2018.
7. "U.S. Courthouse, Richmond, VA," U.S. General Services Administration, accessed October 22, 2022, https://www.gsa.gov/historic-buildings/lewis-f-powell-jr-us-courthouse-richmond-va; "Seven Witnesses Oppose Penal Center," *RTD,* November 3, 1970; "Decision of Judge Merhige Awaiting Results of Tests," *CV,* November 5, 1970.
8. Bill Jobes, "Court Delays Ruling on Prison Location," *DP,* November 4, 1970; Bacigal, "A Judge Remembers," 2–3.

9. *Ely v. Velde 1*, 1093–94 for quotations (Merhige's emphasis); "Recent Development, Ely v. Velde: The Application of Federal Environmental Policy to Revenue Sharing Programs," *Duke Law Journal* 1972: 667–79, at 674.
10. *Ely v. Velde 1*, 1093–94 (Merhige's emphasis); "Ely v. Velde," 674.
11. Jerry Simpson, "Brown: Penal Center to 'Fit In,'" *DP*, March 18, 1971; "Green Springs Group Will Carry on Fight," *DP*, January 25, 1971; Jerry Simpson, "Judge Refuses Louisa Again," *DP*, February 5, 1971.
12. "Two National Groups Join Prison Fight," *DP*, June 18, 1971; Moody to Garvey, January 27, 1971, DHR.
13. Biddle to Johnson, March 30, 1971, DHR; Jerry Simpson, "Art Commission OKs Green Springs Prison Plan," *DP*, April 4, 1971; "Two National Groups"; *Green Springs Association Newsletter* [hereafter, *GSA Newsletter*], June 28, 1971, Welch Papers.
14. Jerry Simpson, "Sold to State for Penal Unit," *DP*, January 29, 1971; Deborah Murdock, e-mail to author, May 28, 2018; Jerry Simpson, "Federal Officials Hear Plea by Green Springs Delegation," *DP*, February 17, 1971; Rae Ely interview, November 24, 2010.
15. Patricia Nixon to Frederick Hartt, May 24, 1971, Welch Papers.
16. "Residents of Old Virginia Spa Oppose Prison Facility Plan," *WAPO*, April 25, 1971.
17. Dorothy Mench, "TV News Filmed in Green Springs," *DP*, August 19, 1971.
18. *Ely v. Velde*, U.S. Court of Appeals, Fourth Circuit, 451 F.2d 1130, argued August 23, 1971, decided November 8, 1971 [hereafter, *Ely 1 Appeal*]; *GSA Newsletter*, September 17, 1971; "Louisa Case in Appeals Court," *DP*, August 23, 1971; Ken Ringle, "Court Ruling Sets Back Va. Prison Plans," *WAPO*, November 10, 1971.
19. "Court Ruling"; Harry S. Raleigh, Jr., "Case Comments," *Notre Dame Lawyer* 47 (1972): 1042–77, at 1043.
20. Raleigh, "Case Comments," 1051–54; *Ely 1 Appeal*, at 16, quoted in Raleigh, 1052–3; *Calvert Cliffs Coordinating Committee Inc. v. United States Atomic Energy Commission*, 449 F. 2nd, 1109 (D.C. Circuit, 1971), cited in Raleigh, "Case Comments," 1053.
21. *Ely 1 Appeal*, 7; Raleigh, "Case Comments, 1051.
22. Ringle, "Court Ruling"; Mike Steele, "State to Go Ahead with Prison," *DP*, November 10, 1971.
23. "Case Comments," 1050 and 1054; appeals court decision quoted in "Comment," 1052.
24. "Case Comments," 1056.
25. "Virginia to Proceed on Prison," *News-Virginian*, November 10, 1971.
26. "Chance to Reconsider," *RTD*, November 12, 1971.
27. "VA. Mulls Decision on Penal Site," *WAPO*, December 4, 1971; James N. Woodson, "Environmental Reports Must Now Accompany New Jail Fund Pleas," *RTD*, December 3, 1971.
28. VHLC minutes, November 16, 1971, 215–16; Moody to Biddle, January 21, 1972, DHR.
29. "Penal Center Will Not Hurt Environment"; "Study Holds Prison Not Harmful"; DWI Press Release; "An Objective Report?" *RTD*, December 19, 1971.
30. Bob Gibson, e-mail to author, December 29, 2020.

31. Ed Grimsley interview, June 9, 2014.
32. Sanders to Tuck, cover letter, January 11, 1972; Sanders to LEAA, January 10, 1972, DHR.
33. Letter cited in VHLC chronology; Fishburne to Minter, March 6, 1972; McDermott to Moody, January 25, 1972; Biddle to Smith, February 10, 1972, DHR; Claude Burrows, "Gains by Penal Site Foes Seen," *RTD*, February 15, 1972; "Court Fights May Delay Louisa Facility 2 Years," *RTD*, February 18, 1972; "Waste Not," *RTD*, February 14, 1972.
34. Jerry Simpson, "Green Springs Hearing to View Key Resolution," *DP*, February 28, 1972; "Green Springs Hearing Cancelled," *DP*, February 29, 1972; "Ode," *DP*, March 6, 1972.
35. Historic Green Springs Association letter (Ely) to members, May 2, 1972, Welch Papers.

Chapter 9. The Women's Ground War

1. Rae Ely interview, December 22, 2010.
2. Jerry Simpson, "Governor Gets Petition," *DP*, January 11, 1972; Simpson, "Holton Meets with Green Springs Delegation, Receives Petition Opposing Prison Location," *CV*, January 13, 1972; Rae Ely interview December 22, 2010.
3. Simpson, "Holton Meets."
4. Simpson, "Holton Meets"; "Governor Gets Petition."
5. Simpson, "Holton Meets"; Holton to Mrs. R. A Murdock, January 11, 1972, Welch Papers.
6. Simpson, "Governor Gets Petition."
7. Simpson, "Governor Gets Petition."
8. Simpson, "Governor Gets Petition."
9. Agee, Whitlock, and Krahenbill interviews.
10. Krahenbill interview.
11. Rae Ely interviews, August 5 and December 30, 2010.
12. Rae Ely interview, August 5, 2010.
13. Rae Ely interview, December 30, 2010.
14. Rae Ely interview, December 30, 2010.

Chapter 10. Courting Bureaucrats

1. Rae Ely interview, December 17, 2010.
2. Megan Rosenfield and Paul G. Edwards, "Major Reynolds: Virginia Name, Virginia Money," *WAPO*, April 20, 1977, accessed October 3, 2022, https://www.washingtonpost.com/archive/local/1977/04/20/major-reynolds-virginia-name-virginia-money/cd5e340d-1e67-4236-80f7-d4820f7c1d5e/; Rebecca Hanmer interview, January 10, 2010.
3. Rae Ely interview, December 17, 2010; Daniel Carpenter, *The Forging of Bureaucratic Autonomy: Reputations, Networks, and Policy Innovation in Executive Agencies, 1862–1928* (Princeton, NJ: Princeton University Press, 2002).

4. Hanmer interview; Christine Neuberger, "Keysville: Town to Mark 100 Years of Solitude," *RTD*, September 6, 1987.
5. Bruce Blanchard interview, January 12, 2012.
6. Bob Craig, "U.S. Green Springs Report to Be Challenged in Court," *DP*, August 9, 1972; "LEAA Files Impact Report with Environmental Council," *CV*, August 10, 1972; "Green Springs—Again," *RTD*, August 13, 1972.
7. "Green Springs—Again"; Roger Miller, "Merhige Won't Stop Prison Impact Study," *DP*, August 14, 1972.
8. A-95 Information Officer, Division of State Planning and Community Affairs, to Moody, August 1, 1972; Moody to Lauer, August 15, 1972, DHR.
9. "Louisa No Prison Site, Report Says," *DP*, August 25, 1972.
10. "Louisa No Prison Site."
11. "Louisa No Prison Site."
12. "The Impact Report," *RTD*, August 27, 1972; Rae Ely letter to Dear Fellow Members, September 25, 1972, Welch Papers.
13. Hanmer interview.
14. Hanmer interview.
15. Hanmer interview; Hanmer resume, undated, provided to author in December 16, 2015 e-mail.
16. Ann Carey McFeatters, *Sandra Day O'Connor: Justice in the Balance* (Albuquerque, NM: University of New Mexico Press, 2006), 45–47; "Sandra Day O'Connor's Peninsula Ties," *San Mateo Daily Journal*, June 14, 2018, accessed October 15, 2020, https://www.smdailyjournal.com/news/local/sandra-day-o-connor-s-peninsula-ties/article_f6d00d70-67a5-11e8-9bc3-a33b5eb945f0.html.
17. Hanmer interview; Rivlin CV on the Brookings Institution website, accessed October 3, 2022, https://www.brookings.edu/wp-content/uploads/2016/07/rivlin-cv_-2018.pdf; John Dean, *The Rehnquist Choice: The Untold Story of the Nixon Appointment That Redefined the Supreme Court* (New York: Simon & Schuster, 2001), 113.
18. Nixon Secret Tapes, 1:32:30, accessed October 4, 2022, http://web2.millercenter.org/rmn/audiovisual/whrecordings/chron2/rmn_e581a.mp3. "Richard Nixon, John N. Mitchell, and Stephen B. Bull on 30 September 1971," Richard Nixon Telephone Tapes, Oval Office Recordings, Conversation 581-4, Miller Center of Public Affairs, University of Virginia; "Richard Nixon and John B. Connally on 24 September 1971," Conversation 010-009, Presidential Recordings Digital Edition [Nixon Telephone Tapes 1971, ed. Ken Hughes] (Charlottesville, VA: University of Virginia Press, 2014).
19. Rosenfield, and Edwards "Major Reynolds"; Hanmer interview; *GSA Newsletter*, September 25, 1972, EOF.
20. Hanmer interview; Green Springs compendium, "Comments and Information on Environmental Impact of Proposed Reception and Diagnostic Center in Green Springs," EOF.
21. Neuberger, "Keysville"; Jennifer Buckman, "Longtime Keysville Mayor Dies at 86," *RTD*, January 5, 2002; "Keysville Ready for New Phone Service," *RTD*, September 2, 1991; Hanmer interview.
22. Hanmer interview.
23. Hanmer interview.

24. Blanchard interview as edited by Bruce Blanchard in December 5, 2022 e-mail from Mary Josie Blanchard to author.
25. Edited Blanchard interview.
26. Edited Blanchard interview.
27. Edited Blanchard interview.
28. Hanmer interview.
29. Edited Blanchard interview.
30. Lyons to Madden, September 21, 1972, DHR; Helen Dewar, "Site Criticism Clouds Virginia Prison Project," *WAPO*, September 27, 1972.
31. "Interior Critical of Prison," DP, September 27, 1972. "How Much Longer?" *RTD*, September 28, 1972; "The History of the Richmond Times-Dispatch," *RTD*, December 3, 2014, accessed October 4, 2022, https://richmond.com/the-history-of-the-richmond-times-dispatch/article_5d7412c0-8f5f-11e3-a538-0017a43b2370.html.
32. BOS to Edward Grimsley; "Louisa Supervisors Write Times-Dispatch Facts on Diagnostic Center Site," *CV*, October 5, 1972.
33. "Louisa Supervisors."
34. Roger Miller, "Federal Money Won't Build Louisa Prison," *DP*, October 7, 1972; Peter Bacque, "Challenge Tossed Green Springs," *DP*, October 11, 1972.
35. Miller, "Federal Money"; Bacque, "Challenge Tossed": Helen Dewar, "Louisa County Now Girds to Fight Mining Project," *WAPO*, October 6, 1972.

Chapter 11. Public-Private Partnership

1. Governor's Press Release, attached to October 12, 1972, H. Peter Pudner, Historian-Editor, VHLC, to Members of the Commission, DHR.
2. Governor's Press Release; Bacque, "Challenge Tossed."
3. Claude Burrows, "State May Drop Louisa Project," *RTD*, October 11, 1972; Loth interview.
4. *Life* magazine 69, no. 1 (July 4, 1970): 28; Rae Ely interview, December 22, 2010.
5. Rae Ely interview, December 22, 2010.
6. "Green Springs Praised," *DP*, October 26, 1970.
7. Bacque, "Challenge Tossed"; Helen Dewar, "Holton Acts to Dump Va. Prison Site," *WAPO*, October 11, 1972; Jean Purcell, "Reaction in Louisa Is Mixed," *RTD*, October 11, 1972.
8. Burrows, "State May Drop Louisa Project"; Roger Miller, "Strip Mining in Green Springs?" *DP*, October 4, 1972; Dewar, "Louisa County Now Girds."
9. Rae Ely interview, December 22, 2010.
10. Rae Ely interview, December 22, 2010.
11. Helen Dewar, "Residents Oppose Plan for Penal Facility," *WAPO*, April 25, 1971; Jean Purcell, "Holton Says Center in Louisa Definite," *RTD*, September 12, 1971; "Prison Foes Extend Effort," *RTD*, December 2, 1970.
12. Note attached to "Prison Foes," DHR.
13. Alexander to Abbott, January 4, 1972, 2, attached as Appendix VI to VHLC minutes, March 21, 1972, DHR.
14. Moody to Murtagh, Keeper of the National Register, January 12, 1972, DHR.

15. Murtagh to SLOs, April 18, 1972, DHR.
16. Margaret T. Peters, *Conserving the Commonwealth: The Early Years of the Environmental Movement in Virginia* (Charlottesville, VA: University of Virginia Press, 2008); "Conservation and Open-Space Easement Donations, Virginia CLE, 2008," provided by David Kudravetz, I-1, 15; John Frisbee III, "Virginia Open Space Easements Are Extra Preservation Tool," *Preservation News*, May 1, 1971: 5.
17. Brian Balogh, *A Government Out of Sight: The Mystery of National Authority in Nineteenth-Century America* (New York: Cambridge University Press, 2007); *The Associational State: American Governance in the Twentieth Century* (Philadelphia: University of Pennsylvania Press, 2015); Christopher P. Loss, *Between Citizens and State: The Politics of Higher Education in the Twentieth Century* (Princeton, NJ: Princeton University Press, 2012); Brent Cebul, *Illusions of Progress*; Greta Krippner, *Capitalizing on Crisis: The Political Origins of the Rise of Finance* (Cambridge, UK: Cambridge University Press, 2012); Lily Geismer, *Left Behind: The Democrats' Failed Attempt to Solve Inequality* (New York: Public Affairs, 2022).
18. Bruce J. Schulman, *The Seventies: The Great Shift in American Culture, Society, and Politics* (New York: Free Press, 2001), 246, 248; Suleiman Osman, " 'We're Doing It Ourselves': The Unexpected Origins of New York City's Public-Private Parks during the 1970s Fiscal Crisis," *Journal of Planning History* 16, no. 2 (2016): 162–74, at 169; Osman, *The Invention of Brownstone Brooklyn: Gentrification and the Search for Authenticity in Postwar New York* (Oxford: Oxford University Press, 2012).
19. Osman, " 'We're Doing It Ourselves,' " 169, quotation at 170.
20. "Resolution," Appendix III, DHR.
21. Draft letter from Elizabeth Nolting, President, to Members of the Green Springs Association, October 15, 1972, EOF; "Agreement," October 29, 1972, Welch Papers.
22. "Master Map of Green Springs," October 21, 1972, EOF; Nolting to Fishburne, October 30, 1972, DHR.
23. Bracketts inventory of Green Springs easements, Bracketts Archive; Map of GS Easements; Green Springs Easements Fact Sheet, EOF.
24. Nolting to Fishburne, October 30, 1972; Holton to Congressman Kenneth Robinson, November 1, 1972, DHR; Roger Miller, "Green Springs Residents Join State for Study," *DP*, November 20, 1972; "Green Springs Landowners Indicate Easements to Be Given on 6,307 Acres," *CV*, December 7, 1972.
25. Nolting to Members, December 9, 1972, EOF; Claude Burrows, "Green Springs Battle Ebbs Till Next Round," *RTD*, December 10, 1972; Loth interview. Peter Bacque, "Green Springs Residents Say Demands Met," *DP*, December 5, 1972; Gilliam to Fishburne, December 1, 1972, DHR; "Green Springs Landowners Indicate."
26. "Green Springs Landowners Indicate."
27. Loth interview; Junius Fishburne interview, June 6, 2018.
28. Fishburne to Commission, "Green Springs Historic District," February 14, 1973, DHR.
29. Minutes of the Landmark Committee, Appendix II, VHLC minutes, February 20, 1973, 264, DHR.
30. "Springs' Acres Named," *DP*, February 21, 1973; "A Historic District," *RTD*, February 26, 1973.

Chapter 12. Vermiculite

1. Peter Bacque, "Stormy Controversies Strike Louisa County in '73," *DP*, December 31, 1973.
2. Peers to VHLC, March 1, 1973, attached to Abbott to Peers, March 7, 1973, DHR; Dave Dawson, "Board Appeals Green Springs Decision," *DP*, March 15, 1973; "Court Asked to Void Historic Designation," *RTD*, March 15, 1973; see also attachment from Quatro Hubbard with full minutes, March 15, 1973, DHR.
3. "Mrs. Nininger Tells 50-Year Restoration and Love of Land," *CV*, July 11, 1974.
4. "Green Springs: Finis?" *Roanoke Times*, March 1, 1973.
5. "Green Springs: Finis?"
6. Meade Palmer, *Green Springs, Louisa County, Virginia: A Land Use Study*, December 1973, 16, 20; Robert Hopkins, "Geology of Western Louisa County, Virginia" (Ph.D. diss., Cornell University, 1960).
7. Green Springs Nomination for Historic District narrative, February 20, 1973, 1, DHR; Dave Dawson, "Who Is Grace?" *DP*, June 10, 1973.
8. Lyall to Editor, *CV*, June 14, 1973.
9. Arie de Geus, "The Living Company," *Harvard Business Review*, March–April 1997: 2, 4.
10. Patricia A. Dreyfus, "W. R. Grace & Company," September 1, 1972, 26–29, quotation at 29.
11. "Oil Dependence and Foreign Relations," Council on Foreign Relations, accessed December 30, 2020, https://www.cfr.org/timeline/oil-dependence-and-us-foreign-policy.
12. Thomas Lyall's letter to the ninth-grade science class is reprinted in *CV*, October 12, 1972.
13. Dean Levi, "Green Springs Battle Lines," *News Leader*, November 17, 1972.
14. Fishburne to Ogg, October 24, 1972, attached to Fishburne to Ogg, November 9, 1972, DHR.
15. Levi, "Green Springs Battle Lines."
16. "HLC Designate Historic Area in Louisa County This Week," *CV*, February 22, 1973.
17. Dorothy Mench, "Green Springs Rule Condemned," *DP*, February 22, 1973; untitled resolution, February 21, 1973, attached to Fishburne to Agee, February 28, 1973, DHR; "Louisa Hits Historic Tag," *RTD*, February 23, 1973; "HLC Designate Historic Area."
18. Mr. and Mrs. Lewis Dobbins to VHLC, February 23, 1973, attached to Fishburne to Dobbins, March 6, 1973; Fishburne to Dobbins, February 28, 1973; Dobbins to Fishburne, March 1, 1973, attached to Fishburne to Dobbins, March 6, 1973, DHR.
19. "GS Area Gets National Tag," *DP*, March 13, 1973; Jean Purcell, "GS Gets Historic Listing," *RTD*, March 13, 1973, for Ely quotation.
20. Dorothy Mench, "Louisa Still Fighting Green Springs," *DP*, March 7, 1973; Dave Dawson, "Board Appeals GS Decision," *DP*, March 15, 1973; "Court Asked to Void Historic Designation," *RTD*, March 15, 1973.
21. "County Landowners Join Supervisors in Noting Appeal of VHLC Designation," *CV*, March 15, 1973.

22. Peers to Connally, attached to Murtagh to Peers, April 30, 1973; Murtagh to Peers, April 30, 1973; M. F. and Norma Peers to Murtagh, May 21, 1973, attached to Murtagh to Peers, May 24, 1973, DHR.
23. L. J. Hash to Project Lou File, Visit Lou Area, March 15, 1973, HGSI 91, Antitrust Collection.
24. Hash to Lyall, March 20, 1973; O. M. Favorito to H. A. Brown regarding VA Historic Landmarks Act, April 3, 1973, Antitrust Collection; Lou Cannon, "Nixon Asks Hill to Act on Ecology," *WAPO*, February 15, 1973; James Morton Turner and Andrew C. Isenberg, *The Republican Reversal* (Cambridge, MA: Harvard University Press, 2018).
25. John R. Nolon, "The National Land Use Policy Act," *Pace Environmental Law Review* 13, no, 519 (1996), accessed August 30, 2019, http://digitalcommons.pace.edu/pelr/vol13/iss2/6; James W. Curlin and Robert K. Lane, "National Land Use Policy Legislation, 93d Congress: An Analysis of Legislative Proposals and State Laws," Congressional Research Service (U.S. Government Printing Office: Washington, D.C., 1973); see also "Senate Votes Bill to Authorize $1 Billion for Land-Use Grants," *Wall Street Journal*, June 22, 1973; George C. Wilson, "Morton Shifts on Land-Use Bill," *WAPO*, June 11, 1974; "Ruckelshaus Favors Aid for States on Land Use," *NYT*, April 2, 1973; Richard D. Lyons, "House Vote Kills Bill on Land Use," *NYT*, June 12, 1974.
26. Favorito to Brown, April 3, 1973.
27. "Firm Indicates Further Interest in GS," *RTD*, April 20, 1973; quotation from "Supervisors Hold Three Public Hearings," *CV*, April 26, 1973; "Request of Pit Mining Given Louisa Commission," *DP*, April 25, 1973.
28. For an outstanding discussion of how Nixon cynically ran roughshod over local prerogatives in criminal justice, see Hinton, *From Great Society*.
29. "Release from Governor's Office," March 30, 1973, Appendix IV, March 30, 1973, in April 1973 minutes, DHR; Helen Dewar, "Virginia Prison Site Decided," *WAPO*, March 31, 1973; Peter Bacque, "Holton Orders Prison Construction to Begin in Historic Green Springs," *DP*, March 31, 1973.
30. Dewar, "Virginia Prison Site Decided"; Bacque, "Holt Orders Prison Construction to Begin."
31. Dewar, "Virginia Prison Site Decided"; Bacque, "Holton Orders Prison Construction to Begin."
32. "The Green Springs Sonata," *DP*, April 4, 1973; "The Final Word on Green Springs?" *World News*, April 3, 1973.
33. "Green Springs: Finis?"; *GSA Newsletter*, ca. April 1, 1973, Welch Papers.

Chapter 13. The Conflict Expands

1. Lennart Heimer, "Future of Green Springs Discussed," *RTD*, May 12,1973; "A Question of Values," *DP*, May 27, 1973.
2. David D. Ryan, "State Gets GS 'Jolt,' " *RTD*, July 19, 1973.
3. National Park Service, "Expanding the Register," in *The NPHA and NPS: A History*, 2007, accessed October 7, 2022, https://www.nps.gov/parkhistory/online_books/mackintosh5/chap2.htm.

4. "GS Area Gets National Tag;" Ernest Connally to Assistant Secretary for Fish and Wildlife and Parks, re "Green Springs Easements," August 31, 1973, ARC ID 41681673, Virginia SP Green Springs Historic District, Digitized National Historic Landmarks Nomination File, RG 79, Records of the National Park Service, 1785–2006, National Archives [hereafter, GS NHL Nomination File].
5. Department of the Interior, press release, "Douglas P. Wheeler Appointed," November 7, 1972 (in author's possession); also see Wheeler interview, July 30, 2019; Chairman of the National Advisory Board on National Parks, Historic Sites, Buildings and Monuments to Secretary of the Interior, re "Report on Overview of National Parks Operations," September 9, 1971, Papers of Rogers C. B. Morton, box 314, folder 6, 1971, Advisory Committee, Special Collections Research Center, University of Kentucky Library, Margaret King Library.
6. Connecticut's Act Concerning the Preservation of Wetlands and Tidal Marsh and Estuarine Systems was passed in 1969 (PA 695); cited in David G. Casagrande, *The Full Circle: A Historical Context for Urban Salt Marsh Restoration* (New Haven, CT: Center for Coastal and Watershed Systems, Yale School of Forestry and Environmental Studies, 1997), 26; Brenneman interview, August 19, 2015.
7. Matt Schudel, "Nathaniel P. Reed, Leader in Efforts to Protect Endangered Wildlife and Wetlands, Dies at 84," *WAPO*, July 13, 2018; Wheeler interview; photograph in Richard Sandomir, "Nathaniel Reed, 84, Champion of Florida's Environment, Is Dead," *NYT*, July 13, 2018; "Oral History with Nathaniel Reed," University of Florida Digital Collection, December 18, 2000, accessed March 8, 2023, https://original-ufdc.uflib.ufl.edu/UF00004804/00001/2x.
8. Sandomir, "Nathaniel Reed"; Paul Milazzo, *Unlikely Environmentalists: Congress and Clean Water, 1945–1975* (Lawrence, KS: University Press of Kansas, 2006); Turner and Isenberg, *Republican Reversal*.
9. Sandomir, "Nathaniel Reed."
10. Wheeler interview; Connally, "Green Springs Easements."
11. Connally, "Green Springs Easements;" the Connally memo, judging from initials at the bottom, was most likely written by Bob Utley; for Utley's role, see Barry Mackintosh, NHPA and the NPS: A History (Washington, D.C., History Division, National Park Service, Department of the Interior, 1986), accessed October 10, 2022, https://www.nps.gov/parkhistory/online_books/mackintosh5/chap4.htm.
12. Connally, "Green Springs Easements."
13. Connally, "Green Springs Easements."
14. Green Springs Easements Fact Sheet; see also Nathaniel Reid to Elizabeth Nolting, January 19, 1977, GS NHL Nomination File; Mackintosh, *Historic Sites Survey*; Wheeler interview; Stephen J. Small, *The Federal Tax Law of Conservation Easements* (Washington, D.C.: Land Trust Alliance, 1986 [1997]), I–1.
15. Acting Solicitor, Conservation and Wildlife, to Assistant Secretary for Fish, Wildlife and Parks, Department of the Interior, October 10, 1973, 1, 3, Appendix B-25, in Russell L. Brenneman, "Should 'Easements' Be Used to Protect National Historic Landmarks?" (Hartford, CT: National Park Service, 1975); Mackintosh, *Historic Sites Survey*.

16. Connally to Wheeler, Program of Easements for Historic Properties, December 26, 1973, GS NHL Nomination File.
17. Robert M. Utley to OAHP, January 9, 1974, GS NHL Nomination File.
18. Hartt to Morton, January 14, 1974, GS NHL Nomination File.
19. Handwritten note from ENC to Utley, March 3, 1974, forwarding previous memo from Connally to Wheeler, December 26, 1973; A. R. Mortenson, Director, Office of Archeology and Historic Preservation, to Assistant Director, Park Historic Preservation, re "Draft of Proposal for Establishment of Easements for National Historic Landmarks," March 22, 1974, GS NHL Nomination File.
20. Mortenson, "Draft of Proposal."
21. Mortenson, "Draft of Proposal."
22. Utley to Connally, re "Easements," April 3, 1974, GS NHL Nomination File.
23. Benjamin Levy and Katherine Cole, "Report on Green Springs Historic District for the Secretary of the Interior's Advisory Board on National Parks, Historic Sites, Buildings and Monuments," April 1974, Historic Sites Survey, Office of Archeology and Historic Preservation, National Park Service, GS NHL Nomination File.
24. "Tentative Agenda," NHL Advisory Board, attached to Liaison Officer letter to Members, March 14, 1974; this is contained in the April 1974 Advisory Board minutes, in the Advisory Board Meeting Minutes series of the NHL Program Records, Washington, D.C. [hereafter, Advisory Board Meeting Minutes].
25. Chair of Advisory Board to Morton, NHL April 1974 Advisory Board minutes, April 24, 1974, Advisory Board Meeting Minutes.
26. Ely, e-mail to author re "Grace," February 24, 2019.
27. Ely, e-mail to author, April 14, 2015; "Ben A. Franklin, 78, Reporter for The Times, Dies," *NYT*, November 22, 2005, accessed August 19, 2019, https://www.nytimes.com/2005/11/22/business/media/ben-a-franklin-78-reporter-for-the-times-dies.html; Deborah Murdock interview.
28. Ben A. Franklin, "Promise of Mining Riches Splits Historic VA Area," *NYT*, April 21, 1974.
29. Peter Bacque, "Green Springs in Line for Historic Designation," *DP*, April 26, 1974.
30. Bacque, "Green Springs in Line" (emphasis in original).
31. Felix Larkin, President, Grace and Co., to Morton, May 1, 1974, Bracketts Archive.
32. Mr. and Mrs. M. F. Peers to Rogers, handwritten, May 2, 1974, DHR.
33. Mr. and Mrs. M. F. Peers to Rogers.

Chapter 14. Echoes of Vietnam

1. For an extended discussion of the impact of the Vietnam metaphor, see Brian Balogh, "From Metaphor to Quagmire: The Domestic Legacy of the Vietnam War," in Charles E. Neu, ed., *After Vietnam: Legacies of a Lost War* (Baltimore, MD: Johns Hopkins University Press, 2000), 24–55.
2. "Governor Holton and the Battle of GS," *WAPO*, September 4, 1973; "Green Springs and the River Kwai," *DP*, August 29, 1973; Holton cartoon by Bill Nelson,

"Holton's Vietnam: It only hurts when he laughs," cover, *Richmond Mercury* 1, no. 52 (September 1973); Mary Edwards, "The Historic District That Was," *Richmond Mercury* 1, no. 52 (September 1973): 4.
3. Rae to Hiram, November 13, 1973; Rae draft letter to Hiram, February 28, 1974, EOF.
4. "Grace Briefed on Mining Regs," *DP*, July 19, 1973; Jean Purcell, "Grace Debate Continues," *RTD*, July 29, 1973.
5. "W. R. Grace and Company Granted Public Hearing by Louisa County Planning Commission," *CV*, July 26, 1973.
6. "Grace Tour Scored," letter to editor, *DP*, July 30, 1973; "Officials to See Carolina Mining," *DP*, August 15, 1973.
7. "Officials to See Carolina Mining"; Rae Ely interview, February 16, 2011.
8. Pilatus Fact Sheet, attached to Jérôme Zbinden, Executive Assistant to the Chairman, Pilatus Aircraft, Ltd., e-mail to author, May 3, 2019; Rae Ely, e-mail to author, May 3, 2019; Ely interview, February 16, 2011.
9. Rae Ely interview, February 16, 2011.
10. Peter Bacque, "Tempers Flare at Louisa Hearing," *DP*, September 19, 1973; "Planning Commission Delays Action on Zoning Request by W. R. Grace & Co.," *CV*, September 20, 1973.
11. Bacque, "Tempers Flare"; "Planning Commission Delays"; John Hart, "In 1968, Francis Chester and His Wife, Diane, Relocated from Long Island, NY, to Virginia's Alleghany Mountains to Tend Sheep," *Farm Progress*, May 22, 2018, accessed August 3, 2021, https://www.farmprogress.com/livestock/francis-chester-moved-new-york-virginia-be-shepherd; "Historic Group, Grace Square Off," *DP*, September 18, 1973; "Grace Hearing Turns Stormy," *RTD*, September 19, 1973; Jean Purcell, "Verbal Sparks Fly," *RTD*, September 20, 1973.
12. Bacque, "Tempers Flare"; "Planning Commission Delays"; "Supervisors Again Tie on Rezoning," *CV*, April 25, 1974.
13. "Planning Commission Favors Rezoning," *CV*, October 25, 1973; Peter Bacque, "Strip Mining Is a Go," *DP*, October 23, 1973.
14. "Louisa Must Now Choose," *DP*, October 23, 1973.
15. "Louisa Board Sets Strip Mining Bond," *RTD*, November 23, 1973.
16. "W. R. Grace Withdraws Application," *CV*, November 29, 1973; "A Sad Day for Louisa," *DP*, November 25, 1973.
17. Peter Bacque, "Prison Protesters Picnic Peacefully," *DP*, September 16, 1973.
18. "Green Springs to Spring Plans," *DP*, August 19, 1973; Helen Dewar, "Morton Asks for Change in Site for Green Springs Prison," *WAPO*, August 21, 1973.
19. Bruce Blanchard interview.
20. "VA Sets Up Phone Complaint Line," *WAPO*, September 21, 1973.
21. Rogers C. B. Morton to Linwood Holton, August 18, 1973, attached to Fall 1973 *GSA Newsletter*, EOF.
22. George C. Wilson, "Sunset at Presqu'ile," *WAPO Magazine*, March 18, 1979; J. Y. Smith, "Rogers C. B. Morton Dies, Politician, Farmer, Outdoorsman," *WAPO*, April 20, 1979.

23. Patricia McArver, "Rogers Morton, 1915–1979," *Woodberry Forest Bulletin* 18, no. 2 (Summer 1979): 7–8; Wilson, "Sunset at Presqu'ile"; Smith, "Rogers C. B. Morton Dies."
24. Blanchard interview; Schudel, "Nathaniel P. Reed, Leader."
25. "Virginia Sargeant Reynolds," obituary, *DP*, February 4, 2014, accessed October 10, 2022, https://dailyprogress.com/obituaries/reynolds-virginia/article_0551b885-83ee-5676-a441-54fb2c3a15b7.html; Rae Ely, e-mail to author, February 7, 2014; edited Blanchard interview.
26. "Holton Won't Halt Work on Disputed Jail," *WAPO*, August 24, 1973; "Work Starts," *WAPO*, August 28, 1973; Chick Larsen cartoon, August 26, 1973 (likely *RTD*), DHR.
27. "Prison Site Shift Asked by Morton," *WAPO*, September 1, 1973; for date of second letter, see *GSA Newsletter*, ca. September 1, 1973; George Bowles and Peter Bacque, "Word Battle Continues on Louisa Prison," *DP*, September 1, 1973.
28. "Governor Holton and the Battle of Green Springs," *WAPO*, September 4, 1973.
29. Wertsch interview; Edwards, "The Historic District That Was."
30. Edwards, "The Historic District That Was"; "All Out of Step But Linwood," *RTD*, September 9, 1973; the cartoon itself is undated, but a letter to the editor in the *RTD*, dated September 18, 1973, from J. Ellison Loth, refers to the September 9, 1973 *RTD* cartoon by the same name.
31. Linwood Holton, "Letter to the Editor: Governor Holton Takes Issue with a Post Editorial on Green Springs," *WAPO*, September 9, 1973.
32. Holton, "Letter to the Editor."
33. "Red Herring in Green Springs," *DP*, September 15, 1973.
34. Ely Office Meeting Agenda, October 28, 1973, EOF.
35. Rae to Hiram, November 13, 1973, EOF.
36. Hiram diary, entries for January 1, 1974, and November 12, 1973, EOF.
37. Hiram diary, entries for January 1, 1974, and November 12 and December 16, 1973, EOF.
38. Rae draft letter to Hiram, February 28, 1974, EOF.

Chapter 15. Genteel Civility

1. Clare White, "Rae Fought a Prison and Won," *Roanoke Times*, June 23, 1974 (my emphasis).
2. White, "Rae Fought."
3. Peter Bacque, "RIP: Has GS Been Laid to Rest?" *DP*, February 13, 1974.
4. Ben Paviour, "Two-Term Virginia Governors Rare, But Not Unprecedented," *Community Ideas Station*, April 19, 2019; Helen Dewar, "Mills Godwin," *WAPO*, October 11, 1973; C. Matthew West, *A Time for Moderation: J. Sargeant Reynolds and Virginia's New Democrats* (Hanover, PA: Virginia Historical Society, 2019), 39; J. H. Hershman, Jr., "Massive Resistance," *Encyclopedia Virginia*, June 29, 2011, accessed March 9, 2023, https://encyclopediavirginia.org/entries/massive-resistance/#:~:text=Massive%20Resistance%20was%20a%20policy,of%20Education%20of%20Topeka%2C%20Kansas.

5. James L. Bugg, Jr., "Mills Edwin Godwin, Jr.: A Man for All Seasons," in Edward Younger and James Tice Moore, eds., *The Governors of Virginia, 1860–1978* (Charlottesville, VA: University of Virginia Press, 1982); James R. Sweeney, "Bridge to the New Dominion: Virginia's 1965 Gubernatorial Election," *Virginia Magazine of History and Biography* 125 (2017): 246–88, at 248.
6. Dewar, "Mills Goodwin."
7. James Sweeny, "Henry E. Howell (1920–1997)," *Encyclopedia Virginia*, December 22, 2021, accessed October 11, 2022, https://encyclopediavirginia.org/entries/howell-henry-e-1920–1997/; Helen Dewar, "Howell Bids for Governor," *WAPO*, April 8, 1973; Shelley Rolfe, "Howell Is Perpetual Motion Study," *RTD*, August 12, 1973; Helen Dewar, "Howell-Goodwin Gubernatorial Race Heats Up Fast in Hills of Virginia," *WAPO*, August 19, 1973.
8. Virginia Department of Elections, "1973 Governor General Election," Historical Elections Database, accessed October 11, 2022, http://historical.elections.virginia.gov/elections/view/48534/; Helen Dewar and Paul G. Edwards, "Godwin Voters: Rich, White, Conservative," *WAPO*, November 8, 1973.
9. Letter from Henry Howell to Edwin W. Mephis, June 25, 1973, Henry Howell Papers Archive, Old Dominion University, box 113, folder 12; "Consultants Oppose Green Springs Prison," *DP*, November 25, 1973; George M. Kelley, "Godwin Vows Quick Attention to Penal Reform," *WAPO*, January 5, 1974.
10. Peter Bacque, "Court Asked to Halt New Prison on Federal Environmental Grounds," *DP*, January 9, 1974.
11. "Time to Correct an Error," *DP*, January 13, 1974; undated printed sketch, Welch Collection.
12. "Time to Correct an Error"; "Out of Green Springs," *RTD*, January 28, 1974.
13. Helen Dewar, "Jail Facility Plan Falters in VA," *WAPO*, February 8, 1974; Dewar, "Godwin Seeks Building Delay," *WAPO*, February 12, 1974; Steve Stinson, "Prison Deferral Met with Mixed Feelings: GS Catches Breath," *DP*, February 12, 1974.
14. "A Corner Gently Turned," *DP*, February 13, 1974; Stinson, "Prison Deferral."
15. "Corner Gently Turned."
16. "Corner Gently Turned"; Bacque, "RIP."
17. Bacque, "RIP"; "After Four Years a Small Woman Wins Giant Battle," *DP*, February 24, 1974.
18. Peter Bacque, "Push for Prison on Again," *DP*, March 6, 1974; "Supervisors Again Request Completion of Diagnostic Center in Louisa County," *CV*, March 7, 1974.
19. "Decision Upheld," *DP*, March 6, 1974; George M. Kelley, "Mecklenburg Prison Is Set; Louisa Facility Likely," *WAPO*, April 25, 1974; "Never Again," *RTD*, March 20, 1974.
20. "New Prison Gets Go-Ahead," *DP*, April 25, 1974.
21. "Gov. Sets Prison Hearing," *DP*, May 4, 1974; "Relief for GS," *WAPO*, May 13, 1974; "The Prison Hearing," *RTD*, May 14, 1974; *Ely v. Velde*, United States Court of Appeals, Fourth Circuit—497 F. 2nd 252, argued January 8, 1974, decided May 8, 1974; "VA Is Told to Comply on Jail Site," *WAPO*, May 9, 1974; "Green Springs Prison Suit Goes to Judge Merhige," *DP*, May 9, 1974.

22. "Injunctions, the National Environmental Policy Act of 1969, and the Fourth Circuit's Chimera of Revocability," *Iowa Law Review* 362 (1974): 362–76.
23. "Relief for Green Springs," *WAPO*, May 13, 1974.
24. Helen Dewar, "Prison Site Chosen as Historic District," *WAPO*, May 14, 1974; Shelley Rolfe, "Green Springs Gets Final View by Godwin," *RTD*, May 15, 1974.
25. Rolfe, "Green Springs Gets Final View."
26. Rolfe, "Green Springs Gets Final View."
27. Rolfe, "Green Springs Gets Final View"; Peter Bacque, "Both Sides Air Arguments at Godwin Prison Hearing," *DP*, May 15, 1974.
28. "Godwin Meets with Green Springs Backers, Foes," *DP*, May 15, 1974; Bacque, "Both Sides Air Arguments."
29. "About Green Springs," *News Leader*, May 17, 1974.
30. Peter Bacque, "The Curtain Falls Suddenly, and Finally on Green Springs," *DP*, June 14, 1974; Helen Dewar, "VA Drops Prison Plan for Louisa," *WAPO*, June 14, 1974.
31. Bacque, "Curtain Falls."
32. Dewar, "VA Drops Prison Plan."
33. Dewar, "VA Drops Prison Plan."
34. "Godwin's Decision," *RTD*, June 14, 1974; "Congratulations Governor Godwin," *DP*, June 14, 1974.
35. "Victory in GS," *WAPO*, June 21, 1974.
36. Peter Bacque, "Calm Settles on Green Springs," *DP*, June 16, 1974.
37. Bacque, "Calm."
38. White, "Rae Fought a Prison"; Sandra Kelly, e-mail to author, August 20, 2019.
39. White, "Rae Fought,"
40. White, "Rae Fought."
41. Nolting letter to Members, ca. July 1, 1974, EOF.
42. Nolting letter to Members.
43. Rae Ely, phone interview with author (not recorded), January 3, 2021, noted in e-mail to self.

Chapter 16. Guys and Dames

1. Gary Everhardt to Secretary, re "Proposal to Acquire Preservation Easements at Green Springs" (and attached letters), April 13, 1977, GS NHL Nomination File.
2. Chief, Division of Land Acquisition, through Assistant Director Resource Management, to Associate Director, Park System Management, re "Unanticipated Ramifications of a Program for the Protection of National Historic Landmarks," May 9, 1974, Easements file in Green Springs Papers Series of the NHL Program Records, Washington, D.C.: NPS [hereafter, Easements File, GS Papers].
3. Chief . . . "Unanticipated Ramifications," 6.
4. Bill Connolly, "Senate Urged to Protect Mount Vernon," *RTD*, June 5, 1974; Paul Hodge, "Marshall Hall May Close in Fall," *WAPO*, August 18, 1977; see also, 1974—Public Law 93–444.

5. Ken Ringle, "View from Mt. Vernon Is Bitter," *WAPO*, September 5, 1971; "Bolton, Frances Payne, United States House of Representatives," accessed October 12, 2022, https://history.house.gov/People/Listing/B/BOLTON,-Frances-Payne-(B000607)/.
6. "Bolton."
7. Ringle, "View"; Accokeek Foundation—Correspondence, 1954–1959, Operation Overview Collection, Archives of the Mount Vernon Ladies' Association; Frances Bolton—Correspondence, 1962–1969, Washington Library at Mount Vernon [hereafter, Washington Library].
8. Washington Suburban Sanitary Commission file, 1960–1974, Washington Library.
9. Marshall Hall—Piscataway Matters Hearing, March 25, 1971, House of Representatives, Subcommittee on National Parks and Recreation of the Committee on Interior and Insular Affairs, Washington, D.C.; Public Law 87–362; Ringle, "View."
10. Ringle, "View"; "Statement of George B. Hartzog Jr.," Marshall Hall—Piscataway Matters Hearing, 48.
11. Ringle, "View."
12. Ringle, "View."
13. Ringle, "View"; Chief . . ., "Unanticipated Ramifications."
14. Chief . . ., "Unanticipated Ramifications," 5, 6.
15. Chief . . ., "Unanticipated Ramifications," 5, 6.
16. Associate Director, Professional Services to Director, re "Input for Meeting with Assistant Secretary and Under Secretary," July 16, 1974, Easements File, GS Papers.
17. "Louisa Supervisors Fight Historic Tag," *DP*, July 22, 1974.
18. Peter Bacque, "Oral Arguments Over in Historic District Case," *DP*, July 24, 1974; "Landmark-County Case Concluded," *CV*, July 25, 1974.
19. Whitlock to Berry, Petitioner Memorandum of Fact and Law, 21–22, 25.
20. Whitlock, Petitioner Memorandum, 28, 30.
21. Whitlock, Petitioner Memorandum, 32.
22. Associate Director, Professional Services, to Director, re "Input for Meeting with Assistant Secretary and Under Secretary, August. 12–16," August 13, 1974; EAC to Utley, September 13 [1974], Easements File, Green Springs Papers, Advisory Board Meeting Minutes. series of the National Historic Landmark Program Records, Washington, D.C.: NPS [hereafter, Easements File, GS Papers].
23. Chairman, Advisory Board to Secretary of the Interior, re Easements on National Historic Landmarks, October 10, 1974, Easements File, GS Papers.
24. Chief, Division of Land Acquisition to Assistant Chief, Administration, Division of Land Acquisition, re Restrictive (Development) Easements Over Registered Historic Landmarks, October 9, 1974, 1, Easements File, GS Papers.
25. Chief . . . Restrictive, 2; Blanchard interview.
26. Chief . . . Restrictive, 2–3.
27. Edited Blanchard interview.
28. Edited Blanchard interview.
29. Edited Blanchard interview.
30. "Jury Probe Head's 1974's Top Stories," *DP*, January 1, 1975.
31. Bill McKelway, "Mrs. Ely's War: 'Mama vs. Otis Brown' No Game," *RTD*, February 2, 1975.

32. McKelway, "Ely's War"; Lynn Darling, e-mail to author, September 30, 2019.
33. McKelway, "Mrs. Ely's War."
34. McKelway, "Mrs. Ely's War."
35. Handwritten notes, January 1, 1974 and entries, March 17, November 14, and November 17, 1974; list is from December 2, 1974 entry, EOF.
36. Meyer Friedman and Ray H. Rosenman, *Type A Behavior and Your Heart* (New York: Knopf, 1974); Denise Grady, "Meyer Friedman, 'Type A' Theorist, Dies at 90," *NYT*, May 1, 2001, accessed, October 12, 2022, https://www.nytimes.com/2001/05/01/us/meyer-friedman-type-a-theorist-dies-at-90.html; Hiram Ely, typed summary attached to handwritten notes, January 1, 1974, at the December 5, 1974 entry, EOF.
37. Ely, typed summary.
38. Friedman and Rosenman, *Type A Behavior*, 56 for quotation, 56–57 for origins of theory.

Chapter 17. Repurposing Civil Rights Strategies

1. Peter Bacque, "Strip Mining Hearing Resolves Very Little," *DP*, January 17, 1974.
2. Bacque, "Strip Mining."
3. Undated *DP* editorial, reprinted in *CV* next to "Random Reflections" article, February 14, 1974; "Strip Mining Bill Delayed," *WAPO*, February 6, 1974; "Supervisors Minutes," *CV*, February 7, 1974.
4. "Strip Mining Bill Delayed"; "Supervisors Minutes," *CV*, February 28, 1974; "Louisa Supervisors Fail to Accept Offer to Discuss Mining," *CV*, March 7, 1974.
5. Peter Bacque, "Louisa Supervisors Split Over Strip Mining: Tiebreaker Called In," *DP*, April 18, 1974; paid ad, "Reclamation of Surface Mine Site—Is It Possible?" *CV*, March 14, 1974.
6. "Which Do You Want . . . Production or Destruction?" Citizens of Louisa paid ad, *CV*, April 4, 1974; "Reclamation of Surface Mine Site–Is It Possible?"
7. Bacque, "Supervisors Split"; "Grace Rezoning Request Goes to Tie Breaker," *CV*, April 18, 1974; "Tiebreaker to Decide VA Mining Case," *WAPO*, April 19, 1974; "The Week of Decision: Will Green Springs Be Mined?" *DP*, May 5, 1974; Peter Bacque, "Daniel's Disqualification Leaves Louisa Perplexed," *DP*, May 8, 1974.
8. Bacque, "Daniel's Disqualification."
9. Bacque, "Daniel's Disqualification."
10. Peter Bacque, "Judge Won't Compel Vote," *DP*, June 15, 1974; "Louisa Official Refuses to Vote on Mining Bid," *WAPO*, June 15, 1974.
11. Alan Cooper and Jean Purcell, "Effort to Force Louisa Vote Fails," *RTD*, June 15, 1974.
12. Charles Hite, "Delay Asked on Louisa Tie Breaker Decision," *DP*, June 24, 1975; "Tie Breaker Fails to Break Tie," *CV*, June 26, 1975; Hite, "2nd Green Springs Zoning Suit Filed," *DP*, February 20, 1975; "Louisa Supervisors Wrangle Over Legal Representation," *CV*, February 27, 1975; Hite, "Daniel Again Refused to Break Deadlock," *DP*, March 5, 1975.
13. Peter Bacque, "Hung Jury Ends Louisa Trial," *DP*, March 22, 1975.

14. Fry Opinion, April 9, 1975, in Circuit Court of Louisa County, *E. H. Nininger et al. v. Louisa County Board of Supervisors*, 195, 198, 200–201, EOF.
15. "Travail at Green Springs," *News Virginian*, April 11, 1975; "It's Back to the Trenches," *DP*, April 16, 1975.
16. Charles Hite, "Board Expected to Consider Strip Ruling," *DP*, April 16, 1975.
17. R. H. Deeds, "Troy Applauds Louisa Mining Decision," letter to the editor, *DP*, April 24, 1975.
18. Peter Bacque, "Judge Refuses Petition," *DP*, July 2, 1975.
19. Charles Hite, "HGSI Record Request Nixed," *DP*, July 15, 1975; "Javor, Henry J.," obituary, *DP*, November 14, 2014, updated November 19, 2014, accessed January 3, 2021, https://dailyprogress.com/obituaries/javor-henry-j/article_ba5ed724-8d86-55bb-9a75-cba50da09e6d.html.
20. Charles Hite, "Tiebreaker in Louisa Quits," *DP*, July 16, 1975.
21. Hite, "Tiebreaker"; Charles Hite, "Louisa Suit Filed to Halt Tiebreaker," *DP*, August 2, 1975.
22. "Judge Refuses to Unseat Tie Breaker; Jesse Martin Refuses to Vote at Tuesday's Meeting," *CV*, August 7, 1975; "Judge Harold Purcell Names Jesse Martin Co. Tie Breaker," *CV*, July 24, 1975; Jeremy Slayton, "Former State Legislator Harold Purcell Dies," *RTD*, July 17, 2007, accessed January 31, 2021, https://richmond.com/entertainment/former-state-legislator-harold-purcell-dies/article_6373f35b-3fb1-570a-b526-0a80c370a7d7.html.
23. Peter Bacque, "Louisa Tie Breaker Named by Judge," *DP*, July 25, 1975; Gouldman interview, January 2, 2020.
24. Gouldman interview; Hite, "Louisa Suit Filed"; Allen Short, "Jurist Due Tie-Breaker Controversy," *RTD*, August 14, 1975; Hite, "Halt Tiebreaker" and "Injunction Against Louisa Tiebreaker Denied," *DP*, August 5, 1975.
25. Hite, "Louisa Suit Filed"; Allen Short, "Louisa Suit to Test Tie-Breaker Law," *RTD*, August 3, 1975; Hite, "Injunction Against Louisa Tiebreaker Denied"; "Request Barred to Deny Seating of Tie-Breaker," *RTD*, August 5, 1975.
26. Charles Hite, "Louisa Hearing Block Sought," *DP*, August 14, 1975; "Seating Delay Denied," *RTD*, August 19, 1975.
27. Charles Hite and Richard Long, "Strip Mine Issue Boils: Court Delays Ruling," *DP*, August 15, 1975; Hite, "HGSI Case May Go to Federal Court," *DP*, August 19, 1975.
28. Charles Hite, "U.S. Court to Hear Louisa Challenge," *DP*, August 28, 1975; Hite, "Voting Rights at Issue in Louisa Challenge," *DP*, August 30, 1975.
29. Alexander Keyssar, *The Right to Vote: The Contested History of Democracy in the United States* (New York: Basic Books, 2009), 264; for an outstanding study of these techniques in Richmond, see Julian Hayter, *The Dream Is Lost: Voting Rights and the Politics of Race in Richmond, Virginia* (Lexington, KY: University Press of Kentucky, 2017), 67 for Virginia statistic.
30. "Louisa Challenge"; *Allen v. State Board of Elections*, 393 U.S. 544 (1969); John P. MacCoon, "The Enforcement of the Preclearance Requirement of Section 5 of the Voting Rights Act of 1965," *Catholic University Law Review* 29, no. 1 (1979): 107–28.
31. Allen Short, "Tie Breaker Case Taken to U.S. Court," *RTD*, August 29, 1975.
32. "Louisa Challenge."

33. "Louisa Challenge"; Charles Hite and Richard Long, "Louisa Rezoning Plan Approved," *DP*, September 4, 1975.
34. Charles Hite, "Voting Rights at Issue in Louisa Challenge," *DP*, August 30, 1975.
35. "Louisa Plan," *RTD*, May 7, 1964; "Louisa School Board Delays Action on NAACP Petition," *RTD*, May 22, 1964.
36. *Greene v. County School Board of New Kent County*, 391 U.S. 430 (1968); "School Board Rejects Desegregation," *WAPO*, May 9, 1969.
37. Drumheller notes, 1–2, Oral History Collection, Louisa County Historical Society.
38. Jean Purcell, "HEW Favors September 1970 for Total Mixing in Louisa," *RTD*, August 30, 1969, 4; Drumheller notes, 7–8.
39. Stephens interview.
40. Stephens interview.
41. Stephens interview.
42. Greg Jones interview, November 27, 2019.
43. Stephens interview.
44. Bacque, "Named by Judge"; Hite, "Tiebreaker Denied."
45. Charles Hite, "Tiebreaker Casts Deciding Vote," *DP*, September 4, 1975; Rosenfeld, "Historic-Area Strip Mining"; Hite and Long, "Louisa Rezoning Plan Approved"; "Hearing Draws 120 in Louisa," *RTD*, September 4, 1975.
46. Allen Short, "Candidate Was Paid Sale Fee," *RTD*, September 9, 1975; Short, "Mining Battle Overtones Seen in Election," *RTD*, October 19, 1975.
47. "Strip Mining Backers Win Big in Louisa," *RTD*, November 5, 1975; Charles Hite, "Voters Favor Strip Mining," *DP*, November 5, 1975.
48. VVL CO. WRG 68/DTX 32, December 10, 1975, 3, Antitrust Collection.
49. Peter Bacque, "Strip Mining Foes Will Continue Fight," *DP*, November 10, 1975.
50. Allen Shot, "Green Springs Suit Moot, Judges Told," *RTD*, January 27, 1976; "Louisa to Reopen Stripmining Issue," *WAPO*, January 10, 1976.
51. Legal notes for three-judge case, January 26, 1976, EOF; Allen Short, "Louisa Mining Opponents Hindered by Suit Dismissal," *RTD*, June 5, 1976; Injunctive and Declaratory Judgement, *Historic Green Springs Inc., et al. v. Board of Supervisors of Louisa County, et al.*, Dismissed.

Chapter 18. The Problem of Asbestos

1. Associated Press, "Thomas S. Kleppe, 87, Interior Secretary, Dies," *NYT*, March 10, 2007, accessed October 15, 2022, https://www.nytimes.com/2007/03/10/obituaries/10kleppe.html; Kleppe to J. Peter Grace, March 1, 1976, Easements File, GS Papers.
2. Kleppe to Grace, March 1, 1976.
3. Ben Franklin, "Interior Chief Calls on Company Not to Strip Mine Virginia, Land," *NYT*, March 10, 1976; Ray McGrath, "Landmark Status Defended," *DP*, March 10, 1976.
4. Allen Short, "Kleppe Asks Grace to Forgo Mining," *RTD*, March 10, 1976.
5. "Chairman A. G. Johnson Comments on Request by Secretary of Interior," *CV*, March 11, 1976; Pat Wechsler, "Kleppe's Action Criticized," *DP*, March 24, 1976.

6. "Farmland and River," *NYT*, March 22, 1976; "Mine Firm to Release Louisa Plan," *WAPO*, March 23, 1976.
7. H. D. N. Hill, "Random Reflections," *CV*, March 25, 1976; "The Secretary of Interior Unwarranted Meddling in Green Springs Mining Issue," *CV*, March 25, 1976; "Grace Co. Accused of Bad Faith," *Preservation News*, August 1976.
8. "Louisa Board Votes to Open 97% of County to Mining," *WAPO*, June 25, 1976; Ray McGrath, "Ordinance Opens Louisa to Mining," *DP*, June 24, 1976; "Black Wednesday," *DP*, June 26, 1976.
9. Allen Short, "Louisa Board Grants Approval for Mining at Green Springs," *RTD*, June 8, 1976; "Supervisors Approve CUP for Vermiculite Mining Green Springs: First in Green Springs," *CV*, June 10, 1976; Gregory Light, "Open Pit Mining Approved," *DP*, June 8, 1976; "Federal Judges Dismiss Tie-Breaker Suit, Historic Green Springs Files Another Suit," *CV*, June 10, 1976.
10. Allen Short, "Louisa May Feel Montana Problem," *RTD*, September 3, 1976.
11. Short, "Louisa May Feel"; "Grace Official Corrects False Statements about Vermiculite Mining in Montana and Louisa Co.," *CV*, September 9, 1976.
12. Michael Moss and Adrianne Appel, "Protecting the Product: A Special Report: Company's Silence Countered Safety Fears About Asbestos," *NYT*, July 9, 2001.
13. Allen Short, "Problem of Asbestos Comes with Vermiculite," *RTD*, September 19, 1976.
14. Paul Richter, "Mining Danger Claimed," *DP*, September 21, 1976; Allen Short, "Experts Call Vermiculite Potential Health Hazard," *RTD*, September 21, 1976; Short, "Asbestos Findings Confirmed," *RTD*, September 26, 1976.
15. Short, "Asbestos Findings Confirmed"; "Mining Suit's Plaintiffs Ask Delay," *RTD*, October 1, 1976; Short "Mining Opponents Win Round: Asbestos Tests to Be Taken," *RTD*, October 2, 1976; Paul Richter, "Mining Suit Delay Denied," *DP*, October 2, 1976.
16. Allen Short, "Foes of Mining Lose Time Plea," *RTD*, October 29, 1976.
17. "Court Rules in Favor of Supervisors in Two Green Springs Mining Cases," *CV*, November 18, 1976.
18. Allen Short, "Approval Expected for Louisa Mining," *RTD*, December 9, 1976.
19. Peg Brickley, "5 Takeaways from the W. R. Grace Bankruptcy," *Wall Street Journal*, February 3, 2014, accessed October 15, 2022, https://blogs.wsj.com/briefly/2014/02/03/5-takeaways-from-the-w-r-grace-bankruptcy/.
20. Mark R. Powell, *Science at EPA: Information in the Regulatory Process* (New York: Routledge, 2000), 304–06; Moss and Appel, "Protecting the Product"; William E. Schmidt, "Huge Cost of Removing Asbestos Daunts Schools," *NYT*, October 5, 1983, accessed October 22, 2022, https://www.nytimes.com/1983/10/05/us/huge-costs-of-removing-asbestos-daunts-schools.html; "Screening for Toxic Substances," *WAPO*, October 1, 1974.
21. Mark Matthews, "Libby's Dark Secret: For Decades, Mine Dust Has Been Killing People in Libby, Montana. Why Didn't Anyone Do Anything About It?" *High Country News*, March 13, 2000, accessed October 15, 2022, https://www.hcn.org/issues/174/5619; Patrick Klemz, "Saving Grace," *Missoula Independent*, December 18, 2008.

22. Klemz, "Saving Grace"; Powell, *Science at EPA,* 321; Matthews, "Dark Secret."
23. Matthews, "Dark Secret."

Chapter 19. A Formidable New Foe

1. Marsha Blakemore and Bill Miller, "Road to Success Has Produced Foes," *RTD,* July 29, 1979; Margaret Ball Sansom, "Former Knoxvillian, Dies," *Knoxville News-Sentinel,* April 16, 1995; CIA routing slip attached to "1968–1969 White House Fellows" press release, September 12, 1968, attached to Frank Gannon, e-mail to author, October 10, 2019.
2. "1968–1969 White House Fellows"; Robert L. Sansom, *The Economics of Insurgency in the Mekong Delta of Vietnam* (Cambridge, MA: MIT Press, 1970), xiv, xv; Sansom, *The Impact of an Insurgent War on the Traditional Economy of the Mekong River Delta Region of South Vietnam* (Oxford: University of Oxford, 1969).
3. Gannon interview, October 9, 2019; Gannon, e-mail to author, October 10, 2019.
4. Gannon interview; "1968–1969 White House Fellows"; Nixon White House Files, Richardson to Kissinger, September 19, 1969, https://www.nixonlibrary.gov/sites/default/files/virtuallibrary/releases/dec10/dec10/dec10_34.pdf; National Security Decision Memorandum 23, Kissinger to Secretaries of Defense, State and Director of CIA, NSC Institutional Files (H-Files), box H—211, September 16, 1969, https://fas.org/irp/offdocs/nsdm-nixon/nsdm-23.pdf; Robert L. Sansom, *The New American Dream Machine: Toward a Simpler Lifestyle in an Environmental Age* (Garden City, NY: Anchor Books, 1976), vii; Daniel Guttman, "The Energy Hustle: Getting Rich by Serving Two Masters," *New Republic,* March 11, 1978: 16–19, at 17.
5. Guttman, "Energy Hustle; Blackmere and Miller, "Road to Success"; Sansom Crossexam, September 18, 2000, 881, Antitrust.
6. Sansom, *New American Dream Machine,* 21 and ch. 8.
7. Sansom, *New American* Dream *Machine,* 185–87; Shapley, "The Electric War," *NYT,* January 16, 1977.
8. Sansom, *New American Dream Machine,* 91–92.
9. Sansom to Ford, March 27, 1976, WHCF, Name File (Sansom), Gerald Ford Presidential Library (hereafter, Ford Library).
10. Sansom to Ford, March 27, 1976; Jack Anderson and Les Whitten, "A White House Aide Intervenes," *WAPO,* September 29, 1976; Sansom to Connor, March 29, 1976, Ford Library.
11. Allen Short, "U.S. Agency Said to Accept Green Springs Easements," *RTD,* September 5, 1976.
12. Anderson and Whitten, "White House Aide."
13. Anderson and Whitten, "White House Aide."
14. Anderson and Whitten, "White House Aide"; *Ukiah Daily Journal,* September 28, 1976.
15. Public Law 94-429, 90, Section 9 94-929, at STAT 1343-4, September 28, 1976, accessed October 16, 2022, https://www.govinfo.gov/content/pkg/STATUTE-90/

pdf/STATUTE-90-Pg1342.pdf#page=2; Rae Ely interview, February 24, 2011; Alan Short, "Law May Aid Louisa Solution," *RTD*, September 30, 1976; Carleton Knight III, "Ford Signs 4 Preservation Bills," *Preservation News*, November 1976.
16. "Oversight Provided for VA Stripmining," *WAPO*, October 1, 1976; Short, "Law May Aid"; "New Law Clouds Green Springs Mining Plan," *DP*, September 30, 1976.
17. Rae Ely interview, February 24, 2011.
18. Gordon Chaplin, "O Louisa!" *WAPO*, Potomac Section, October 3, 1976.

Chapter 20. Local Affairs and the Law of the Land

1. Gallup began systematically polling the choice between environmental protection and growth in 1984, with 61 percent of Americans choosing "protection of the environment should be given priority, even at the risk of curbing economic growth," versus 28 percent who chose "economic growth should be given priority, even if the environment suffers to some extent"; Lydia Saad, "Preference for Environment Over Economy Largest since 2000," *Gallup News*, April 4, 2019, accessed August 18, 2022, https://news.gallup.com/poll/248243/preference-environment-economy-largest-2000.aspx; "Questions Health Risks of Farming Asbestos-Soil in Green Springs Area," *CV*, March 24, 1977.
2. Albert G. Johnson to Cecil Andrus, March 17, 1977, Easements File, GS Papers; Nicholas Dawidoff, "The Riddle of Jimmy Carter," *Rolling Stone*, February 2, 2011, accessed October 16, 2022, https://www.rollingstone.com/politics/politics-news/the-riddle-of-jimmy-carter-181915/.
3. Statement by Jerry L. Rogers, April 22, 1977, Public Hearing: Green Springs Easements, Easements File, GS Papers.
4. Short, "U.S. Agency Said"; minutes of the Historic Preservation Committee, Historic Green Springs, Inc., September 13, 1976, EOF.
5. "Supervisors Want Chance to Reiterate Stand to Interior Department National Officials," *CV*, September 9, 1976; Allen Short, "Louisa Easements Taken," *RTD*, January 21, 1977.
6. "Ford Signs Bill Aiding Landmarks," *RTD*, October 12, 1976.
7. Benjamin Levy, Green Springs Historic District Report on the Sufficiency of Easements on Land in Green Springs, November 23, 1976, 13, EOF.
8. Levy, Green Springs Historic District Report, 20; cover note from Assistant Secretary of the Interior for Fish and Wildlife and Parks, January 24, 1977, EOF.
9. Reed to Nolting, January 19, 1977, Easements File, GS Papers; Ray McGrath, "Park Service to Control Green Springs Easements," *DP*, January 21, 1977; Short, "Louisa Easements Taken."
10. Allen Short, "Back Green Springs Loan, Mining Company Asks U.S.," *RTD*, February 7, 1977.
11. Short, "Back Green Springs Loan"; "Louisa Backs Mining Request," *DP*, February 9, 1977; "Three County Groups Endorse FHA Mining Loan Application," *CV*, February 24, 1977.

12. Short, "Back Green Springs Loan"; Paul Richter, "Impact Study Likely for Louisa Mining," *DP*, March 16, 1977; Paul Richter, "Mining Firm Seeks to Avoid Louisa Site Impact Study," *DP*, March 19, 1977; Marsha Blakemore, "Mine Study for Loan Ordered," *RTD*, April 7, 1977.
13. Allen Short, "Andrus to Accept Louisa Easements," *RTD*, March 19, 1977; Paul Richter, "Hearing Set April 22 on Green Springs Land," *DP*, March 20, 1977; Jimmy Carter, "The Environment—The President's Message to the Congress," *Environmental Law Reporter* 7 (1977): 50057–50068, at 50064; "Statement of J. Destry Jarvis, Nationals Parks and Conservation Association," Hearing Before the Senate Subcommittee on Parks, Recreation, and Renewable Resources, 96th Cong. 2nd sess., April 17, 1980, 367–68.
14. Johnson to Andrus, March 17, 1977; Andrus to Johnson, April 20, 1977, Easements File, GS Papers.
15. " 'Purcell Subdivision' with 86 Lots in Green Springs District Recorded in Co. Clerk's Office," *CV*, April 21, 1977.
16. Notes on Hearing, April 24, 1977, Easements File, GS Papers; "Interior Department Announces Hearing on G.S. Easements," *CV*, April 7, 1977; Megan Rosenfeld, "History, Vermiculite Forces Clash Anew in Louisa," *WAPO*, April 23, 1977; Allen Short, "150 Hear Pleas on Easements, Louisa Mining," *RTD*, April 23, 1977; Paul Richter, "155 Ask to Speak at Green Springs Easements Hearing Friday," *DP*, April 20, 1977; Rae Ely interview, February 16, 2011 for quotation; "Opponents, Proponents Express Strong Feelings," *CV*, April 28, 1977.
17. Statement by Jerry L. Rogers; "Agenda: Public Hearing, Will's Chapel Meeting House," April 22, 1977, Easements File, GS Papers.
18. Statement by Jerry L. Rogers.
19. Notes on Hearing; "Opponents, Proponents."
20. Notes on Hearing; Short, "150 Hear Pleas."
21. "Statement of W. R. Grace & Co. in Opposition," Will's Chapel Hearing Materials, Easements File, GS Papers.
22. Rosenfeld, "Forces Clash"; "Opponents, Proponents"; Short, "150 Hear Pleas."
23. Notes on Hearing; Richter, "155 Ask to Speak"; Paul Richter, "Louisa Easements Debated," *DP*, April 23, 1977.
24. Notes on Hearing.
25. Richter, "Louisa Easements Debated"; Notes on Hearing.
26. Draft, Assistant Secretary for Fish and Wildlife and Parks, to Director, National Park Service, re "Proposed Acceptance of Historic Preservation Easements"; Secretary to Director, April 13, 1977, Easements File, GS Papers.
27. Paul Richter, "Blaze Destroys Louisa Chapel," *DP*, May 10, 1977; Rae Ely, e-mail exchange with author, April 1, 2020; Paul Richter. "Green Springs Fire Deliberate," *DP*, May 13, 1977; Marsha Blakemore, "Probing of Fire Goes On," *RTD*, May 12, 1977.
28. Richter, "Green Springs Fire Deliberate"; Blakemore, "Probing of Fire"; Paul Richter, "Louisa Offers Reward for Arsonist," *DP*, May 16, 1977; Richter, "State Investigators Have Suspect in Green Springs Chapel Fire," *DP*, November 8, 1977.
29. Allen Short, "Study Won't Be Conducted of Green Springs Mine Plan," *RTD*, April 25, 1977.

30. Short, "Study Won't Be Conducted"; Paul Richter, "Green Springs Mine Impact Study Unlikely," *DP*, April 25, 1977; "Green Springs Case Opens," *DP*, April 27, 1977; Allen Short, "Green Springs Suit Filed Here," *RTD*, April 27, 1977.
31. Allen Short, "Mining Loan Guarantee May Proceed," *RTD*, April 28, 1977; Paul Richter, "Mining Case Delayed," *DP*, April 28, 1977.
32. Short, "Zoning, Mining Confrontations Create Louisa's Second Civil War," *RTD*, May 1, 1977.
33. Short, "Mining Loan"; Paul Richter, "Louisa to Ask for Federal Disaster Aid," *DP*, June 29, 1977; Richter, "Louisa Needs Airport to Boost Economy," *DP*, June 7, 1977.

Chapter 21. Preservationists as Lobbyists

1. Allen Short, "U.S. Signs Scenic Easements to Preserve Green Springs," *RTD*, September 10, 1978; "News from Historic Green Springs," ca. October 1, 1978, EOF; Rae Ely interview, February 8, 2011.
2. *U.S. vs. NPS: Virginians Defending the Bill of Rights*, Virginians for Property Rights pamphlet (in author's possession), 13.
3. Rae Ely interview, February 8, 2011; Ben A. Franklin, "Landmark Designations Are Upheld by New Law," *NYT*, December 14, 1980; Franklin, "Judge Backs Down in Face of Changes in Preservation Law," *NYT*, July 27, 1981.
4. Allen Short, "Opposition Stalls Mining Company," *RTD*, May 5, 1977; *HGSI v. Bergland*, 497 F. Supp. 839, 1980, 3.
5. Paul Richter, "Green Springs Case Argued," *DP*, June 4, 1977.
6. "Environmental Review and Negative Declaration," June 14, 1977; "Reconsideration of Designation as National Historic Landmark and Listing on National Register," June 23, 1977, Easements File, GS Papers.
7. Paul Richter, "Green Springs Review Set," *DP*, June 29, 1977.
8. Richter, "Green Springs Review Set"; Paul Richter, "Judge Rejects Vermiculite Mining Company's Request," *DP*, July 8, 1977.
9. "Statement of Robert L. Sansom," July 27, 1977, Easements File, GS Papers; Paul Richter, "Interior Won't Set Limits in Green Springs," *DP*, July 28, 1977.
10. Paul Richter, "Green Springs Historic Status Reconsidered," *DP*, July 27, 1977; Richter, "Interior Won't Set Limits"; Allen Short, "Government May Enter Louisa Fight," *RTD*, July 28, 1977.
11. H. D. N. Hill, "Random Reflections," *CV*, August 11, 1977.
12. Paul Richter, "U.S. Orders Mine Impact Study," *DP*, July 29, 1977; Allen Short, "Louisa Study to Be Made After All," *RTD*, July 29, 1977.
13. Associate Director, Management and Operations to Associate Director, Preservation of Historic Properties, re "Green Springs National Historic District," November 21, 1977; Associate Director, Preservation of Historic Properties to Associate Director, Management and Operations re "Green Springs Historic District—Mining in the Parks Study," November 29, 1977, Easements File, GS Papers.
14. Director to Assistant Secretary, November 25, 1977, Easements File, GS Papers.

15. Assistant Secretary for Fish and Wildlife and Parks to Secretary, December 2, 1977, signed "Enclosure" by Andrus, December 13, 1977; News Release, Department of the Interior, December 15, 1977, Easements File, GS Papers; "Green Springs Section Is Historical Landmark," *Northern Virginia Daily*, December 16, 1977.
16. Ben Franklin, *NYT*, December 18, 1977.
17. Senior Historian, Historic Site Survey Division to Chief, Office of Archeology and Historic Preservation, re "Green Springs: Management of Easements," December 20, 1977, Easements File, GS Papers.
18. Acting Assistant Director, Cultural Resources, to Director, re "Easements on the Properties Within the Green Springs National Historic Landmark District," February 15, 1979, Easements File, GS Papers.
19. Allen Short, "Vermiculite Firm Has Loan Accord," *RTD*, December 16, 1977.
20. Short, "Vermiculite Firm"; "Firm Drops Loan Application," *Roanoke Times*, November 30, 1977.
21. Strong to Bumpers, November 7, 1977, Green Springs Correspondence, DHR.
22. Bumpers to Andrus, November 22, 1977; Myshak to Bumpers, January 4, 1978, DHR.
23. Marsha Blakemore, "Virginia Vermiculite Ready to Mine in Green Springs," *RTD*, February 7, 1978; "Richest Vermiculite Deposit in the World Being Mined in Green Springs District of County," *CV*, April 29, 1979.
24. *Historic Green Springs v. Bergland*, 497 F. Supp. 839, Civ. A No. 77–0230-R, U.S. District Court for the Eastern District of VA, Richmond Div., 12–14.
25. *Green Springs v. Bergland*, 12, 11, 14.
26. *Green Springs v. Bergland*, 6.
27. Ben A. Franklin, "Appeal Weighed as Judge Voids U.S. 'Landmark,' " *NYT*, August 13, 1980; Paul W. Edmondson, "Historic Preservation Regulation and Procedural Due Process," *Ecology Law Quarterly* 9, no. 4 (1981): 743–76, at 775.
28. "Radioactive Waste: National Regulations Needed," *Daily Press* (Newport News), February 13, 1979.
29. Rae Ely interview, February 8, 2011.
30. Rae Ely interview, February 8, 2011.
31. Rae Ely interviews February 8 and 24, 2011;"Today in Congress," *WAPO*, April 17, 1980; "National Heritage Policy Act of 1979," Hearing Before the Senate Subcommittee on Parks, Recreation, and Renewable Resources, 96th Cong. 2nd sess., April 17, 1980, 1–517; Marilyn Bethany, "Sharing History," *NYT*, April 13, 1980.
32. Bethany, "Sharing History."
33. United States Senate, Committee on Energy and Natural Resources, National Historic Preservation Act Amendments of 1980: Report to Accompany S. 3116 (Washington, D.C.: U.S. Government Printing Office, 1980); United States House of Representatives, Committee on Interior and Insular Affairs, National Historic Preservation Act Amendments of 1980: Report Together with Additional Views (to Accompany H.R. 5496), 126 Cong. Rec. 29829 (Washington, D.C.: U.S. Government Printing Office, 1980); Franklin, "Landmark Designations."
34. Ely interview, February 24, 2011.
35. Franklin, "Landmark Designations"; Franklin, "Judge Backs Down."

36. Ely to Weingarten, January 15, 1981, EOF; Ely interview, February 8, 2011.
37. Robert Sansom, *US vs. NPS*, 1, 11.
38. On authorship of this section, see Thomas interview, June 18, 2020. She could not confirm that Sansom actually wrote this section, but did confirm that he "provided it." The description tracks closely with Sansom's public testimony on Green Springs and with portions of the arguments presented by VVL during its extensive litigation; Sansom, *US vs. NPS*, 13, 15.
39. Lois Marie Gibbs, *Love Canal: My Story* (Albany, NY: SUNY Press, 1982); Susan Saiter, "Local Opposition Is Stalling Development of Waste Sites," *NYT,* June 18, 1983; William Glaberson, "The 'Not in My Backyard' Movement Is Now a Potent Anti-development Force," *NYT,* June 19, 1988.
40. Robert Sansom to David Jones (Supervisor, Madison County), March 9, 1991 (in author's possession).
41. Sansom to Young, February 22, 1995, DTX 38, Antitrust.

Chapter 22. Wife or Environmentalist?

1. Rae to Hiram, May 31, June 28, 1976, EOF.
2. Rae Ely's application is cited in Albert R. Turnbull to UVa Law School Faculty, April 17, 1980, 5 (in author's possession).
3. Rae Ely interview, January 4, 2011.
4. Rae to Hiram, June 28, 1976.
5. Rae to Hiram, June 28, 1976.
6. Rae to Hiram, June 28, 1976.
7. Hiram to Rae, August 11, 1976; Rae to Hiram, August 17, attached to August 11, 1976 letter from Hiram, EOF.
8. Petition for Appeal, Supreme Court of Virginia, May 21, 1982, 5–6; Decree of Separate Maintenance, Louisa County Circuit Court, Judge Vance M. Fry, September 2, 1977, 1; Singer to Hiram Ely, May 18, 1977, EOF.
9. For date of original decree and description of initial appeals, see Decree of Separate Maintenance, September 2, 1977, 1; see also Singer to Hiram Ely, May 18, 1977.
10. Decree of Separate Maintenance, 2–3; agreement on property, 4; Rae Ely interview, December 30, 2010.
11. Motion for Temporary Injunction, Louisa County Circuit Court, June 16, 1978, 1; Callaghan to Trembly, September 21, 1977; Bill of Particulars, Circuit Court of City of Charlottesville, July 24, 1980, 3, EOF.
12. Rae Ely to Callaghan, May 6, 1978, EOF.
13. Rae to Hiram, September 12, 1978; Motion for Temporary Injunction, 4, 3; Bill of Particulars, 2–3.
14. Hiram to Rae, August 21, 1978, EOF.
15. Hiram to Rae, October 23, 1978, EOF.
16. Rae to Hiram, August 22, 1978, EOF.
17. Rae to Hiram, August 22, 1978, EOF; Rae Ely interview, December 20, 2010; Circuit Court of Louisa County, Final Settlement Trial Memorandum #2, October 23, 1978, EOF.

18. Rae Ely interviews, December 30, 2010, and January 4, 2011.
19. Rae Ely interview, December 30, 2010.
20. Rae Ely interview, December 30, 2010; Final Settlement Trial Memo #2, 6–7.
21. Rich Collins to Director of Admissions, St. John's College, January 19, 1979; Franklin to Director of Admissions, January 20, 1979 (in author's possession).
22. Ely interview December 30, 2010; Albert R. Turnbull to UVa Law School Faculty, April 17, 1980 (in author's possession).
23. Rae Ely interview, December 30, 2010.
24. Joel Weingarten interview, August 14, 2020; Ely interview, December 30, 2020.
25. Weingarten interview, August 14, 2020; Ely interview, December 30, 2020.
26. Rae Ely interview, December 30, 2020; Joel M. Weingarten, "Prelude to the Destruction of Israel," *NYT,* March 27, 1979.
27. Harry S. Truman Scholarship website, https://www.truman.gov/our-history, accessed August 14, 2020; Conklin Truman Scholarship evaluation, November 21, 1979 (in author's possession).
28. Weingarten interview, August 14, 2020.
29. Ely's application is cited in Turnbull to UVa Law School Faculty, 5.
30. A. E. Dick Howard interview, January 2, 2015; University of Virginia School of Law, "Women Who Led the Way: A Timeline of Trailblazers at UVa Law," accessed October 19, 2022, https://www.law.virginia.edu/uvalawyer/article/women-who-led-way; Foundation Class Profiles, RG 32/107-11, Law School Foundation Class Profiles and Commencement Exercises, 1965–2014, University of Virginia Law Library; Boyd to Turnbull, January 23, 1980 (in author's possession).
31. Bergin to Turnbull, April 17, 1980 (in author's possession).
32. Charles Goetz interview, March 4, 2011; Howard interview, January 2, 2015.
33. Howard interview, January 2, 2015.
34. Rae to Weingarten, January 15, 1981, EOF; Rae Ely interview, January 4, 2011; Goetz interview, March 4, 2011.
35. Rae Ely interview, January 4, 2011, January 18, 2001; Bill McKelway and Carlos Santos, "Blaze Destroys Villa in Green Springs," *RTD,* January 29, 1982.
36. Rae Ely interviews, January 4 and 18, 2001.
37. Ely interview, January 4, 2001; Hiram to Add, February 17, 1982, EOF.
38. Ely interviews, January 4 and 18, 2001; Ed Lowrey interview, August 25, 2020.
39. Ruth S. Intress, "Preservationist's Bid for Villa Tops Them All," *RTD,* March 6, 1986; Rae Ely interview, January 18, 2001; Bruce Potter, "Lengthy Divorce Case Embroils Louisa Court," *RTD,* January 24, 1986.
40. Potter, "Lengthy Divorce Case."
41. Bruce Potter, "Deadline Is Monday," *RTD,* February 26, 1986; Potter, "Lengthy Divorce Case."
42. Rae Ely interview, January 18, 2001; Potter, "Deadline Is Monday."
43. Ruthe S. Intress, "Ruined Villa Inspires Hot Court Battle," *RTD,* March 2, 1986; Intress, "Preservationists Bid."
44. Intress, "Ruined Villa and "Preservationists Bid"; Ely interview, January 18, 2001.
45. Intress, "Preservationist's Bid."

Chapter 23. A Silk Jungle

1. Ridge Schuyler interview, May 8, 2020.
2. Rae Ely interview, February 1, 2011.
3. Rae Ely interview, February 8, 2011.
4. For this estimate, see Poling to Favorito, "CPD's Vermiculite Reserves," May 23, 1991, DTX 301 Antitrust.
5. Ned Gumble interview, September 15, 2017.
6. Poling to Locke, February 14, 1991, WRG, 177, DTX 138, Antitrust; Gumble interview.
7. *Va. Vermiculite, Ltd. v. W. R. Grace & Co.*, Conn, 144 F. Supp. 2d at 558 (W.D. Va., 2001) [hereafter, *Va. Vermiculite*, 144 F. Supp. 2d at 558], facts 91–95; "Trip to Virginia: April 23/25," May 20, 1991, attached to Poling to Locke, May 28, 1991, WRG 169, DTX 134, Antitrust.
8. Rae Ely interview, February 1, 2011.
9. Rae Ely interview, February 1, 2011.
10. Rae Ely interview, February 1, 2011.
11. Rae Ely interview, February 1, 2011; *Va. Vermiculite*, 144 F. Supp. 2d at 558, facts 108–09.
12. Rae Ely interview, February 8, 2011.
13. Rae Ely interview, March 8, 2001.
14. Rae Ely interview, March 8, 2001.
15. *Va. Vermiculite*, 144 F. Supp. 2d at 558, fact 111.
16. *Va. Vermiculite*, 144 F. Supp. 2d at 558, fact 121; Poling to Locke, "Discussions with VV," September 19, 1991, WRG 175, DTX 137, Antitrust.
17. *Va. Vermiculite*, 144 F. Supp. 2d at 558, facts 128–30; Poling to Sansom, September 23, 1991, WRG 57, DTX 7, Antitrust.
18. Rae Ely interview, March 17, 2011; *Va. Vermiculite*, 144 F. Supp. 2d at 558, facts 140–41, quotation at fact 147.
19. Rae Ely interview, March 17, 2011; *Va. Vermiculite*, 144 F. Supp. 2d at 558, facts 141–48; Ely to Kohnken, May 13, 1992, PDX 117, PTX 354.
20. Poling to Bettacchi, June 27, 1992, attached to Bettacchi to Walsh, July 29, 1992, PDX 50, PTX 312; Poling to Walsh, August 10, 1992, PDX 53, PTX 315, Antitrust; Board Meeting, August 2, 1992, EOF.
21. Poling to Walsh, August 26, 1992; Board Meeting minutes, August 2, 1992; W. W. Whitlock to Porter and attached application, September 2, 1992, EOF.
22. Rae Ely interviews, March 17 and 27, 2011.
23. Walsh notes, "Visit with Rae Ely," September 1, 1992, PDX 55, PTX 317, Antitrust.
24. *Va. Vermiculite*, 144 F. Supp. 2d at 558, facts 179, 165; Walsh to Kohnken, September 17, 1992, PDX 61, PTX 320, Antitrust.
25. *Va. Vermiculite*, 144 F. Supp. 2d at 558, fact 179; Walsh to Kohnken, September 17, 1992, EOF.
26. Walsh to Kohnken, September 17, 1992; "Grace Donates Land" (draft), September 14, 1992, PDX 62, PTX 321; "Grace News," September 29, 1992, HGSI 69, DTX 124, Antitrust.

27. Walsh to Kohnken, September 17, 1992.
28. *Va. Vermiculite,* 144 F. Supp. 2d at 558, facts 180–82; tagline from "Grace Donates Land"; Hilda Miller, "Company That Fought to Mine Gives Land, Rights to Opponent," *CV,* October 1, 1992.
29. Miller, "Company That Fought"; "Firm Gives Land to Preservationists," *RTD,* September 30, 1992; "W. R. Grace Gives VA Preservationists 1300 Acres," *WAPO,* October 10, 1992.
30. Notes from the joint meeting of the two general partners for VVL, February 29, 1992, WRG 82, DTX 131; transcript of Robert Sansom Cross-Examination, September 18. 2000, 937, Antitrust.
31. Gumble interview.
32. *Va. Vermiculite,* 144 F. Supp. 2d at 558, facts 63–69, 84–85; *Historic Green Springs Inc. v. Brandy Farm, Ltd.,* 32 VA, Cir. 98 (1993) [Louisa Circuit Court] [hereafter, *HGSI v. Brandy Farm*]; Gumble interview.
33. Gumble interview; *HGSI v. Brandy Farm.*
34. Rae Ely interview, March 17, 2011; Gumble interview.
35. Rae Ely to Favorito, November 18, 1992, PDX 76, PTX 333 Antitrust; *Va. Vermiculite,* 144 F. Supp. 2d at 558, facts 214–15; Gumble interview.
36. Rae Ely to Favorito, November 18, 1992, PDX 76, PTX 333 Antitrust; *Va. Vermiculite,* 144 F. Supp. 2d at 558, facts 214–15; Gumble interview.
37. Whitlock to Porter, attached to Whitlock to Sansom, January 2, 1993, WRG 114, DTX 17, Antitrust.
38. Poling to Walsh, February 23, 1993, PDX 85, PTX 340, Antitrust.
39. HGSI Board Meeting notes, December 13, 1993, and January 5, 1994, EOF.
40. HGSI Board minutes, June 15, 1993; Favorito to Ely, June 16, 1993, WRG 221, DTX 110, EOF; Rae Ely interview, July 4, 2020.
41. M. F. Peers Direct Examination, September 15, 2000, 498, Antitrust; on loss in court, see *VVL v. Grace,* 269 and 288.
42. M. F. Peers to Peter Grace, August 16, 1993, attached to Grace to Bettacchi, August 19, 1993, PDX 112, PTX 352, Antitrust.
43. M. F. Peers to Peter Grace (emphasis in original).
44. *Va. Vermiculite,* 144 F. Supp. 2d at 558, facts 269–70, 288 for loss on appeal; Carlos Santos, "In Louisa, the Gift Is Bittersweet," *RTD,* November 22, 1993.
45. *Va. Vermiculite,* 144 F. Supp. 2d at 558, facts 271–75, 290–92; A. D. Peers to Greg Poling, January 3, 1994, WRG 247, DTX 141; the Peerses informed the Virginia Division of Minerals and Mining on February 25, 1995 that they had executed a mining agreement with VVL on their property: Alfred and Elizabeth Peers to Division of Minerals and Mining, EOF.
46. *Va. Vermiculite,* 144 F. Supp. 2d at 558.

Chapter 24. "A Female in Your Face"

1. *Virginia Vermiculite v. W. R. Grace,* U.S. District Court, W.D. Virginia, Charlottesville Division, April 22, 1997, 965 F. Supp. At 802 (W.D. Va. 1997) [hereafter, *Va.*

Vermiculite, 965 F. Supp. at 802]; *Va. Vermiculite, Ltd. v. W. R. Grace & Co.*, 156 F. 3d at 535 (4th Cir. 2001) [hereafter, *Va. Vermiculite*, 156 F. 3d at 535].
2. *Va. Vermiculite*, 965 F. Supp. at 808, 817.
3. Francis X. Clines, "An Environmental Suit with the Roles Switched," *NYT*, February 20, 2000; *Va. Vermiculite*, 965 F. Supp. at 182.
4. Charles Montange interview, March 1, 2016.
5. Penelope Canan and George W. Pring, "Strategic Lawsuits Against Public Participation," *Social Problems* 35, no. 5 (1988): 506–19; Canan and Pring, "Studying Strategic Lawsuits Against Public Participation: Mixing Quantitative and Qualitative Approaches," *Law & Society Review* 22, no. 2 (1988): 385–95; Alice Glover and Marcus Jimison, "SLAPP Suits: A First Amendment Issue and Beyond," *North Carolina Central Law Journal* 21 (1995): 124–42; Jerome I. Braun, "Increasing SLAPP Protections: Unburdening the Right of Petition in California," *UC Davis Law Review* 32 (1999): 967–1078; for quotation, see John J. Fried, "Debate Rages Over Developers' Lawsuits to Hinder Public Participation," *Chicago Tribune*, June 23, 1991; Stephanie Simon, "Nader Suits Up to Strike Back Against Slapps," *Wall Street Journal*, July 9, 1991.
6. Rae Ely interview, March 8, 2011.
7. Gumble interview; Leri Thomas interview, June 18, 2000; David Izakowitz interview, September 4, 2017; Izakowitz, e-mail to author, October 26, 2022.
8. Izakowitz interview; Goetz interview.
9. Izakowitz interview.
10. Gumble interview; Izakowitz interview.
11. Izakowitz interview.
12. Izakowitz interview.
13. Izakowitz interview.
14. *Va. Vermiculite*, 965 F. Supp. at 802; Goetz interview.
15. Rae Ely interviews, July 4, 2020, and March 8, 2011; for Bausch, Charles Montange interview, March 1, 2016.
16. Montange interview.
17. Rae Ely interview, March 8, 2011.
18. Rae Ely interview, March 8, 2011; Goetz interview.
19. Montange interview.
20. Montange interview.
21. HGSI Board minutes, March 11, 1995, EOF; e-mail notes to files after unrecorded interviews with Rae Ely at Hawkwood, January 2 and 11, 2021.
22. Izakowitz interview.
23. Izakowitz interview.
24. *Va. Vermiculite*, 965 F. Supp. at 807.
25. *Va. Vermiculite*, 965 F. Supp. at 812.
26. *Va. Vermiculite*, 965 F. Supp. at 813, 816.
27. Charles H. Montange, SCOTUS Brief in Opposition, *VVL v. HGSI*, Petition for Writ of Cert., no. 02–1167, 8 (in author's possession); *Va. Vermiculite*, 965 F. Supp. at 811.
28. *Va. Vermiculite*, 156 F. 3d at 535, 541.
29. William Horne, "Strings Attached," *Preservation News*, February 1999.

30. Montange, SCOTUS Brief, 9; *Virginia Vermiculite v. W. R. Grace*, United States District Court, W.D. Virginia, Charlottesville Division, May 4, 2000, 98 F. Supp. 2d 729 (W.D. VA 2000) [hereafter, *Va. Vermiculite*, 98 F. Supp. 2d 729]; at 730 for Schwartz.
31. The legal standards for scheduling such a hearing were established by *Daubert v. Merrell Dow Pharmaceuticals, Inc.*, 509 U.S. 579, 592–93, 125 L. Ed. 2d 469, 113 S. Ct. 2786 (1993); *Va. Vermiculite*, 98 F. Supp. 2d at 730.
32. *Va. Vermiculite*, 98 F. Supp. 2d at 740; Goetz interview.
33. Montange interview.
34. Montange interview; Goetz interview.
35. Rae Ely interview, March 8, 2011; *Lightweight News* 62, no. 1 (March 2011): 2, accessed January 11, 2021, https://www.vermiculite.org/wp-content/uploads/2014/10/Lightweight-News-March-2011_1.pdf; for rough date of Ellicott engagement, see HGSI Board meeting minutes, April 7, 1999, EOF.
36. Izakowitz interview.
37. *Va. Vermiculite*, 98 F. Supp. 2d at 575 and 576, note 16.
38. *Va. Vermiculite*, 98 F. Supp. 2d at 554 and 591, quotation at 590.
39. Goetz interview.
40. Michael, James Harry Jr., Federal Judicial Center, accessed July 17, 2020, https://www.fjc.gov/history/judges/michael-james-harry-jr; Ed Lowrey interview; Montange interview; Clines, "Environmental Suit."
41. Montange interview.
42. Gumble re-cross-examination, September 15, 2000, 494, Antitrust.
43. Goetz interview.
44. Rae Ely interview, March 8, 2011.
45. Rae Ely interview, March 8, 2011.
46. Rae Ely interview, March 8, 2011.
47. Montange interview; Sansom cross-examination, September 18, 2000, Antitrust Trial, 941, 976.
48. Montange interview.
49. Andrew Schneider, "Tenacious Ladies Vindicated," *Seattle Post Intelligencer*, October 4, 2000.
50. Hearing on Workplace Safety and Asbestos Contamination, July 31, 2001, S. Hrg. 107–269, at 1 (Washington, D.C.: U.S. Government Printing Office, 2002).
51. United States District Court for the Western District of Virginia, Virginia Vermiculite, Ltd.'s "Motion to Modify and Quash Subpoena," filed August 30, 2000, granted September 12, 2000; quotation at paragraph 4; Montange interview.
52. *Va. Vermiculite*, 144 F. Supp. 2d at 608.
53. Adrienne Schwisow, "Historic Green Springs Cleared," *RTD*, May 30, 2001; Einer R. Elhauge, Harvard Law School, accessed July 17, 2020, https://hls.harvard.edu/faculty/directory/10234/Elhauge.
54. Montange interview.
55. United States Court of Appeals for the Fourth Circuit 307 F. 3d 277; argued May 6, 2002, decided October 4, 2002, 277, quotation at 281.
56. *Virginia Vermiculite, LLC v. The Historic Green Springs, Inc.*, 02–1167 Supreme Court of the United States 538 U.S. 998, April 28, 2003; Goetz interview.

57. Deana Meredith, "Court Sides with Historic Green Springs," *CV*, May 2, 2003; Olivia S. Choe, "A Missed Opportunity: Nonprofit Antitrust Liability in *Virginia Vermiculite, Ltd. v. Historic Green Springs, Inc.*," *Yale Law Journal* 113, no. 2 (November 2003): 533–40, at 534, 540.
58. Montange interview; Goetz interview.

Epilogue

1. Spring Creek Home Owners Association, May 24, 2012, notes by author.
2. Rae Ely, e-mails to author, May 24 and 25, 2012.
3. "Joint Pipeline Going Under," *CV*, August 12, 2010; Elizabeth Wilkerson, "Fluvanna, Louisa Eying Water Plan at Zion Crossroads," *RTD*, July 24, 1996; Deana Meredith, "Who Will Manage Zion X-Roads Water/Sewer?" *CV*, March 13, 2003.
4. Deanna Meredith, "Former Prison Site Could Be Site for Green Springs Park," *CV*, October 25, 2001; Patrick Hickerson, "Zion Crossroads Investment Plan Passes," *DP*, February 2, 1999.
5. Hickerson, "Investment Plan Passes"; Melissa Scott Sinclair, "Preservation Group Takes State to Court," *DP*, December 18, 2002; Deanna Meredith, "Planners Approve Public Utility at Zion Crossroads," *CV*, January 28, 1999; "Supervisors OK Tower and Water," *CV*, February 4, 1999; "Water to Be Drawn from Green Springs," *CV*, February 24, 2005; Deana Meredith, "Who Will Manage," *CV*, March 13, 2003; "Permanent Power Plans on Hold for Zion Crossroads Water," *CV*, May 3, 2001; Melissa Scott Sinclair, "Waters Run Deep," *Style*, April 23, 2003.
6. Sinclair, "Waters Run Deep."
7. Patrick Hickerson, "Green Springs-Zion Crossroads Water Plan," *DP*, February 1, 1999; "Losing Battle: Spring Creek Wells Targeted," *CV*, March 10, 2005; "Proffers," May 25, 2001, attached to Complaint for Declaratory Judgment, Injunctive Relief and Damages, *HGSI v. Virginia Western Land Company, LLC and Charles D. Kincannon* in the Circuit Court for Louisa County, March 23, 2005 [hereafter, HGSI Complaint 2005]; "Proffers," May 25, 2001, attached to HGSI Complaint 2005; "Permanent Power Plans on Hold"; "Spring Creek Decision Tabled," *CV*, June 7, 2001.
8. Sinclair, "Waters Run Deep," 21; Exhibit A to original contract, attached to HGSI Complaint 2005; Contract of Purchase and Sale, January 22, 2002, attached to HGSI Complaint 2005.
9. Rae Ely to Governor Mark Warner, March 28, 2002 (in author's possession); Rae Ely to Friends and Neighbors, March 29, 2002 (in author's possession); *HGSI and Landowners v. Charles D. Kincannon and the Commonwealth of Virginia*, Bill of Complaint for Declaratory Judgment and Request for Temporary and Permanent Injunctive Relief, Circuit Court for Louisa County, March 11, 2002 [hereafter, HGSI Complaint 2002], 9.
10. HGSI Complaint 2002, 9–10; Sinclair, "Preservation Group Takes State to Court."
11. Sinclair, "Preservation Group Takes State to Court"; Austin Graham, "Historic District Lawsuit Begins," *DP*, March 31, 2003; Deana Meredith, "Historic Green Springs Inc. Battles Developer and Commonwealth," *CV*, April 10, 2003.

12. F. Ward Harkrader, Jr. to David S. Bailey, re "*Historic Greensprings Inc., et al. v. Charles Kincannon, et al.*, June 25, 2003, attached to HGSI Complaint 2005.
13. Deanna Meredith, "Lawsuit Filed Over Green Springs Water," *DP*, June 14, 2004; HGSI Complaint,2005, 16, 19.
14. Rex Murphy, "Comments for Planning Commission and Board of Supervisors Joint Meeting," February 23, 2005 (in author's possession).
15. David Hendrick, "At a Crossroads: Community Eyes Resources as Area Experiences Major Growth," *DP*, June 20, 2005; Greg Dorazio, "Lowe's Site Plan Approved," *CV*, April 5, 2007; "Liquid Assets," *DP*, June 20, 2004.
16. David Hendrick, "At a Crossroads: Residential Growth Is Assured, But What Will Follow?" *DP*, July 2, 2006.
17. "Liquid Assets"; "Judge OKs Pumping in District," *DP*, December 21, 2006; Petition for Appeal in the Supreme Court of Virginia, *HGSI v. VWLC and Louisa County*, May 21, 2007 [hereafter, Petition for Appeal].
18. Petition for Appeal, 3; Supreme Court of Virginia cases number 071076 (confirmed in phone conversation with Terrance Morris, an associate in the Clerk of the Court's office, May 18, 2021.)
19. Conversation with Meredith, property manager at Stonegate, May 18, 2021, for number of apartments.
20. Committee on House Resources, Subcommittee on National Parks, Recreation and Public Lands, Hearing on National Preservation Act, April 21, 2005, accessed January 2, 2023, https://www.govinfo.gov/content/pkg/CHRG-109hhrg20807/html/CHRG-109hhrg20807.htm; see also L. M. Schwartz, "Historic Easement Challenged in US and Virginia Courts," Virginia Land Rights Coalition, accessed May 22, 2021, http://www.vlrc.org/articles/158.html.
21. Supreme Court of Virginia, *U.S. v. Blackman*, Upon Questions of Law Certified by the United States District Court for the Western District of Virginia, Opinion, Justice Lawrence L. Koontz, June 9, 2005 [hereafter, Va. Supreme Court Blackman], 2–3.
22. Va. Supreme Court Blackman, 3; Schwartz, "Easement Challenged," 4.
23. Va. Supreme Court Blackman, 3
24. Va. Supreme Court Blackman, 4, 1, 5, 16; Deana Meredith, "Green Springs Catalyst for Landmark Decision," *CV*, June 16, 2005.
25. Va. Supreme Court Blackman, 15–16.
26. Blackman testimony, April 21, 2005; Blackman, "Property Law Today: The New Feudalism," October 22, 2005.
27. *U.S. v. Blackman*, in the U.S. Court for the Western District of Virginia, decided October 19, 2005, Memorandum Opinion, Judge Norman K. Moon, 3, at 5, 16; U.S. Court of Appeals for the Fourth Circuit, *U.S. v. Blackman*, Decided May 31, 2007, at 5; "Man Worked on House Without OK, Must Pay," *RTD*, January 30, 2006.
28. Virginia Land Rights Coalition, accessed May 22, 2021, http://www.vlrc.org/about.html.
29. Schwartz, "Easement Challenged."
30. Schwartz, "Easement Challenged."
31. "Green Springs," NPS, accessed May 23, 2021, https://www.nps.gov/grsp/index.htm.

32. *Roanoke Times*, "Green Springs Decision," April 4, 1973.
33. Rae Ely, e-mail update to Louisa County Community, August 13, 2019 (in author's possession); Allison Wrabel, "Monacan Tribe Pushes Against Water Project," *DP*, August 13, 2019.
34. James River Water Project (JRWP), Timmons Group, accessed October 26, 2022, https://www.timmons.com/project/james-river-water-project/; David Holtzman, "Federal Panel Intervenes in Louisa County Water Dispute," *CV*, July 12, 2019; Allison Wrabel, "Under Pressure, Fluvanna OKs Permit for Water Project," *DP*, January 21, 2016.
35. Gregory S. Schneider, "Virginia's Monacan Tribe Uses New Federal Status to Take a Stand for What Could Be Its Long-Lost Capital," *WAPO*, January 5, 2020.
36. Schneider, "Virginia's Monacan Tribes"; Mouer to Fluvanna and Louisa Administrators and Boards of Supervisors, November 9, 2014, letter provided to author by Jeffrey Hantman in e-mail of May 28, 2021; L. Daniel Mouer, "Monacan Archaeology and Ethnohistory," in *Piedmont Archaeology*, ed. Mark Wittkofski (Richmond, VA: Virginia Historic Landmarks Commission, 1984), 21–39, at 26; Cultural Heritage Partners website "timeline," accessed May 28, 2021, http://www.culturalheritagepartners.com/wp-content/uploads/2020/09/SaveRassawekTimeline_9-23-2020.pdf [hereafter, CHP timeline].
37. Schneider, "Virginia's Monacan Tribes."
38. CHP timeline.
39. CHP timeline.
40. Schneider, "Virginia's Monacan Tribes"; Encyclopedia Virginia staff, Monacan Indian Nation, December 14, 2020, in *Encyclopedia Virginia*, accessed October 26, 2022, https://encyclopediavirginia.org/entries/monacan-indian-nation; Public Law 115–121, accessed May 30, 2021, https://www.congress.gov/bill/115th-congress/house-bill/984/text.
41. Remarks of Marion F. Werkheiser, Managing Partner, Cultural Heritage Partners, PLLC, and Legal Counsel to the Monacan Indian Nation at the James River Water Authority Public Meeting Spring Creek Golf Course, August 13, 2019, CHP, accessed May 30, 2021, http://www.culturalheritagepartners.com/wp-content/uploads/2019/08/JRWAMeeting8_13_2019-1.pdf.
42. Remarks of Marion F. Werkheiser.
43. Remarks of Marion F. Werkheiser.

ACKNOWLEDGMENTS

TWO EDS HAVE HELPED ME WITH every step of this journey, kindly pausing each time they raced several steps ahead of me. Ed Ayers was able to see the historical vistas that stretched far beyond Green Springs' 14,000 acres and gently nudged me to explore them without losing the reader along the way. His panoramic grasp of history did not prevent him from noticing every misplaced comma in the many drafts he read. Nor did it ever stop him from excising exclamation points! Ed Russell read those drafts with the same care, subtly sifting through what I hoped would be an argument, distilling its essence. I always came away from his written comments and our conversations believing that these crucial refinements were my own. Both Eds were cheerleaders and critics; consolers and coaches. Leaders in their fields of southern (Ayers) and environmental (Russell) history, each graciously welcomed this newcomer into worlds they had long since mastered.

Several other historians offered invaluable assistance at crucial points along the way. Lily Geismer and Bryant Simon, the two readers for Yale University Press, delivered constructive criticism that significantly improved the book. They were kind enough to identify themselves and continue the conversation after they submitted their reports. I am grateful for the time and thought that they invested in my work. Mel Leffler, who answered the call whenever I found the courage to show him portions of the manuscript, delivered the keen constructive criticism that he has consistently provided over the course of my career.

I am indebted to a far longer list of scholars for assistance that ranges from advice about the literature in their fields to expert criticism of portions of my manuscript. They include Jacob Anbinder, Yoni Appelbaum, Monica Blair, Brent Cebul, Christy Chapin, Nathan Connolly, Gareth Davies, Bart Elmore, Kate Epstein, Lou Galambos, George Gilliam, Jeff Hantman, Claudrena Harold, Julian Hayter, Sarah Igo, Trish Kahle, Andrew Kahrl, Matt Lassiter, Caroline Lee, Phyllis Leffler, Shane Lin, Chris Loss, Beth Meyer, Sarah Milov, Quinn Mulroy, Margaret O'Mara, Peter Onuf, Suleiman Osman, Jess Phelps, Sarah Phillips, Emily Prifogle, Adam Rome, Brian Rosenwald, Laura Phillips Sawyer, Bruce Schulman, Lori Schuyler, Jim Sparrow, Tom Sugrue, Alan Taylor, Will Thomas, Billy Wayson, and Michael Willrich.

I also benefited from the scholarship and research of many graduate research assistants at the University of Virginia. Erik Erlandson, Leif Fredrickson, Jim Lawson, Evan McCormick, and Nic Wood worked smartly, selflessly, and tirelessly. So too the UVa undergraduates who worked on this book: Hailey Chapman, Selena Coles, Erica Hinchman, Anne Jordan, Rebekah Madigan, Fallon Moore, Sarah Rigazio, and Emily Whalen. I would also like to thank Matt West for sharing his work on Virginia politics.

I received outstanding comments from scholars in a number of seminars and workshops, including the Nature and Culture Seminar at the University of Kansas; the Center for Cultural Landscapes at the University of Virginia School of Architecture; the Virginia Tech Department of History; the Seminar at Johns Hopkins University; a panel at the American Society for Legal History; the Contemporary History Colloquium at the Smithsonian Institution; and the Rothermere American Institute at Oxford University. I also received generous assistance from librarians and archivists, including Loren Moulds at the University of Virginia Law School; Jim Ambuske and Rebecca Baird at Mount Vernon; James Alvey, Noel Harrison, and John Sprinkle at the National Park Service; Judy Thomas and Keith Weimer at the University of Virginia Library; Elaine Taylor and Karleen Kovalcik at the Louisa County Historical Society; Hamilton Lombard at the Weldon Cooper Center; Quatro Hubbard at the Virginia Department of Historic Resources; and Clara Altman at the Federal Judicial Center.

Generous institutional support was provided by the University of Virginia College of Arts and Sciences; the UVa Corcoran Department of History; the Miller Center of Public Affairs, where Sheila Blackford, Sean Gallagher, Mike

ACKNOWLEDGMENTS

Greco, Julie Gronlund, and Guian McKee were particularly helpful; and the Jefferson Scholars Foundation, where Jeff Bialy, Lew Burrus, Ben Skipper, Linda Winecoff, and Jimmy Wright were particularly helpful. A great deal of assistance came from noninstitutional sources. I could not have written this book without the hundreds of hours that Rae Ely poured into interviews, e-mails, and phone calls. She allowed me complete access to her files on all matters relating to Green Springs. Nor could this book have been written without the interviews that dozens of people made time for. Thank you for the care and effort that went into these. Several people knowledgeable about the Battle of Green Springs and Virginia politics went beyond interviews to offer valuable primary sources and insight. I would like to thank Richard Bland, Michael Bowles, Chris Ely, Jane Fisher, Bob Gibson, Ned Gumble, Kristin Hicks, David Holzman, Kat Imhoff, David Izakowitz, David Kudravetz, Steve Lucas, Barbara Moore-Savidge, Angus Murdock, Deborah Murdock, Tammy Purcell, Edmund Rennolds, Jeff Schapiro, Jay Taylor, Leri Thomas, Billy Wayson, Amanda Welch, and Mary Wertch.

I would like to thank the staff at Yale University Press. I also benefited from the advice and editing skill of Tim Mennel and Bill Strachan. Michael McGandy has offered wise counsel at every stage of the project. My agent, Geri Thoma, was kind enough to take on this book at the end of a long, distinguished career and when she retired, John Schline stepped in and did not miss a beat. His encouragement, counsel, and criticism were remarkable.

Patience has been the universal quality shared by my friends and family as I worked on this book. I want to thank my friends who have endured long conversations about tie-breakers who don't break ties and terms like *exfoliation*, which they convinced me to excise from the text. Among the friends who have patiently endured all of this are David and Joan Anderson, Wayne and Janet Bush, Neil Brander, Greg Doull, Chris Hobbie, Elenana Moore, Adrian Owens, David Polk, Aran Shetterly, Margot Shetterly, Brian, Grace, and Marcy Wagner, and Jon Zimmerman. Steve Golub read and edited portions of the manuscript, improving each draft I sent him. Barbara Salisbury read the entire manuscript, offering both wise counsel and support.

Fortunately, my family had little choice about listening to me talk about the book. My cousin, Bobby Balogh, quickly turned the conversation to the Miami Hurricanes—an unfortunate choice, given the way their seasons have gone. My brother, Michael Balogh, and his wife, Katie Tanaka, were models of patience, when they might easily have attended to far more important matters. My children, Dustin, Jake, and Carmen Balogh, had been through this before—they responded like real pros. Kathy Craig, to whom this work is dedicated, has helped with every aspect of this book, reading, editing, criticizing, suggesting, but always encouraging. Her curiosity, sophisticated understanding of human nature, and finely tuned literary sensibilities are infused through every page, as is my love for her.

INDEX

Figures are indicated by page number accompanied with italicized "f."

Abbott, Stanley, 115, 119, 120
Abourezk, James, 71
Accokeek Foundation, 172, 178
Adams, Eugenia, 28–29
Administrative Procedures Act (1946), 234
Advisory Council on Historic Preservation, 228, 297
Agee, Dean: Board of Supervisors rezoning deadlock and, 185; on easement donation to Interior Department, 221; environmental impact statement authored by, 92; on Federal reach in Louisa County, 223; on HGSI, 212; on historical Green Springs, 42; on Louisa County economic development, 44; on national landmark designation, 164; on prison construction proposal, 42, 48–49, 132, 167; property rights and, 293; on Purcell, 48
Agnew, Spiro, 17, 148
agriculture and forestry in historic Green Springs, 19, 33–34, 79, 119, 125, 211
Alamo, 4, 137, 142

Alexander, Edward, 78, 115
Allen v. State Board of Elections (U.S. 1969), 191
Almond, Lindsay, Jr., 46
Anderson, Jack, 209, 269
Andrus, Cecil D., 218, 230–32, 234
antitrust allegations: asbestos hazards and, 281, 282; expert testimony in, 276–78, 282–83; Historic Green Springs, Inc. subject to, 271–83; non-profit liability and, 283–84; as SLAPP, 275; W. R. Grace land donation and, 267; Zion Crossroads development and, 287
anti-Vietnam War movement: direct citizen action influenced by, 7, 37; Hickel and, 107; historical scholarship influenced by, 37; women in, 53
Army Corps of Engineers, 297, 298
asbestos, 198–99, 202–5, 259, 261, 281–82, 284
Askew, John B., 35, 36
Association for the Preservation of Virginia Antiquities, 78
Atkins, Donald Lee, 35, 38, 56, 100, 291, 294

Atkins, Frances Anne, 38, 291
Attica Prison uprising (1971), 152

Bacque, Peter, 122, 161, 167
Bailey, David S., 288
Bausch, Karl, 272
Beame, Abe, 117
Bergin, Tom, 249
Bergland, Bob, 222
Bergland decision (1980). *See Historic Green Springs Inc. v. Bergland*
Berry, David F., 176
Berry, Edward D., 252–53
Bethany, Merilyn, 236
Biddle, James, 78, 87, 93
Black Americans: Federal protections for, 214; HGSI and, 49; Louisa County and, 192–95, 197; prison construction proposal and, 194; vermiculite mining and, 49, 194–95; voter suppression and, 18, 45–46, 190. *See also* race and racism; segregation and desegregation
Blackman, Peter F., 290–94
Blackman, United States v. (Va. 2005), 291–93
Blanchard, Bruce: background and career of, 107; easement procurement and, 142–43, 178–79, 217, 221, 231; Ely and, 101, 108–9, 134–35, 142–43; Hanmer and, 101, 106–8; Morton and, 151, 157
block grants, 69, 74, 75, 77, 87, 91, 163
Bolton, Chester, 172
Bolton, Frances Payne, 172–73
BOS. *See* Louisa County Board of Supervisors
Boswell's Tavern, 78–79, 122
Bowles, George, 144
Boyd, T. Munford "Munny," 249
Bracketts Plantation, 35–36, 39, 58
Brandy Farm vermiculite reserves, 259–60, 265–66
Branham, Kenneth, 295
Brenneman, Russell, 135

Brown, B. B., 222
Brown, Otis L.: *Ely 1* appeal (1971) and, 91; environmental impact statement and, 92–93; on Murdock's Green Springs history, 43; prison construction proposal and, 18–20, 35, 36, 67, 82, 87; Virginia Historic Landmarks Commission and, 78, 80
Brown v. Board of Education (U.S. 1954), 68, 84, 192
Bumpers, Dale, 233–34
Burger, Warren, 105
Butler, John Q., 128, 184, 186, 187, 195
Byrd, Harry F., Jr., 45
Byrd, Harry F., Sr., 45–47
Byrd organization: citizen action vs., 5, 18, 130; death of Harry Byrd, Sr. and, 45; Ely's citizen group challenging, 5; Godwin and, 157, 158; local control as tenet of, 46; political power of, 45–46; prison construction proposal and, 18–19; racism and, 5, 6, 46; vermiculite mining and, 123; voter suppression by, 18, 45–46, 123. *See also* courthouse crowd

Calvert Cliffs (D.C. Circuit 1971), 89
Carr, Dabney, 42
Carson, Rachel: *Silent Spring*, 136
Carter, Jimmy, 214–15, 218, 228, 237
Celebrezze, Anthony J., 104
Central Virginian: on *Blackman* (2005), 292; Lyall's letters in, 125–26, 202; on national landmark designation, 129, 230; on nuclear power plant in Louisa County, 18; on prison construction proposal, 109, 161; on Purcell subdivision, 218; on rezoning conflict, 148, 186; on vermiculite mining, 184–85, 200, 234; on W. R. Grace land donation proposal, 261–62; on Zion Crossroads development, 287
Champion, Jane, 270
Chaplin, Gordon, 212
Cheney, Dick, 236–37, 238

Chester, Francis, 148
Chisolm, Leroy, 221
Choe, Olivia S., 283–84
Christian Youth Ranch, 24, 58
citizen activism. *See* direct action; women; *specific activists and activist organizations*
Citizens Committee for Fair Taxation, 65
A Civil Action (book and film), 204
Civil Rights Act (1964), 68
civil rights movement: environmental movement and, 180; federalism and, 6, 68, 71, 192, 195, 214; historical scholarship influenced by, 37; historic preservation adopting strategies from, 9, 37, 184, 188, 190–92, 197, 212; Merhige as judge in cases involving, 84; participatory politics from, 9; women in, 53
class divide. *See* poverty and class divide
Clean Water Act (1972), 104, 130
Clines, Francis, 267, 279
Coffey, Darren, 289
Cole, Katherine, 141
Coles, George M., 186
Collins, Rich, 245
Colonial Williamsburg, 40, 127, 142, 212
community associations as public-private partnerships, 116–17
Conklin, Patrick, 247–48
Connally, Ernest Allan, 129, 137–40, 171, 175–79
Connor, James E., 209, 210
conservation. *See* environmental movement; historic preservation
conservative politicians and organizations, 47, 53, 113, 158, 208
conservative press, 45, 59, 92, 281
courthouse crowd: Byrd organization and, 45; citizen activism and, 10, 294; civil rights movement and, 192; Rae Ely, attitudes toward, 97–98; Hanmer and, 106; historic preservation and, 44, 100, 176; local agenda of, 5, 18–19; Louisa County economic development and, 43, 44, 122–23; Nixon and, 9; prison construction proposal and, 32, 49, 67; property rights and, 5, 294; segregation and, 5, 49; vermiculite mining and, 148, 189
Crigler, B. Waugh, 274, 280
criminal justice reform: Holton's policy of, 13–14, 16–17; New Federalism and, 70–71; Nixon and, 13, 70–71, 73–74; picket federalism and, 77, 81; prison construction proposal and, 17–18, 80–81, 102–3, 159, 160, 165, 166; public opinion on, 17
Cultural Heritage Partners, 298
cultural landscapes. *See* historic preservation
Curtis, R. E., 215

Dade County Children's Home, 23–24
Daily Progress: easement issue in, 113; on elimination of zoning restrictions, 201; Ely as Citizen of the Year in, 179; Ely's relationship with, 67; on national landmark status, 142; on prison construction proposal, 35, 40, 56–57, 93–94, 110, 144, 153, 159–62, 166; on vermiculite mining, 133, 147, 148, 187; on Zion Crossroads development, 289
Daniel, Griffith B., 185–88
Darling, Lynn, 180
Davies, Jane, 77–78
Davis, Alexander Jackson, 40, 41, 77–78
Deeds, R. H., 187
Democratic Party, 13, 15, 18, 46, 70, 158. *See also specific politicians*
Department of Health, Education, and Welfare, 192, 195
Department of the Interior: Blanchard's role in, 106–7; easement procurement and, 134–41, 171, 178–79, 214–22, 227, 229–32, 291; Ely's relationship with, 72, 101, 108–9, 149–51, 199, 236; Green Springs

Department of the Interior (*continued*)
national landmark status and, 6, 81, 234–35; Green Springs vermiculite mining and, 199–200, 233–34; on prison construction proposal, 8, 102, 109–10; public-private partnership and, 117; Virginia Historic Landmarks Commission and, 77, 80. *See also* National Park Service

Dewar, Helen, 88, 158

direct action: anti-Vietnam War movement and, 7, 37; Byrd organization and, 5, 18, 130; civil rights movement and, 9, 197; Federal access through, 9; NIMBY activism and, 235; petition drive against prison construction, 95–97; picnic protest, 149; political scene adapting to, 124; Sansom on, 208; SLAPPs and, 268–69; vermiculite mining and, 130–31

Dobbins, J. Lewis and Martha H., 128, 131, 147

Duncan, Hugh (Rae's first husband), 3, 24–25

DWI. *See* Virginia Department of Welfare and Institutions

Eardley, Carl, 229

easements: antitrust suit against HGSI and, 268; Eastern View and, 291; Ely's procurement of, 113–15, 119–21, 128, 132, 217; Green Springs historic district and, 4, 8, 112–15, 117–18, 119–21, 128–29, 131, 134, 209, 216–19; historic preservation and, 116, 135, 221, 232, 284, 292; Holton and, 111, 114, 117–21, 124–25, 292; Mount Vernon and, 171–75; National Park Service oversight of, 8, 113, 134–41, 171–72, 175–79, 216–17, 232–33, 290–94; prison construction proposal and, 111–15, 152, 175; property rights and, 140, 173, 175, 176, 220, 230, 232, 290–93; public access to, 295; public-private partnership and, 8, 112–13, 135–36, 152; role of, 111–13, 294–95; tax benefits of, 294; vermiculite mining and, 114, 178, 199, 230. *See also* Department of the Interior; Virginia Historic Landmarks Commission

Eastern View estate, 38, 291–94

Edwards, Mary, 152

Edwards, Paul G., 158

EIS. *See* environmental impact statements

Eisenhower, Dwight D., 14–15

Eisenhower, Mamie, 26

Electric Home and Farm Authority, 44

Elhauge, Einer R., 282–83

Ellicott, Graham, 277

Ellis, Claire, 54

Ely, Addison (father of Hiram), 25

Ely, Addison (son of Rae and Hiram), 28, 29, 156, 246

Ely, Hiram (Hi), Jr. (son from Hiram's first marriage), 27–28

Ely, Hiram (Rae's second husband): background and career of, 25–26, 26*f*; domestic struggles and divorce proceedings, 145–46, 154–55, 181–82, 240–45, 251–53; easement donation and, 114; *Ely 1* initial suit filed by (1971), 74–75; Green Springs Association and, 54, 59, 63; marriage to Rae, 3–4, 21–22, 25–27, 31, 34, 95, 98–99; move to Florida, 251; move to Green Springs, 4, 21, 28–31, 79; prison construction proposal and, 32, 34–35; Rae's leadership and, 62–64, 95, 98–99, 156

Ely, Hope (daughter from Hiram's first marriage), 27

Ely, Nathaniel (ancestor of Hiram), 25

Ely, Rae: on antitrust suit against HGSI, 279–80, 283–84; character and abilities, 5–6, 21–22, 54, 58, 61–62, 93, 97, 246, 284, 286; childhood, 3, 21–24, 58; children of, 28, 29, 31, 54, 156, 246; creation of Green Springs National Historic Landmark District,

4–5, 133, 139, 141, 227; domestic struggles and divorce proceedings, 145–46, 154–55, 181–82, 240–45, 251–53; fashion and appearance as tools of, 1–2, 54, 60, 73, 254–55, 257, 259; Federal relationships cultivated by, 8, 72, 100–101, 103–8, 134–37, 139–40, 149–51, 209, 215, 236; home tour initiative, 57–60, 62; law practice of, 254, 270, 272; marriage to Duncan (first husband), 3, 24–25; marriage to Ely (second husband), 3–4, 21–22, 25–27, 31, 34, 95, 98–99; media relationships cultivated by, 67, 92–93, 101, 119, 141–42, 199; move to Green Springs (Louisa County), 4, 21, 28–31, 79; New Federalism and, 8, 71–72; participatory politics of, 9–10, 95–97, 149–50, 180; photos of, 61f, 299f; at St. John's College, Annapolis, 245–48; at University of Virginia School of Law, 241, 248–50; Whitlock on, 177; women's political engagement and, 53–55, 62, 156, 167–68, 180, 270. *See also* prison construction proposal; *specific court cases and names of persons with whom Rae interacted and issues in which she took role*

Ely, Sherri (Rae's daughter from her first marriage), 25, 29, 54, 246

Ely, Todd (son of Rae and Hiram), 28, 29, 156, 246

Ely v. Velde: Eastern District of Virginia (Merhige, 1971) (*Ely 1*), 85–87, 159; Eastern District of Virginia (Merhige, 1973) (*Ely 2*), 154, 162; filing of initial suit by Hiram Ely, 74–75; FmHA suit compared to, 223; Fourth Circuit Court of Appeals (1971) (*Ely 1*), 8, 89–92; Fourth Circuit Court of Appeals (1974) (*Ely 2*), 157, 159, 162–63; preservation and environmental networks mobilized by, 87–89

eminent domain, 143, 173, 215

Emroch, Emanuel (Manny): on asbestos dangers, 203; on easement donation to Interior Department, 215; as Ely's choice of attorney, 55–56, 58, 62, 72–74; *Ely 2* arguments of (1974), 159; University of Illinois environmental impact study and, 102; Virginia Historic Landmarks Commission report and, 80

Endangered Species Act (1973), 136

Energy and Environmental Analysis, Inc., 207

Engel, George, 21–23, 29, 40, 253, 284

enslaved people, 33, 39

Environmental Defense Fund, 72, 234

environmental impact statements (EIS): Blanchard's rejection of, 108–9; easement donation to Interior Department and, 218, 221; *Ely 1* (1971) and, 75, 91–92, 154; Federal influence through, 105–6; FmHA and, 218, 222–23, 228, 230–31; insider knowledge of, 101, 104; University of Illinois analysis suppressed, 102–3; vermiculite mining and, 199, 217–18

environmental movement: civil rights movement and, 180; Ely and, 94, 180; Great Society and, 64; highway construction and, 65–66; historical scholarship influenced by, 37; historic preservation linked to, 41, 93; Holton and, 14, 16–17, 62–63, 66, 80, 82; industrial chemical pollution and, 204–5; Montange and, 272; natural resource conservation and, 126; New Federalism and, 72; Nixon and, 130, 136; Potter and, 65; prison construction proposal and, 35–36, 41, 62–63, 167; quality of life demands in, 6, 7, 64; Reed and, 136; Sansom and, 208; women in, 53–54, 63, 66

Environmental Protection Agency (EPA): asbestos regulation and, 204; Ely's relationship with, 72, 101, 104; Hanmer and, 104; Sansom and, 207

Equal Employment Opportunity Commission (EEOC), 71

Farmers Home Administration (FmHA): environmental impact statements and, 218, 222–23, 228, 230–31; Virginia Vermiculite, Inc. loan from, 217, 222–23, 230–31, 233
Favorito, Mario, 130, 258, 263, 266
federalism: Byrd organization and, 45; civil rights movement and, 6, 68, 71, 192, 195, 214; court access and, 6, 71; direct citizen action and, 9; easement donation program and, 112, 134–43, 171–73, 175, 177–79, 214–22; *Ely 1* (1971) and, 75, 86–87, 90–91, 297; *Ely 2* (1974) and, 162–63; Green Springs Association and, 71–72, 75, 109; historic preservation and, 6, 9, 100; Holton and, 100; Merhige on, 85; New Deal and, 44–45; New Federalism, 8–9, 68–72, 75, 83, 86, 131, 140, 175, 239; picket fence federalism, 76, 81, 87, 100; prison construction proposal and, 70–75, 89–91, 106, 152; Purcell and, 47; tribal recognition and, 297–98; zoning and, 130
feminist movement: direct citizen action and, 7; domestic relationships and, 242; Ely and, 240; historical scholarship influenced by, 37; women's political engagement and, 7, 53. *See also* gender and gender norms
Fishburne, Junius, 80, 102, 120, 127, 128
Fisher, Eunice, 59, 221
Flemington, New Jersey, 3, 25, 28
Fluvanna County Board of Supervisors, 295–96
FmHA. *See* Farmers Home Administration
Ford, Gerald, 8, 198, 215–16
Franklin, Ben A., 141–42, 199, 232, 235, 237, 246, 247

Friedman, Milton, 113
Fry, Vance, 186–87, 203–4, 243

Gale, Christopher and Pamela, 113, 116
Gannon, Frank, 207
Garland, Ray L., 14, 16
Garvey, Robert, 87
gender and gender norms: Ely and, 61–62, 98, 180, 249, 269–70; Ely divorce proceedings and, 240, 242–44; prison resistance movement and, 63; Sansom and, 270–71; in Virginia politics, 96–97. *See also* feminist movement; women
General Electric Company, 66–67
Gibbs, Lois Marie, 238
Glaberson, William, 238
Godwin, Mills, 15, 47, 156–66, 175
Goetz, Charles, 238, 249, 270, 273, 276–80, 284
Goldstein, Joseph I., 173–74, 221
Goldwater, Barry, 69
Gouin, Clara, 66
Gouldman, Clyde, 189–91
Grace, Peter: Ely and, 1, 8, 200–201, 254, 256–59, 262, 269; *Forbes* profile, 126; Kleppe and, 199, 200; Peers and, 265–66. *See also* W. R. Grace & Co.
Granade, Warner, 253
Granger, Ann Hill, 263
Great Society, 14, 64, 177
Green Springs, Virginia: agricultural advantages in, 33–34, 79, 119, 125, 211; class divisions in Louisa County and, 4, 9, 19, 33–34, 56, 124–25; easement procurement in preservation of, 112–15, 117–18, 128–29, 131, 209; Elys' move to, 4, 21, 28–31, 79; environmental movement and, 94; history of, 32–34, 39–41, 43, 74, 80; land-use policy in, 5; map, *ii*; as national historic landmark district, 2, 4–5, 112, 115–16, 118–21, 125, 128–29, 133–34, 137–41, 199, 211, 219, 227–32, 234, 237, 288–89; transportation infra-

structure and, 47, 80, 81. *See also* prison construction proposal; vermiculite mining

Green Springs Association: easement procurement and, 112, 113, 118; *Ely 1* (1971) and, 74, 75, 90; Rae Ely's leadership in, 53, 61–64, 95; federalism and, 71–72, 75, 109; public-private partnership and, 117; reorganized as Historic Green Springs, Inc., 118. *See also* Historic Green Springs, Inc.

Green Springs Cattle & Grain Farm, 252–53

Green v. County School Board of New Kent County (U.S. 1968), 84

Grimsley, Ed, 92–93, 109

Group Against Smog and Pollution (GASP), 54, 66

Group Against Smokers and Pollution (GASP), 66

Gumble, Ned, 255, 262, 263, 269–71

Hanmer, Rebecca, 101, 103–8
Hanslin, Lars, 230, 233
Harkrader, F. Ward, Jr., 288–89
Harris, Richard N., 91–92
Harris, Stephen C., 220
Hartt, Frederick, 81–82, 88–89, 139
Hash, L. J., 130, 131
Hatfield, Ethel Abercrombie (Rae's mother), 22–23
Hatfield, Rae. *See* Ely, Rae
Hatfield, Ray Vinton (Rae's father), 3, 22–23
Hawkwood, John, 273
Hawkwood estate: auctioning of, 252–53; domestic unrest and, 98–99; in Ely divorce proceedings, 241–45, 252–53; Ely's purchase of and living at, 29–32; fire at, 241, 250–51; historical pedigree of, 39–41, 77–78; historic preservation and, 53, 253, 284; nomination to landmark registers, 79, 81; photo of, 30*f*; Reynolds family and, 35, 105, 151

Haynsworth, Clement, 89
Heimer, Hanne, 203, 212
Heimer, Lennart, 133
Heller, Walter, 69
Hendrick, David, 289
Henry, Patrick, 42
Herbst, Robert L., 221, 229, 231
HGSI. *See* Historic Green Springs, Inc.
Hickel, Walter, 107, 150
Higginbotham, Samuel Page, II, 186, 220
highway construction. *See* transportation infrastructure
Hill, H. D. N., 200, 230
Hill, J. M., 129, 131, 195
Historic Green Springs, Inc. (HGSI): antitrust suit against, 271–83; asbestos dangers and, 198, 203–5, 264; Black public opinion on, 49; easement donation to Interior Department, 138, 179, 215, 219–22, 227, 233; easement procurement and, 118–19, 124–25, 267–68; *Ely 2* (Eastern District of Virginia, 1973) and, 154; *Ely 2* (Fourth Circuit Court of Appeals, 1974) and, 159, 162–63; environmental impact statements and, 222–23; Federal relationship with, 8, 134; Godwin's prison construction decision and, 165, 168; Green Springs Association reorganized as, 118; Higginbotham on, 186, 188; Holton's 1973 prison announcement and, 132; Mount Vernon Ladies' Association compared to, 172; national historic landmark designation and, 133–34, 227–29, 232; property rights claims against, 176–77; rezoning conflict and, 187–91, 195, 197, 215; vermiculite mining and, 122–24, 147–48, 196–97, 200–202; Will's Chapel fire and, 222; W. R. Grace land donation to, 256–64, 267, 275, 280, 283; Zion Crossroads development and, 287–90. *See also* Green Springs Association

Historic Green Springs Inc. v. Bergland (Eastern District of Virginia, 1980), 227–28, 234–39, 280

Historic Green Springs Inc. v. Brandy Farm, Ltd. (Louisa Circuit Court, 1993), 264–65

historic preservation: civil rights movement strategies adopted in, 9, 37, 184, 188, 190–92, 197, 212; conceptions of history in, 6, 32–33, 36, 40, 75, 79, 235; of districts as national historic landmarks, 115–16, 141, 235; easement donations and, 116, 135, 221, 232, 284, 292; environmental movement linked to, 41, 93; federalism and, 6, 9, 100; Hawkwood and, 53, 253, 284; Native American history and, 295–98; prison construction proposal and, 32–33, 38–41, 77–82, 108–9; public-private partnership and, 39–40, 108, 218, 233, 295; women in, 61. *See also specific agencies, organizations, legal measures, and proposed developments*

Historic Sites Act (1935), 137, 141

history, changing conception of, 7, 10, 32–33, 36, 40, 75, 79, 235, 295

Holladay, Mary Jane Boggs, 39

Holland, Ross, 232–33

Holton, Abner Linwood, Jr., 13–20; background of, 14–15; citizen activism of women confronting, 10, 95–97; criminal justice reform and, 13–14, 16–17; easement procurement and, 111, 114, 117–21, 124–25, 292; *Ely 2* (1973) and, 131–32, 149–53, 167; environmental movement and, 14, 16–17, 62–63, 66, 80, 82; Federal funding withdrawal and, 110, 152, 163; federalism and, 100; Green Springs historic district and, 128, 216; Louisa County vote for, 46; New Federalism and, 70; prison construction proposal and, 4, 7–9, 17–20, 20f, 32, 34, 38, 44, 67, 77–82; Sansom compared to, 269; school integration and, 15–16, 16f, 84;

Vietnam comparisons to prison construction fight, 4, 109, 144–46, 145f, 150, 296; Virginia Historic Landmarks Commission and, 76, 78, 79

Holton, Woody, 19

Howard, A. E. Dick, 119, 248–50

Howell, Henry, 158

Hruska, Roman, 74

Humphrey, Hubert, 15

Hutchinson, Ira J., 231

Illick, Joseph, 37

Indian Tribes of Virginia Recognition Act (2018), 297–98

integration of Louisa County High School, 5

interracial dating, 194

Interstate 64 (I-64), 44, 47, 81, 286

"Ivy Valley" manufacturing facility proposal, 66–67

Izakowitz, David, 269–71, 274, 277–79

Jackson, Henry (Scoop), 88

James River, 286

James River Water Authority (JRWA), 295–99

Javor, Henry, 188

Jefferson, Thomas, 33, 37, 42, 159, 238, 296

Jim Crow. *See* segregation and desegregation

jobs and economic gains: FmHA and, 217; prison construction creating, 9, 18–20, 32, 44, 49, 88, 103, 164; Sansom and, 271; vermiculite mining and, 122–23, 126–27, 146, 189, 195, 209, 227

Johnson, A. D. (Sambo), 164, 200, 203, 214–15, 217, 218

Johnson, Lady Bird, 141, 142, 178

Johnson, Lyndon: appendectomy scar cartoon, 145; civil rights movement and, 68; crime policy of, 73–74; electoral victory, 13; Great Society speech,

64; Merhige appointed by, 84; Vietnam War and, 144
Jones, Greg, 194, 197

Kelly, Sandra, 167
Kennedy, John F., 18, 73, 136, 173
Kennon, Gladys, 212
Kennon, Henry, 59, 187–88, 222
Keune, Russell, 119
Keysville, Virginia, 106
Kincannon, Charles D., 287–88
King, James, 184, 196, 200, 217
Kinoy, Mrs. Arthur, 53, 66
Kirk, Claude, 136
Kissinger, Henry, 207
Kleppe, Thomas, 198–201, 208–10, 231
Kohnken, Donald, 257, 259
Koontz, Lawrence L., 292
Krahenbill, Chauncey, 36, 56–57, 100
Krahenbill, Doris, 36, 56–57, 98, 100, 168
Kube, Ed, 287
Ku Klux Klan, 84

Lafayette, Marquis de, 42, 79, 164
landmark preservation. *See* national historic landmark status; National Historic Preservation Act; National Register of Historic Places; National Trust for Historic Preservation; Virginia Historic Landmarks Commission; Virginia Landmarks Register
Land Trust Alliance, 275
Larkin, Felix, 143
Larsen, Chick, 151, 153
Lassiter, A. R., 184, 196
Law Enforcement Assistance Administration (LEAA): creation of, 73–74; *Ely 1* (1971) and, 74–75, 86, 89–90; environmental impact statement of, 101–3, 107–10; picket fence federalism and, 77; prison construction grant from, 74–75
Lefcoe, Vann H., 91, 133–34
Lekto, Arlene, 208

Levine, David, 145
Levy, Benjamin, 140, 141, 216–17, 229
Lewis, James Fielding, 28–29
Libby (Montana) vermiculite mines, 198, 202–5, 281–82
Lille, Mildred, 105
Lintecum, Lee, 289
Lloyd, Robert L., 196
Longsworth, Nellie, 236
Loth, Calder, 78–79, 111, 120
Louisa and Mineral Industrial Development Corporation, 217
Louisa Chamber of Commerce, 217
Louisa County: Byrd organization and economic development in, 42–43, 45–46; class divisions in, 4, 9, 19, 33–34, 56, 124–25; economic stimulus, prison construction promoted as, 9, 18–20, 32, 44, 49, 88, 103, 164; Elys' move to, 4, 21, 28–29; Hanmer on, 101; nuclear reactor siting in, 18, 42, 45, 161, 223; Purcell's power in, 5, 46–48, 227; race relations in, 192–95
Louisa County Board of Supervisors (BOS): Brandy Farm vermiculite reserves and, 263–64; Federal aid received by, 223; Green Springs historic district and, 127–29, 176, 238; National Park Service easement donation and, 217; as oligarchy, 101; prison construction supported by, 109, 127, 161–62, 164; rezoning deadlock in, 185–91; vermiculite mining and, 200–204, 217; W. R. Grace closed sessions with, 114; W. R. Grace rezoning requests and, 131, 146, 148–49, 153, 183–86, 195–97; Zion Crossroads development and, 286–87, 289; zoning requirements eliminated by, 201
Louisa County Water Authority, 285, 289–90
Love Canal calamity, 204, 238
Loving, Bryce, 67
Lowe, David, 75
Luttig, Michael, 275, 283

Lyall, Thomas: on easement donation to Interior Department, 220; Green Springs national landmark status and, 129–31, 234; rezoning requests, 131, 146, 184; on vermiculite mining, 125–27, 201–2

Madoff, Michelle, 53–54, 66
Marshall Hall amusement park, 174
Martin, Frances, 63
Martin, Jesse, 189–90, 196, 197
McCumber, David, 204
McKelway, Bill, 179–81
Mench, Dorothy, 89
Merhige, Robert R.: background of, 83–85; Board of Supervisors rezoning stalemate and, 190–91; Ely on, 237; *Ely v. Velde* decision (Eastern District of Virginia, 1971) (*Ely 1*), 85–87; *Ely v. Velde* decision (Eastern District of Virginia, 1973) (*Ely 2*), 154, 162, 234; *Historic Green Springs Inc. v. Bergland* (Eastern District of Virginia, 1980), 222–23, 227, 234–38, 280; University of Illinois environmental impact study, release ordered by, 102
Metropolitan Coalition for Clean Air, 65
Michael, James H., 267, 274–76, 278–83
Michels, Franklin P., 219
mining. *See* vermiculite mining; Virginia Vermiculite, Inc. and Virginia Vermiculite, Ltd.; W. R. Grace & Co.
Mining in the Parks Act (1976), 210–11, 216, 231, 236, 264
Minter, George, 90
Monacan Indian Nation, 295–99
Monokote (insulation product), 202
Montange, Charles, 268, 272–74, 277, 279–84
Montgomery Citizens Planning Association, 65
Moody, James, 77, 79–83, 86, 92, 115
Moon, Norman K., 293
Moore, Richard L., 199–200

Morris, Roger, 205
Morrow, Duncan, 142–43
Mortensen, A. R., 139–40
Morton, Rogers: Blanchard and, 107; easement donations and, 137–41, 143, 177, 231; national historic landmark designation and, 140–43, 157, 163; National Land Use Policy Act's failure to pass and, 130; prison construction proposal and, 8, 149–53, 166
Mouer, L. Daniel, 296
Mount Vernon, 4, 212, 221
Mount Vernon Ladies' Association, 171–73
Murdock, Angus: background and education of, 36–38; easement procurement and, 119; Elys and, 38–41, 58; move to Eastern View in Louisa County, 38, 291; "A Private Opinion of the Future of the Green Springs" (essay), 32–33, 39–41, 43, 74, 80; South Carolina mine survey by, 146–47, 153
Murdock, Deborah: *Ely 1* (1971) and, 88; Elys and, 38–41, 57–58, 60, 73; HGSI leadership and, 168; Holton and, 96; marriage, 36–37
Murphy, Rex, 289
Murray, Patty, 282
Murtagh, William J., 115, 119, 129
Muskie, Edmund, 69
Myshak, Richard, 234

Nader, Ralph, 53, 269
National Association for the Advancement of Colored People (NAACP), 71, 72, 192
National Conference of State Historic Preservation Officers, 218
National Endowments for the Arts and Humanities, 64, 119
National Environmental Policy Act (NEPA, 1970): activists' use of, 6, 73, 83; *Ely 1* (1971) and, 86–90; Jackson and, 88; Nixon and, 130

National Heritage Policy Act (1980), 236–37
National Heritage Trust, 218
national historic landmark status: agency contention over, 141–43; coveted designation, 125, 133–34, 137–38, 163, 288; Ely's determination, 9, 55, 57, 83, 111–12, 228, 235–36, 246, 253; Green Springs as first created in a rural district, 3, 4–5, 157, 211; litigation challenging validity of, 227–33, 280; National Heritage Policy Act's passage (1980) and, 236–37. *See also* National Historic Preservation Act; National Register of Historic Places; National Trust for Historic Preservation; *specific court cases*
National Historic Preservation Act (NHPA, 1966): *Ely 1* (trial and appeal, 1971) and, 86, 87, 89–90; *Ely 2* (appeal, 1974), 159, 163; Federal access through, 73; FmHA environmental impact statement waiver and, 223; local control as risk to, 83; Nunes conducting hearings on amendments, 290–92; Sanders on, 93
National Institute of Occupational Safety and Health (NIOSH), 203
National Land Use Policy Act (proposed), 130
National Park Service (NPS): Blackman's house renovation and, 291–93; easement oversight and, 8, 113, 134–41, 171–72, 175–79, 216–17, 232–33, 290–94; Rae Ely's relationship with, 101, 108; Green Springs historic district and, 128; Mount Vernon conservation and, 171–75; public-private partnership and, 117; Sansom on, 238–39. *See also* National Register of Historic Places
National Register of Historic Places: Green Springs historic district nomination to, 112, 115–16, 118–21, 125, 128–29, 133–34, 229, 231–32; Green Springs plantations on, 77, 79; Hawkwood and Westend added to, 81; public-private partnership and, 116
National Trust for Historic Preservation: in antitrust suit against HGSI, 275; *Blackman* (2005) and, 291–92; on easement donation to Interior Department, 221; Ely and, 78; *Ely 1* (1971) and, 85; Federal officials allied with, 81, 100; Holton and, 77; prison construction proposal and, 80–82, 92; public-private partnership and, 218
Native American history, 295–99
Natural Resources Defense Council, 72, 87
Nature Conservancy, 85, 112, 117, 215, 284, 291
Nelson, Bill, 145, 145f
NEPA. *See* National Environmental Policy Act
New Deal, 8, 14, 44–45, 49, 117
New Federalism, 8–9, 68–72, 75, 83, 86, 131, 140, 175, 239
New York City public-private partnerships, 116–17
New York Times: on asbestos in W. R. Grace products, 202, 281–82; on *Bergland* decision, 235; Ely's relationships with, 141, 199; on Green Springs vermiculite mining, 200; Holton's school integration support in, 15; Kleppe's letter in, 199, 200; on legislative reversal of *Bergland* decision, 228; NIMBYs in, 7; on woman activists, 53, 65–66
NHPA. *See* National Historic Preservation Act
Nichols, Freddy, 38
NIMBY (not in my backyard): coinage of in response to quality of life issues, 7, 235, 271; media portrayals of, 10, 238; property rights and, 293; Sansom on, 228; SLAPPs and, 268; as template for other anti-development initiatives, 9–10

Nininger, Elizabeth Craig and Elgin, 123, 131, 183, 186–87, 196
NIOSH (National Institute of Occupational Safety and Health), 203
Nixon, Pat, 88–89
Nixon, Richard: block grants and, 77; citizen activism and, 71; crime policies of, 74; environmental movement and, 130, 136; Godwin and, 158; mining interests and, 122; New Federalism of, 8–9, 68–72, 75, 83, 86, 175, 239; picket fence federalism and, 81, 87; Republican ideology and, 13; Sansom on, 208; Vietnam War and, 144; on women in government, 105
Nolting, Carl, 35–36, 58
Nolting, Elisabeth Aiken: background of, 35–36, 58–59; defining historic preservation area, 118–19; easement offer to Interior Department, 138, 217; on *Ely 2* loss at District Court level, 154; Green Springs Association, role in, 59, 88; HGSI role of, 168; prison construction opposed by, 36
North Anna nuclear power plant. *See* nuclear reactor siting in Louisa County
not in my backyard. *See* NIMBY
NPS. *See* National Park Service
Nuckols, Harry, 193
nuclear reactor siting in Louisa County, 18, 42, 45, 161, 223
Nunes, Devin, 290–92, 294

Occupational Safety and Health Administration (OSHA), 204
O'Connor, Sandra Day, 104
Ogg, Earl: easement procurement and, 113–14; electoral victories, 196; environmental impact statement authored by, 92; Green Springs historic district and, 43–44, 127; on job creation from prison construction, 88; Purcell family and, 46

oligarchy, 6, 9, 101, 106. *See also* Byrd organization; courthouse crowd
O'Neal, Tip, 100
OPEC (Organization of Petroleum Exporting Countries), 126
Open-Space Land Act (1966), 111, 116

Palmer, Meade, 119, 125, 139
participatory politics. *See* direct action; *specific political movements*
partisan politics: crime policies and, 70–71, 74; Godwin and, 157–58; ideology in, 13, 15–16; New Federalism and, 69; public-private partnerships and, 8. *See also* conservative politicians and organizations; progressives
Patton, Robin, 280
Peers, A. D. (Icky), 164, 265
Peers, Millard Filmore and Norma: Green Springs historic district and, 129, 220; property rights and, 143, 293; vermiculite mining support of, 123, 127–29, 131, 196, 213; on W. R. Grace land donation, 265–66
Perkins, William: Ely and, 55; on Interior Department's easement acceptance, 220; on vermiculite mining, 2, 149, 186, 195, 197, 201, 203
picket fence federalism, 76, 81, 87, 100
Piscataway Park, 171–72, 174, 178
Point of Fork, 296–97
Poling, Greg, 255, 258, 264, 265
Poore, Earl, 196
Potter, Neal, 65
poverty and class divide: environmental movement and, 66; Great Society speech and, 64; in Louisa County, 4, 9, 19, 33–34, 56, 124
Preservation Action, 237
Preservation Virginia, 298
prison construction proposal (diagnostic center), 87; Black public opinion on, 194; block grant funding for, 70–71,

74, 77, 91; costs and details, 17–20, 20f, 96, 159; courthouse crowd and, 32, 49, 67; criminal justice reform and, 17–18, 80–81, 102–3, 159, 160, 165, 166; easement procurement and, 111–15, 152, 175; Ely leading opposition to, 20, 22, 30f, 32–35, 39, 55–64, 61f, 74–75, 95–97; environmental impact statement for, 101–2; environmental movement's opposition to, 35–36, 41, 62–63, 167; Federal funding withdrawal, 110, 152, 163; Federal jurisdiction over, 70–75, 89–91, 106, 152; Godwin's termination of, 156–57, 160–66, 175; historic preservation in resistance to, 32–33, 38–41, 77–82, 108–9, 141; Holton's plans, 4, 7–9, 17–20, 20f, 32, 34, 38, 44, 67, 77–82, 132; initial mobilization of resistance to, 32, 34–36; jobs arguments for, 18–20, 32, 44, 48–49, 88, 103, 164; location choice, 4, 18–20, 67, 74; media coverage of, 35, 40, 56–57, 91–94, 109, 110, 153, 159–63, 166, 295; Morton and, 149–53, 166; National Trust for Historic Preservation and, 80–82, 92; public opinion on, 48–49; Purcell and land deal for, 47–48, 108; University of Illinois environmental impact study and, 102–3, 109–10; Vietnam comparisons to, 4, 109, 144–46, 145f, 150, 296; water supply for, 286–87; Willey and, 159. *See also* criminal justice reform; *Ely v. Velde*; Holton, Abner Linwood, Jr.

progressives: Holton's criminal justice reform and, 14, 17; Nixon pursuing moderately progressive domestic policy, 13; property rights arguments against, 177; public-private partnership and, 113; quality of life demands of, 6, 66

property rights: courthouse crowd's agenda and, 5; creation of Green Springs historic district and, 129, 176–77; HGSI's easement procurement and, 125; local majorities resenting government interference in, 6, 9, 34; national landmark status and, 142–43, 163, 290–91; National Land Use Policy Act and, 130; property values as issue, 32, 41, 53, 117, 127, 174, 295; vermiculite mining and, 123, 131, 183, 186–87; water rights and, 285–90. *See also* easements

Property Rights Foundation of America, 292–93

public-private partnership: community associations and, 116–17; cost effectiveness of, 216; easements and, 112–13, 135–36, 152; historic preservation of Green Springs and, 39–40, 108, 218, 233, 295; Louisa County economic development and, 43; National Trust for Historic Preservation and, 81, 100, 218; Nature Conservancy and, 117; New Deal and, 44–45; political support for, 8

Purcell, Charles, 251–52

Purcell, Francis H. and Fredericka S., 201

Purcell, Harold: background of, 46–47; Board of Supervisors rezoning stalemate and, 185, 188–89; Ely and, 48, 251–52; Hawkwood auction and, 252; Louisa County economic development and, 43, 47–48; political power of, 5, 46–48, 227; prison construction proposal and, 18–19; property rights and, 293; recusal from mining issues, 183

Purcell, John S., 43

Purcell, Richard (Dickie), 19, 35, 132, 152, 218–19, 221, 253

quality of life: class conflict in issues of, 64, 201; environmental movement and, 6, 180; historic preservation and, 252; NIMBYism and, 7, 235, 271 race and racism: Byrd organization and, 5, 6, 46; civil rights legislation, 68; courthouse crowd and, 49, 192; environmental movement and, 66; Godwin and, 157–58; interracial dating, 194; Louisa County history of, 9, 192–95; New Federalism and, 70; Nixon and, 13, 68, 70; quality of life issues and, 64; Tuition Reimbursement Plan for white Virginians, 29. *See also* segregation and desegregation

Rails to Trails Conservancy, 272

Rassawek (Monacan ancestral capital), 297–99

Raynor, Pete, 134

Reagan, Ronald, 13, 17, 113

Reed, Nathaniel P.: background of, 136–38; on Green Springs easement donation, 134, 177, 217, 231; supporting opposition to prison construction, 151, 164

rehabilitation. *See* criminal justice reform; prison construction proposal

Republican Party, 14–15, 70, 122. *See also specific politicians*

revenue sharing, 69–70, 75

Reynolds, Richard S., 35, 100, 101, 151

Reynolds, Virginia Sargeant, 35, 100

Richards, Thomas, 112, 114, 119, 215

Richmond Mercury: female reporter's advantage, 180; on Holton's prison construction woes, 144–45, 145f; on Holton's stubbornness, 152

Richmond Times-Dispatch: on asbestos dangers of vermiculite mining, 196, 198, 202, 205; on Byrd organization, 45; on creation of Green Springs National Historic Landmark District, 121; on easement procurement, 115; Ely's interview in, 179–81; on Hawkwood auction, 253; Holton criticized by, 109; on LEAA's environmental impact study, 102, 103; on prison construction proposal, 91–93, 160, 162, 163, 166; on Sansom, 207; on W. R. Grace land donation proposal, 262

Ritchie, John, 16, 132

Rivlin, Alice, 105

Roanoke Times, 124, 132, 156, 167, 295

Robert E. Lee Elementary School (Charlottesville), 29

Robinson, J. Kenneth, 211

Rockefeller, Nelson, 13

Rogers, Jerry, 128, 215, 219

Romney, George, 13

Roosevelt, Franklin D., 44–45

Rosenfeld, Megan, 195–96

Rostow, Walt, 207

Ruckelshaus, William, 101, 103, 105–6, 130, 208

Safe Streets Act (1968), 70, 73–74, 86, 90

Sanders, Irwin Taylor, II, 93, 105

Sanner, Timothy, 289

Sansom, John C., 206

Sansom, Robert: antitrust suit against W. R. Grace and HGSI by, 266–69, 274, 276–78, 282–83; on asbestos dangers, 203; background and career of, 206–8, 270–71; easement donation to Interior Department and, 220–21, 227, 229–30; *The Economics of Insurgency*, 207; Ely and, 206, 228, 269–71, 274; FmHA loan and, 217, 222–23, 230–31, 233; gender norms and, 270–71; "Historic Green Springs: Where Preservationists Cut Their Teeth" (case study), 238; Holton compared to, 269; on legislative overturn of *Bergland*, 237–38, 280; on Mining in the Parks Act, 210–11; *The New American Dream Machine: Toward a Simpler Lifestyle in an Environmental Age* (book), 208; on protected properties as inaccessible to public, 295; *U.S. vs. NPS* (pamphlet), 237–38, 292; vermiculite mining and, 201, 203–4, 208–10, 233–34, 259–63, 269;

W. R. Grace negotiations and, 255, 258, 261
Save Lake Superior Association, 208
Schneider, Andrew, 204, 281–82, 293
Schneider, Gregory S., 296
schools. *See* segregation and desegregation
Schwartz, Chair L. M., 293, 294
Schwartz, Seth, 276, 278
Scott, William L., 88
segregation and desegregation: Byrd organization and, 45; courthouse crowd and, 49; Federal policy undermining, 68, 71, 72; Godwin and, 157–58; Holton's electoral victory and, 15; Louisa County's history of, 5, 192–95, 197; Merhige and, 84, 85; oligarchy and, 6; Tuition Reimbursement Plan, 29
Seiberling, John, 236
Selikoff, Irving J., 202, 204–5
Shapley, Deborah, 208
Shapp, Milton, 184
Shenandoah National Park, 117
Sherman Antitrust Act (1980), 267, 274–75, 278, 283
Short, Allen, 202, 205, 209, 223
Sierra Club, 65
Simms, William C., 146
Simpson, Jerry, 63, 95–97
SLAPPs (Strategic Lawsuits Against Public Participation), 268–69, 275, 277
Sobeloff, Simon E., 89
South Anna River, 47
Spong, William B., 88
sprawl: Ely's move to Green Springs and, 4, 28, 79; highway construction and, 28, 65; preservation efforts against, 120, 148
Spring Creek subdivision and Homeowners Association, 285–90
Stanford, Ray and Sue, 24
State and Local Fiscal Assistance Act (1972), 70

Stephens, Lewis, 49, 193–94, 197
Stewart, Philip O., 171–72, 174–79, 220, 221
Stokes, Samuel N., 221
strip mining. *See* vermiculite mining
Strong, William A., 233
Sutherland, Marvin M., 204
Sweeny, William, 189

Taylor, Henry, 58, 77, 81
Taylor and Parrish Construction Company, 77
Temple, Ed, 82
Tennessee Valley Authority, 44
Thomas, Leri, 269
Thomasson, John, 195
Tidal Lands Preservation Act (Connecticut, 1969), 135
Train, Russel, 152
transportation infrastructure: environmental protest against, 65–66; exurban sprawl and, 28, 65; Green Springs and, 47, 80, 81; picket fence federalism and, 76
Tredegar Iron Works (Richmond), 37
Trevilians, Battle of (1864), 43–44
Troy, Anthony, 191
Truman Scholarship Program, 247–48, 250
Tuition Reimbursement Plan (Virginia), 29
Turner, Melvin, 148

United States v. See name of opposing party
University of Illinois environmental impact study, 102–3, 109–10
University of Virginia School of Law, 241, 248–50
U.S. Conference of Mayors Special Committee on Historic Preservation: *With Heritage So Rich*, 65
Utley, Robert M., 139–41, 171

Vashti Industrial School for Girls (Georgia), 3, 24, 97

Velde, Richard, 74
Verdier, Ruby, 98
vermiculite mining, 4, 122–32; asbestos dangers in, 198–99, 202–5, 259, 261, 281–82, 284; Black public opinion on, 49, 194–95; commercial uses, 125, 230; conditional use permits for, 199, 234, 255, 261, 263–64; easements and, 114, 178, 199, 230; Franklin's reporting on, 142; Green Springs historic district and, 129–30, 211–13, 231–32; land reclamation and, 146, 184, 284; national landmark status and, 141; natural resource conservation and, 125; property rights and, 123, 131, 183, 186–87; rezoning conflict and, 184–85; Sansom's lobbying for, 208–10, 233–34, 269. *See also* Virginia Vermiculite, Inc. and Virginia Vermiculite, Ltd.; W. R. Grace & Co.
VHLC. *See* Virginia Historic Landmarks Commission
Vietnam War: Federal austerity and, 116; prison construction fight compared to, 4, 109, 144–46, 145f, 150, 296; Sansom and, 206–7; troop withdrawal from, 144–46, 148. *See also* anti-Vietnam War movement
Virginia Commission for the Arts, 63, 87
Virginia Department of Conservation and Economic Development, 204
Virginia Department of Historic Resources, 296–98
Virginia Department of Welfare and Institutions (DWI), 90, 92–93, 96, 102–3, 109–10, 124
Virginia Historic Landmarks Commission (VHLC): easements and, 82, 111–13, 115, 117–19, 124–25, 153, 216; *Ely 1* (1971) and, 83, 87, 92; Green Springs historic district and, 118–21, 129, 131, 176; prison construction proposal and, 77–82, 102, 153; public-private partnership and, 117; University of Illinois environmental impact study and, 102; vermiculite mining and, 123, 127–28

Virginia Landmarks Register, 79, 81, 120–21
Virginia Land Rights Coalition (VLRC), 293
Virginia State Penitentiary (Richmond), 4, 17, 152
Virginia Vermiculite, Inc. and Virginia Vermiculite, Ltd. (VVI and VVL): antitrust suit against W. R. Grace and HGSI, 266–69, 274, 276–78, 282–83; on asbestos dangers, 203; Brandy Farm reserves and, 259–60, 262–66; conditional use permits and, 199, 261, 263–64; expansion strategy of, 196, 259; financing and loans to, 217, 222–23, 230–31, 233; Green Springs landmark designation and, 228–32, 234–35; land reclamation by, 284; mining clearance for, 201, 204, 234; National Park Service and, 262; W. R. Grace negotiations with, 255–56, 258–60, 262–63
VLRC (Virginia Land Rights Coalition), 293
voter suppression, 18, 45–46, 190
Voting Rights Act (1965), 45, 68, 183, 190–92, 195, 197, 274
VVI and VVL. *See* Virginia Vermiculite, Inc. and Virginia Vermiculite, Ltd.

Wall, Cecil, 174
Wallace, George, 13, 15, 17
Wal-Mart, 285, 287, 289
Walsh, Robert, 259–61, 264
Warner, Mark, 288
Warren, Earl, 17, 191
Washington Post: on asbestos regulation, 204; on Green Springs vermiculite mining, 211–13; on prison construction proposal, 152, 153, 163, 165–67; on Sansom's mining lobbying efforts,

209–10; on W. R. Grace land donation proposal, 262
Washington Suburban Sanitary Commission, 173
water rights, 285–90
Watts, David A., 138
Weingarten, Joel, 246–48
Welch, Amanda, 287
Welch, Lilas, 205
Werkheiser, Marion, 298–99
Westend plantation, 77, 79, 81, 211
Wheeler, Douglas P., 135–38, 216, 217, 231
White, Clare, 33–34, 156, 167–68
white supremacy, 46, 84. *See also* race and racism
Whitlock, Robert, 43, 146
Whitlock, W. W.: on asbestos dangers, 203; Board of Supervisors (BOS) rezoning deadlock and, 185; Green Springs historic district and, 128–29; on Hawkwood auction, 253; "Petitioner Memorandum of Fact and Law" (as counsel for BOS), 176–77; on race in Louisa County, 192, 194–95; vermiculite mining and, 203, 263–64
Whitten, Les, 209
Willey, Edward E., 159, 160
Will's Chapel Meeting House, 219, 221–22
Winston, Carson S., 128, 132, 166, 184, 185
Winters, Harrison, 89
Woburn (Massachusetts) water supply pollution, 204
women: Bolton and, 172; Ely and political engagement of, 5, 53–55, 62, 156, 167–68, 180, 270; environmental movement and, 53–54, 63, 66; Federal employment of, 104–5; historic preservation and, 61; political engagement of, 6–7, 10, 53–54, 124, 156;

prison construction proposal and, 67, 168; at University of Virginia School of Law, 241, 248–49. *See also* feminist movement; gender and gender norms
W. R. Grace & Co.: antitrust suit against, 271–72, 275, 278, 279, 282; asbestos dangers and, 202–5, 281; bankruptcy, 204; corporate identity of, 126; Ely as shareholder, 1–3; expansion strategy of, 130, 133; Green Springs historic district and, 129–30; on Green Springs landmark status, 143; Kleppe and, 199–200; land donation to Historic Green Springs, Inc., 256–64, 267, 275, 280, 283; land purchase by, 122; Libby (Montana) vermiculite mines of, 198, 202–5, 281–82; Louisa County Board of Supervisors and, 114; May 1976 shareholders' meeting, 1–3, 198, 200–201; rezoning requests, 131, 146–49, 153, 183–86, 195–97; South Carolina mining operation of, 146–47; tax revenue from, 148; vermiculite interests of, 125–27, 130, 232, 255; Virginia Vermiculite's negotiations with, 255–56, 258–60, 262–63; Woburn (Massachusetts) water supply pollution and, 204

Young, Don, 239
Youth for Christ, 24, 58

Zion Crossroads development, 286–90, 295
zoning laws: historic preservation and, 135; Louisa County Board of Supervisors and, 201; National Land Use Policy Act and, 130; prison construction proposal and, 152; rezoning for apartment complex in Louisa County, 285; SLAPPs and, 268
Zonolite Company, 205